· · · · · · ·

Thomas Bulfinch

1796–1867

The United States was still a very young country when Thomas Bulfinch was born in 1796 in Newton, Massachusetts, close to many famous sites of the recent Revolutionary War.

His father, Charles Bulfinch, a prominent architect, saw that his son received perhaps the best education then available in America: a traditional curriculum strong in the ancient classics, both Greek and Latin, beginning at the Boston Latin School, then progressing to Phillips Exeter Academy and Harvard University. After graduation in 1814, Bulfinch returned to his old school, Boston Latin, to teach for a year. He then entered business, something for which he apparently was ill-suited.

When his father was appointed architect of the new Capitol Building, Thomas moved with the family to Washington, D.C., in 1818, but in 1825 he returned for good to Boston. He never married, but kept household with his various brothers and sisters. In 1837, he began to work at the Merchant Bank of Boston, where he remained the rest of his life, holding a series of modest positions. Unambitious, he was content to drone away his days so long as he could save his energies for after-hours work as an amateur scholar and writer.

Although Bulfinch lived near the intellectual circle of Emerson, Thoreau, and Hawthorne, he was too shy to seek out such famous figures. Instead, he immersed himself in the past. Ever since his teaching days, he had been interested in helping young students, and his life work became a series of books making ancient literature accessible in fresh, modern English.

The Age of Fable (1855) is a rich treasury of ancient mythology—Greek, Roman, Celtic, Oriental, and Norse. *The Age of Chivalry* (1858) and *Legends of Charlemagne* (1863) retell medieval legends and romances. Bulfinch never received much glory for his accomplishments, but his books were immediately successful and became classics themselves, read by generations of students.

Thomas Bulfinch

BULFINCH'S MYTHOLOGY
THE AGE
OF FABLE

COURAGE
BOOKS

an imprint of
RUNNING PRESS
Philadelphia, Pennsylvania

The text of this volume is reprinted from a first edition of *The Age of Fable*,
published by Allen & Farnham, Cambridge, Massachusetts, in 1855,
and made available through the courtesy of The Bancroft Library,
University of California, Berkeley.

The essay "Myths and the Modern World" by Michael Grant is excerpted from
Myths of the Greeks and Romans by Michael Grant,
copyright © 1965 by Meredian Books—The World Publishing Company.
Reprinted by permission of Weidenfeld & Nicholson Ltd., London.

The essay "Greek Myth and the Poets" by Charles Grosvenor Osgood is reprinted from
the introduction to *Classical Myths in English Literature* by Dan S. Norton and Peter
Rushton, copyright © 1952 by Holt, Rinehart & Winston, Inc.
Reprinted by permission of Holt, Rinehart & Winston, Inc., New York.

Canadian representatives: General Publishing Co., Ltd.,
30 Lesmill Road, Don Mills, Ontario M3B 2T6.

International representatives: Worldwide Media Services, Inc.,
115 East Twenty-third Street, New York, NY 10010.

9   8   7   6   5   4   3   2
Digit on the right indicates the number of this printing.

Library of Congress Cataloging-in-Publication Number 90–55347
ISBN 0–89471–881–9

Cover design by Toby Schmidt,
Typography: Times Roman and Plantin
by Commcor Communications Corporation,
Philadelphia, Pennsylvania
Augustea Open by Letraset
Printed and bound in the United States of America
by Bertelsmann Printing and Manufacturing Corporation.

Published by Courage Books, an imprint of Running Press Book Publishers,
125 South Twenty-second Street, Philadelphia, Pennsylvania 19103.

To
HENRY WADSWORTH LONGFELLOW,
The Poet Alike Of The Many And Of The Few.
This Attempt To Popularize
Mythology,
And Extend The Enjoyment Of Elegant Literature,
Is Respectfully Inscribed.

Contents

THE LINEAGE OF THE GODS

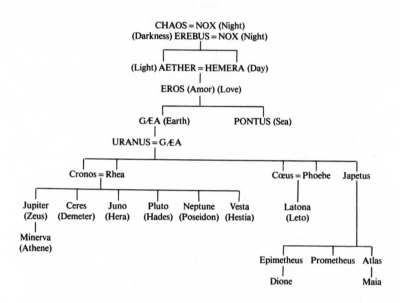

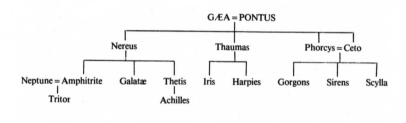

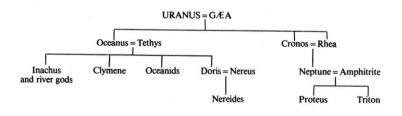

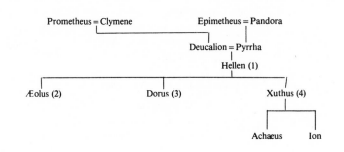

ZEUS (JUPITER)

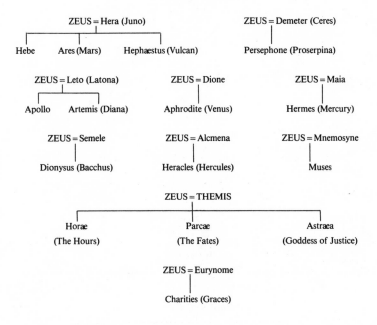

(1) Ancestor of the Greeks
(2) Ancestor of the Æolians
(3) Ancestor of the Dorians
(4) Ancestor of the Achæans and Ionians

·······

Preface

If no other knowledge deserves to be called useful but that which helps to raise our station in society, then mythology has no claim to the appellation. But if that which tends to make us happier and better can be called useful, then we claim that epithet for our subject. For mythology is the handmaid of literature; and literature is one of the best allies of virtue and promoters of happiness.

Without a knowledge of mythology much of the elegant literature of our own language cannot be understood and appreciated. When Byron calls Rome "the Niobe of nations," or says of Venice, "She looks a Sea-Cybele fresh from ocean," he calls up to the mind of one familiar with our subject illustrations more vivid and striking than the pencil could furnish, but which are lost to the reader ignorant of mythology. Milton abounds in similar allusions.The short poem "Comus" contains more than thirty such, and the ode "On the Morning of the Nativity" half as many. Through "Paradise Lost" they are scattered profusely. This is one reason why we often hear persons by no means illiterate say that they cannot enjoy Milton. But were these persons to add to their more solid acquirements the easy learning of this little volume, much of the poetry of Milton which has appeared to them "harsh and crabbed" would be found "musical as is Apollo's lute." Our citations, taken from more than twenty-five poets, from Spenser to Longfellow, will show how general has been the practice of borrowing illustrations from mythology.

The prose writers also avail themselves of the same source of elegant and suggestive illustration. One can hardly take up a number of the Edinburgh or Quarterly Review without meeting with instances. In Macaulay's article on Milton there are twenty such.

But how is mythology to be taught to one who does not learn it through the medium of the languages of Greece and Rome? To devote study to a species of learning which relates wholly to false marvels and obsolete faiths, is not to be expected of the general reader in a practical age like this. The time even of the young is claimed by so many sciences of facts and things, that little can be spared for set treatises on a science of mere fancy.

But may not requisite knowledge of the subject be acquired by reading the ancient poets in translation? We reply, the field is too extensive for a preparatory course; and these very translations require some previous knowledge of the subject to make them intelligible. Let any one who doubts it read the first page of the *Æneid,* and see what he can make of "the hatred of Juno," the "decree of the Parcæ," the "judgment of Paris," and the "honors of Ganymede," without this knowledge.

Shall we be told that answers to such queries may be found in notes, or by a reference to the Classical Dictionary? We reply, the interruption of one's reading by either process is so annoying that most readers prefer to let an allusion pass unapprehended rather than submit to it. Moreover, such sources give us only the dry facts without any of the charm of the original narrative; and what is a poetical myth when stripped of its poetry? The story of Ceyx and Halcyone, which fills a chapter in our book, occupies but eight lines in the best (Smith's) Classical Dictionary; and so of others.

Our book is an attempt to solve this problem, by telling the stories of mythology in such a manner as to make them a source of amusement. We have endeavored to tell them correctly, according to the ancient authorities, so that when the reader finds them referred to he may not be at a loss to recognize the reference. Thus we hope to teach mythology not as a study, but as a relaxation from study; to give our work the charm of a story-book, yet by means of it to impart a knowledge of an important branch of education. The index at the end will adapt it to the purpose of reference, and make it a Classical Dictionary for the parlor.

Most of the classical legends in this book are derived from Ovid and Virgil. They are not literally translated, for, in the author's opinion, poetry translated into literal prose is very unattractive reading. Neither are they in verse, as well for other reasons as from a conviction that to translate faithfully under all the embarrassments of rhyme and measure is impossible. The attempt has been made to tell the stories in prose, preserving so much of the poetry as resides in the thoughts and is separable from the language itself, and omitting those amplifications which are not suited to the altered form.

The Northern mythological stories are copied with some abridgment from Mallet's Northern Antiquities. These chapters, with those on Oriental and Egyptian mythology, seemed necessary to complete the subject, though it is believed these topics have not usually been presented in the same volume with the classical fables.

The poetical citations so freely introduced are expected to answer several valuable purposes. They will tend to fix in memory the leading fact of each story, they will help to the attainment of a correct pronunciation of the proper names, and they will enrich the memory with many gems of poetry, some of them such as are most frequently quoted or alluded to in reading and conversation.

Having chosen *mythology as connected with literature* for our province, we have endeavored to omit nothing which the reader of elegant literature is likely to find occasion for. Such stories and parts of stories as are offensive to pure taste and good morals are not given. But such stories are not often referred to, and if they occasionally should be, the English reader need feel no mortification in confessing his ignorance of them.

Our book is not for the learned, nor for the theologian, nor for the philosopher, but for the reader of English literature, of either sex, who wishes to comprehend the allusions so frequently made by public speakers, lecturers, essayists, and poets, and those which occur in polite conversation.

We trust our young readers will find it a source of entertainment; those more advanced a useful companion in their reading; those who travel, and visit museums and galleries of art, an interpreter of paintings and sculptures; those who mingle in cultivated society, a key to allusions which are occasionally made; and last of all, those in advanced life, pleasure in retracing a path of literature which leads them back to the days of childhood, and revives at every step the associations of the morning of life.

The permanency of those associations is beautifully expressed in the well-known lines of Coleridge, in "The Piccolomini," Act II, Scene 4.

"The intelligible forms of ancient poets,
 The fair humanities of old religion,
 The Power, the Beauty, and the Majesty
 That had their haunts in dale or piny mountains,
 Or forest, by slow stream, or pebbly spring,
 Or chasms and watery depths; all these have vanished;
 They live no longer in the faith of reason;
 But still the heart doth need a language; still
 Doth the old instinct bring back the old names;
 Spirits or gods that used to share this earth
 With man as with their friend; and at this day
 'Tis Jupiter who brings whate'er is great,
 And Venus who brings every thing that's fair."

BULFINCH'S MYTHOLOGY

O, ye delicious fables! where the wave
  And the woods were peopled, and the air, with things
So lovely! why, ah! why has science grave
  Scattered afar your sweet imaginings?

BARRY CORNWALL

Introduction

The religions of ancient Greece and Rome are extinct. The so-called divinities of Olympus have not a single worshipper among living men. They belong now not to the department of theology, but to those of literature and taste. There they still hold their place, and will continue to hold it, for they are too closely connected with the finest productions of poetry and art, both ancient and modern, to pass into oblivion.

We propose to tell the stories relating to them which have come down to us from the ancients, and which are alluded to by modern poets, essayists, and orators. Our readers may thus at the same time be entertained by the most charming fictions which fancy has ever created, and put in possession of information indispensable to every one who would read with intelligence the elegant literature of his own day.

In order to understand these stories, it will be necessary to acquaint ourselves with the ideas of the structure of the universe, which prevailed among the Greeks—the people from whom the Romans, and other nations through them, received their science and religion.

The Greeks believed the earth to be flat and circular, their own country occupying the middle of it, the central point being either Mount Olympus, the abode of the gods, or Delphi, so famous for its oracle.

The circular disk of the earth was crossed from west to east, and divided into two equal parts by the *Sea,* as they called the Mediterranean, and its continuation the Euxine, the only seas with which they were acquainted.

Around the earth flowed the *River Ocean,* its course being from south to north on the western side of the earth, and in a contrary direction on the eastern side. It flowed in a steady, equable current, unvexed by storm or tempest. The sea, and all the rivers on earth, received their waters from it.

The northern portion of the earth was supposed to be inhabited by a happy race named the Hyperboreans, dwelling in everlasting bliss and spring beyond the lofty mountains whose caverns were supposed to send forth the piercing blasts of the north wind, which chilled the people of Hellas (Greece). Their country was inaccessible by land or sea. They lived exempt from disease or old age, from toils and warfare. Moore has given us the "Song of a Hyperborean," beginning

"I come from a land in the sun-bright deep,
    Where golden gardens glow,
Where the winds of the north, becalmed in sleep,
    Their conch shells never blow."

On the south side of the earth, close to the stream of Ocean, dwelt a people happy and virtuous as the Hyperboreans. They were named the Æthiopians. The gods favored them so highly that they were wont to leave at times their Olympian abodes, and go to share their sacrifices and banquets.

On the western margin of the earth, by the stream of Ocean, lay a happy place named the Elysian Plain, whither mortals favored by the gods were transported without tasting of death, to enjoy an immortality of bliss. This happy region was also called the "Fortunate Fields," and the "Isles of the Blessed."

We thus see that the Greeks of the early ages knew little of any real people except those to the east and south of their own country, or near the coast of the Mediterranean. Their imagination meantime peopled the western portion of this sea with giants, monsters, and enchantresses; while they placed around the disk of the earth, which they probably regarded as of no great width, nations enjoying the peculiar favor of the gods, and blessed with happiness and longevity.

The Dawn, the Sun, and the Moon were supposed to rise out of the Ocean, on the eastern side, and to drive through the air, giving light to gods and men. The stars also, except those forming the Wain or Bear, and others near them, rose out of and sank into the stream of Ocean. There the sun-god embarked in a winged boat, which conveyed him round by the northern part of the earth, back to his place of rising in the east. Milton alludes to this in his "Comus."

"Now the gilded car of day
    His golden axle doth allay
    In the steep Atlantic stream,
    And the slope Sun his upward beam
    Shoots against the dusky pole,
    Pacing towards the other goal
    Of his chamber in the east."

The abode of the gods was on the summit of Mount Olympus, in Thessaly. A gate of clouds, kept by the goddesses named the Seasons, opened to permit the passage of the Celestials to earth, and to receive them on their return. The gods had their separate dwellings; but all, when summoned, repaired to the palace of Jupiter, as did also those deities whose usual abode was the earth, the waters, or the underworld. It was also in the great hall of the palace of the Olympian king that the gods feasted each day on ambrosia and nectar, their food and drink, the latter being handed round by the lovely goddess Hebe. Here they conversed of the affairs of heaven and earth; and as they quaffed their nectar, Apollo, the god of music, delighted them with the tones of his lyre, to which the Muses sang in responsive strains. When the sun was set, the gods retired to sleep in their respective dwellings.

The following lines from the *Odyssey* will show how Homer conceived of Olympus:

> "So saying, Minerva, goddess azure-eyed,
> Rose to Olympus, the reputed seat
> Eternal of the gods, which never storms
> Disturb, rains drench, or snow invades, but calm
> The expanse and cloudless shines with purest day.
> There the inhabitants divine rejoice
> Forever."   *Cowper*

The robes and other parts of the dress of the goddesses were woven by Minerva and the Graces, and every thing of a more solid nature was formed of the various metals. Vulcan was architect, smith, armorer, chariot builder, and artist of all work in Olympus. He built of brass the houses of the gods; he made for them the golden shoes with which they trod the air or the water, and moved from place to place with the speed of the wind, or even of thought. He also shod with brass the celestial steeds, which whirled the chariots of the gods through the air, or along the surface of the sea. He was able to bestow on his workmanship self-motion, so that the tripods (chairs and tables) could move of themselves in and out of the celestial hall. He even endowed with intelligence the golden handmaidens whom he made to wait on himself.

Jupiter, or Jove (Zeus), though called the father of gods and men, had himself a beginning. Saturn (Cronos) was his father, and Rhea (Ops) his mother. Saturn and Rhea were of the race of Titans, who were the children of Earth and Heaven, which sprang from Chaos, of which we shall give a further account in our next chapter.

There is another cosmogony, or account of the creation, according to which Earth, Erebus, and Love were the first of beings. Love (Eros) issued from the egg of Night, which floated on Chaos. By his arrows and torch he pierced and vivified all things, producing life and joy.

Saturn and Rhea were not the only Titans. There were others, whose names were Oceanus, Hyperion, Iapetus, and Ophion, males; and Themis, Mnemosyne, Eurynome, females. They are spoken of as the elder gods, whose dominion was afterwards transferred to others. Saturn yielded to Jupiter, Oceanus to Neptune, Hyperion to Apollo. Hyperion was the father of the Sun, Moon, and Dawn. He is therefore the original sun-god, and is painted with the splendor and beauty which were afterwards bestowed on Apollo.

"Hyperion's curls, the front of Jove himself." *Shakespeare*

Ophion and Eurynome ruled over Olympus till they were dethroned by Saturn and Rhea. Milton alludes to them in "Paradise Lost." He says the heathens seem to have had some knowledge of the temptation and fall of man,

> "And fabled how the serpent, whom they called
> Ophion, with Eurynome, (the wide-
> Encroaching Eve perhaps) had first the rule
> Of high Olympus, thence by Saturn driven.

The representations given of Saturn are not very consistent; for on the one hand his reign is said to have been the golden age of innocence and purity, and on the other he is described as a monster who devoured his own children.* Jupiter, however, escaped this fate, and when grown up espoused Metis (Prudence), who administered a draught to Saturn which caused him to disgorge his children. Jupiter, with his brothers and sisters, now rebelled against their father Saturn, and his brothers the Titans; vanquished them, and imprisoned some of them in Tartarus, inflicting other penalties on others. Atlas was condemned to bear up the heavens on his shoulders.

On the dethronement of Saturn, Jupiter with his brothers Neptune (Poseidon) and Pluto (Dis) divided his dominions. Jupiter's portion was the heavens, Neptune's the ocean, and Pluto's the realms of the dead. Earth and Olympus were common property. Jupiter was king of gods and men. The thunder was his weapon, and he bore a shield called Aegis, made for him by Vulcan. The eagle was his favorite bird, and bore his thunderbolts.

Juno (Hera) was the wife of Jupiter, and queen of the gods. Iris, the goddess of the rainbow, was her attendant and messenger. The peacock was her favorite bird.

Vulcan (Hephæstos), the celestial artist, was the son of Jupiter and Juno. He was born lame, and his mother was so displeased at the sight of him that she flung him out of heaven. Other accounts say that Jupiter kicked him out for taking part with his mother, in a quarrel which occurred between them. Vulcan's lameness, according to this account, was the consequence of his fall. He was a whole day falling, and at last alighted in the Island of Lemnos, which was thenceforth sacred to him. Milton alludes to this story in "Paradise Lost," Book I.

> "From morn
> To noon he fell, from noon to dewy eve,
> A summer's day; and with the setting sun
> Dropped from the zenith, like a falling star,
> On Lemnos, the Ægean isle."

Mars (Ares), the god of war, was the son of Jupiter and Juno. Phœbus Apollo, the god of archery, prophecy, and music, was the

---

*This inconsistency arises from considering the Saturn of the Romans the same with the Grecian deity Cronos (Time), which, as it brings an end to all things which have had a beginning, may be said to devour its own offspring.

son of Jupiter and Latona, and brother of Diana (Artemis). He was god of the sun, as Diana, his sister, was the goddess of the moon.

Venus (Aphrodite), the goddess of love and beauty, was the daughter of Jupiter and Dione. Others say that Venus sprang from the foam of the sea. The zephyr wafted her along the waves to the Isle of Cyprus, where she was received and attired by the Seasons, and then led to the assembly of the gods. All were charmed with her beauty, and each one demanded her for his wife. Jupiter gave her to Vulcan, in gratitude for the service he had rendered in forging thunderbolts. So the most beautiful of the goddesses became the wife of the most ill-favored of the gods. Venus possessed an embroidered girdle called Cestus, which had the power of inspiring love. Her favorite birds were swans and doves, and the plants sacred to her were the rose and the myrtle.

Cupid (Eros), the god of love, was the son of Venus. He was her constant companion; and, armed with bow and arrows, he shot the darts of desire into the bosoms of both gods and men. There was a deity named Anteros, who was sometimes represented as the avenger of slighted love, and sometimes as the symbol of reciprocal affection. The following legend is told of him:

Venus, complaining to Themis that her son Eros continued always a child, was told by her that it was because he was solitary, and that if he had a brother he would grow apace. Anteros was soon afterwards born, and Eros immediately was seen to increase rapidly in size and strength.

Minerva (Pallas-Athene), the goddess of wisdom, was the offspring of Jupiter, without a mother. She sprang forth from his head, completely armed. Her favorite bird was the owl, and the plant sacred to her the olive.

Byron, in "Childe Harold," alludes to the birth of Minerva, thus:

"Can tyrants but by tyrants conquered be,
And Freedom find no champion and no child,
Such as Columbia saw arise, when she
Sprang forth a Pallas, armed and undefiled?
Or must such minds be nourished in the wild,
Deep in the unpruned forest, 'midst the roar
Of cataracts, where nursing Nature smiled
On infant Washington? Has earth no more
Such seeds within her breast, or Europe no such shore?"

Mercury (Hermes) was the son of Jupiter and Maia. He presided over commerce, wrestling, and other gymnastic exercises, even over thieving, and every thing, in short, which required skill and dexterity. He was the messenger of Jupiter, and wore a winged cap and winged shoes. He bore in his hand a rod entwined with two serpents, called the Caduceus.

Mercury is said to have invented the lyre. He found, one day, a tortoise, of which he took the shell, made holes in the opposite edges of it, and drew cords of linen through them, and the instrument was complete. The cords were nine, in honor of the nine Muses. Mercury gave the lyre to Apollo, and received from him in exchange the caduceus.*

Ceres (Demeter) was the daughter of Saturn and Rhea. She had a daughter named Proserpine (Persephone), who became the wife of Pluto, and queen of the realms of the dead. Ceres presided over agriculture.

Bacchus (Dionysus), the god of wine, was the son of Jupiter and Semele. He represents not only the intoxicating power of wine, but its social and beneficent influences likewise, so that he is viewed as the promoter of civilization, and a lawgiver and lover of peace.

The Muses were the daughters of Jupiter and Mnemosyne (Memory). They presided over song, and prompted the memory. They were nine in number, to each of whom was assigned the presidence over some particular department of literature, art, or science. Calliope was the muse of epic poetry, Clio of history, Euterpe of lyric poetry, Melpomene of tragedy, Terpsichore of choral dance and song, Erato of love poetry, Polyhymnia of sacred poetry, Urania of astronomy, Thalia of comedy.

The Graces were goddesses presiding over the banquet, the dance, and all social enjoyments and elegant arts. They were three in number. Their names were Euphrosyne, Aglaia, and Thalia.

Spenser describes the office of the Graces thus:

> "These three on men all gracious gifts bestow
> Which deck the body or adorn the mind,
> To make them lovely or well-favored show;
> As comely carriage, entertainment kind,
> Sweet semblance, friendly offices that bind,
> And all the complements of courtesy;
> They teach us how to each degree and kind
> We should ourselves demean, to low, to high,
> To friends, to foes; which skill men call Civility."

The Fates were also three—Clotho, Lachesis, and Atropos. Their office was to spin the thread of human destiny, and they were armed with shears, with which they cut it off when they pleased. They were the daughters of Themis (Law), who sits by Jove on his throne to give him counsel.

The Erinnyes, or Furies, were three goddesses who punished by their secret stings the crimes of those who escaped or defied public justice. The heads of the Furies were wreathed with serpents, and their whole appearance was terrific and appalling. Their names were Aleeto,

---

*From this origin of the instrument, the word "shell" is often used as synonymous with "lyre," and figuratively for music and poetry. Thus Gray, in his ode on the "Progress of Poesy," says,—

> "O Sovereign of the willing soul,
> Parent of sweet and solemn-breathing airs,
> Enchanting shell! the sullen Cares
> And frantic Passions hear thy soft control."

Tisiphone, and Megæra. They were also called Eumenides.

Nemesis was also an avenging goddess. She represents the righteous anger of the gods, particularly towards the proud and insolent.

Pan was the god of flocks and shepherds. His favorite residence was in Arcadia.

The Satyrs were deities of the woods and fields. They were conceived to be covered with bristly hair, their heads decorated with short, sprouting horns, and their feet like goats'.

Momus was the god of laughter, and Plutus the god of wealth.

Roman Divinities

The preceding are Grecian divinities, though received also by the Romans. Those which follow are peculiar to Roman mythology.

Saturn was an ancient Italian deity. It was attempted to identify him with the Grecian god Cronos, and fabled that after his dethronement by Jupiter, he fled to Italy, where he reigned during what was called the Golden Age. In memory of his beneficent dominion, the feast of Saturnalia was held every year in the winter season. Then all public business was suspended, declarations of war and criminal executions were postponed, friends made presents to one another, and the slaves were indulged with great liberties. A feast was given them at which they sat at table, while their masters served them, to show the natural equality of men, and that all things belonged equally to all, in the reign of Saturn.

Faunus, the grandson of Saturn, was worshipped as the god of fields and shepherds, and also as a prophetic god. His name in the plural, Fauns, expressed a class of gamesome deities, like the Satyrs of the Greeks.

Quirinus was a war god, said to be no other than Romulus, the founder of Rome, exalted after his death to a place among the gods.

Bellona, a war goddess.

Terminus, the god of landmarks. His statue was a rude stone or post, set in the ground to mark the boundaries of fields.

Pales, the goddess presiding over cattle and pastures.

Pomona presided over fruit trees.

Flora, the goddess of flowers.

Lucina, the goddess of childbirth.

Vesta (the Hestia of the Greeks) was a deity presiding over the public and private hearth. A sacred fire, tended by six virgin priestesses called Vestals, flamed in her temple. As the safety of the city was held to be connected with its conservation, the neglect of the virgins, if they let it go out, was severely punished, and the fire was rekindled from the rays of the sun.

Liber is the Latin name of Bacchus; and Mulciber of Vulcan.

Janus was the porter of heaven. He opens the year, the first month being named after him. He is the guardian deity of gates, on which account he is commonly represented with two heads, because every door looks two ways. His temples at Rome were numerous. In war time the gates of the principal one were always open. In peace they were closed; but they were shut only once between the reign of Numa and that of Augustus.

The Penates were the gods who were supposed to attend to the welfare and prosperity of the family. Their name is derived from Penus, the pantry, which was sacred to them. Every master of a family was the priest to the Penates of his own house.

The Lares, or Lars, were also household gods, but differed from the Penates in being regarded as the deified spirits of mortals. The family Lars were held to be the souls of the ancestors, who watched over and protected their descendants. The words Lemur and Larva more nearly correspond to our word Ghost.

The Romans believed that every man had his Genius, and every woman her Juno; that is, a spirit who had given them being, and was regarded as their protector through life. On their birthdays men made offerings to their Genius, women to their Juno.

A modern poet thus alludes to some of the Roman gods:

> "Pomona loves the orchard,
>   And Liber loves the vine,
> And Pales loves the straw-built shed
>   Warm with the breath of kine;
> And Venus loves the whisper
>   Of plighted youth and maid,
> In April's ivory moonlight,
>   Beneath the chestnut shade."

Macaulay, "Prophecy of Capys"

N.B.—It is to be observed that in proper names the final *e* and *es* are to be sounded. Thus Cybele and Penates are words of three syllables. But Proserpine and Thebes are exceptions, and to be pronounced as English words. In the Index at the close of the volume, we shall mark the accented syllable, in all words which appear to require it.

· · · · · · ·

2

Prometheus and Pandora

The creation of the world is a problem naturally fitted to excite the liveliest interest of man, its inhabitant. The ancient pagans, not having the information of the subject which we derive from the pages of Scripture, had their own way of telling the story, which is as follows:

Before earth, and sea, and heaven were created, all things wore one aspect, to which we give the name of Chaos—a confused and shapeless mass, nothing but dead weight, in which, however, slumbered the seeds of things. Earth, sea, and air were all mixed up together; so the earth was not solid, the sea was not fluid, and the air was not transparent. God and Nature at last interposed, and put an end to this discord, separating earth from sea, and heaven from both. The fiery part, being the lightest, sprang up, and formed the skies; the air was next in weight and place. The earth, being heavier, sank below; and the water took the lowest place, and buoyed up the earth.

Here some god—it is not known which—gave his good offices in arranging and disposing the earth. He appointed rivers and bays their places, raised mountains, scooped out valleys, distributed woods, fountains, fertile fields, and stony plains. The air being cleared, the stars began to appear, fishes took possession of the sea, birds of the air, and four-footed beasts of the land.

But a nobler animal was wanted, and Man was made. It is not known whether the creator made him of divine materials, or whether in the earth, so lately separated from heaven, there lurked still some heavenly seeds. Prometheus took some of this earth, and kneading it up with water, made man in the image of the gods. He gave him an upright stature, so that while all other animals turn their faces downward, and look to the earth, he raises his to heaven, and gazes on the stars.

Prometheus was one of the Titans, a gigantic race, who inhabited the earth before the creation of man. To him and his brother Epimetheus was committed the office of making man, and providing him and all other animals with the faculties necessary for their preservation. Epimetheus undertook to do this, and Prometheus was to overlook his work, when it was done. Epimetheus accordingly proceeded to bestow upon the different animals the various gifts of courage, strength, swiftness, sagacity; wings to one, claws to another, a shell covering to a third, etc. But when man came to be provided for, who was to be superior to all other animals, Epimetheus had been so prodigal of his resources that he had nothing left to bestow upon him. In his perplexity he resorted to his brother Prometheus, who, with the aid of Minerva, went up to heaven, and lighted his torch at the chariot of the sun, and brought down fire to man. With this gift man was more than a match for all other animals. It enabled him to make weapons wherewith to subdue them; tools with which to cultivate the earth; to warm his dwelling, so as to be comparatively independent of climate; and finally to introduce the arts and to coin money, the means of trade and commerce.

Woman was not yet made. The story (absurd enough!) is, that Jupiter made her, and sent her to Prometheus and his brother, to punish them for their presumption in stealing fire from heaven; and man, for accepting the gift. The first woman was named Pandora. She was made in heaven, every god contributing something to perfect her. Venus gave her beauty, Mercury persuasion, Apollo music, etc. Thus equipped, she was conveyed to earth, and presented to Epimetheus, who gladly accepted her, though cautioned by his brother to beware of Jupiter and his gifts. Epimetheus had in his house a jar, in which were kept certain noxious articles, for which, in fitting man for his new abode, he had had no occasion. Pandora was seized with an eager curiosity to know what this jar contained; and one day she slipped off the cover and looked in. Forthwith there escaped a multitude of plagues for hapless man—such as gout, rheumatism, and colic for his body, and envy, spite, and revenge for his mind—and scattered themselves far and wide. Pandora hastened to replace the lid; but, alas! the whole contents of the jar had escaped, one thing only excepted, which lay at the bottom, and that was *hope*. So we see at this day, whatever evils are abroad, hope never entirely leaves us; and while we have *that*, no amount of other ills can make us completely wretched.

Another story is, that Pandora was sent in good faith, by Jupiter, to bless man; that she was furnished with a box, containing her marriage presents, into which every god had put some blessing. She opened the box incautiously, and the blessings all escaped, *hope* only excepted. This story seems more probable than the former; for how could *hope,* so precious a jewel as it is, have been kept in a jar full of all manner of evils, as in the former statement?

The world being thus furnished with inhabitants, the first age was an age of innocence and happiness, called the *Golden Age.* Truth and right prevailed, though not enforced by law, nor was there any magistrate to threaten or punish. The forest had not yet been robbed of its trees to furnish timbers for vessels, nor had men built fortifications round their towns. There were no such things as swords, spears, or helmets. The earth brought forth all things necessary for man, without his labor in ploughing or sowing. Perpetual spring reigned, flowers sprang up without seed, the rivers flowed with milk and wine, and yellow honey distilled from the oaks.

Then succeeded the *Silver Age,* inferior to the golden but better than that of brass. Jupiter shortened the spring, and divided the year into seasons. Then, first, men had to endure the extremes of heat and cold, and houses became necessary. Caves were the first dwellings, and leafy coverts of the woods, and huts woven of twigs. Crops would no longer grow without planting. The farmer was obliged to sow the seed, and the toiling ox to draw the plough.

Next came the *Brazen Age,* more savage of temper, and readier to the strife of arms, yet not altogether wicked. The hardest and worst was the *Iron Age.* Crime burst in like a flood; modesty, truth, and honor fled. In their places came fraud and cunning, violence, and the wicked love of gain. Then seamen spread sails to the wind, and the trees were torn from the mountains to serve for keels to ships, and vex the face of the ocean. The earth, which till now had been cultivated in common, began to be divided off into possessions. Men were not satisfied with what the surface produced, but must dig into its bowels, and draw forth from thence the ores of metals. Mischievous *iron,* and more mischievous *gold,* were produced. War sprang up, using both as weapons; the guest was not safe in his friend's house; and sons-in-law and fathers-in-law, brothers and sisters, husbands and wives, could not trust one another. Sons wished their fathers dead, that they might come to the inheritance; family love lay prostrate. The earth was wet with slaughter, and the gods abandoned it, one by one, till Astræa* alone was left, and finally she also took her departure.

Jupiter, seeing this state of things, burned with anger. He summoned the gods to council. They obeyed the call, and took the road to the palace of heaven. The road, which any one may see in a clear night, stretches across the face of the sky, and is called the Milky Way. Along the road stand the palaces of the illustrious gods; the common people of the skies live apart, on either side. Jupiter addressed the assembly. He set forth the frightful condition of things on the earth, and closed by announcing his intention to destroy the whole of its inhabitants, and provide a new race, unlike the first, who would be more worthy of life, and much better worshippers of the gods. So saying he took a thunderbolt, and was about to launch it at the world, and destroy it by burning; but recollecting the danger that such a conflagration might set heaven itself on fire, he changed his plan, and resolved to drown it. The north wind, which scatters the clouds, was chained up; the south was sent out, and soon covered all the face of heaven with a cloak of pitchy darkness. The clouds, driven together, resound with a crash; torrents of rain fall; the crops are laid low; the year's labor of the husbandman perishes in an hour. Jupiter, not satisfied with his own waters, calls on his brother Neptune to aid him with his. He lets loose the rivers, and pours them over the land. At the same time, he heaves the land with an earthquake, and brings in the reflux of the ocean over the shores. Flocks, herds, men, and houses are swept away, and temples, with their sacred enclosures, profaned. If any edifice remained standing, it was overwhelmed, and its turrets lay hid beneath the waves. Now all was sea, sea without shore. Here and there an individual remained on a projecting hill-top, and a few, in boats, pulled the oar where they had lately driven the plough. The fishes swim among the tree-tops; the anchor is let down into a garden. Where the graceful lambs played but now, unwieldy sea calves gambol. The wolf swims among the sheep, the yellow lions and tigers struggle in the water. The strength of the wild boar serves him not, nor his swiftness the stag. The birds fall with weary wing into the water, having found no land for a

---

*The goddess of innocence and purity. After leaving earth, she was placed among the stars, where she became the constellation Virgo—the Virgin. Themis (Justice) was the mother of Astræa. She is represented as holding aloft a pair of scales, in which she weighs the claims of opposing parties.

It was a favorite idea of the old poets, that these goddesses would one day return, and bring back the Golden Age. Even in a Christian Hymn, the Messiah of Pope, this idea occurs.

"All crimes shall cease, and ancient fraud shall fail,
Returning Justice lift aloft her scale,
Peace o'er the world her olive wand extend,
And white-robed Innocence from heaven descend."

See, also, Milton's "Hymn to the Nativity," stanzas xiv and xv.

resting-place. Those living beings whom the water spared fell a prey to hunger.

Parnassus alone, of all the mountains, overtopped the waves; and there Deucalion, and his wife Pyrrha, of the race of Prometheus, found refuge—he a just man, and she a faithful worshipper of the gods. Jupiter, when he saw none left alive but this pair, and remembered their harmless lives and pious demeanor, ordered the north winds to drive away the clouds, and disclose the skies to earth, and earth to the skies. Neptune also directed Triton to blow on his shell, and sound a retreat to the waters. The waters obeyed, and the sea returned to its shores, and the rivers to their channels. Then Deucalion thus addressed Pyrrha: "O wife, only surviving woman, joined to me first by the ties of kindred and marriage, and now by a common danger, would that we possessed the power of our ancestor Prometheus, and could renew the race as he at first made it! But as we cannot, let us seek yonder temple, and inquire of the gods what remains for us to do." They entered the temple, deformed as it was with slime, and approached the altar, where no fire burned. There they fell prostrate on the earth, and prayed the goddess to inform them how they might retrieve their miserable affairs. The oracle answered, "Depart from the temple with head veiled and garments unbound, and cast behind you the bones of your mother." They heard the words with astonishment. Pyrrha first broke silence: "We cannot obey; we dare not profane the remains of our parents." They sought the thickest shades of the wood, and revolved the oracle in their minds. At length Deucalion spoke: "Either my sagacity deceives me, or the command is one we may obey without impiety. The earth is the great parent of all; the stones are her bones; these we may cast behind us; and I think this is what the oracle means. At least, it will do no harm to try." They veiled their faces, unbound their garments, and picked up stones, and cast them behind them. The stones (wonderful to relate) began to grow soft, and assume shape. By degrees, they put on a rude resemblance to the human form, like a block half finished in the hands of the sculptor. The moisture and slime that were about them became flesh; the stony part became bones; the veins remained veins, retaining their name, only changing their use. Those thrown by the hand of the man became men, and those by the woman became women. It was a hard race, and well adapted to labor, as we find ourselves to be at this day, giving plain indications of our origin.

The comparison of Eve to Pandora is too obvious to have escaped Milton, who introduces it in Book IV of "Paradise Lost":

"More lovely than Pandora, whom the gods
  Endowed with all their gifts; and O, too like
  In sad event, when to the unwiser son
  On Japhet brought by Hermes, she insnared

Mankind with her fair looks, to be avenged
On him who had stole Jove's authentic fire.''

Prometheus and Epimetheus were sons of Iapetus, which Milton changes to Japhet.

Prometheus has been a favorite subject with poets. He is represented as the friend of mankind, who interposed in their behalf when Jove was incensed against them, and who taught them civilization and the arts. But as, in so doing, he transgressed the will of Jupiter, he drew down on himself the anger of the ruler of gods and men. Jupiter had him chained to a rock on Mount Caucasus, where a vulture preyed on his liver, which was renewed as fast as devoured. This state of torment might have been brought to an end at any time by Prometheus, if he had been willing to submit to his oppressor; for he possessed a secret which involved the stability of Jove's throne, and if he would have revealed it, he might have been at once taken into favor. But that he disdained to do. He has therefore become the symbol of magnanimous endurance of unmerited suffering, and strength of will resisting oppression.

Byron and Shelly have both treated this theme. The following are Byron's lines:

"Titan! to whose immmortal eyes
    The sufferings of mortality,
    Seen in their sad reality,
Were not as things that gods despise;
What was thy pity's recompense?
A silent suffering, and intense;
The rock, the vulture, and the chain;
All that the proud can feel of pain;
The agony they do not show;
The suffocating sense of woe.

"Thy godlike crime was to be kind;
    To render with thy precepts less
    The sum of human wretchedness,
And strengthen man with his own mind.
    And, baffled as thou wert from high,
    Still, in thy patient energy,
In the endurance and repulse
    Of thine impenetrable spirit,
Which earth and heaven could not convulse,
    A mighty lesson we inherit.''

Byron also employs the same allusion, in his ode to Napoleon Bonaparte:

"Or, like the thief of fire from heaven,
    Wilt thou withstand the shock?
And share with him—the unforgiven—
    His vulture and his rock?''

Apollo and Daphne – Pyramus and Thisbe – Cephalus and Procris

The slime with which the earth was covered by the waters of the flood produced an excessive fertility, which called forth every variety of production, both bad and good. Among the rest, Python, an enormous serpent, crept forth, the terror of the people, and lurked in the caves of Mount Parnassus. Apollo slew him with his arrows—weapons which he had not before used against any but feeble animals, hares, wild goats, and such game. In commemoration of this illustrious conquest he instituted the Pythian games, in which the victor in feats of strength, swiftness of foot, or in the chariot race, was crowned with a wreath of beech leaves; for the laurel was not yet adopted by Apollo as his own tree.

The famous statue of Apollo called the Belvedere represents the god after this victory over the serpent Python. To this Byron alludes in his "Childe Harold," IV 161:

> "The lord of the unerring bow,
> The god of life, and poetry, and light,
> The Sun, in human limbs arrayed, and brow
> All radiant from his triumph in the fight.
> The shaft has just been shot; the arrow bright
> With an immortal's vengeance; in his eye
> And nostril, beautiful disdain, and might,
> And majesty flash their full lightnings by,
> Developing in that one glance the Deity."

Apollo and Daphne

Daphne was Apollo's first love. It was not brought about by accident, but by the malice of Cupid. Apollo saw the boy playing with his bow and arrows; and being himself elated with his recent victory over Python, he said to him, "What have you to do with warlike weapons, saucy boy? Leave them for hands worthy of them. Behold the conquest I have won by means of them over the vast serpent who stretched his poisonous body over acres of the plain! Be content with your torch, child, and kindle up your flames, as you call them, where you will, but presume not to meddle with my weapons."

Venus's boy heard these words, and rejoined, "Your arrows may strike all things else, Apollo, but mine shall strike you." So saying, he took his stand on a rock of Parnassus, and drew from his quiver two arrows of different workmanship, one to excite love, the other to repel it. The former was of gold and sharp pointed, the latter blunt and tipped with lead. With the leaden shaft he struck the nymph Daphne, the daughter of the river god Peneus, and with the golden one Apollo, through the heart. Forthwith the god was seized with love for the maiden, and she abhorred the thought of loving. Her delight was in woodland sports and in the spoils of the chase. Many lovers sought her, but she spurned them all, ranging the woods, and taking no thought of Cupid nor of Hymen. Her father often said to her, "Daughter, you owe me a son-in-law; you owe me grandchildren." She, hating the thought of marriage as a crime, with her beautiful face tinged all over with blushes, threw her arms around her father's neck, and said, "Dearest father, grant me this favor, that I may always remain unmarried, like Diana." He consented, but at the same time said, "Your own face will forbid it."

Apollo loved her, and longed to obtain her; and he who gives oracles to all the world was not wise enough to look into his own fortunes. He saw her hair flung loose over her shoulders, and said, "If so charming in disorder, what would it be if arranged?" He saw her eyes bright as stars; he saw her lips, and was not satisfied with only seeing them. He admired her hands and arms, naked to the shoulder, and whatever was hidden from view he imagined more beautiful still. He followed her; she fled, swifter than the wind, and delayed not a moment at his entreaties. "Stay," said he, "daughter of Peneus; I am not a foe. Do not fly me as a lamb flies the wolf, or a dove the hawk. It is for love I pursue you. You make me miserable, for fear you should fall and hurt yourself on these stones, and I should be the cause. Pray run slower, and I will follow slower. I am no clown, no rude peasant. Jupiter is my father, and I am lord of Delphos and Tenedos, and know all things, present and future. I am the god of song and the lyre. My arrows fly true to the mark; but alas! an arrow more fatal than mine has pierced my heart! I am the god of medicine, and know the virtues of all healing plants. Alas! I suffer a malady that no balm can cure!"

The nymph continued her flight, and left his plea half uttered. And even as she fled she charmed him. The wind blew her garments, and her unbound hair streamed loose behind her. The god grew impatient to find his wooings thrown away, and, sped by Cupid, gained upon her in the race. It was like a hound pursuing a hare, with open jaws ready to seize, while the feebler animal darts forward, slipping from the very grasp. So flew the god and the virgin—he on the wings of love, and she on those of fear. The pursuer is the more rapid, however, and gains upon her, and his panting breath blows upon her hair. Her strength begins to fail, and, ready to sink, she calls upon her father, the river god: "Help me, Peneus! open the earth to enclose me, or change my form, which has brought me into this danger!" Scarcely had she spoken, when a stiffness seized all her limbs; her bosom began to be enclosed in a tender bark; her hair became leaves; her arms became branches; her foot stuck fast in the ground, as a root; her face became a tree-top, retaining nothing of its former self but its beauty. Apollo stood amazed. He touched the stem, and felt the flesh tremble under the new bark. He embraced the branches, and lavished kisses on the wood. The branches shrank from his lips. "Since you cannot be my wife," said he, "you shall assuredly be my tree. I will wear you for my crown; I will decorate with you my harp and my quiver; and when the great Roman conquerors lead up the triumphal pomp to the Capitol, you shall be woven into wreaths for their brows. And, as eternal youth is mine, you also shall be always green, and your leaf know no decay." The nymph, now changed into a Laurel tree, bowed its head in grateful acknowledgment.

That Apollo should be the god both of music and poetry will not appear strange, but that medicine should also be assigned to his province, may. The poet Armstrong, himself a physician, thus accounts for it:—

"Music exalts each joy, allays each grief,
    Expels diseases, softens every pain;
    And hence the wise of ancient days adored
    One power of physic, melody, and song."

The story of Apollo and Daphne is often alluded to by the poets. Waller applies it to the case of one whose amatory verses, though they did not soften the heart of his mistress, yet won for the poet wide-spread fame.

"Yet what he sung in his immortal strain,
    Though unsuccessful, was not sung in vain.
    All but the nymph that should redress his wrong,
    Attend his passion and approve his song.
    Like Phœbus thus, acquiring unsought praise,
    He caught at love and filled his arms with bays."

The following stanza from Shelley's "Adonais" alludes to Byron's early quarrel with the reviewers:

"The herded wolves, bold only to pursue;
    The obscene ravens, clamorous o'er the dead;
    The vultures, to the conqueror's banner true,
    Who feed where Desolation first has fed,
    And whose wings rain contagion; how they fled,
    When like Apollo, from his golden bow,
    The Pythian of the age one arrow sped
    And smiled! The spoilers tempt no second blow;
    They fawn on the proud feet that spurn them as they go."

Pyramus and Thisbe

Pyramus was the handsomest youth, and Thisbe the fairest maiden, in all Babylonia, where Semiramis reigned. Their parents occupied adjoining houses; and neighborhood brought the young people together, and acquaintance ripened into love. They would gladly have married, but their parents forbade. One thing however they could not forbid—that love should glow with equal ardor in the bosoms of both. They conversed by signs and glances, and the fire burned more intensely for being covered up. In the wall that parted the two houses there was a crack, caused by some fault in the structure. No one had remarked it before, but the lovers discovered it. What will not love discover! It afforded a passage to the voice; and tender messages used to pass backward and forward through the gap. As they stood, Pyramus on this side, Thisbe on that, their breaths would mingle. "Cruel wall," they said, "why do you keep two lovers apart? But we will not be ungrateful. We owe you, we confess, the privilege of transmitting loving words to willing ears." Such words they uttered on different sides of the wall; and when night came and they must say farewell, they pressed their lips upon the wall, she on her side, he on his, as they could come no nearer.

Next morning, when Aurora had put out the stars, and the sun had melted the frost from the grass, they met at the accustomed spot. Then, after lamenting their hard fate, they agreed that next night, when all was still, they would slip away from watchful eyes, leave their dwellings and walk out into the fields; and to insure a meeting, repair to a well-known edifice, standing without the city's bounds, called the Tomb of Ninus, and that the one who came first should await the other at the foot of a certain tree. It was a white mulberry tree, and stood near a cool spring. All was agreed on, and they waited impatiently for the sun to go down beneath the waters and night to rise up from them. Then cautiously Thisbe stole forth, unobserved by the family, her head covered with a veil, made her way to the monument and sat down under the tree. As she sat alone in the dim light of the evening she descried a lioness, her jaws reeking with recent slaughter, approaching the fountain to slake her thirst. Thisbe fled at the sight, and sought refuge in the hollow of a rock. As she fled she dropped her veil. The lioness, after drinking at the spring, turned to retreat to the woods, and seeing the veil on the ground, tossed and rent it with her bloody mouth.

Pyramus, having been delayed, now approached the place of meeting. He saw in the sand the footsteps of the lion, and the color fled from his cheeks at the sight. Presently he found the veil all rent and bloody. "O, hapless girl," said he, "I have been the cause of thy death! Thou, more worthy of life than I, hast fallen the first victim. I will follow. I am the guilty cause, in tempting thee forth to a place of such peril, and not being myself on the spot to guard thee. Come forth, ye lions, from the rocks, and tear this guilty body with your teeth." He took up the veil, carried it with him to the appointed tree, and covered it with kisses and with tears. "*My* blood also shall stain your texture," said he, and drawing his sword plunged it into his heart. The blood spurted from the wound, and tinged the white mulberries of the tree all red; and sinking into the earth reached the roots, so that the red color mounted through the trunk to the fruit.

By this time, Thisbe, still trembling with fear, yet wishing not to disappoint her lover, stepped cautiously forth, looking anxiously for the youth, eager to tell him the danger she had escaped. When she came to the spot and saw the changed color of the mulberries she doubted whether it was the same place. While she hesitated she saw the form of one struggling in the agonies of death. She started back, a shudder ran through her frame as a ripple on the face of the still water when a sudden breeze sweeps over it. But as soon as she recognized her lover, she screamed and beat her breast; embracing the lifeless body, pouring tears into its wounds, and imprinting kisses on the cold lips. "O, Pyramus," she cried, "what has done this? Answer me, Pyramus; it is your own Thisbe that speaks. Hear me, dearest, and lift that drooping head!" At the name of Thisbe Pyramus opened his eyes, then closed them again. She saw her veil stained with blood and the scabbard empty of its sword. "Thy own hand has slain thee, and for my sake," she said. "I too can be brave for once, and my love is as strong as thine. I will follow thee in death, for I have been the cause; and death, which alone could part us, shall not prevent my joining thee. And ye, unhappy parents of us both, deny us not our united request. As love and death have joined us, let one tomb contain us. And thou, tree, retain the marks of slaughter. Let thy berries still serve for memorials of our blood." So saying she plunged the sword into her breast. Her parents ratified her wish, the gods also ratified it. The two bodies were buried in one sepulchre, and the tree ever after brought forth purple berries, as it does to this day.

Moore, in the "Sylph's Ball," speaking of Davy's Safety Lamp, is reminded of the wall that separated Thisbe and her lover:

"O for that Lamp's metallic gauze,
    That curtain of protecting wire,
  Which Davy delicately draws
    Around illicit, dangerous fire!

"The wall he sets 'twixt Flame and Air,
    (Like that which barred young Thisbe's bliss)
  Through whose small holes this dangerous pair
    May see each other, but not kiss."

In Mickle's translation of the *Lusiad* occurs the following allusion to the story of Pyramus and Thisbe, and the metamorphosis of the mulberries. The poet is describing the Island of Love.

"——here each gift Pomona's hand bestows
In cultured garden, free uncultured flows,
The flavor sweeter and the hue more fair
Than e'er was fostered by the hand of care.
The cherry here in shining crimson glows,
And stained with lovers' blood, in pendent rows,
The mulberries o'erload the bending boughs."

If any of our young readers can be so hard-hearted as to enjoy a laugh at the expense of poor Pyramus and Thisbe, they may find an opportunity by turning to Shakespeare's play of the "Midsummer Night's Dream," where it is most amusingly burlesqued.

Cephalus and Procris

Cephalus was a beautiful youth and fond of manly sports. He would rise before the dawn to pursue the chase. Aurora saw him when she first looked forth, fell in love with him and stole him away. But Cephalus was just married to a charming wife whom he devotedly loved. Her name was Procris. She was a favorite of Diana, the goddess of hunting, who had given her a dog which could outrun every rival, and a javelin which would never fail of its mark; and Procris gave these presents to her husband. Cephalus was so happy in his wife that he resisted all the entreaties of Aurora, and she finally dismissed him in displeasure, saying, "Go, ungrateful mortal, keep your wife, whom, if I am not much mistaken, you will one day be very sorry you ever saw again."

Cephalus returned, and was as happy as ever in his wife and his woodland sports. Now it happened some angry deity had sent a ravenous fox to annoy the country; and the hunters turned out in great strength to capture it. Their efforts were all in vain; no dog could run it down; and at last they came to Cephalus to borrow his famous dog, whose name was Lelaps. No sooner was the dog let loose than he darted off, quicker than their eye could follow him. If they had not seen his footprints in the sand they would have thought he flew. Cephalus and others stood on a hill and saw the race. The fox tried every art; he ran in a circle and turned on his track, the dog close upon him, with open jaws, snapping at his heels, but biting only the air. Cephalus was about to use his javelin, when suddenly he saw both dog and game stop instantly. The heavenly powers who had given both, were not willing that either should conquer. In the very attitude of life and action they were turned into stone. So lifelike and natural did they look, you would have thought, as you looked at them, that one was going to bark, the other to leap forward.

Cephalus, though he had lost his dog, still continued to take delight in the chase. He would go out at early morning, ranging the woods and hills unaccompanied by any one, needing no help, for his javelin was a sure weapon in all cases. Fatigued with hunting, when the sun got high he would seek a shady nook where a cool stream flowed, and, stretched on the grass, with his garments thrown aside, would enjoy the breeze. Sometimes he would say aloud, "Come, sweet breeze, come and fan my breast, come and allay the heat that burns me." Some one passing by one day heard him talking in this way to the air, and, foolishly believing that he was talking to some maiden, went and told the secret to Procris, Cephalus's wife. Love is credulous. Procris, at the sudden shock, fainted away. Presently recovering she said, "It cannot be true; I will not believe it unless I myself am a witness to it." So she waited, with anxious heart, till the next morning, when Cephalus went to hunt as usual. Then she stole out after him, and concealed herself in the place where the informer directed her. Cephalus came as he was wont when tired with sport, and stretched himself on the green bank, saying,

"Come, sweet breeze, come and fan me; you know how I love you! you make the groves and my solitary rambles delightful." He was running on in this way when he heard, or thought he heard, a sound as of a sob in the bushes. Supposing it some wild animal, he threw his javelin at the spot. A cry from his beloved Procris told him that the weapon had too surely met its mark. He rushed to the place, and found her bleeding, and with sinking strength endeavoring to draw forth from the wound the javelin, her own gift. Cephalus raised her from the earth, strove to stanch the blood, and called her to revive and not to leave him miserable, to reproach himself with her death. She opened her feeble eyes, and forced herself to utter these few words: "I implore you if you have ever loved me, if I have ever deserved kindness at your hands, my husband, grant me this last request; do not marry that odious Breeze!" This disclosed the whole mystery; but alas! what advantage to disclose it now? She died; but her face wore a calm expression, and she looked pityingly and forgivingly on her husband when he made her understand the truth.

Moore, in his "Legendary Ballads," has one on Cephalus and Procris, beginning thus:

"A hunter once in a grove reclined,
    To shun the noon's bright eye,
And oft he wooed the wandering wind
    To cool his brow with its sigh.
While mute lay even the wild bee's hum,
    Nor breath could stir the aspen's hair,
His song was still, 'Sweet Air, O come!'
    While Echo answered, 'Come, sweet Air!' "
· · · · · · ·

4
Juno and Her Rivals,
Io and Callisto — Diana and
Actæon — Latona and the Rustics

Juno one day perceived it suddenly grow dark, and immediately suspected that her husband had raised a cloud to hide some of his doings that would not bear the light. She brushed away the cloud, and saw her husband, on the banks of a glassy river, with a beautiful heifer standing near him. Juno suspected the heifer's form concealed some fair nymph of mortal mould—as was, indeed, the case; for it was Io, the daughter of the river god Inachus, whom Jupiter had been flirting with, and, when he became aware of the approach of his wife, had changed into that form.

Juno joined her husband, and noticing the heifer praised its beauty, and asked whose it was, and of what herd. Jupiter, to stop questions, replied that it was a fresh creation from the earth. Juno asked to have it as a gift. What could Jupiter do? He was loath to give his mistress to his wife; yet how refuse so trifling a present as a simple heifer? He could not, without exciting suspicion; so he consented. The goddess was not yet relieved of her suspicions; so she delivered the heifer to Argus, to be strictly watched.

Now Argus had a hundred eyes in his head, and never went to sleep with more than two at a time, so that he kept watch of Io constantly. He suffered her to feed through the day, and at night tied her up with a vile rope round her neck. She would have stretched out her arms to implore freedom of Argus, but she had no arms to stretch out, and her voice was a bellow that frightened even herself. She saw her father and her sisters, went near them, and suffered them to pat her back, and heard them admire her beauty. Her father reached her a tuft of grass, and she licked the outstretched hand. She longed to make herself known to him, and would have uttered her wish; but, alas! words were wanting. At length she bethought herself of writing, and inscribed her name—it was a short one—with her hoof on the sand. Inachus recognized it, and discovering that his daughter, whom he had long sought in vain, was hidden under this disguise, mourned over her, and, embracing her white neck, exclaimed, "Alas! my daughter, it would have been a less grief to have lost you altogether!" While he thus lamented, Argus, observing, came and drove her away, and took his seat on a high bank, from whence he could see all round in every direction.

Jupiter was troubled at beholding the sufferings of his mistress, and calling Mercury told him to go and despatch Argus. Mercury made haste, put his winged slippers on his feet, and cap on his head, took his sleep-producing wand, and leaped down from the heavenly towers to the earth. There he laid aside his wings; and kept only his wand, with which he presented himself as a shepherd driving his flock. As he strolled on he blew upon his pipes. These were what are called the Syrinx or Pandean pipes. Argus listened with delight, for he had never seen the instrument before. "Young man," said he, "come and take a seat by me on this stone. There is no better place for your flock to graze in than hereabouts, and here is a pleasant shade such as shepherds love." Mercury sat down, talked, and told stories till it grew late, and played upon his pipes his most soothing strains, hoping to lull the watchful eyes to sleep, but all in vain; for Argus still contrived to keep some of his eyes open though he shut the rest.

Among other stories, Mercury told him how the instrument on which he played was invented. "There was a certain nymph, whose name was Syrinx, who was much beloved by the satyrs and spirits of the wood; but she would have none of them, but was a faithful worshipper of Diana, and followed the chase. You would have thought it was Diana herself, had you seen her in her hunting dress, only that her bow was of horn and Diana's of silver. One day, as she was returning from the chase, Pan met her, told her just this, and added more of the same sort. She ran away, without stopping to hear his compliments, and he pursued till she came to the bank of the river, where he overtook her, and she had only time to

call for help on her friends the water nymphs. They heard and consented. Pan threw his arms around what he supposed to be the form of
the nymph, and found he embraced only a tuft of reeds! As he breathed
a sigh, the air sounded through the reeds, and produced a plaintive
melody. The god, charmed with the novelty, and with the sweetness of
the music, said, 'Thus, then, at least, you shall be mine.' And he took
some of the reeds, and placing them together, of unequal lengths, side
by side, made an instrument which he called Syrinx, in honor of the
nymph.'' Before Mercury had finished his story he saw Argus's eyes all
asleep. As his head nodded forward on his breast, Mercury with one
stroke cut his neck through, and tumbled his head down the rocks. O,
hapless Argus! the light of your hundred eyes is quenched at once! Juno
took them and put them as ornaments on the tail of her peacock, where
they remain to this day.

But the vengeance of Juno was not yet satiated. She sent a gadfly to
torment Io, who fled over the whole world from its pursuit. She swam
through the Ionian Sea, which derived its name from her, then roamed
over the plains of Illyria, ascended Mount Hæmus, and crossed the
Thracian strait, thence named the Bosphorus (cowford), rambled on
through Seythia, and the country of the Cimmerians, and arrived at last
on the banks of the Nile. At length Jupiter interceded for her, and upon
his promising not to pay her any more attentions Juno consented to
restore her to her form. It was curious to see her gradually recover her
former self. The coarse hairs fell from her body, her horns shrank up,
her eyes grew narrower, her mouth shorter; hands and fingers came instead of hoofs to her forefeet; in fine there was nothing left of the
heifer, except her beauty. At first she was afraid to speak for fear she
should low, but gradually she recovered her confidence and was
restored to her father and sisters.

In a poem dedicated to Leigh Hunt, by Keats, the following allusion
to the story of Pan and Syrinx occurs:

"So did he feel who pulled the boughs aside,
  That we might look into a forest wide,
                *   *   *   *
Telling us how fair trembling Syrinx fled
Arcadian Pan, with such a fearful dread.
Poor nymph—poor Pan—how he did weep to find
Nought but a lovely sighing of the wind
Along the reedy stream; a half-heard strain,
Full of sweet desolation, balmy pain.''

Callisto

Callisto was another maiden who excited the jealousy of Juno, and
the goddess changed her into a bear. "I will take away," said she, "that
beauty with which you have captivated my husband." Down fell
Callisto on her hands and knees; she tried to stretch out her arms in

supplication—they were already beginning to be covered with black hair. Her hands grew rounded, became armed with crooked claws, and served for feet; her mouth, which Jove used to praise for its beauty, became a horrid pair of jaws; her voice, which if unchanged would have moved the heart to pity, became a growl, more fit to inspire terror. Yet her former disposition remained, and with continual groaning, she bemoaned her fate, and stood upright as well as she could, lifting up her paws to beg for mercy; and felt that Jove was unkind, though she could not tell him so. Ah, how often, afraid to stay in the woods all night alone, she wandered about the neighborhood of her former haunts; how often, frightened by the dogs, did she, so lately a huntress, fly in terror from the hunters! Often she fled from the wild beasts, forgetting that she was now a wild beast herself; and, bear as she was, was afraid of the bears.

One day a youth espied her as he was hunting. She saw him and recognized him as her own son, now grown a young man. She stopped and felt inclined to embrace him. As she was about to approach, he, alarmed, raised his hunting spear, and was on the point of transfixing her, when Jupiter, beholding, arrested the crime, and snatching away both of them, placed them in the heavens as the Great and Little Bear.

Juno was in a rage to see her rival so set in honor, and hastened to ancient Tethys and Oceanus, the powers of ocean, and in answer to their inquiries, thus told the cause of her coming. "Do you ask why I, the queen of the gods, have left the heavenly plains and sought your depths. Learn that I am supplanted in heaven—my place is given to another. You will hardly believe me; but look when night darkens the world, and you shall see the two of whom I have so much reason to complain exalted to the heavens, in that part where the circle is the smallest, in the neighborhood of the pole. Why should any one hereafter tremble at the thought of offending Juno, when such rewards are the consequence of my displeasure! See what I have been able to effect! I forbade her to wear the human form—she is placed among the stars! So do my punishments result—such is the extent of my power! Better that she should have resumed her former shape, as I permitted Io to do. Perhaps he means to marry her, and put me away! But you, my foster-parents, if you feel for me, and see with displeasure this unworthy treatment of me, show it, I beseech you, by forbidding this guilty couple from coming into your waters." The powers of the ocean assented, and consequently the two constellations of the Great and Little Bear move round and round in heaven, but never sink, as the other stars do, beneath the ocean.

Milton alludes to the fact that the constellation of the Bear never sets, when he says,

"Let my lamp at midnight hour
 Be seen in some high lonely tower,
 Where I may oft outwatch the Bear," etc.

And Prometheus, in J.R. Lowell's poem, says,

"One after one the stars have risen and set,
  Sparkling upon the hoar frost of my chain;
  The Bear that prowled all night about the fold
  Of the North-star, hath shrunk into his den,
  Scared by the blithesome footsteps of the Dawn."

The last star in the tail of the Little Bear is the Pole-star, called also the Cynosure. Milton says,

"Straight mine eye hath caught new pleasures
  While the landscape round it measures.
            *   *   *   *
  Towers and battlements it sees
  Bosomed high in tufted trees,
  Where perhaps some beauty lies
  The Cynosure of neighboring eyes."

The reference here is both to the Pole-star as the guide of mariners, and to the magnetic attraction of the North. He calls it also the "Star of Arcady," because Callisto's boy was named Arcas, and they lived in Arcadia. In "Comus," the brother, benighted in the woods, says,

              "——Some gentle taper!
  Though a rush candle, from the wicker hole
  Of some clay habitation, visit us
  With thy long levelled rule of streaming light,
  And thou shalt be our star of Arcady,
  Or Tyrian Cynosure."

Diana and Actæon

Thus, in two instances, we have seen Juno's severity to her rivals; now let us learn how a virgin goddess punished an invader of her privacy.

It was midday, and the sun stood equally distant from either goal, when young Actæon, son of King Cadmus, thus addressed the youths who with him were hunting the stag in the mountains:

"Friends, our nets and our weapons are wet with the blood of our victims; we have had sport enough for one day, and to-morrow we can renew our labors. Now, while Phœbus parches the earth, let us put by our implements and indulge ourselves with rest."

There was a valley thick enclosed with cypresses and pines, sacred to the huntress queen, Diana. In the extremity of the valley was a cave, not adorned with art, but nature had counterfeited art in its construction, for she had turned the arch of its roof with stones as delicately fitted as if by the hand of man. A fountain burst out from one side, whose open basin was bounded by a grassy rim. Here the goddess of the woods used to come when weary with hunting and lave her virgin limbs in the sparkling water.

One day, having repaired thither with her nymphs, she handed her javelin, her quiver, and her bow to one, her robe to another, while a third unbound the sandals from her feet. Then Crocale, the most skilful of them, arranged her hair, and Nephele, Hyale, and the rest drew water in capacious urns. While the goddess was thus employed in the labors of the toilet, behold Actæon, having quitted his companions, and rambling without any especial object, came to the place, led thither by his destiny. As he presented himself at the entrance of the cave, the nymphs, seeing a man, screamed and rushed towards the goddess to hide her with their bodies. But she was taller than the rest and overtopped them all by a head. Such a color as tinges the clouds at sunset or at dawn, came over the countenance of Diana thus taken by surprise. Surrounded as she was by her nymphs, she yet turned half away, and sought with a sudden impulse for her arrows. As they were not at hand, she dashed the water into the face of the intruder, adding these words:"Now go and tell, if you can, that you have seen Diana unapparelled." Immediately a pair of branching stag's horns grew out of his head, his neck gained in length, his ears grew sharp-pointed, his hands became feet, his arms long legs, his body was covered with a hairy spotted hide. Fear took the place of his former boldness, and the hero fled. He could not but admire his own speed; but when he saw his horns in the water, "Ah, wretched me!" he would have said, but no sound followed the effort. He groaned, and tears flowed down the face which had taken the place of his own. Yet his consciousness remained. What shall he do?—go home to seek the palace, or lie hid in the woods? The latter he was afraid, the former he was ashamed, to do. While he hesitated the dogs saw him. First Melampus, a Spartan dog, gave the signal with his bark, then Pamphagus, Dorceus, Lelaps, Theron, Nape, Tigris, and all the rest, rushed after him swifter than the wind. Over rocks and cliffs, through mountain gorges that seemed impracticable, he fled and they followed. Where he had often chased the stag and cheered on his pack, his pack now chased him, cheered on by his huntsmen. He longed to cry out, "I am Actæon; recognize your master!" but the words came not at his will. The air resounded with the bark of the dogs. Presently one fastened on his back, another seized his shoulder. While they held their master, the rest of the pack came up and buried their teeth in his flesh. He groaned—not in a human voice, yet certainly not in a stag's—and falling on his knees, raised his eyes, and would have raised his arms in supplication, if he had had them. His friends and fellow-huntsmen cheered on the dogs, and looked everywhere for Actæon, calling on him to join the sport. At the sound of his name, he turned his head, and heard them regret that he should be away. He earnestly wished he was. He would have been well pleased to see the exploits of his dogs, but to feel them was too much. They were all around him, rending and tearing; and it was not till they had torn his life out, that the anger of Diana was satisfied.

In Shelley's poem "Adonais" is the following allusion to the story of Actæon:

" 'Midst others of less note came one frail form,
A phantom among men; companionless
As the last cloud of an expiring storm,
Whose thunder is its knell; he, as I guess,
Had gazed on Nature's naked loveliness,
Actæon-like, and now he fled astray
With feeble steps o'er the world's wilderness;
And his own Thoughts, along that rugged way,
Pursued like raging hounds their father and their prey."

Stanza 31

The allusion is probably to Shelley himself.

Latona and the Rustics

Some thought the goddess in this instance more severe than was just, while others praised her conduct as strictly consistent with her virgin dignity. As usual, the recent event brought older ones to mind, and one of the by-standers told this story. "Some countrymen of Lycia once insulted the goddess Latona, but not with impunity. When I was young, my father, who had grown too old for active labors, sent me to Lycia to drive thence some choice oxen, and there I saw the very pond and marsh where the wonder happened. Near by stood an ancient altar, black with the smoke of sacrifice and almost buried among the reeds. I inquired whose altar it might be, whether of Faunus or the Naiads or some god of the neighboring mountain, and one of the country people replied, 'No mountain or river god possesses this altar, but she whom royal Juno in her jealousy drove from land to land, denying her any spot of earth whereon to rear her twins. Bearing in her arms the infant deities, Latona reached this land, weary with her burden and parched with thirst. By chance she espied in the bottom of the valley this pond of clear water, where the country people were at work gathering willows and osiers. The goddess approached, and kneeling on the bank would have slaked her thirst in the cool stream, but the rustics forbade her. 'Why do you refuse me water?' said she; 'water is free to all. Nature allows no one to claim as property the sunshine, the air, or the water. I come to take my share of the common blessing. Yet I ask it of you as a favor. I have no intention of washing my limbs in it, weary though they be, but only to quench my thirst. My mouth is so dry that I can hardly speak. A draught of water would be nectar to me; it would revive me, and I would own myself indebted to you for life itself. Let these infants move your pity, who stretch out their little arms as if to plead for me'; and the children, as it happened, were stretching out their arms.

"Who would not have been moved with these gentle words of the goddess? But these clowns persisted in their rudeness; they even added jeers and threats of violence if she did not leave the place. Nor was this all. They waded into the pond and stirred up the mud with their feet, so as to make the water unfit to drink. Latona was so angry that she ceased to mind her thirst. She no longer supplicated the clowns, but lifting her hands to heaven exclaimed, 'May they never quit that pool, but pass their lives there!' And it came to pass accordingly. They now live in the water, sometimes totally submerged, then raising their heads above the surface or swimming upon it. Sometimes they come out upon the bank, but soon leap back again into the water. They still use their base voices in railing, and though they have the water all to themselves, are not ashamed to croak in the midst of it. Their voices are harsh, their throats bloated, their mouths have become stretched by constant railing, their necks have shrunk up and disappeared, and their heads are joined to their bodies. Their backs are green, their disproportioned bellies white, and in short they are now frogs, and dwell in the slimy pool.''

This story explains the allusion in one of Milton's sonnets, "On the detraction which followed upon his writing certain treatises."

"I did but prompt the age to quit their clogs
    By the known laws of ancient liberty,
    When straight a barbarous noise environs me
  Of owls and cuckoos, asses, apes and dogs.
  As when those hinds that were transformed to frogs
    Railed at Latona's twin-born progeny,
    Which after held the sun and moon in fee."

The persecution which Latona experienced from Juno is alluded to in the story. The tradition was that the future mother of Apollo and Diana, flying from the wrath of Juno, besought all the islands of the Ægean to afford her a place of rest, but all feared too much the potent queen of heaven to assist her rival. Delos alone consented to become the birthplace of the future deities. Delos was then a floating island; but when Latona arrived there, Jupiter fastened it with adamantine chains to the bottom of the sea, that it might be a secure resting-place for his beloved. Byron alludes to Delos in his "Don Juan":

"The isles of Greece! the isles of Greece!
    Where burning Sappho loved and sung,
  Where grew the arts of war and peace,
    Where Delos rose and Phœbus sprung!"

• • • • • • •

5

Phaeton

Phaeton was the son of Apollo and the nymph Clymene. One day a schoolfellow laughed at the idea of his being the son of the god, and Phaeton went in rage and shame and reported it to his mother. "If," said he, "I am indeed of heavenly birth, give me, mother, some proof of it, and establish my claim to the honor." Clymene stretched forth her hands towards the skies, and said, "I call to witness the Sun which looks down upon us, that I have told you the truth. If I speak falsely, let this be the last time I behold his light. But it needs not much labor to go and inquire for yourself; the land whence the Sun rises lies next to ours. Go and demand of him whether he will own you as a son." Phaeton heard with delight. He travelled to India, which lies directly in the regions of sunrise; and, full of hope and pride, approached the goal whence his parent begins his course.

The palace of the Sun stood reared aloft on columns, glittering with gold and precious stones, while polished ivory formed the ceilings, and silver the doors. The workmanship surpassed the material;* for upon the walls Vulcan had represented earth, sea and skies, with their inhabitants. In the sea were the nymphs, some sporting in the waves, some riding on the backs of fishes, while others sat upon the rocks and dried their sea-green hair. Their faces were not all alike, nor yet unlike—but such as sisters' ought to be.* The earth had its towns and forests and rivers and rustic divinities. Over all was carved the likeness of the glorious heaven; and on the silver doors the twelve signs of the zodiac, six on each side.

Clymene's son advanced up the steep ascent, and entered the halls of his disputed father. He approached the paternal presence, but stopped at a distance, for the light was more than he could bear. Phœbus, arrayed in a purple vesture, sat on a throne which glittered as with diamonds. On his right hand and his left stood the Day, the Month, and the Year, and, at regular intervals, the Hours. Spring stood with her head crowned with flowers, and Summer, with garment cast aside, and a garland formed of spears of ripened grain, and Autumn, with his feet stained with grape-juice, and icy Winter, with his hair stiffened with hoar frost. Surrounded by these attendants, the Sun, with the eye that sees every thing, beheld the youth dazzled with the novelty and splendor of the scene, and inquired the purpose of his errand. The youth replied, "O, light of the boundless world, Phœbus, my father—if you permit me to use that name—give me some proof, I beseech you, by which I may be known as yours." He ceased; and his father, laying aside the beams that shone all around his head, bade him approach, and embracing him, said, "My son, you deserve not to be disowned, and I confirm what your mother has told you. To put an end to your doubts, ask what you will, the gift shall be yours. I call to witness that dreadful lake, which I never saw, but which we gods swear by in our most solemn engagements." Phaeton immediately asked to be permitted for one day to drive the chariot of the sun. The father repented of his promise; thrice and four times he shook his radiant head in warning. "I have spoken rashly," said he; "this only request I would fain deny. I beg you to withdraw it. It is not a safe boon, nor one, my Phaeton, suited to your youth and strength. Your lot is mortal, and you ask what is beyond a mortal's power. In your ignorance you aspire to do that which not even the gods

*See Proverbial Expressions, page 271.

themselves may do. None but myself may drive the flaming car of day. Not even Jupiter, whose terrible right arm hurls the thunderbolts. The first part of the way is steep, and such as the horses when fresh in the morning can hardly climb; the middle is high up in the heavens, whence I myself can scarcely, without alarm, look down and behold the earth and sea stretched beneath me. The last part of the road descends rapidly, and requires most careful driving. Tethys, who is waiting to receive me, often trembles for me lest I should fall headlong. Add to all this, the heaven is all the time turning round and carrying the stars with it. I have to be perpetually on my guard lest that movement, which sweeps every thing else along, should hurry me also away. Suppose I should lend you the chariot, what would you do? Could you keep your course while the sphere was revolving under you? Perhaps you think that there are forests and cities, the abodes of gods, and palaces and temples on the way. On the contrary, the road is through the midst of frightful monsters. You pass by the horns of the Bull, in front of the Archer, and near the Lion's jaws, and where the Scorpion stretches its arms in one direction and the Crab in another. Nor will you find it easy to guide those horses, with their breasts full of fire that they breathe forth from their mouths and nostrils. I can scarcely govern them myself, when they are unruly and resist the reins. Beware, my son, lest I be the donor of a fatal gift; recall your request while yet you may. Do you ask me for a proof that you are sprung from my blood? I give you a proof in my fears for you. Look at my face—I would that you could look into my breast, you would there see all a father's anxiety. Finally," he continued, "look round the world and choose whatever you will of what earth or sea contains most precious—ask it and fear no refusal. This only I pray you not to urge. It is not honor, but destruction you seek. Why do you hang round my neck and still entreat me? You shall have it if you persist—the oath is sworn and must be kept—but I beg you to choose more wisely."

He ended; but the youth rejected all admonition, and held to his demand. So, having resisted as long as he could, Phœbus at last led the way to where stood the lofty chariot.

It was of gold, the gift of Vulcan; the axle was of gold, the pole and wheels of gold, the spokes of silver. Along the seat were rows of chrysolites and diamonds, which reflected all around the brightness of the sun. While the daring youth gazed in admiration, the early Dawn threw open the purple doors of the east, and showed the pathway strewn with roses. The stars withdrew, marshalled by the Daystar, which last of all retired also. The father, when he saw the earth beginning to glow, and the Moon preparing to retire, ordered the Hours to harness up the horses. They obeyed, and led forth from the lofty stalls the steeds full fed with ambrosia, and attached the reins. Then the father bathed the face of his son with a powerful unguent, and made him capable of enduring the brightness of the flame. He set the rays on his head, and, with a foreboding sigh, said, "If, my son, you will in this at least heed my advice, spare the whip and hold tight the reins. They go fast enough of their own accord; the labor is to hold them in. You are not to take the straight road directly between the five circles, but turn off to the left. Keep within the limit of the middle zone, and avoid the northern and the southern alike. You will see the marks of the wheels, and they will serve to guide you. And, that the skies and the earth may each receive their due share of heat, go not too low, or you will set the earth on fire; the middle course is safest and best.* And now I leave you to your chance, which I hope will plan better for you than you have done for yourself. Night is passing out of the western gates and we can delay no longer. Take the reins; but if at last your heart fails you, and you will benefit by my advice, stay where you are in safety, and suffer me to light and warm the earth." The agile youth sprang into the chariot, stood erect and grasped the reins with delight, pouring out thanks to his reluctant parent.

Meanwhile the horses fill the air with their snortings and fiery breath, and stamp the ground impatient. Now the bars are let down, and the boundless plain of the universe lies open before them. They dart forward and cleave the opposing clouds, and outrun the morning breezes which started from the same eastern goal. The steeds soon perceived that the load they drew was lighter than usual; and as a ship without ballast is tossed hither and thither on the sea, so the chariot, without its accustomed weight, was dashed about as if empty. They rush headlong and leave the travelled road. He is alarmed, and knows not how to guide them; nor, if he knew, has he the power. Then, for the first time, the Great and Little Bear were scorched with heat, and would fain, if it were possible, have plunged into the water; and the Serpent which lies coiled up round the north pole, torpid and harmless, grew warm, and with warmth felt its rage revive. Boötes, they say, fled away, though encumbered with his plough, and all unused to rapid motion.

When hapless Phaeton looked down upon the earth, now spreading in vast extent beneath him, he grew pale and his knees shook with terror. In spite of the glare all around him, the sight of his eyes grew dim. He wished he had never touched his father's horses, never learned his parentage, never prevailed in his request. He is borne along like a vessel that flies before a tempest, when the pilot can do no more and betakes himself to his prayers. What shall he do? Much of the heavenly road is left behind, but more remains before. He turns his eyes from one direction to the other; now to the goal whence he began his course, now to the realms of sunset which he is not destined to reach. He loses his self-command, and knows not what to do—whether to draw tight the reins or throw them loose; he forgets the names of the horses. He sees with terror the monstrous forms scattered over the surface of heaven. Here the Scorpion extended his two great arms, with his tail and crooked claws stretching over two signs of the zodiac. When the boy beheld him, reeking with poison and menacing with his fangs, his courage failed, and the reins fell from his hands. The horses, when they felt them loose

*See Proverbial Expressions, page 271.

on their backs, dashed headlong, and unrestrained went off into unknown regions of the sky, in among the stars, hurling the chariot over
pathless places, now up in high heaven, now down almost to the earth.
The moon saw with astonishment her brother's chariot running beneath
her own. The clouds begin to smoke, and the mountain tops take fire;
the fields are parched with heat, the plants wither, the trees with their
leafy branches burn, the harvest is ablaze! The forest-clad mountains
burned, Athos and Taurus and Tmolus and Œte; Ida, once celebrated for
fountains, but now all dry; the Muses' mountain Helicon, and Hæmus;
Ætna, with fires within and without, and Parnassus, with his two peaks,
and Rhodope, forced at last to part with his snowy crown. Her cold
climate was no protection to Scythia, Caucasus burned, and Ossa and
Pindus, and, greater than both, Olympus; the Alps high in air, and the
Apennines crowned with clouds.

Then Phaeton beheld the world on fire, and felt the heat intolerable.
The air he breathed was like the air of a furnace and full of burning
ashes, and the smoke was of a pitchy darkness. He dashed forward he
knew not whither. Then, it is believed, the people of Æthiopia became
black by the blood being forced so suddenly to the surface, and the Libyan desert was dried up to the condition in which it remains to this day.
The Nymphs of the fountains, with dishevelled hair, mourned their
waters, nor were the rivers safe beneath their banks; Tanais smoked,
and Caicus, Xanthus and Meander; Babylonian Euphrates and Ganges,
Tagus with golden sands, and Cayster where the swans resort. Nile fled
away and hid his head in the desert, and there it still remains concealed.
Where he used to discharge his waters through seven mouths into the sea,
there seven dry channels alone remained. The earth cracked open, and
through the chinks light broke into Tartarus, and frightened the king of
shadows and his queen. The sea shrank up. Where before was water, it
became a dry plain; and the mountains that lie beneath the waves lifted
up their heads and became islands. The fishes sought the lowest depths,
and the dolphins no longer ventured as usual to sport on the surface. Even
Nereus, and his wife Doris, with the Nereids, their daughters, sought the
deepest caves for refuge. Thrice Neptune essayed to raise his head above
the surface, and thrice was driven back by the heat. Earth, surrounded
as she was by waters, yet with head and shoulders bare, screening her
face with her hand, looked up to heaven, and with a husky voice called
on Jupiter.

"O, ruler of the gods, if I have deserved this treatment, and it is your
will that I perish with fire, why withhold your thunderbolts? Let me at
least fall by your hand. Is this the reward of my fertility, of my obedient
service? Is it for this that I have supplied herbage for cattle, and fruits
for men, and frankincense for your altars? But if I am unworthy of
regard, what has my brother Ocean done to deserve such a fate? If neither
of us can excite your pity, think, I pray you, of your own heaven, and
behold how both the poles are smoking which sustain your palace,
which must fall if they be destroyed. Atlas faints, and scarce holds up

his burden. If sea, earth, and heaven perish, we fall into ancient Chaos. Save what yet remains to us from the devouring flame. O, take thought for our deliverance in this awful moment!''

Thus spoke Earth, and overcome with heat and thirst, could say no more. Then Jupiter omnipotent, calling to witness all the gods, including him who had lent the chariot, and showing them that all was lost unless some speedy remedy were applied, mounted the lofty tower from whence he diffuses clouds over the earth, and hurls the forked lightnings. But at that time not a cloud was to be found to interpose for a screen to earth, nor was a shower remaining unexhausted. He thundered, and brandishing a lightning bolt in his right hand launched it against the charioteer, and struck him at the same moment from his seat and from existence! Phaeton, with his hair on fire, fell headlong, like a shooting star which marks the heavens with its brightness as it falls, and Eridanus, the great river, received him and cooled his burning frame. The Italian Naiads reared a tomb for him, and inscribed these words upon the stone:

> "Driver of Phœbus' chariot, Phaeton,
>   Struck by Jove's thunder, rest beneath this stone.
>   He could not rule his father's car of fire,
>   Yet was it much so nobly to aspire." *

His sisters, the Heliades, as they lamented his fate, were turned into poplar trees, on the banks of the river, and their tears, which continued to flow, became amber as they dropped into the stream.

Milman, in his poem of "Samor," makes the following allusion to Phaeton's story:

> "As when the palsied universe aghast
>   Lay . . . mute and still,
>   When drove, so poets sing, the Sun-born youth
>   Devious through Heaven's affrighted signs his sire's
>   Ill-granted chariot. Him the Thunderer hurled
>   From th' empyrean headlong to the gulf
>   Of the half-parched Eridanus, where weep
>   Even now the sister trees their amber tears
>   O'er Phaeton untimely dead."

In the beautiful lines of Walter Savage Landor, descriptive of the Sea-shell, there is an allusion to the Sun's palace and chariot. The water-nymph says,

> "——I have sinuous shells of pearly hue
>   Within, and things that lustre have imbibed
>   In the sun's palace porch, where when unyoked
>   His chariot wheel stands midway in the wave.
>   Shake one and it awakens; then apply
>   Its polished lip to your attentive ear,
>   And it remembers its august abodes,
>   And murmurs as the ocean murmurs there."

Gebir, Book I

*See Proverbial Expressions, page 271.

Midas—Baucis and Philemon

Bacchus, on a certain occasion, found his old school-master and foster-father, Silenus, missing. The old man had been drinking, and in that state wandered away, and was found by some peasants, who carried him to their king, Midas. Midas recognized him, and treated him hospitably, entertaining him for ten days and nights with an unceasing round of jollity.On the eleventh day he brought Silenus back, and restored him in safety to his pupil. Whereupon Bacchus offered Midas his choice of a reward, whatever he might wish. He asked that whatever he might touch should be changed into *gold*. Bacchus consented, though sorry that he had not made a better choice. Midas went his way, rejoicing in his new-acquired power, which he hastened to put to the test. He could scarce believe his eyes when he found a twig of an oak, which he plucked from the branch, become gold in his hand. He took up a stone; it changed to gold. He touched a sod; it did the same. He took an apple from the tree; you would have thought he had robbed the garden of the Hesperides. His joy knew no bounds, and as soon as he got home, he ordered the servants to set a splendid repast on the table. Then he found to his dismay that whether he touched bread, it hardened in his hand; or put a morsel to his lips, it defied his teeth. He took a glass of wine, but it flowed down his throat like melted gold.

In consternation at the unprecedented affliction, he strove to divest himself of his power; he hated the gift he had lately coveted. But all in vain; starvation seemed to await him. He raised his arms, all shining with gold, in prayer to Bacchus, begging to be delivered from his glittering destruction. Bacchus, merciful deity, heard and consented. "Go," said he, "to the River Pactolus, trace the stream to its fountain-head, there plunge your head and body in, and wash away your fault and its punishment." He did so, and scarce had he touched the waters before the gold-creating power passed into them, and the river sands became changed into *gold,* as they remain to this day.

Thenceforth Midas, hating wealth and splendor, dwelt in the country, and became a worshipper of Pan, the god of the fields. On a certain occasion Pan had the temerity to compare his music with that of Apollo, and to challenge the god of the lyre to a trial of skill. The challenge was accepted, and Tmolus, the mountain god, was chosen umpire. The senior took his seat, and cleared away the trees from his ears to listen. At a given signal Pan blew on his pipes, and with his rustic melody gave great satisfaction to himself and his faithful follower Midas, who happened to be present. Then Tmolus turned his head toward the Sun-god, and all his trees turned with him. Apollo rose; his brow wreathed with Parnassian laurel, while his robe of Tyrian purple swept the ground. In his left hand he held the lyre, and with his right hand struck the strings. Ravished with the harmony, Tmolus at once awarded the victory to the god of the lyre, and all but Midas acquiesced in the judgment. He dissented, and questioned the justice of the award. Apollo would not suffer such a depraved pair of ears any longer to wear the human form, but caused them to increase in length, grow hairy, within and without, and movable on their roots; in short, to be on the perfect pattern of those of an ass.

Mortified enough was King Midas at this mishap; but he consoled himself with the thought that it was possible to hide his misfortune, which he attempted to do by means of an ample turban or head-dress. But his hair-dresser of course knew the secret. He was charged not to mention it, and threatened with dire punishment if he presumed to disobey. But he found it too much for his discretion to keep such a secret; so he went out into the meadow, dug a hole in the ground, and stooping down, whispered the story, and covered it up. Before long a thick bed of reeds sprang up in the meadow, and as soon as it had gained its growth, began whispering the story, and has continued to do so, from that day to this, every time a breeze passes over the place.

The story of King Midas has been told by others with some variations. Dryden, in the "Wife of Bath's Tale," makes Midas's queen the betrayer of the secret.

> "This Midas knew, and durst communicate
> To none but to his wife his ears of state."

Midas was king of Phrygia. He was the son of Gordius, a poor countryman, who was taken by the people and made king, in obedience to the command of the oracle, which had said that their future king should come in a wagon. While the people were deliberating, Gordius with his wife and son came driving his wagon into the public square.

Gordius, being made king, dedicated his wagon to the deity of the oracle, and tied it up in its place with a fast knot. This was the celebrated *Gordian knot,* which, in after times it was said, whoever should untie should become lord of all Asia. Many tried to untie it, but none succeeded, till Alexander the Great, in his career of conquest, came to Phrygia. He tried his skill with as ill success as others, till growing impatient he drew his sword and cut the knot. When he afterwards succeeded in subjecting all Asia to his sway, people began to think that he had complied with the terms of the oracle according to its true meaning.

Baucis and Philemon

On a certain hill in Phrygia stand a linden tree and an oak, enclosed by a low wall. Not far from the spot is a marsh, formerly good habitable land, but now indented with pools, the resort of fen-birds and cormorants. Once on a time, Jupiter, in human shape, visited this country, and with him his son Mercury (he of the caduceus), without his wings. They presented themselves as weary travellers, at many a door, seeking rest and shelter, but found all closed, for it was late, and the inhospitable inhabitants would not rouse themselves to open for their reception. At last a humble mansion received them, a small thatched cottage, where Baucis, a pious old dame, and her husband Philemon, united when young, had grown old together. Not ashamed of their poverty, they made it endurable by moderate desires and kind dispositions. One need not look there for master or for servant; they two were the whole household, master and servant alike. When the two heavenly guests crossed the humble threshold, and bowed their heads to pass under the low door, the old man placed a seat, on which Baucis, bustling and attentive, spread a cloth, and begged them to sit down. Then she raked out the coals from the ashes, and kindled up a fire, fed it with leaves and dry bark, and with her scanty breath blew it into a flame. She brought out of a corner split sticks and dry branches, broke them up, and placed them under the small kettle. Her husband collected some pot-herbs in the garden, and she shred them from the stalks, and prepared them for the pot. He reached down with a forked stick a flitch of bacon hanging in the chimney, cut a small piece, and put it in the pot to boil with the herbs, setting away the rest for another time. A beechen bowl was filled with warm water, that their guests might wash. While all was doing, they beguiled the time with conversation.

On the bench designed for the guests was laid a cushion stuffed with sea-weed; and a cloth, only produced on great occasions, but ancient and coarse enough, was spread over that. The old lady, with her apron on, with trembling hand set the table. One leg was shorter than the rest, but a piece of slate put under restored the level. When fixed, she rubbed the table down with some sweet-smelling herbs. Upon it she set some of chaste Minerva's olives, some cornel berries preserved in vinegar, and added radishes and cheese, with eggs lightly cooked in the ashes. All were served in earthen dishes, and an earthen-ware pitcher, with wooden cups, stood beside them. When all was ready, the stew, smoking hot, was set on the table. Some wine, not of the oldest, was added; and for dessert, apples and wild honey; and over and above all, friendly faces, and simple but hearty welcome.

Now while the repast proceeded, the old folks were astonished to see that the wine, as fast as it was poured out, renewed itself in the pitcher, of its own accord. Struck with terror, Baucis and Philemon recognized their heavenly guests, fell on their knees, and with clasped hands implored forgiveness for their poor entertainment. There was an old goose, which they kept as the guardian of their humble cottage; and they bethought them to make this a sacrifice in honor of their guests. But the goose, too nimble, with the aid of feet and wings, for the old folks, eluded their pursuit, and at last took shelter between the gods themselves. They forbade it to be slain; and spoke in these words: "We are gods. This inhospitable village shall pay the penalty of its impiety;

you alone shall go free from the chastisement. Quit your house, and come with us to the top of yonder hill.'' They hastened to obey, and, staff in hand, labored up the steep ascent. They had reached to within an arrow's flight of the top, when turning their eyes below, they beheld all the country sunk in a lake, only their own house left standing. While they gazed with wonder at the sight, and lamented the fate of their neighbors, that old house of theirs was changed into a *temple*. Columns took the place of the corner posts, the thatch grew yellow and appeared a gilded roof, the floors became marble, the doors were enriched with carving and ornaments of gold. Then spoke Jupiter in benignant accents: "Excellent old man, and woman worthy of such a husband, speak, tell us your wishes; what favor have you to ask of us?'' Philemon took counsel with Baucis a few moments; then declared to the gods their united wish. "We ask to be priests and guardians of this your temple; and since here we have passed our lives in love and concord, we wish that one and the same hour may take us both from life, that I may not live to see her grave, nor be laid in my own by her.'' Their prayer was granted. They were the keepers of the temple as long as they lived. When grown very old, as they stood one day before the steps of the sacred edifice, and were telling the story of the place, Baucis saw Philemon begin to put forth leaves, and old Philemon saw Baucis changing in like manner. And now a leafy crown had grown over their heads, while exchanging parting words, as long as they could speak. "Farewell, dear spouse,'' they said, together, and at the same moment the bark closed over their mouths. The Tyanean shepherd still shows the two trees, standing side by side, made out of the two good old people.

The story of Baucis and Philemon has been imitated by Swift, in a burlesque style, the actors in the change being two wandering saints, and the house being changed into a church, of which Philemon is made the parson. The following may serve as a specimen:

"They scarce had spoke, when, fair and soft,
  The roof began to mount aloft;
  Aloft rose every beam and rafter;
  The heavy wall climbed slowly after.
  The chimney widened and grew higher,
  Became a steeple with a spire.
  The kettle to the top was hoist,
  And there stood fastened to a joist,
  But with the upside down, to show
  Its inclination for below;
  In vain, for a superior force,
  Applied at bottom, stops its course;
  Doomed ever in suspense to dwell,
  'Tis now no kettle, but a bell.
  A wooden jack, which had almost
  Lost by disuse the art to roast,
  A sudden alteration feels,

Increased by new intestine wheels;
And, what exalts the wonder more,
The number made the motion slower;
The flier, though 't had leaden feet,
Turned round so quick you scarce could see't;
But slackened by some secret power,
Now hardly moves an inch an hour.
The jack and chimney, near allied,
Had never left each other's side
The chimney to a steeple grown,
The jack would not be left alone;
But up against the steeple reared,
Became a clock, and still adhered;
And still its love to household cares
By a shrill voice at noon declares,
Warning the cook-maid not to burn
That roast meat which it cannot turn.
The groaning chair began to crawl,
Like a huge snail, along the wall;
There stuck aloft in public view,
And with small change, a pulpit grew.
A bedstead of the antique mode,
Compact of timber many a load,
Such as our ancestors did use,
Was metamorphosed into pews,
Which still their ancient nature keep
By lodging folks disposed to sleep."

. . . .

7

Proserpine — Glaucus and Scylla

When Jupiter and his brothers had defeated the Titans and banished them to Tartarus, a new enemy rose up against the gods. They were the giants Typhon, Briareus, Enceladus, and others. Some of them had a hundred arms, others breathed fire. They were finally subdued and buried alive under Mount Ætna, where they still sometimes struggle to get loose, and shake the whole island with earthquakes. Their breath comes up through the mountain, and is what men call the eruption of the volcano.

The fall of these monsters shook the earth, so that Pluto was alarmed, and feared that his kingdom would be laid open to the light of day. Under this apprehension, he mounted his chariot, drawn by black horses, and took a circuit of inspection to satisfy himself of the extent of the damage. While he was thus engaged, Venus, who was sitting on Mount Eryx playing with her boy Cupid, espied him, and said, "My son, take your darts with which you conquer all, even Jove himself, and send one into the breast of yonder dark monarch, who rules the realm of Tartarus. Why should he alone escape? Seize the opportunity to extend your empire and mine. Do you not see that even in heaven some despise our power? Minerva the wise, and Diana the huntress, defy us; and there is that daughter of Ceres, who threatens to follow their example. Now do you, if you have any regard for your own interest or mine, join these two in one." The boy unbound his quiver, and selected his sharpest and truest arrow; then, straining the bow against his knee, he attached the string, and, having made ready, shot the arrow with its barbed point right into the heart of Pluto.

In the value of Enna there is a lake embowered in woods, which screen it from the fervid rays of the sun, while the moist ground is covered with flowers, and Spring reigns perpetual. Here Proserpine was playing with her companions, gathering lilies and violets, and filling her basket and her apron with them, when Pluto saw her, loved her, and carried her off. She screamed for help to her mother and her companions; and when in her fright she dropped the corners of her apron and let the flowers fall, childlike she felt the loss of them as an addition to her grief. The ravisher urged on his steeds, calling them each by name, and throwing loose over their heads and necks his iron-colored reins. When he reached the River Cyane, and it opposed his passage, he struck the riverbank with his trident, and the earth opened and gave him a passage to Tartarus.

Ceres sought her daughter all the world over. Bright-haired Aurora, when she came forth in the morning, and Hesperus, when he led out the stars in the evening, found her still busy in the search. But it was all unavailing. At length weary and sad, she sat down upon a stone, and continued sitting nine days and nights, in the open air, under the sunlight and moonlight and falling showers. It was where now stands the city of Eleusis, then the home of an old man named Celeus. He was out in the field, gathering acorns and blackberries, and sticks for his fire. His little girl was driving home their two goats, and as she passed the goddess, who appeared in the guise of an old woman, she said to her, "Mother"—and the name was sweet to the ears of Ceres—"why do you sit here alone upon the rocks?" The old man also stopped, though his load was heavy, and begged her to come into his cottage, such as it was. She declined, and he urged her. "Go in peace," she replied, "and be happy in your daughter; I have lost mine." As she spoke, tears—or something like tears, for the gods never weep—fell down her cheeks upon her bosom. The compassionate old man and his child wept with her. Then said he, "Come with us, and despise not our humble roof; so may your daughter be restored to you in safety." "Lead on," said she, "I cannot resist that appeal!" So she rose from the stone and went with them. As they walked he told her that his only son, a little boy, lay very sick, feverish and sleepless. She stopped and gathered some poppies. As they entered the cottage, they found all in great distress, for the boy seemed past hope of recovery. Metanira, his mother, received her kindly, and the goddess stooped and kissed the lips of the sick child. Instantly the paleness left his face, and healthy vigor returned to his body. The whole family were delighted—that is, the father, mother, and little girl, for they were all; they had no servants. They spread the table, and put upon it curds and cream, apples, and honey in the comb. While they ate, Ceres mingled poppy juice in the milk of the boy. When night came and all was still, she arose, and taking the sleeping boy moulded his limbs with her hands, and uttered over him three times a solemn charm, then went and laid him in the ashes. His mother who had been watching what her guest was doing, sprang forward with a cry and snatched the child from the fire. Then Ceres assumed her own form, and a divine splendor shone all around. While they were overcome with astonishment, she said, "Mother, you have been cruel in your fondness to your son. I would have made him immortal, but you have frustrated my attempt. Nevertheless, he shall be great and useful. He shall teach men the use of the plough, and the rewards which labor can win from the cultivated soil." So saying, she wrapped a cloud about her, and mounting her chariot rode away.

Ceres continued her search for her daughter, passing from land to land, and across seas and rivers, till at length she returned to Sicily, whence she at first set out, and stood by the banks of the River Cyane, where Pluto made himself a passage with his prize to his own dominions. The river nymph would have told the goddess all she had witnessed, but dared not, for fear of Pluto; so she only ventured to take up the girdle which Proserpine had dropped in her flight, and waft it to the feet of the mother. Ceres, seeing this, was no longer in doubt of her loss, but she did not yet know the cause, and laid the blame on the innocent land. "Ungrateful soil," she said, "which I have endowed with fertility and clothed with herbage and nourishing grain, no more shall you enjoy my favors." Then the cattle died, the plough broke in the furrow, the seed failed to come up; there was too much sun, there was too much rain; the birds stole the seeds—thistles and brambles were the only growth. Seeing this, the fountain Arethusa interceded for the land. "Goddess," said she, "blame not the land; it opened unwillingly to yield a passage to your daughter. I can tell you of her fate, for I have seen her. This is not my native country; I came hither from Elis. I was a woodland nymph, and delighted in the chase. They praised my beauty, but I cared nothing for it, and rather boasted of my hunting exploits. One day I was returning from the wood, heated with exercise, when I came to a stream silently flowing, so clear that you might count the pebbles on the bottom. The willows shaded it, and the grassy bank sloped down to the water's edge. I approached, I touched the water with my foot. I stepped in knee-deep, and not content with that, I laid my garments on the willows and went in. While I sported in the water, I heard an indistinct murmur coming up as out of the depths of the stream; and made haste to escape to the nearest bank. The voice said, "Why do you fly, Arethusa? I am Alpheus, the god of this stream." I ran, he pursued; he was not more swift than I, but he was stronger, and gained upon me, as my strength failed. At last, exhausted, I cried for help to Diana. 'Help me, goddess! help your votary!' The goddess heard, and wrapped me suddenly in a thick cloud. The river god looked now this way and now that, and twice came close to me, but could not find me. 'Arethusa! Arethusa!' he cried. O, how I trembled—like a lamb that hears the wolf growling outside the fold. A cold sweat came over me, my hair flowed down in streams; where my foot stood there was a pool. In short, in less time than it takes to tell I became a fountain. But in this form Alpheus knew me, and attempted to mingle his stream with mine. Diana cleft the ground, and I, endeavoring to escape him, plunged into the cavern, and through the bowels of the earth came out here in Sicily. While I passed through the lower parts of the earth, I saw your Proserpine. She was sad, but no longer showing alarm in her countenance. Her look was such as became a queen—the queen of Erebus; the powerful bride of the monarch of the realms of the dead.''

When Ceres heard this, she stood for a while like one stupefied; then turned her chariot towards heaven, and hastened to present herself before the throne of Jove. She told the story of her bereavement, and implored Jupiter to interfere to procure the restitution of her daughter. Jupiter consented on one condition, namely, that Proserpine should not during her stay in the lower world have taken any food; otherwise, the Fates forbade her release. Accordingly, Mercury was sent, accompanied by Spring, to demand Proserpine of Pluto. The wily monarch consented; but alas! the maiden had taken a pomegranate which Pluto offered her, and had sucked the sweet pulp from a few of the seeds. This was enough to prevent her complete release; but a compromise was made, by which she was to pass half the time with her mother, and the rest with her husband Pluto.

Ceres allowed herself to be pacified with this arrangement, and restored the earth to her favor. Now she remembered Celeus and his family, and her promise to his infant son Triptolemus. When the boy grew up, she taught him the use of the plough, and how to sow the seed. She took him in her chariot, drawn by winged dragons, through all the countries of the earth, imparting to mankind valuable grains, and the knowledge of agriculture. After his return, Triptolemus built a magnificent temple to Ceres in Eleusis, and established the worship of the goddess, under the name of the Eleusinian mysteries, which in the splendor and solemnity of their observance, surpassed all other religious celebrations among the Greeks.

There can be little doubt of this story of Ceres and Proserpine being an allegory. Proserpine signifies the seed-corn which when cast into the ground lies there concealed—that is, she is carried off by the god of the underworld; it reappears—that is, Proserpine is restored to her mother. Spring leads her back to the light of day.

Milton alludes to the story of Proserpine in "Paradise Lost," Book IV:

> "Not that fair field
> On Enna where Proserpine gathering flowers,
> Herself a fairer flower, by gloomy Dis
> Was gathered, which cost Ceres all that pain
> To seek her through the world,——
> * * * * might with this Paradise
> Of Eden strive."

Hood, in his "Ode to Melancholy," uses the same allusion very beautifully:

> "Forgive, if somewhile I forget,
>   In woe to come the present bliss;
> As frighted Proserpine let fall
>   Her flowers at the sight of Dis."

The River Alpheus does in fact disappear underground, in part of its course, finding its way through subterranean channels, till it again appears on the surface. It was said that the Sicilian fountain Arethusa was the same stream, which, after passing under the sea, came up again in Sicily. Hence the story ran that a cup thrown into the Alpheus appeared again in Arethusa. It is this fable of the underground course of Alpheus that Coleridge alludes to in his poem of "Kubla Khan":

> "In Xanadu did Kubla Khan
>   A stately pleasure-dome decree,
> Where Alph, the sacred river, ran
> Through caverns measureless to man,
>   Down to a sunless sea."

In one of Moore's juvenile poems he thus alludes to the same story, and to the practice of throwing garlands or other light objects on his stream to be carried downward by it, and afterwards reproduced at its emerging:

> "O my beloved, how divinely sweet
> Is the pure joy when kindred spirits meet!
> Like him the river god, whose waters flow,
> With love their only light, through caves below,
> Wafting in triumph all the flowery braids
> And festal rings, with which Olympic maids
> Have decked his current, as an offering meet
> To lay at Arethusa's shining feet.
> Think, when he meets at last his fountain bride,
> What perfect love must thrill the blended tide!
> Each lost in each, till mingling into one,
> Their lot the same for shadow or for sun,
> A type of true love, to the deep they run."

The following extract from Moore's "Rhymes on the Road" gives an account of a celebrated picture by Albano, at Milan, called a Dance of Loves:

" 'Tis for the theft of Enna's flower from earth
These urchins celebrate their dance of mirth,
    Round the green tree, like fays upon a heath;—
      Those that are nearest linked in order bright,
    Check after check, like rosebuds in a wreath;
    And those more distant showing from beneath
      The others' wings their little eyes of light.
While see! among the clouds, their eldest brother,
    But just flown up, tells with a smile of bliss,
This prank of Pluto to his charmed mother,
    Who turns to greet the tidings with a kiss."

Glaucus and Scylla

Glaucus was a fisherman. One day he had drawn his nets to land, and had taken a great many fishes of various kinds. So he emptied his net, and proceeded to sort the fishes on the grass. The place where he stood was a beautiful island in the river, a solitary spot, uninhabited, and not used for pasturage of cattle, nor ever visited by any but himself. On a sudden, the fishes, which had been laid on the grass, began to revive and move their fins as if they were in the water; and while he looked on astonished, they one and all moved off to the water, plunged in and swam away. He did not know what to make of this, whether some god had done it, or some secret power in the herbage. "What herb has such a power?" he exclaimed; and gathering some of it, he tasted it. Scarce had the juices of the plant reached his palate when he found himself agitated with a longing desire for the water. He could no longer restrain himself, but bidding farewell to earth, he plunged into the stream. The gods of the water received him graciously, and admitted him to the honor of their society. They obtained the consent of Oceanus and Tethys, the sovereigns of the sea, that all that was mortal in him should be washed away. A hundred rivers poured their waters over him. Then he lost all sense of his former nature and all consciousness. When he recovered, he found himself changed in form and mind. His hair was sea-green, and trailed behind him on the water; his shoulders grew broad, and what had been thighs and legs assumed the form of a fish's tail. The sea-gods complimented him on the change of his appearance, and he fancied himself rather a good-looking personage.

One day Glaucus saw the beautiful maiden Scylla, the favorite of the water-nymphs, rambling on the shore, and when she had found a sheltered nook, laving her limbs in the clear water. He fell in love with her, and showing himself on the surface, spoke to her, saying such things as he thought most likely to win her to stay; for she turned to run immediately on the sight of him, and ran till she had gained a cliff overlooking the sea. Here she stopped and turned round to see whether it was a god or a sea animal, and observed with wonder his shape and color. Glaucus partly emerging from the water, and supporting himself against a rock, said, "Maiden, I am no monster, nor a sea animal, but a god; and neither Proteus nor Triton ranks higher than I. Once I was a mortal, and followed the sea for a living; but now I belong wholly to it.'' Then he told the story of his metamorphosis, and how he had been promoted to his present dignity, and added, ''But what avails all this if it fails to move your heart?'' He was going on in this strain, but Scylla turned and hastened away.

Glaucus was in despair, but it occurred to him to consult the enchantress, Circe. Accordingly he repaired to her island—the same where afterwards Ulysses landed, as we shall see in one of our later stories. After mutual salutations, he said, ''Goddess, I entreat your pity; you alone can relieve the pain I suffer. The power of herbs I know as well as any one, for it is to them I owe my change of form. I love Scylla. I am ashamed to tell you how I have sued and promised to her, and how scornfully she has treated me. I beseech you to use your incantations, or potent herbs, if they are more prevailing, not to cure me of my love—for that I do not wish—but to make her share it and yield me like return.'' To which Circe replied, for she was not insensible to the attractions of the sea-green deity, ''You had better pursue a willing object; you are worthy to be sought, instead of having to seek in vain. Be not diffident, know your own worth. I protest to you that even I, goddess though I be, and learned in the virtues of plants and spells, should not know how to refuse you. If she scorns you, scorn her; meet one who is ready to meet you half way, and thus make a due return to both at once.'' To these words Glaucus replied, ''Sooner shall trees grow at the bottom of the ocean, and seaweed on the top of the mountains, than I will cease to love Scylla, and her alone.''

The goddess was indignant, but she could not punish him, neither did she wish to do so, for she liked him too well; so she turned all her wrath against her rival, poor Scylla. She took plants of poisonous powers and mixed them together, with incantations and charms. Then she passed through the crowd of gambolling beasts, the victims of her art, and proceeded to the coast of Sicily, where Scylla lived. There was a little bay on the shore to which Scylla used to resort, in the heat of the day, to breathe the air of the sea, and to bathe in its waters. Here the goddess poured her poisonous mixture, and muttered over it incantations of mighty power. Scylla came as usual and plunged into the water up to her waist. What was her horror to perceive a brood of serpents and barking monsters surrounding her! At first she could not imagine they were a part of herself, and tried to run from them, and to drive them away; but as she ran she carried them with her, and when she tried to touch her limbs, she found her hands touch only the yawning jaws of monsters. Scylla remained rooted to the spot. Her temper grew as ugly as her form, and she took pleasure in devouring hapless mariners who came within her grasp. Thus she destroyed six of the companions of Ulysses, and tried to wreck the ships of Æneas, till at last she was turned into a rock, and as such still continues to be a terror to mariners.

Keats, in his "Endymion," has given a new version of the ending of "Glaucus and Scylla"—Glaucus consents to Circe's blandishments, till he by chance is witness to her transactions with her beasts. Disgusted with her treachery and cruelty, he tries to escape from her, but is taken and brought back, when with reproaches she banishes him, sentencing him to pass a thousand years in decrepitude and pain. He returns to the sea, and there finds the body of Scylla, whom the goddess has not transformed but drowned. Glaucus learns that his destiny is that, if he passes his thousand years in collecting all the bodies of drowned lovers, a youth beloved of the gods will appear and help him. Endymion fulfils this prophecy, and aids in restoring Glaucus to youth, and Scylla and all the drowned lovers to life.

The following is Glaucus's account of his feelings after his "sea-change":

> "I plunged for life or death. To interknit
> One's senses with so dense a breathing stuff
> Might seem a work of pain; so not enough
> Can I admire how crystal-smooth it felt,
> And buoyant round my limbs. At first I dwelt
> Whole days and days in sheer astonishment;
> Forgetful utterly of self-intent,
> Moving but with the mighty ebb and flow.
> Then like a new-fledged bird that first doth show
> His spreaded feathers to the morrow chill,
> I tried in fear the pinions of my will.
> 'Twas freedom! and at once I visited
> The ceaseless wonders of this ocean-bed," etc.

Keats

. . . .

8

Pygmalion – Dryope – Venus and Adonis – Apollo and Hyacinthus

Pygmalion saw so much wickedness in women that he came at last to abhor the sex, and resolved to live unmarried. He was a sculptor, and had made with wonderful skill a statue of ivory, so beautiful that no living woman came anywhere near it. It was indeed the perfect semblance of a maiden that seemed to be alive, and only prevented from moving by modesty. His art was so perfect that it concealed itself; and its product looked like the workmanship of nature. Pygmalion admired his own work, and at last fell in love with the counterfeit creation. Oftentimes he laid his hand upon it as if to assure himself whether it were living or not, and could not even then believe that it was only ivory. He caressed it, and gave it presents such as young girls love—bright shells and polished stones, little birds and flowers of various hues, beads and amber. He put raiment on its limbs, and jewels on its fingers, and a necklace about its neck. To the ears he hung earrings, and strings of pearls upon the breast. Her dress became her, and she looked not less charming than when unattired. He laid her on a couch spread with cloths of Tyrian dye, and called her his wife, and put her head upon a pillow of the softest feathers, as if she could enjoy their softness.

The festival of Venus was at hand—a festival celebrated with great pomp at Cyprus. Victims were offered, the altars smoked, and the odor of incense filled the air. When Pygmalion had performed his part in the solemnities, he stood before the altar and timidly said, "Ye gods, who can do all things, give me, I pray you, for my wife"—he dared not say "my ivory virgin," but said instead—"one like my ivory virgin." Venus, who was present at the festival, heard him and knew the thought he would have uttered; and as an omen of her favor, caused the flame on the altar to shoot up thrice in a fiery point into the air. When he returned home, he went to see his statue, and leaning over the couch, gave a kiss to the mouth. It seemed to be warm. He pressed its lips again, he laid his hand upon the limbs; the ivory felt soft to his touch, and yielded to his fingers like the wax of Hymettus. While he stands astonished and glad, though doubting, and fears he may be mistaken, again and again with a lover's ardor, he touches the object of his hopes. It was indeed alive! The veins when pressed yielded to the finger and again resumed their roundness. Then at last the votary of Venus found words to thank the goddess, and pressed his lips upon lips as real as his own. The virgin felt the kisses and blushed, and opening her timid eyes to the light, fixed them at the same moment on her lover. Venus blessed the nuptials she had formed, and from this union Paphos was born, from whom the city, sacred to Venus, received its name.

Schiller, in his poem the "Ideals," applies this tale of Pygmalion to the love of nature in a youthful heart. The following translation is furnished by a friend:

"As once with prayers in passion flowing,
    Pygmalion embraced the stone,
Till from the frozen marble glowing,
    The light of feeling o'er him shone,
So did I clasp with young devotion
    Bright nature to a poet's heart;
Till breath and warmth and vital motion
    Seemed through the statue form to dart.

"And then, in all my ardor sharing.
    The silent form expression found;
Returned my kiss of youthful daring,
    And understood my heart's quick sound.
Then lived for me the bright creation,
    The silver rill with song was rife;
The trees, the roses shared sensation,
    An echo of my boundless life."

S. G. B.

Dryope

Dryope and Iole were sisters. The former was the wife of Andræmon, beloved by her husband, and happy in the birth of her first child. One day the sisters strolled to the bank of a stream that sloped gradually down to the water's edge, while the upland was overgrown with myrtles. They were intending to gather flowers for forming garlands for the altars of the nymphs, and Dryope carried her child at her bosom, a precious burden, and nursed him as she walked. Near the water grew a lotus plant, full of purple flowers. Dryope gathered some and offered them to the baby, and Iole was about to do the same, when she perceived blood dropping from the places where her sister had broken them off the stem. The plant was no other than the nymph Lotis, who, running from a base pursuer, had been changed into this form. This they learned from the country people when it was too late.

Dryope, horror-struck when she perceived what she had done, would gladly have hastened from the spot, but found her feet rooted to the ground. She tried to pull them away, but moved nothing but her upper limbs. The woodiness crept upward, and by degrees invested her body. In anguish she attempted to tear her hair, but found her hands filled with leaves. The infant felt his mother's bosom begin to harden, and the milk cease to flow. Iole looked on at the sad fate of her sister, and could render no assistance. She embraced the growing trunk, as if she would hold back the advancing wood, and would gladly have been enveloped in the same bark. At this moment, Andræmon, the husband of Dryope, with her father, approached; and when they asked for Dryope, Iole pointed them to the new-formed lotus. They embraced the trunk of the yet warm tree, and showered their kisses on its leaves.

Now there was nothing left of Dryope but her face. Her tears still flowed and fell on her leaves, and while she could she spoke. "I am not guilty. I deserve not this fate. I have injured no one. If I speak falsely, may my foliage perish with drought and my trunk be cut down and burned. Take this infant and give it to a nurse. Let it often be brought and nursed under my branches, and play in my shade; and when he is old enough to talk, let him be taught to call me mother, and to say with sadness, 'My mother lies hid under this bark.' But bid him be careful of river banks, and beware how he plucks flowers, remembering that every bush he sees may be a goddess in disguise. Farewell, dear husband, and sister, and father. If you retain any love for me, let not the axe wound me, nor the flocks bite and tear my branches. Since I cannot stoop to you, climb up hither and kiss me; and while my lips continue to feel, lift up my child that I may kiss him. I can speak no more, for already the bark advances up my neck, and will soon shoot over me. You need not close my eyes, the bark will close them without your aid." Then the lips ceased to move, and life was extinct; but the branches retained for some time longer the vital heat.

Keats, in "Endymion," alludes to Dryope, thus:

"She took a lute from which there pulsing came
A lively prelude, fashioning the way
In which her voice should wander. 'Twas a lay
More subtle-cadenced, more forest-wild
Than Dryope's lone lulling of her child;" etc.

Venus and Adonis

Venus, playing one day with her boy Cupid, wounded her bosom with one of his arrows. She pushed him away, but the wound was deeper than she thought. Before it healed she beheld Adonis, and was captivated with him. She no longer took any interest in her favorite resorts —Paphos, and Cnidos, and Amathos, rich in metals. She absented herself even from heaven, for Adonis was dearer to her than heaven. Him she followed and bore him company. She who used to love to recline in the shade, with no care but to cultivate her charms, now rambles through the woods and over the hills, dressed like the huntress Diana; and calls her dogs, and chases hares and stags, or other game that it is safe to hunt, but keeps clear of the wolves and bears, reeking with the slaughter of the herd. She charged Adonis, too, to beware of such dangerous animals. "Be brave towards the timid," said she; "courage against the courageous is not safe. Beware how you expose yourself to danger, and put my happiness to risk. Attack not the beasts that Nature has armed with weapons. I do not value your glory so high as to consent to purchase it by such exposure. Your youth, and the beauty that charms Venus, will not touch the hearts of lions and bristly boars. Think of their terrible claws and prodigious strength! I hate the whole race of them. Do you ask me why?" Then she told him the story of Atalanta and Hippomenes, who were changed into lions for their ingratitude to her.

Having given him this warning, she mounted her chariot drawn by swans, and drove away through the air. But Adonis was too noble to heed such counsels. The dogs had roused a wild boar from his lair, and the youth threw his spear and wounded the animal with a sidelong stroke. The beast drew out the weapon with his jaws, and rushed after Adonis, who turned and ran; but the boar overtook him, and buried his tusks in his side, and stretched him dying upon the plain.

Venus, in her swan-drawn chariot, had not yet reached Cyprus, when she heard coming up through mid-air the groans of her beloved, and turned her white-winged coursers back to earth. As she drew near and saw from on high his lifeless body bathed in blood, she alighted, and bending over it beat her breast and tore her hair. Reproaching the Fates, she said, "Yet theirs shall be but a partial triumph; memorials of my grief shall endure, and the spectacle of your death, my Adonis, and of my lamentation shall be annually renewed. Your blood shall be changed into a flower; that consolation none can envy me." Thus speaking, she sprinkled nectar on the blood; and as they mingled, bubbles rose as in a pool on which raindrops fall, and in an hour's time there sprang up a flower of bloody hue like that of the pomegranate. But it is short-lived. It is said the wind blows the blossoms open, and afterwards blows the petals away; so it is called Anemone, or Wind Flower, from the cause which assists equally in its production and its decay.

Milton alludes to the story of Venus and Adonis in his "Comus":

"Beds of hyacinth and roses
    Where young Adonis oft reposes,
    Waxing well of his deep wound
    In slumber soft, and on the ground
    Sadly sits th' Assyrian queen;" etc.

Apollo and Hyacinthus

Apollo was passionately fond of a youth named Hyacinthus. He accompanied him in his sports, carried the nets when he went fishing, led the dogs when he went to hunt, followed him in his excursions in the mountains, and neglected for him his lyre and his arrows. One day they played a game of quoits together, and Apollo, heaving aloft the discus, with strength mingled with skill, sent it high and far. Hyacinthus watched it as it fell, and excited with the sport ran forward to seize it, eager to make his throw, when the quoit bounded from the earth and struck him in the forehead. He fainted and fell. The god, as pale as himself, raised him and tried all his art to stanch the wound and retain the flitting life, but all in vain; the hurt was past the power of medicine. As when one has broken the stem of a lily in the garden it hangs its head and turns its flowers to the earth, so the head of the dying boy, as if too heavy for his neck, fell over on his shoulder. "Thou diest, Hyacinth," so spoke Phœbus, "robbed of thy youth by me. Thine is the suffering, mine is the crime. Would that I could die for thee! But since that may not be, thou shalt live with me in memory and in song. My lyre shall celebrate thee, my song shall tell thy fate, and thou shalt become a flower inscribed with my regrets." While Apollo spoke, behold the blood which had flowed on the ground and stained the herbage, ceased to be blood; but a flower of hue more beautiful than the Tyrian sprang up, resembling the lily, if it were not that this is purple and that silvery white. And this was not enough for Phœbus; but to confer still greater honor, he marked the petals with his sorrow, and inscribed "Ah! ah!" upon them, as we see to this day. The flower bears the name of Hyacinthus, and with every returning spring revives the memory of his fate.

It was said that Zephyrus (the West-wind), who was also fond of Hyacinthus and jealous of his preference of Apollo, blew the quoit out of its course to make it strike Hyacinthus. Keats alludes to this in his "Endymion," where he describes the lookers-on at the game of quoits:

"Or they might watch the quoit-pitchers, intent
    On either side, pitying the sad death
    Of Hyacinthus, when the cruel breath

Of Zephyr slew him; Zephyr penitent,
Who now ere Phœbus mounts the firmament,
  Fondles the flower amid the sobbing rain."

An allusion to Hyacinthus will also be recognized in Milton's "Lyicidas":

"Like to that sanguine flower inscribed with woe."

· · · · · · ·

9

Ceyx and Halcyone: or, The Halcyon Birds

Ceyx was king of Thessaly, where he reigned in peace, without violence or wrong. He was son of Hesperus, the Day-star, and the glow of his beauty reminded one of his father. Halcyone, the daughter of Æolus, was his wife, and devotedly attached to him. Now Ceyx was in deep affliction for the loss of his brother, and direful prodigies following his brother's death made him feel as if the gods were hostile to him. He thought best therefore to make a voyage to Claros in Ionia, to consult the oracle of Apollo. But as soon as he disclosed his intention to his wife Halcyone, a shudder ran through her frame, and her face grew deadly pale. "What fault of mine, dearest husband, has turned your affection from me? Where is that love of me that used to be uppermost in your thoughts? Have you learned to feel easy in the absence of Halcyone? Would you rather have me away?" She also endeavored to discourage him, by describing the violence of the winds, which she had known familiarly when she lived at home in her father's house, Æolus being the god of the winds, and having as much as he could do to restrain them. "They rush together," said she, "with such fury that fire flashes from the conflict. But if you must go," she added, "dear husband, let me go with you, otherwise I shall suffer, not only the real evils which you must encounter, but those also which my fears suggest."

These words weighed heavily on the mind of King Ceyx, and it was no less his own wish than hers to take her with him, but he could not bear to expose her to the dangers of the sea. He answered therefore consoling her as well as he could, and finished with these words: "I promise, by the rays of my father the Day-star, that if fate permits I will return before the moon shall have twice rounded her orb." When he had thus spoken he ordered the vessel to be drawn out of the shiphouse, and the oars and sails to be put aboard. When Halcyone saw these preparations she shuddered, as if with a presentiment of evil. With tears and sobs she said farewell, and then fell senseless to the ground.

Ceyx would still have lingered, but now the young men grasped their oars and pulled vigorously through the waves, with long and measured strokes. Halcyone raised her streaming eyes, and saw her husband standing on the deck, waving his hand to her. She answered his signal till the vessel had receded so far that she could no longer distinguish his form from the rest. When the vessel itself could no more be seen, she strained her eyes to catch the last glimmer of the sail, till that too disappeared. Then, retiring to her chamber, she threw herself on her solitary couch.

Meanwhile they glide out of the harbor, and the breeze plays among the ropes. The seamen draw in their oars, and hoist their sails. When half or less of their course was passed, as night drew on, the sea began to whiten with swelling waves, and the east wind to blow a gale. The master gave the word to take in sail, but the storm forbade obedience, for such is the roar of the winds and waves his orders are unheard. The men, of their own accord, busy themselves to secure the oars, to strengthen the ship, to reef the sail. While they thus do what to each one seems best, the storm increases. The shouting of the men, the rattling of the shrouds, and the dashing of the waves, mingle with the roar of the thunder. The swelling sea seems lifted up to the heavens, to scatter its foam among the clouds; then sinking away to the bottom assumes the color of the shoal —a Stygian blackness.

The vessel shares all these changes. It seems like a wild beast that rushes on the spears of the hunters. Rain falls in torrents, as if the skies were coming down to unite with the sea. When the lightning ceases for a moment, the night seems to add its own darkness to that of the storm; then comes the flash, rending the darkness asunder, and lighting up all with a glare. Skill fails, courage sinks, and death seems to come on every wave. The men are stupefied with terror. The thought of parents, and kindred, and pledges left at home, comes over their minds. Ceyx thinks of Halcyone. no name but hers is on his lips, and while he yearns for her, he yet rejoices in her absence. Presently the mast is shattered by a stroke of lightning, the rudder broken, and the triumphant surge curling over looks down upon the wreck, then falls, and crushes it to fragments. Some of the seamen, stunned by the stroke, sink, and rise no more; others cling to fragments of the wreck. Ceyx, with the hand that used to grasp the sceptre, holds fast to a plank, calling for help—alas, in vain— upon his father and his father-in-law. But oftenest on his lips was the name of Halcyone. To her his thoughts cling. He prays that the waves may bear his body to her sight, and that it may receive burial at her hands. At length the waters overwhelm him, and he sinks. The Day-star looked dim that night. Since it could not leave the heavens, it shrouded its face with clouds.

In the meanwhile Halcyone, ignorant of all these horrors, counted the days till her husband's promised return. Now she gets ready the garments which he shall put on, and now what she shall wear when he arrives. To all the gods she offers frequent incense, but more than all to Juno. For her husband, who was no more, she prayed incessantly; that he might be safe; that he might come home; that he might not, in his absence, see any one that he would love better than her. But of all these prayers, the last was the only one destined to be granted. The goddess, at length, could not bear any longer to be pleaded with for one already dead, and to have hands raised to her altars, that ought rather to be offering funeral rites. So, calling Iris, she said, "Iris, my faithful messenger, go to the drowsy dwelling of Somnus, and tell him to send a vision to Halcyone, in the form of Ceyx, to make known to her the event."

Iris puts on her robe of many colors, and tinging the sky with her bow, seeks the palace of the King of Sleep. Near the Cimmerian country, a mountain cave is the abode of the dull god, Somnus. Here Phœbus dares not come, either rising, at midday or setting. Clouds and shadows are exhaled from the ground, and the light glimmers faintly. The bird of dawning, with crested head, never there calls aloud to Aurora, nor watchful dog, nor more sagacious goose disturbs the silence. No wild beast, nor cattle, nor branch moved with the wind, nor sound of human conversation, breaks the stillness. Silence reigns there; but from the bottom of the rock the River Lethe flows, and by its murmur invites to sleep. Poppies grow abundantly before the door of the cave, and other herbs, from whose juices Night collects slumbers, which she scatters over the darkened earth. There is no gate to the mansion, to creak on its hinges, nor any watchman; but in the midst, a couch of black ebony, adorned with black plumes and black curtains. There the god reclines, his limbs relaxed with sleep. Around him lie dreams, resembling all various forms, as many as the harvest bears stalks, or the forest leaves, or the seashore sandgrains.

As soon as the goddess entered and brushed away the dreams that hovered around her, her brightness lit up all the cave. The god, scarce opening his eyes, and ever and anon dropping his beard upon his breast, at last shook himself free from himself, and leaning on his arm, enquired her errand—for he knew who she was. She answered, "Somnus, gentlest of the gods, tranquilizer of minds and soother of care-worn hearts, Juno sends you her commands that you despatch a dream to Halcyone, in the city of Trachine, representing her lost husband and all the events of the wreck."

Having delivered her message, Iris hastened away, for she could not longer endure the stagnant air, and as she felt drowsiness creeping over her, she made her escape, and returned by her bow the way she came. Then Somnus called one of his numerous sons—Morpheus—the most expert in counterfeiting forms, and in imitating the walk, the countenance, and mode of speaking, even the clothes and attitudes most characteristic of each. But he only imitates men, leaving it to another to personate birds, beasts, and serpents. Him they call Icelos; and Phantasos is a third, who turns himself into rocks, waters, woods, and other things without life. These wait upon kings and great personages in their sleeping hours, while others move among the common people. Somnus chose, from all the brothers, Morpheus, to perform the command of Iris; then laid his head on his pillow and yielded himself to grateful repose.

Morpheus flew, making no noise with his wings, and soon came to the Hæmonian city, where, laying aside his wings, he assumed the form of Ceyx. Under that form, but pale like a dead man, naked, he stood before the couch of the wretched wife. His beard seemed soaked with water, and water trickled from his drowned locks. Leaning over the bed, tears streaming from his eyes, he said, "Do you recoginze your Ceyx, unhappy wife, or has death too much changed my visage? Behold me, know me, your husband's shade, instead of himself. Your prayers, Halcyone, availed me nothing. I am dead. No more deceive yourself with vain hopes of my return. The stormy winds sunk my ship in the Ægean Sea, waves filled my mouth while it called aloud on you. No uncertain messenger tells you this, no vague rumor brings it to your ears. I come in person, a shipwrecked man, to tell you my fate. Arise! give me tears, give me lamentations, let me not go down to Tartarus unwept." To these words Morpheus added the voice which seemed to be that of her husband; he seemed to pour forth genuine tears; his hands had the gestures of Ceyx.

Halcyone, weeping, groaned, and stretched out her arms in her sleep, striving to embrace his body, but grasping only the air. "Stay!" she cried; "whither do you fly? let us go together." Her own voice awakened her. Starting up, she gazed eagerly around, to see if he was still present, for the servants, alarmed by her cries, had brought a light. When she found him not, she smote her breast and rent her garments. She cares not to unbind her hair, but tears it wildly. Her nurse asks what is the cause of her grief. "Halcyone is no more," she answers, " she perished with her Ceyx. Utter not words of comfort, he is shipwrecked and dead. I have seen him, I have recognized him. I stretched out my hands to seize him and detain him. His shade vanished, but it was the true shade of my husband. Not with the accustomed features, not with the beauty that was his, but pale, naked, and with his hair wet with seawater, he appeared to wretched me. Here, in this very spot, the sad vision stood"—and she looked to find the mark of his footsteps. "This it was, this that my presaging mind foreboded, when I implored him not to leave me, to trust himself to the waves. O, how I wish, since thou wouldst go, thou hadst taken me with thee! It would have been far better. Then I should have had no remnant of life to spend without thee, nor a separate death to die. If I could bear to live and struggle to endure, I should be more cruel to myself than the sea has been to me. But I will not struggle, I will not be separated from thee, unhappy husband. This time, at least, I will keep thee company. In death, if one tomb may not include us, one epitaph shall; if I may not lay my ashes with thine, my name, at least, shall not be separated." Her grief forbade more words, and these were broken with tears and sobs.

It was now morning. She went to the sea shore, and sought the spot where she last saw him, on his departure. "While he lingered here, and cast off his tacklings, he gave me his last kiss." While she reviews every object, and strives to recall every incident, looking out over the sea, she descries an indistinct object floating in the water. At first she was in doubt what it was, but by degrees the waves bore it nearer, and it was plainly the body of a man. Though unknowing of whom, yet, as it was of some ship-wrecked one, she was deeply moved, and gave it her tears, saying, "Alas! unhappy one, and unhappy, if such there be, thy wife!" Borne by the waves, it came nearer. As she more and more nearly views it, she trembles more and more. Now, now it approaches the shore. Now marks that she recognizes appear. It is her husband! Stretching out her trembling hands towards it, she exclaims, "O, dearest husband, is it thus you return to me?"

There was built out from the shore a mole, constructed to break the assaults of the sea, and stem its violent ingress. She leaped upon this barrier and (it was wonderful she could do so) she flew, and striking the air with wings produced on the instant, skimmed along the surface of the water, an unhappy bird. As she flew, her throat poured forth sounds full of grief, and like the voice of one lamenting. When she touched the mute and bloodless body, she enfolded its beloved limbs with her new-formed wings, and tried to give kisses with her horny beak. Whether Ceyx felt it, or whether it was only the action of the waves, those who looked on doubted, but the body seemed to raise its head. But indeed he did feel it, and by the pitying gods both of them were changed into birds. They mate and have their young ones. For seven placid days, in winter time, Halcyone broods over her nest, which floats upon the sea. Then the way is safe to seamen. Æolus guards the winds and keeps them from disturbing the deep. The sea is given up, for the time, to his grandchildren.

The following lines from Byron's "Bride of Abydos" might seem borrowed from the concluding part of this description, if it were not stated that the author derived the suggestion from observing the motion of a floating corpse.

"As shaken on his restless pillow,
　His head heaves with the heaving billow;
　That hand, whose motion is not life,
　Yet feebly seems to menace strife,
　Flung by the tossing tide on high,
　Then levelled with the wave——"

Milton in his "Hymn to the Nativity" thus alludes to the fable of the Halcyon:

"But peaceful was the night
　Wherein the Prince of light
　　His reign of peace upon the earth began;
　The winds with wonder whist
　Smoothly the waters kist
　　Whispering new joys to the mild ocean,
　Who now hath quite forgot to rave
　While birds of calm sit brooding on the charmed wave."

Keats also in "Endymion" says,

"O magic sleep! O comfortable bird
That broodest o'er the troubled sea of the mind
Till it is hushed and smooth."
. . . .
10

Vertumnus and Pomona

The Hamadryads were Wood-nymphs. Pomona was of this class, and no one excelled her in love of the garden and the culture of fruit. She cared not for forests and rivers, but loved the cultivated country and trees that bear delicious apples. Her right hand bore for its weapon not a javelin, but a pruning-knife. Armed with this, she busied herself at one time to repress the too luxuriant growths, and curtail the branches that straggled out of place; at another, to split the twig and insert therein a graft, making the branch adopt a nursling not its own. She took care, too, that her favorites should not suffer from drought, and led streams of water by them that the thirsty roots might drink. This occupation was her pursuit, her passion; and she was free from that which Venus inspires. She was not without fear of the country people, and kept her orchard locked, and allowed not men to enter. The Fauns and Satyrs would have given all they possessed to win her, and so would old Sylvanus, who looks young for his years, and Pan, who wears a garland of pine leaves around his head. But Vertumnus loved her best of all; yet he sped no better than the rest. O, how often, in the disguise of a reaper, did he bring her corn in a basket, and looked the very image of a reaper! With a hay band tied round him, one would think he had just come from turning over the grass. Sometimes he would have an ox-goad in his hand, and you would have said he had just unyoked his weary oxen. Now he bore a pruning-hook, and personated a vinedresser; and again with a ladder on his shoulder, he seemed as if he was going to gather apples. Sometimes he trudged along as a discharged soldier, and again he bore a fishing-rod as if going to fish. In this way, he gained admission to her, again and again, and fed his passion with the sight of her.

One day he came in the guise of an old woman, her gray hair surmounted with a cap, and a staff in her hand. She entered the garden and admired the fruit. "It does you credit, my dear," she said, and kissed her, not exactly with an old woman's kiss. She sat down on a bank, and looked up at the branches laden with fruit which hung over her. Opposite was an elm entwined with a vine loaded with swelling grapes. She praised the tree and associated vine, equally. "But," said she, "if the tree stood alone, and had no vine clinging to it, it would have nothing to attract or offer us but its useless leaves. And equally the vine, if it were not twined round the elm, would lie prostrate on the ground. Why will you not take a lesson from the tree and the vine, and consent to unite yourself with some one? I wish you would. Helen herself had not more numerous suitors, nor Penelope, the wife of shrewd Ulysses. Even while you spurn them, they court you—rural deities and others of every kind that frequent these mountains. But if you are prudent and want to make a good alliance, and will let an old woman advise you—who loves you better than you have any idea of—dismiss all the rest and accept Vertumnus, on my recommendation. I know him as well as he knows himself. He is not a wandering deity, but belongs to these mountains. Nor is he like too many of the lovers nowadays, who love any one they happen to see; he loves you, and you only. Add to this, he is young and handsome, and has the art of assuming any shape he pleases, and can make himself just what you command him. Moreover, he loves the same things that you do, delights in gardening, and handles your apples with admiration. But now he cares nothing for fruits, nor flowers, nor any thing else, but only yourself. Take pity on him, and fancy him speaking now with my mouth. Remember that the gods punish cruelty, and that Venus hates a hard heart, and will visit such offences sooner or later. To prove this, let me tell you a story, which is well known in Cyprus to be a fact; and I hope it will have the effect to make you more merciful.

"Iphis was a young man of humble parentage, who saw and loved Anaxarete, a noble lady of the ancient family of Teucer. He struggled long with his passion, but when he found he could not subdue it, he came a suppliant to her mansion. First he told his passion to her nurse, and begged her as she loved her foster-child to favor his suit. And then he tried to win her domestics to his side. Sometimes he committed his vows to written tablets, and often hung at her door garlands which he had moistened with his tears. He stretched himself on her threshold, and uttered his complaints to the cruel bolts and bars. She was deafer than the surges which rise in the November gale; harder than steel from the German forges, or a rock that still clings to its native cliff. She mocked and laughed at him, adding cruel words to her ungentle treatment, and gave not the slightest gleam of hope.

"Iphis could not any longer endure the torments of hopeless love, and, standing before her doors, he spake these last words: 'Anaxarete, you have conquered, and shall no longer have to bear my importunities. Enjoy your triumph! Sing songs of joy, and bind your forehead with laurel,— you have conquered! I die; stony heart, rejoice! This at least I can do to gratify you, and force you to praise me; and thus shall I prove that the love of you left me but with life. Nor will I leave it to rumor to tell you of my death. I will come myself, and you shall see me die, and feast your eyes on the spectacle. Yet, O ye gods, who look down on mortal woes, observe my fate! I ask but this; let me be remembered in coming ages, and add those years to my fame which you have reft from my life.' Thus he said, and, turning his pale face and weeping eyes towards her mansion, he fastened a rope to the gate-post, on which he had often hung garlands, and putting his head into the noose, he murmured, 'This garland at least will please you, cruel girl!' and falling hung suspended with his neck broken. As he fell he struck against the gate, and the sound was as the sound of a groan. The servants opened the door and found him dead, and with exclamations of pity raised him and carried him home to his mother, for his father was not living. She received the dead body of her son, and folded the cold form to her bosom, while she poured forth the sad words which bereaved mothers utter. The mournful funeral passed through the town, and the pale corpse was borne on a bier to the place of the funeral pile. By chance the home of Anaxarete was on the street where the procession passed, and the lamentations of the mourners met the cars of her whom the avenging deity had already marked for punishment.

"'Let us see this sad procession,' said she, and mounted to a turret, whence through an open window she looked upon the funeral. Scarce had her eyes rested upon the form of Iphis stretched on the bier, when they began to stiffen, and the warm blood in her body to become cold. Endeavoring to step back, she found she could not move her feet; trying to turn away her face, she tried in vain; and by degrees all her limbs became stony like her heart. That you may not doubt the fact, the statue still remains, and stands in the temple of Venus at Salamis, in the exact form of the lady. Now think of these things, my dear, and lay aside your scorn and your delays, and accept a lover. So may neither the vernal frosts blight your young fruits, nor furious winds scatter your blossoms!"

When Vertumnus had spoken thus, he dropped the disguise of an old woman, and stood before her in his proper person, as a comely youth. It appeared to her like the sun bursting through a cloud. He would have renewed his entreaties, but there was no need; his arguments and the sight of his true form prevailed, and the Nymph no longer resisted, but owned a mutual flame.

Pomona was the especial patroness of the Apple-orchard, and as such she was invoked by Phillips, the author of a poem on Cider, in blank verse. Thomson in the "Seasons" alludes to him:

"Phillips, Pomona's bard, the second thou
  Who nobly durst, in rhyme-unfettered verse,
  With British freedom, sing the British song."

But Pomona was also regarded as presiding over other fruits, and as such is invoked by Thomson:

"Bear me, Pomona, to thy citron groves,
  To where the lemon and the piercing lime,
  With the deep orange, glowing through the green,
  Their lighter glories blend. Lay me reclined
  Beneath the spreading tamarind, that shakes,
  Fanned by the breeze, its fever-cooling fruit."

Cupid and Psyche

A certain king and queen had three daughters. The charms of the two elder were more than common, but the beauty of the youngest was so wonderful that the poverty of language is unable to express its due praise. The fame of her beauty was so great that strangers from neighboring countries came in crowds to enjoy the sight, and looked on her with amazement, paying her that homage which is due only to Venus herself. In fact Venus found her altars deserted, while men turned their devotion to this young virgin. As she passed along, the people sang her praises, and strewed her way with chaplets and flowers.

This perversion of homage due only to the immortal powers to the exaltation of a mortal gave great offence to the real Venus. Shaking her ambrosial locks with indignation, she exclaimed, "Am I then to be eclipsed in my honors by a mortal girl? In vain then did that royal shepherd whose judgment was approved by Jove himself, give me the palm of beauty over my illustrious rivals, Pallas and Juno. But she shall not so quietly usurp my honors. I will give her cause to repent of so unlawful a beauty."

Thereupon she calls her winged son Cupid, mischievous enough in his own nature, and rouses and provokes him yet more by her complaints. She points out Psyche to him and says, "My dear son, punish that contumacious beauty; give thy mother a revenge as sweet as her injuries are great; infuse into the bosom of that haughty girl a passion for some low, mean, unworthy being, so that she may reap a mortification as great as her present exultation and triumph."

Cupid prepared to obey the commands of his mother. There are two fountains in Venus's garden, one of sweet waters, the other of bitter. Cupid filled two amber vases, one from each fountain, and suspending them from the top of his quiver, hastened to the chamber of Psyche, whom he found asleep. He shed a few drops from the bitter fountain over her lips, though the sight of her almost moved him to pity; then touched her side with the point of his arrow. At the touch she awoke, and opened eyes upon Cupid (himself invisible),which so startled him that in his confusion he wounded himself with his own arrow. Heedless of his wound his whole thought now was to repair the mischief he had done, and he poured the balmy drops of joy over all her silken ringlets.

Psyche, henceforth frowned upon by Venus, derived no benefit from all her charms. True, all eyes were cast eagerly upon her, and every mouth spoke her praises; but neither king, royal youth, nor plebeian presented himself to demand her in marriage. Her two elder sisters of moderate charms had now long been married to two royal princes; but Psyche, in her lonely apartment, deplored her solitude, sick of that beauty, which while it procured abundance of flattery, had failed to awaken love.

Her parents, afraid that they had unwittingly incurred the anger of the gods, consulted the oracle of Apollo, and received this answer: "The virgin is destined for the bride of no mortal lover. Her future husband awaits her on the top of the mountain. He is a monster whom neither gods nor men can resist."

This dreadful decree of the oracle filled all the people with dismay, and her parents abandoned themselves to grief. But Psyche said, "Why, my dear parents, do you now lament me? You should rather have grieved when the people showered upon me undeserved honors, and with one voice called me a Venus. I now perceive that I am a victim to that name. I submit. Lead me to that rock to which my unhappy fate has destined me." Accordingly, all things being prepared, the royal maid took her place in the procession, which more resembled a funeral than a nuptial pomp, and with her parents, amid the lamentations of the people, ascended the mountain, on the summit of which they left her alone, and with sorrowful hearts returned home.

While Psyche stood on the ridge of the mountain, panting with fear and with eyes full of tears, the gentle Zephyr raised her from the earth and bore her with an easy motion into a flowery dale. By degrees her mind became composed, and she laid herself down on the grassy band to sleep. When she awoke refreshed with sleep, she looked round and beheld near by a pleasant grove of tall and stately trees. She entered it, and in the midst discovered a fountain, sending forth clear and crystal waters, and fast by, a magnificent palace whose august front impressed the spectator that it was not the work of mortal hands, but the happy retreat of some god. Drawn by admiration and wonder she approached the building and ventured to enter. Every object she met filled her with pleasure and amazement. Golden pillars supported the vaulted roof, and the walls were enriched with carvings and paintings representing beasts of the chase and rural scenes, adapted to delight the eye of the beholder. Proceeding onward she perceived that besides the apartments of state there were others filled with all manner of treasures, and beautiful and precious productions of nature and art.

While her eyes were thus occupied, a voice addressed her, though she saw no one, uttering these words: "Sovereign lady, all that you see is yours. We whose voices you hear are your servants and shall obey all your commands with our utmost care and diligence. Retire therefore to your chamber and repose on your bed of down, and when you see fit repair to the bath. Supper awaits you in the adjoining alcove when it pleases you to take your seat there."

Psyche gave ear to the admonitions of her vocal attendants, and after repose and the refreshment of the bath, seated herself in the alcove, where a table immediately presented itself, without any visible aid from waiters or servants, and covered with the greatest delicacies of food and the most nectareous wines. Her ears too were feasted with music from invisible performers; of whom one sang, another played on the lute, and all closed in the wonderful harmony of a full chorus.

She had not yet seen her destined husband. He came only in the hours of darkness and fled before the dawn of morning, but his accents were full of love, and inspired like passion in her. She often begged him to stay and let her behold him, but he would not consent. On the contrary he charged her to make no attempt to see him, for it was his pleasure, for the best of reasons, to keep concealed. "Why should you wish to behold me?" he said; "have you any doubt of my love? Have you any wish ungratified? If you saw me, perhaps you would fear me, perhaps adore me, but all I ask is to love me. I would rather you would love me as an equal than adore me as a god."

This reasoning somewhat quieted Psyche for a time, and while the novelty lasted she felt quite happy. But at length the thought of her parents, left in ignorance of her fate, and of her sisters, precluded from sharing with her the delights of her situation, preyed on her mind and made her begin to feel her palace as but a splendid prison. When her husband came one night, she told him her distress, and at last drew from him an unwilling consent that her sisters should be brought to see her.

So, calling Zephyr, she acquainted him with her husband's commands, and he, promptly obedient, soon brought them across the mountain down to their sister's valley. They embraced her and she returned their caresses. "Come," said Psyche, "enter with me my house and refresh yourselves with whatever your sister has to offer." Then taking their hands she led them into her golden palace, and committed them to the care of her numerous train of attendant voices, to refresh them in her baths and at her table, and to show them all her treasures. The view of these celestial delights caused envy to enter their bosoms, at seeing their young sister possessed of such state and splendor, so much exceeding their own.

They asked her numberless questions, among others what sort of a person her husband was. Psyche replied that he was a beautiful youth, who generally spent the daytime in hunting upon the mountains. The sisters, not satisfied with this reply, soon made her confess that she had never seen him. Then they proceeded to fill her bosom with dark suspicions. "Call to mind," they said, "The Pythian oracle that declared you destined to marry a direful and tremendous monster. The inhabitants of this valley say that your husband is a terrible and monstrous serpent, who nourishes you for a while with dainties that he may by and by devour you. Take our advice. Provide yourself with a lamp and a sharp knife; put them in concealment that your husband may not discover them, and when he is sound asleep, slip out of bed, bring forth your lamp and see for yourself whether what they say is true or not. If it is, hesitate not to cut off the monster's head, and thereby recover your liberty."

Psyche resisted these persuasions as well as she could, but they did not fail to have their effect on her mind, and when her sisters were gone, their words and her own curiosity were too strong for her to resist. So she prepared her lamp and a sharp knife, and hid them out of sight of her husband. When he had fallen into his first sleep, she silently rose and uncovering her lamp beheld not a hideous monster, but the most beautiful and charming of the gods, with his golden ringlets wandering over his snowy neck and crimson cheek, with two dewy wings on his shoulders, whiter than snow, and with shining feathers like the tender blossoms of spring. As she leaned the lamp over to have a nearer view of his face a drop of burning oil fell on the shoulder of the god, startled with which he opened his eyes and fixed them full upon her; then, without saying one word, he spread his white wings and flew out of the window. Psyche, in vain endeavoring to follow him, fell from the window to the ground. Cupid, beholding her as she lay in the dust, stopped his flight for an instant and said, "O foolish Psyche, is it thus you repay my love? After having disobeyed my mother's commands and made you my wife, will you think me a monster and cut off my head? But go; return to your sisters, whose advice you seem to think preferable to mine. I inflict no other punishment on you than to leave you forever. Love cannot dwell with suspicion." So saying he fled away leaving poor Psyche prostrate on the ground, filling the place with mournful lamentations.

When she had recovered some degree of composure she looked around her, but the gardens had vanished, and she found herself in the open field not far from the city where her sisters dwelt. She repaired thither and told them the whole story of her misfortunes, at which pretending to grieve, those spiteful creatures inwardly rejoiced; "for now," said they, "he will perhaps choose one of us." With this idea, without saying a word of her intentions, each of them rose early the next morning and ascended the mountain, and having reached the top, called upon Zephyr to receive her and bear her to his lord; then leaping up, and not being sustained by Zephyr, fell down the precipice and was dashed to pieces.

Psyche meanwhile wandered day and night, without food or repose, in search of her husband. Casting her eyes on a lofty mountain having on its brow a magnificent temple, she sighed and said to herself, "Perhaps my love, my lord, inhabits there," and directed her steps thither.

She had no sooner entered than she saw heaps of corn, some in loose ears and some in sheaves, with mingled ears of barley. Scattered about lay sickles and rakes, and all the instruments of harvest, without order, as if thrown carelessly out of the weary reapers' hands in the sultry hours of the day.

This unseemly confusion the pious Psyche put an end to, by separating and sorting every thing to its proper place and kind, believing that she ought to neglect none of the gods, but endeavor by her piety to engage them all in her behalf. The holy Ceres, whose temple it was, finding her so religiously employed, thus spoke to her: "O Psyche, truly worthy of our pity, though I cannot shield you from the frowns of Venus, yet I can teach you how best to allay her displeasure. Go then and voluntarily surrender yourself to your lady and sovereign, and try by modesty and submission to win her forgiveness, and perhaps her favor will restore you the husband you have lost.''

Psyche obeyed the commands of Ceres and took her way to the temple of Venus, endeavoring to fortify her mind and ruminating on what she should say and how best propitiate the angry goddess, feeling that the issue was doubtful and perhaps fatal.

Venus received her with angry countenance. "Most undutiful and faithless of servants,'' said she, "do you at last remember that you really have a mistress? Or have you rather come to see your sick husband, yet laid up of the wound given him by his loving wife? You are so ill-favored and disagreeable that the only way you can merit your lover must be by dint of industry and diligence. I will make trial of your housewifery.'' Then she ordered Psyche to be led to the storehouse of her temple, where was laid up a great quantity of wheat, barley, millet, vetches, beans, and lentils prepared for food for her pigeons, and said, "Take and separate all these grains, putting all of the same kind in a parcel by themselves, and see that you get it done before evening.'' Then Venus departed and left her to her task.

But Psyche, in a perfect consternation at the enormous work, sat stupid and silent, without moving a finger to the inextricable heap.

While she sat despairing, Cupid stirred up the little ant, a native of the fields, to take compassion on her. The leader of the ant hill, followed by whole hosts of his six-legged subjects, approached the heap, and with the utmost diligence taking grain by grain, they separated the pile, sorting each kind to its parcel; and when it was all done, they vanished out of sight in a moment.

Venus at the approach of twilight returned from the banquet of the gods, breathing odors and crowned with roses. Seeing the task done she exclaimed, "This is no work of yours, wicked one, but his, whom to your own and his misfortune you have enticed.'' So saying, she threw her a piece of black bread for her supper and went away.

Next morning Venus ordered Psyche to be called and said to her, "Behold yonder grove which stretches along the margin of the water. There you will find sheep feeding without a shepherd, with golden-shining fleeces on their backs. Go, fetch me a sample of that precious wool gathered from every one of their fleeces.''

Psyche obediently went to the river side, prepared to do her best to execute the command. But the river god inspired the reeds with harmonious murmurs, which seemed to say, "O maiden, severely tried, tempt not the dangerous flood, nor venture among the formidable rams on the other side, for as long as they are under the influence of the rising sun, they burn with a cruel rage to destroy mortals with their sharp horns or rude teeth. But when the noontide sun has driven the cattle to the shade, and the serene spirit of the flood has lulled them to rest, you may then cross in safety, and you will find the woolly gold sticking to the bushes and the trunks of the trees.''

Thus the compassionate river god gave Psyche instructions how to accomplish her task, and by observing his directions she soon returned to Venus with her arms full of the golden fleece; but she received not the approbation of her implacable mistress, who said, "I know very well it is by none of your own doings that you have succeeded in this task, and I am not satisfied yet that you have any capacity to make yourself useful. But I have another task for you. Here, take this box, and go your way to the infernal shades, and give this box to Proserpine and say, 'My mistress Venus desires you to send her a little of your beauty, for in tending her sick son she has lost some of her own.' Be not too long on your errand, for I must paint myself with it to appear at the circle of the gods and goddesses this evening."

Psyche was now satisfied that her destruction was at hand, being obliged to go with her own feet directly down to Erebus. Wherefore, to make no delay of what was not to be avoided, she goes to the top of a high tower to precipitate herself headlong, thus to descend the shortest way to the shades below. But a voice from the tower said to her, "Why, poor unlucky girl, dost thou design to put an end to thy days in so dreadful a manner? And what cowardice makes thee sink under this last danger who hast been so miraculously supported in all thy former?" Then the voice told her how by a certain cave she might reach the realms of Pluto, and how to avoid all the dangers of the road, to pass by Cerberus, the three-headed dog, and prevail on Charon, the ferryman, to take her across the black river and bring her back again. But the voice added, "When Proserpine has given you the box, filled with her beauty, of all things this is chiefly to be observed by you, that you never once open or look into the box nor allow your curiosity to pry into the treasure of the beauty of the goddesses."

Psyche, encouraged by this advice, obeyed it in all things, and taking heed to her ways travelled safely to the kingdom of Pluto. She was admitted to the palace of Proserpine, and without accepting the delicate seat or delicious banquet that was offered her, but contented with coarse bread for her food, she delivered her message from Venus. Presently the box was returned to her, shut and filled with the precious commodity. Then she returned the way she came, and glad was she to come out once more into the light of day.

But having got so far successfully through her dangerous task a longing desire seized her to examine the contents of the box. "What," said she, "shall I, the carrier of this divine beauty, not take the least bit to put on my cheeks to appear to more advantage in the eyes of my beloved husband!" So she carefully opened the box, but found nothing there of any beauty at all, but an infernal and truly Stygian sleep, which being thus set free from its prison, took possession of her, and she fell down in the midst of the road, a sleepy corpse without sense or motion.

But Cupid, being now recovered from his wound, and not able longer to bear the absence of his beloved Psyche, slipping through the smallest crack of the window of his chamber which happened to be left open, flew to the spot where Psyche lay, and gathering up the sleep from her body closed it again in the box, and waked Psyche with a light touch of one of his arrows. "Again," said he, "hast thou almost perished by the same curiosity. But now perform exactly the task imposed on you by my mother, and I will take care of the rest."

Then Cupid, as swift as lightning penetrating the heights of heaven, presented himself before Jupiter with his supplication. Jupiter lent a favoring ear, and pleaded the cause of the lovers so earnestly with Venus that he won her consent. On this he sent Mercury to bring Psyche up to the heavenly assembly, and when she arrived, handing her a cup of ambrosia, he said, "Drink this, Psyche, and be immortal; nor shall Cupid ever break away from the knot in which he is tied, but these nuptials shall be perpetual."

Thus Psyche became at last united to Cupid, and in due time they had a daughter born to them whose name was Pleasure.

The fable of Cupid and Psyche is usually considered allegorical. The Greek name for a *butterfly* is Psyche, and the same word means the *soul*. There is no illustration of the immortality of the soul so striking and beautiful as the butterfly, bursting on brilliant wings from the tomb in which it has lain, after a dull, grovelling, caterpillar existence, to flutter in the blaze of day and feed on the most fragrant and delicate productions of the spring. Psyche then is the human soul, which is purified by sufferings and misfortunes, and is thus prepared for the enjoyment of true and pure happiness.

In works of art Psyche is represented as a maiden with the wings of a butterfly, along with Cupid, in the different situations described in the allegory.

Milton alludes to the story of Cupid and Psyche in the conclusion of his "Comus":

> "Celestial Cupid, her famed son, advanced,
>   Holds his dear Psyche sweet entranced,
>   After her wandering labors long,
>   Till free consent the gods among
>   Make her his eternal bride;
>   And from her fair unspotted side
>   Two blissful twins are to be born,
>   Youth and Joy; so Jove hath sworn."

The allegory of the story of Cupid and Psyche is well presented in the beautiful lines of T. K. Harvey:

> "They wove bright fables in the days of old,
>   When reason borrowed fancy's painted wings;
> When truth's clear river flowed o'er sands of gold,
>   And told in song its high and mystic things!
> And such the sweet and solemn tale of her
>   The pilgrim-heart, to whom a dream was given,

That led her through the world—Love's worshipper—
　　To seek on earth for him whose home was heaven!

"In the full city,—by the haunted fount,—
　　Through the dim grotto's tracery of spars,—
'Mid the pine temples, on the moon-lit mount,
　　Where silence sits to listen to the stars;
In the deep glade where dwells the brooding dove,
　　The painted valley, and the scented air,
She heard far echoes of the voice of Love,
　　And found his footsteps' traces every where.

"But never more they met! since doubts and fears,
　　Those phantom-shapes that haunt and blight the earth,
Had come 'twixt her, a child of sin and tears,
　　And that bright spirit of immortal birth;
Until her pining soul and weeping eyes
Had learned to seek him only in the skies;
Till wings unto the weary heart were given,
And she became Love's angel bride in heaven!"

The story of Cupid and Psyche first appears in the works of Apuleius, a writer of the second century of our era. It is therefore of much more recent date than most of the legends of the Age of Fable. It is this that Keats alludes to in his "Ode to Psyche."

"O latest-born and loveliest vision far
　　Of all Olympus' faded hierarchy!
Fairer than Phœbe's sapphire-regioned star
　　Or Vesper, amorous glow-worm of the sky;
Fairer than these, though temple thou hast none,
　　　Nor altar heaped with flowers;
Nor virgin-choir to make delicious moan
　　　Upon the midnight hours;
No voice, no lute, no pipe, no incense sweet,
　　　From chain-swung censer teeming;
No shrine, no grove, no oracle, no heat
　　　Of pale-mouthed prophet dreaming."

In Moore's "Summer Fete" a fancy ball is described, in which one of the characters personated is Psyche.

"——not in dark disguise to-night
Hath our young heroine veiled her light;—
For see, she walks the earth, Love's own.
　　His wedded bride, by holiest vow
Pledged in Olympus, and made known
　　To mortals by the type which now
　　Hangs glittering on her snowy brow,
That butterfly, mysterious trinket,
Which means the soul, (though few would think it,)
and sparkling thus on brow so white
Tells us we've Psyche here to-night."

· · · · · · ·
12

Cadmus—The Myrmidons

Jupiter, under the disguise of a bull, had carried away Europa, the daughter of Agenor, king of Phœnicia. Agenor commanded his son Cadmus to go in search of his sister, and not to return without her. Cadmus went and sought long and far for his sister, but could not find her, and not daring to return unsuccessful, consulted the oracle of Apollo to know what country he should settle in. The oracle informed him that he should find a cow in the field, and should follow her wherever she might wander, and where she stopped, should build a city and call it Thebes. Cadmus had hardly left the Castalian cave, from which the oracle was delivered, when he saw a young cow slowly walking before him. He followed her close, offering at the same time his prayers to Phœbus. The cow went on till she passed the shallow channel of Cephisus and came out into the plain of Panope. There she stood still, and raising her broad forehead to the sky, filled the air with her lowings. Cadmus gave thanks, and stooping down kissed the foreign soil, then lifting his eyes, greeted the surrounding mountains. Wishing to offer a sacrifice to Jupiter, he sent his servants to seek pure water for a libation. Near by there stood an ancient grove which had never been profaned by the axe, in the midst of which was a cave, thick covered with the growth of bushes, its roof forming a low arch, from beneath which burst forth a fountain of purest water. In the cave lurked a horrid serpent with a crested head and scales glittering like gold. His eyes shone like fire, his body was swollen with venom, he vibrated a triple tongue, and showed a triple row of teeth. No sooner had the Tyrians dipped their pitchers in the fountain, and the ingushing waters made a sound, than the glittering serpent raised his head out of the cave and uttered a fearful hiss. The vessels fell from their hands, the blood left their cheeks, they trembled in every limb. The serpent, twisting his scaly body in a huge coil, raised his head so as to overtop the tallest trees, and while the Tyrians from terror could neither fight nor fly, slew some with his fangs, others in his folds, and others with his poisonous breath.

Cadmus having waited for the return of his men till midday, went in search of them. His covering was a lion's hide, and besides his javelin he carried in his hand a lance, and in his breast a bold heart, a surer reliance than either. When he entered the wood, and saw the lifeless bodies of his men, and the monster with his bloody jaws, he exclaimed, "O faithful friends, I will avenge you, or share your death." So saying he lifted a huge stone and threw it with all his force at the serpent. Such made no impression on the monster. Cadmus next threw his javelin, which met with better success, for it penetrated the serpent's scales, and pierced through to his entrails. Fierce with pain the monster turned back his head to view the wound, and attempted to draw out the weapon with his mouth, but broke it off, leaving the iron point rankling in his flesh. His neck swelled with rage, bloody foam covered his jaws, and the breath of his nostrils poisoned the air around. Now he twisted himself into a circle, then stretched himself out on the ground like the trunk of a fallen tree. As he moved onward, Cadmus retreated before him, holding his spear opposite to the monster's opened jaws. The serpent snapped at the weapon and attempted to bite its iron point. At last Cadmus watching his chance thrust the spear at a moment when the animal's head thrown back came against the trunk of a tree, and so succeeded in pinning him to its side. His weight bent the tree as he struggled in the agonies of death.

While Cadmus stood over his conquered foe, contemplating its vast size, a voice was heard (from whence he knew not, but he heard it distinctly) commanding him to take the dragon's teeth and sow them in the earth. He obeyed. He made a furrow in the ground, and planted the teeth, destined to produce a crop of men. Scarce had he done so when the clods began to move, and the points of spears to appear above the surface. Next helmets with their nodding plumes came up, and next the shoulders and breasts and limbs of men with weapons, and in time a harvest of armed warriors. Cadmus alarmed prepared to encounter a new enemy, but one of them said to him, "Meddle not with our civil war." With that he who had spoken smote one of his earth-born brothers with a sword, and he himself fell pierced with an arrow from another. The latter fell victim to a fourth, and in like manner the whole crowd dealt with each other till all fell slain with mutual wounds, except five survivors. One of these cast away his weapons and said, "Brothers, let us live in peace!" These five joined with Cadmus in building his city, to which they gave the name of Thebes.

Cadmus obtained in marriage Harmonia, the daughter of Venus. The gods left Olympus to honor the occasion with their presence, and Vulcan presented the bride with a necklace of surpassing brilliancy, his own workmanship. But a fatality hung over the family of Cadmus in consequence of his killing the serpent sacred to Mars. Semele and Ino, his daughters, and Actæon and Pentheus, his grandchildren, all perished unhappily, and Cadmus and Harmonia quitted Thebes, now grown odious to them, and emigrated to the country of the Enchelians, who received them with honor and made Cadmus their king. But the misfortunes of their children still weighed upon their minds; and one day Cadmus exclaimed, "If a serpent's life is so dear to the gods, I would I were myself a serpent." No sooner had he uttered the words than he began to change his form. Harmonia beheld it and prayed to the gods to let her share his fate. Both became serpents. They live in the woods, but mindful of their origin, they neither avoid the presence of man, nor do they ever injure any one.

There is a tradition that Cadmus introduced into Greece the letters of the alphabet which were invented by the Phœnicians. This is alluded to by Byron, where, addressing the modern Greeks, he says,

"You have the letters Cadmus gave,
    Think you he meant them for a slave?"

Milton, describing the serpent which tempted Eve, is reminded of the serpents of the classical stories and says,

"—— pleasing was his shape,
And lovely: never since of serpent kind
Lovelier; not those that in Illyria changed
Hermione and Cadmus, nor the god
In Epidaurus."

For an explanation of the last allusion, see EPIDAURUS.

The Myrmidons

The Myrmidons were the soldiers of Achilles, in the Trojan war. From them all zealous and unscrupulous followers of a political chief are called by that name, down to this day. But the origin of the Myrmidons would not give one the idea of a fierce and bloody race, but rather of a laborious and peaceful one.

Cephalus, king of Athens, arrived in the island of Ægina to seek assistance of his old friend and ally Æacus, the king, in his war with Minos, king of Crete. Cephalus was most kindly received, and the desired assistance readily promised. "I have people enough," said Æacus, "to protect myself and spare you such a force as you need." "I rejoice to see it," replied Cephalus, "and my wonder has been raised, I confess, to find such a host of youths as I see around me, all apparently of about the same age. Yet there are many individuals whom I previously knew, that I look for now in vain. What has become of them?" Æacus groaned, and replied with a voice of sadness, "I have been intending to tell you, and will now do so, without more delay, that you may see how from the saddest beginning a happy result sometimes flows. Those whom you formerly knew are now dust and ashes! A plague sent by angry Juno devastated the land. She hated it because it bore the name of one of her husband's female favorites. While the disease appeared to spring from natural causes we resisted it as we best might, by natural remedies; but it soon appeared that the pestilence was too powerful for our efforts, and we yielded. At the beginning the sky seemed to settle down upon the earth, and thick clouds shut in the heated air. For four months together a deadly south wind prevailed. The disorder affected the wells and springs; thousands of snakes crept over the land and shed their poison in the fountains. The force of the disease was first spent on the lower animals, dogs, cattle, sheep, and birds. The luckless ploughman wondered to see his oxen fall in the midst of their work, and lie helpless in the unfinished furrow. The wool fell from the bleating sheep, and their bodies pined away. The horse once foremost in the race contested the palm no more, but groaned at his stall and died an inglorious death. The wild boar forgot his rage, the stag his swiftness, the bears no longer attacked the herds. Every thing languished; dead bodies lay in the roads, the fields, and the woods; the air was poisoned by them. I tell you what is hardly credible, but neither dogs nor birds would touch them, nor starving wolves. Their decay spread the infection. Next the disease attacked the country people, and then the dwellers in the city. At first the cheek was flushed, and the breath drawn with difficulty. The tongue grew rough and swelled, and the dry mouth stood open with its veins enlarged and gasped for the air. Men could not bear the heat of their clothes or their beds, but preferred to lie on the bare ground; and the ground did not cool them, but on the contrary, they heated the spot where they lay. Nor could the physicians help, for the disease attacked them also, and the contact of the sick gave them infection, so that the most faithful were the first victims. At last all hope of relief vanished, and men learned to look upon death as the only deliverer from disease. Then they gave way to every inclination, and cared not to ask what was expedient, for nothing was expedient. All restraint laid aside, they crowded around the wells and fountains and drank till they died, without quenching thirst. Many had not strength to get away from the water, but died in the midst of the stream, and others would drink of it notwithstanding. Such was their weariness of their sick beds that some would creep forth, and if not strong enough to stand, would die on the ground. They seemed to hate their friends, and got away from their homes, as if, not knowing the cause of their sickness, they charged it on the place of their abode. Some were seen tottering along the road, as long as they could stand, while others sank on the earth, and turned their dying eyes around to take a last look, then closed them in death.

"What heart had I left me, during all this, or what ought I to have had, except to hate life and wish to be with my dead subjects? On all sides lay my people strewn like over-ripened apples beneath the tree, or acorns under the storm-shaken oak. You see yonder a temple on the height. It is sacred to Jupiter. O, how many offered prayers there, husbands for wives, fathers for sons, and died in the very act of supplication! How often, while the priest made ready for sacrifice, the victim fell, struck down by disease without waiting for the blow! At length all reverence for sacred things was lost. Bodies were thrown out unburied, wood was wanting for funeral piles, men fought with one another for possession of them. Finally there were none left to mourn; sons and husbands, old men and youths, perished alike unlamented.

"Standing before the altar I raised my eyes to heaven. 'O Jupiter,' I said, 'if thou are indeed my father, and art not ashamed of thy offspring, give me back my people, or take me also away!' At these words a clap of thunder was heard. 'I accept the omen,' I cried; 'O, may it be a sign of a favorable disposition towards me!' By chance there grew by the place where I stood an oak with wide-spreading branches, sacred to Jupiter. I observed a troop of ants busy with their labor, carrying minute grains in their mouths and following one another in a line up the trunk of the tree. Observing their numbers with admiration I said, 'Give me, O father, citizens as numerous as these, and replenish my empty city.' The tree shook and gave a rustling sound with its branches though no wind agitated them. I trembled in every limb, yet I kissed the earth and the tree. I would not confess to myself that I hoped, yet I did hope. Night came on and sleep took possession of my frame oppressed with cares. The tree stood before me in my dreams, with its numerous branches all covered with living, moving creatures. It seemed to shake its limbs and throw down over the ground a multitude of those industrious grain-gathering animals, which appeared to gain in size, and grow larger and larger, and by-and-by to stand erect, lay aside their superfluous legs and their black color, and finally to assume the human form. Then I awoke, and my first impulse was to chide the gods who had robbed me of a sweet vision and given me no reality in its place. Being still in the temple my attention was caught by the sound of many voices without; a sound of late unusual to my ears. While I began to think I was yet dreaming, Telamon, my son, throwing open the temple-gates, exclaimed, 'Father, approach, and behold things surpassing even your hopes!' I went forth; I saw a multitude of men, such as I had seen in my dream, and they were passing in procession in the same manner. While I gazed with wonder and delight they approached, and kneeling hailed me as their king. I paid my vows to Jove, and proceeded to allot the vacant city to the new-born race, and to parcel out the fields among them. I called them Myrmidons from the ant (myrmex) from which they sprang. You have seen these persons; their dispositions resemble those which they had in their former shape. They are a diligent and industrious race, eager to gain, and tenacious of their gains. Among them you may recruit your forces. They will follow you to the war, young in years and bold in heart."

This description of the plague is copied by Ovid from the account which Thucydides, the Greek historian, gives of the plague of Athens. The historian drew from life, and all the poets and writers of fiction since his day, when they have had occasion to describe a similar scene, have borrowed their details from him.

. . . .

13

Nisus and Scylla—Echo and Narcissus—
Clytie—Hero and Leander

Minos, king of Crete, made war upon Megara. Nisus was king of Megara, and Scylla was his daughter. The siege had now lasted six months, and the city still held out, for it was decreed by fate that it should not be taken so long as a certain purple lock, which glittered among the hair of King Nisus, remained on his head. There was a tower on the city walls, which overlooked the plain where Minos and his army were encamped. To this tower Scylla used to repair, and look abroad over the tents of the hostile army. The siege had lasted so long that she had learned to distinguish the persons of the leaders. Minos, in particular, excited her admiration. Arrayed in his helmet, and bearing his shield, she admired his graceful deportment; if he threw his javelin, skill seemed combined with force in the discharge; if he drew his bow, Apollo himself could not have done it more gracefully. But when he laid aside his helmet, and in his purple robes bestrode his white horse with its gay caparisons, and reined in its foaming mouth, the daughter of Nisus was hardly mistress of herself; she was almost frantic with admiration. She envied the weapon that he grasped, the reins that he held. She felt as if she could, if it were possible, go to him through the hostile ranks; she felt an impulse to cast herself down from the tower into the midst of his camp, or to open the gates to him, or to do any thing else, so only it might gratify Minos. As she sat in the tower, she talked thus with herself: "I know not whether to rejoice or grieve at this sad war. I grieve that Minos is our enemy; but I rejoice at any cause that brings him to my sight. Perhaps he would be willing to grant us peace, and receive me as a hostage. I would fly down, if I could, and alight in his camp, and tell him that we yield ourselves to his mercy. But, then, to betray my father! No! rather would I never see Minos again. And yet no doubt it is sometimes the best thing for a city to be conquered, when the conqueror is clement and generous. Minos certainly has right on his side. I think we shall be conquered; and if that must be the end of it, why should not love unbar the gates to him, instead of leaving it to be done by war? Better spare delay and slaughter if we can. And O, if any one should wound or kill Minos! No one surely would have the heart to do it; yet ignorantly, not knowing him, one might. I will, I will surrender myself to him, with my country as a dowry, and so put an end to the war. But how? The gates are guarded, and my father keeps the keys; he only stands in my way. O that it might please the gods to take him away! But why ask the gods to do it? Another woman, loving as I do, would remove with her own hands whatever stood in the way of her love. And can any other woman dare more than I? I would encounter fire and sword to gain my object; but here there is no need of fire and sword. I only need my father's purple lock. More precious than gold to me, that will give me all I wish."

While she thus reasoned night came on, and soon the whole palace was buried in sleep. She entered her father's bedchamber and cut off the fatal lock; then passed out of the city and entered the enemy's camp. She demanded to be led to the king, and thus addressed him: "I am Scylla, the daughter of Nisus. I surrender to you my country and my father's house. I ask no reward but yourself; for love of you I have done it. See here the purple lock! With this I give you my father and his kingdom." She held out her hand with the fatal spoil. Minos shrunk back and refused to touch it. "The gods destroy thee, infamous woman," he exclaimed; "disgrace of our time! May neither earth nor sea yield thee a resting-place! Surely, my Crete, where Jove himself was cradled, shall not be polluted with such a monster!" Thus he said, and gave orders that equitable terms should be allowed to the conquered city, and that the fleet should immediately sail from the island.

Scylla was frantic. "Ungrateful man," she exclaimed, "is it thus you leave me?—me who have given you victory,—who have sacrificed for you parent and country! I am guilty, I confess, and deserve to die, but not by your hand." As the ships left the shore, she leaped into the water, and seizing the rudder of the one which carried Minos, she was borne along, an unwelcome companion of their course. A sea-eagle soaring aloft—it was her father who had been changed into that form—seeing her, pounced down upon her, and struck her with his beak and claws. In terror she let go the ship, and would have fallen into the water, but some pitying deity changed her into a bird. The sea-eagle still cherishes the old animosity; and whenever he espies her in his lofty flight, you may see him dart down upon her, with beak and claws, to take vengeance for the ancient crime.

Echo and Narcissus

Echo was a beautiful nymph, fond of the woods and hills, where she devoted herself to woodland sports. She was a favorite of Diana, and attended her in the chase. But Echo had one failing; she was fond of talking, and whether in chat or argument, would have the last word. One day Juno was seeking her husband, who, she had reason to fear, was amusing himself among the nymphs. Echo by her talk contrived to detain the goddess till the nymphs made their escape. When Juno discovered it, she passed sentence upon Echo in these words: "You shall forfeit the use of that tongue with which you have cheated me, except for that one purpose you are so fond of—*reply.* You shall still have the last word, but no power to speak first."

This nymph saw Narcissus, a beautiful youth, as he pursued the chase upon the mountains. She loved him, and followed his footsteps. O, how she longed to address him in the softest accents, and win him to converse! but it was not in her power. She waited with impatience for him to speak first, and had her answer ready. One day the youth, being separated from his companions, shouted aloud, "Who's here?" Echo replied, "Here." Narcissus looked around, but seeing no one, called out, "Come." Echo answered, "Come." As no one came, Narcissus called again, "Why do you shun me?" Echo asked the same question. "Let us join one another," said the youth. The maid answered with all her heart in the same words, and hastened to the spot, ready to throw her arms about his neck. He started back, exclaiming, "Hands off! I would rather die than you should have me!" "Have me," said she; but it was all in vain. He left her, and she went to hide her blushes in the recesses of the woods. From that time forth she lived in caves and among mountain cliffs. Her form faded with grief, till at last all her flesh shrank away. Her bones were changed into rocks, and there was nothing left to her but her voice. With that she is still ready to reply to any one who calls her and keeps up her old habit of having the last word.

Narcissus's cruelty in this case was not the only instance. He shunned all the rest of the nymphs, as he had done poor Echo. One day a maiden who had in vain endeavored to attract him, uttered a prayer that he might some time or other feel what it was to love and meet no return of affection. The avenging goddess heard and granted the prayer.

There was a clear fountain, with water like silver, to which the shepherds never drove their flocks, nor the mountain goats resorted, nor any of the beasts of the forest; neither was it defaced with fallen leaves or branches; but the grass grew fresh around it, and the rocks sheltered it from the sun. Hither came one day the youth fatigued with hunting, heated and thirsty. He stooped down to drink, and saw his own image in the water; he thought it was some beautiful water-spirit living in the fountain. He stood gazing with admiration at those bright eyes, those locks curled like the locks of Bacchus or Apollo, the rounded cheeks, the ivory neck, the parted lips, and the glow of health and exercise over all. He fell in love with himself. He brought his lips near to take a kiss; he plunged his arms in to embrace the beloved object. It fled at the touch, but returned again after a moment and renewed the fascination. He could not tear himself away; he lost all thought of food or rest, while he hovered over the brink of the fountain gazing upon his own image. He talked with the supposed spirit: "Why, beautiful being, do you shun me? Surely, my face is not one to repel you. The nymphs love me, and you yourself look not indifferent upon me. When I stretch forth my arms you do the same; and you smile upon me and answer my beckonings with the like." His tears fell into the water and disturbed the image. As he saw it depart, he exclaimed, "Stay, I entreat you! Let me at least gaze upon you, if I may not touch you." With this, and much more of the same kind, he cherished the flame that consumed him, so that by degrees he lost his color, his vigor, and the beauty which formerly had so charmed the nymph Echo. She kept near him, however, and when he exclaimed, "Alas! alas!" she answered him with the same words. He pined away and died; and when his shade passed the Stygian river, it leaned over the boat to catch a look of itself in the waters. The nymphs mourned for him, especially the water-nymphs; and when they smote their breasts, Echo smote hers also. They prepared a funeral pile, and would have burned the body, but it was nowhere to be found; but in its place a flower, purple within, and surrounded with white leaves, which bears the name and preserves the memory of Narcissus.

Milton alludes to the story of Echo and Narcissus in the Lady's song in "Comus." She is seeking her brothers in the forest, and sings to attract their attention.

"Sweet Echo, sweetest nymph, that liv'st unseen
    Within thy aery shell
  By slow Meander's margent green,
And in the violet-embroidered vale,
    Where the love-lorn nightingale
Nightly to thee her sad song mourneth well;
Canst thou not tell me of a gentle pair
    That likest thy Narcissus are?
      O, if thou have
    Hid them in some flowery cave,
      Tell me but where,
    Sweet queen of parly, daughter of the sphere,
    So may'st thou be translated to the skies,
  And give resounding grace to all heaven's harmonies."

Milton has imitated the story of Narcissus in the account which he makes Eve give of the first sight of herself reflected in the fountain:

"That day I oft remember when from sleep
I first awaked, and found myself reposed
Under a shade on flowers, much wondering where
And what I was, whence thither brought, and how.
Not distant far from thence a murmuring sound
Of waters issued from a cave, and spread
Into a liquid plain, then stood unmoved
Pure as the expanse of heaven; I thither went
With unexperienced thought, and laid me down
On the green bank, to look into the clear
Smooth lake that to me seemed another sky.
As I bent down to look, just opposite
A shape within the watery gleam appeared,
Bending to look on me. I started back;
It started back; but pleased I soon returned,
Pleased it returned as soon with answering looks
Of sympathy and love. There had I fixed
Mine eyes till now, and pined with vain desire,
Had not a voice thus warned me: 'What thou seest,
What there thou seest, fair creature, is thyself;' " etc.

Paradise Lost, Book IV

No one of the fables of antiquity has been oftener alluded to by the poets than that of Narcissus. Here are two epigrams which treat it in different ways. The first is by Goldsmith:

"ON A BEAUTIFUL YOUTH, STRUCK BLIND BY LIGHTNING"

"Sure 'twas by Providence designed,
    Rather in pity than in hate,
That he should be like Cupid blind,
    To save him from Narcissus' fate."

The other is by Cowper:

"ON AN UGLY FELLOW"

"Beware, my friend, of crystal brook
    Or fountain, lest that hideous hook,
        Thy nose, thou chance to see;
Narcissus' fate would then be thine,
And self-detested thou would'st pine,
    As self-enamoured he."

Clytie

Clytie was a water-nymph and in love with Apollo, who made her no return. So she pined away, sitting all day long upon the cold ground, with her unbound tresses streaming over her shoulders. Nine days she sat and tasted neither food nor drink, her own tears and the chilly dew her only food. She gazed on the sun when he rose, and as he passed through his daily course to his setting; she saw no other object, her face turned constantly on him. At last, they say, her limbs rooted in the ground, her face became a flower, which turns on its stem so as always to face the sun throughout its daily course; for it retains to that extent the feeling of the nymph from whom it sprang.

Hood, in his "Flowers," thus alludes to Clytie:

"I will not have the mad Clytie,
    Whose head is turned by the sun;
The tulip is a courtly quean,
    Whom therefore I will shun;
The cowslip is a country wench,
    The violet is a nun;—
But I will woo the dainty rose,
    The queen of every one."

The sunflower is a favorite emblem of constancy. Thus Moore uses it:

"The heart that has truly loved never forgets,
    But as truly loves on to the close;
As the sunflower turns on her god when he sets
    The same look that she turned when he rose."

Hero and Leander

Leander was a youth of Abydos, a town of the Asian side of the strait which separates Asia and Europe. On the opposite shore, in the town of Sestos, lived the maiden Hero, a priestess of Venus. Leander loved her, and used to swim the strait nightly to enjoy the company of his mistress. But one night a tempest arose and the sea was rough; his strength failed, and he was drowned. The waves bore his body to the European shore, where Hero became aware of his death, and in her despair cast herself down from a tower into the sea and perished.

The story of Leander's swimming the Hellespont was looked upon as fabulous, and the feat considered impossible, till Lord Byron proved its possibility by performing it himself. In the "Bride of Abydos" he says,

"These limbs that buoyant wave hath borne."

The distance in the narrowest part is almost a mile, and there is a constant current setting out from the Sea of Marmora into the Archipelago. Since Byron's time the feat has been achieved by others; but it yet remains a test of strength and skill in the art of swimming sufficient to give a wide and lasting celebrity to any one of our readers who may dare to make the attempt and succeed in accomplishing it.

In the beginning of the second canto of the same poem, Byron thus alludes to this story:

"The winds are high on Helle's wave,
    As on that night of stormiest water,
When Love, who sent, forgot to save
The young, the beautiful, the brave,
    The lonely hope of Sestos' daughter.
O, when alone along the sky
The turret-torch was blazing high,
Though rising gale and breaking foam,
And shrieking sea-birds warned him home;
And clouds aloft and tides below,
With signs and sounds forbade to go,
He could not see, he would not hear
Or sound or sight foreboding fear.
His eye but saw that light of love,
The only star it hailed above;
His ear but rang with Hero's song,
'Ye waves, divide not lovers long.'
That tale is old, but love anew
May nerve young hearts to prove as true."

• • • • • • •

14

Minerva — Niobe

Minerva, the goddess of wisdom, was the daughter of Jupiter. She was said to have leaped forth from his brain, mature, and in complete armor. She presided over the useful and ornamental arts, both those of men—such as agriculture and navigation—and those of women—spinning, weaving, and needle-work. She was also a war-like divinity; but it was defensive war only that she patronized, and she had no sympathy with Mars's savage love of violence and bloodshed. Athens was her chosen seat, her own city, awarded to her as the prize of a contest with

Neptune, who also aspired to it. The tale ran that in the reign of Cecrops, the first king of Athens, the two deities contended for the possession of the city. The gods decreed that it should be awarded to that one who produced the gift most useful to mortals. Neptune gave the horse; Minerva produced the olive. The gods gave judgment that the olive was the more useful of the two, and awarded the city to the goddess; and it was named after her, Athens.

There was another contest, in which a mortal dared to come in competition with Minerva. That mortal was Arachne, a maiden who had attained such skill in the arts of weaving and embroidery that the Nymphs themselves would leave their groves and fountains to come and gaze upon her work. It was not only beautiful when it was done, but beautiful also in the doing. To watch her, as she took the wool in its rude state and formed it into rolls, or separated it with her fingers and carded it till it looked as light and soft as a cloud, or twirled the spindle with skilful touch, or wove the web, or, after it was woven, adorned it with her needle, one would have said that Minerva herself had taught her. But this she denied, and could not bear to be thought a pupil even of a goddess. "Let Minerva try her skill with mine," said she; "if beaten, I will pay the penalty." Minerva heard this and was displeased. She assumed the form of an old woman, and went and gave Arachne some friendly advice. "I have had much experience," said she, "and I hope you will not despise my counsel. Challenge your fellow-mortals as you will, but do not compete with a goddess. On the contrary, I advise you to ask her forgiveness for what you have said, and as she is merciful, perhaps she will pardon you." Arachne stopped her spinning, and looked at the old dame with anger in her countenance. "Keep your counsel," said she, "for your daughters or hand-maids; for my part, I know what I say, and I stand to it. I am not afraid of the goddess; let her try her skill, if she dare venture." "She comes," said Minerva; and dropping her disguise, stood confessed. The Nymphs bent low in homage, and all the bystanders paid reverence. Arachne alone was unterrified. She blushed, indeed; a sudden color dyed her cheek, and then she grew pale. But she stood to her resolve, and with a foolish conceit of her own skill rushed on her fate. Minerva forbore no longer, nor interposed any further advice. They proceed to the contest. Each takes her station and attaches the web to the beam. Then the slender shuttle is passed in and out among the threads. The reed with its fine teeth strikes up the woof into its place and compacts the web. Both work with speed; their skilful hands move rapidly, and the excitement of the contest makes the labor light. Wool of Tyrian dye is contrasted with that of other colors, shaded off into one another so adroitly that the joining deceives the eye, like the bow, whose long arch tinges the heavens, formed by sunbeams reflected from the shower* in which, where the colors meet they seem as one, but at a little distance from the point of contact are wholly different.

*This correct description of the rainbow is literally translated from Ovid.

Minerva wrought on her web the scene of her contest with Neptune. Twelve of the heavenly powers are represented, Jupiter, with august gravity, sitting in the midst. Neptune, the ruler of the sea, holds his trident, and appears to have just smitten the earth, from which a horse has leaped forth. Minerva depicted herself with helmed head, her Ægis covering her breast. Such was the central circle; and in the four corners were represented incidents illustrating the displeasure of the gods at such presumptuous mortals as had dared to contend with them. These were meant as warnings to her rival to give up the contest before it was too late.

Arachne filled her web with subjects designedly chosen to exhibit the failings and errors of the gods. One scene represented Leda caressing the swan, under which form Jupiter had disguised himself; and another, Danae, in the brazen tower in which her father had imprisoned her, but where the god effected his entrance in the form of a golden shower. Still another depicted Europa deceived by Jupiter under the disguise of a bull. Encouraged by the tameness of the animal, Europa ventured to mount his back, whereupon Jupiter advanced into the sea, and swam with her to Crete. You would have thought it was a real bull, so naturally was it wrought, and so natural the water in which it swam. She seemed to look with longing eyes back upon the shore she was leaving, and to call to her companions for help. She appeared to shudder with terror at the sight of the heaving waves, and to draw back her feet from the water.

Arachne filled her canvas with similar subjects, wonderfully well done, but strongly marking her presumption and impiety. Minerva could not forbear to admire, yet felt indignant at the insult. She struck the web with her shuttle, and rent it in pieces; she then touched the forehead of Arachne, and made her feel her guilt and shame. She could not endure it, and went and hanged herself. Minerva pitied her as she saw her suspended by a rope. "Live," she said, "guilty woman!—and that you may preserve the memory of this lesson continue to hang, both you and your descendants, to all future times." She sprinkled her with the juices of aconite, and immediately her hair came off, and her nose and ears likewise. Her form shrank up, and her head grew smaller yet; her fingers cleaved to her side, and served for legs. All the rest of her is body, out of which she spins her thread, often hanging suspended by it, in the same attitude as when Minerva touched her and transformed her into a spider.

Spenser tells the story of Arachne in his "Muiopotmos," adhering very closely to his master Ovid, but improving upon him in the conclusion of the story. The two stanzas which follow tell what was done after the goddess had depicted her creation of the olive tree:

> "Amongst these leaves she made a Butterfly,
>   With excellent device and wondrous slight,
>   Fluttering among the olives wantonly,

That seemed to live, so like it was in sight;
The velvet nap which on his wings doth lie,
The silken down with which his back is dight,
His broad outstretched horns, his hairy thighs,
His glorious colors, and his glistening eyes.'"*

"Which when Arachne saw, as overlaid
And mastered with workmanship so rare,
She stood astonied long, ne aught gainsaid;
And with fast-fixed eyes on her did stare,
And by her silence, sign of one dismayed,
The victory did yield her as her share:
Yet did she inly fret and felly burn,
And all her blood to poisonous rancor turn."

And so the metamorphosis is caused by Arachne's own mortification and vexation, and not by any direct act of the goddess.

The following specimen of old-fashioned gallantry is by Garrick:

UPON A LADY'S EMBROIDERY

"Arachne once, as poets tell,
   A goddess at her art defied,
And soon the daring mortal fell
   The hapless victim of her pride.

O, then beware Arachne's fate;
   Be prudent, Chloe, and submit,
For you'll most surely meet her hate,
   Who rival both her art and wit."

Tennyson, in his "Palace of Art," describing the works of art with which the palace was adorned, thus alludes to Europa:

"——sweet Europa's mantle blew unclasped
   From off her shoulder, backward borne,
From one hand drooped a crocus, one hand grasped
   The mild bull's golden horn."

In his "Princess" there is this allusion to Danae:

"Now lies the earth all Danae to the stars,
And all thy heart lies open unto me."

Niobe

The fate of Arachne was noised abroad through all the country, and served as a warning to all presumptuous mortals not to compare themselves with the divinities. But one, and she a matron too, failed to learn the lesson of humility. It was Niobe, the queen of Thebes. She had in-

*Sir James Mackintosh says of this, "Do you think that even a Chinese could paint the gay colors of a butterfly with more minute exactness than the following lines—'The velvet nap,' etc.?"   *Life*, Vol. II. 246

deed much to be proud of; but it was not her husband's fame, nor her own beauty, nor their great descent, nor the power of their kingdom that elated her. It was her children; and truly the happiest of mothers would Niobe have been, if only she had not claimed to be so. It was on occasion of the annual celebration in honor of Latona and her offspring, Apollo and Diana—when the people of Thebes were assembled, their brows crowned with laurel, bearing frankincense to the altars and paying their vows—that Niobe appeared among the crowd. Her attire was splendid with gold and gems, and her aspect beautiful as the face of an angry woman can be. She stood and surveyed the people with haughty looks. "What folly," said she, "is this!—to prefer beings whom you never saw to those who stand before your eyes! Why should Latona be honored with worship, and none be paid to me? My father was Tantalus, who was received as a guest at the table of the gods; my mother was a goddess. My husband built and rules this city, Thebes, and Phrygia is my paternal inheritance. Wherever I turn my eyes I survey the elements of my power; nor is my form and presence unworthy of a goddess. To all this let me add, I have seven sons and seven daughters, and look for sons-in-law and daughters-in-law of pretensions worthy of my alliance. Have I not cause for pride? Will you prefer to me this Latona, the Titan's daughter, with her two children? I have seven times as many. Fortunate indeed am I, and fortunate I shall remain! Will any one deny this? My abundance is my security. I feel myself too strong for Fortune to subdue. She may take from me much; I shall still have much left. Were I to lose some of my children, I should hardly be left as poor as Latona with her two only. Away with you from these solemnities—put off the laurel from your brows—have done with this worship!" The people obeyed, and left the sacred services uncompleted.

The goddess was indignant. On the Cynthian mountain top, where she dwelt, she thus addressed her son and daughter: "My children, I who have been so proud of you both, and have been used to hold myself second to none of the goddesses except Juno alone, begin now to doubt whether I am indeed a goddess. I shall be deprived of my worship altogether unless you protect me." She was proceeding in this strain, but Apollo interrupted her. "Say no more," said he; "speech only delays punishment." So said Diana also. Darting through the air, veiled in clouds, they alighted on the towers of the city. Spread out before the gates was a broad plain, where the youth of the city pursued their warlike sports. The sons of Niobe were there with the rest—some mounted on spirited horses richly caparisoned, some driving gay chariots. Ismenos, the first-born, as he guided his foaming steeds, struck with an arrow from above, cried out, "Ah me!"—dropped the reins and fell lifeless. Another, hearing the sound of the bow—like a boatman who sees the storm gathering and makes all sail for the port—gave the rein to his horses and attempted to escape. The inevitable arrow overtook him as he fled. Two others, younger boys, just from their tasks, had gone to the playground to have a game of wrestling. As they stood breast to breast, one arrow pierced them both. They uttered a cry together, together cast a parting look around them, and together breathed their last. Alphenor, an elder brother, seeing them fall hastened to the spot to render assistance, and fell stricken in the act of brotherly duty. One only was left, Ilioneus. He raised his arms to heaven to try whether prayer might not avail. "Spare me, ye gods!" he cried, addressing all, in his ignorance that all needed not his intercessions; and Apollo would have spared him, but the arrow had already left the string, and it was too late.

The terror of the people and grief of the attendants soon made Niobe acquainted with what had taken place. She could hardly think it possible; she was indignant that the gods had dared and amazed that they had been able to do it. Her husband, Amphion, overwhelmed with the blow, destroyed himself. Alas! how different was this Niobe from her who had so lately driven away the people from the sacred rites, and held her stately course through the city, the envy of her friends, now the pity even of her foes! She knelt over the lifeless bodies, and kissed, now one, now another of her dead sons. Raising her pallid arms to heaven, "Cruel Latona," said she, "feed full your rage with my anguish! Satiate your hard heart, while I follow to the grave my seven sons. Yet where is your triumph? Bereaved as I am, I am still richer than you, my conqueror." Scarce had she spoken, when the bow sounded and struck terror into all hearts except Niobe's alone. She was brave from excess of grief. The sisters stood in garments of mourning over the biers of their dead brothers. One fell, struck by an arrow, and died on the corpse she was bewailing. Another, attempting to console her mother, suddenly ceased to speak, and sank lifeless to the earth. A third tried to escape by flight, a fourth by concealment, another stood trembling, uncertain what course to take. Six were now dead, and only one remained, whom the mother held clasped in her arms, and covered as it were with her whole body. "Spare me one, and that the youngest! O, spare me one of so many!" she cried; and while she spoke, that one fell dead. Desolate she sat, among sons, daughters, husband, all dead, and seemed torpid with grief. The breeze moved not her hair, no color was on her cheek, her eyes glared fixed and immovable, there was no sign of life about her. Her very tongue cleaved to the roof of her mouth, and her veins ceased to convey the tide of life. Her neck bent not, her arms made no gesture, her foot no step. She was changed to stone, within and without. Yet tears continued to flow; and, borne on a whirlwind to her native mountain, she still remains, a mass of rock, from which a trickling stream flows, the tribute of her never-ending grief.

The story of Niobe has furnished Byron with a fine illustration of the fallen condition of modern Rome:

"The Niobe of nations! there she stands,
  Childless and crownless in her voiceless woe;
  An empty urn within her withered hands,
  Whose holy dust was scattered long ago;

The Scipios' tomb contains no ashes now;
The very sepulchres lie tenantless
Of their heroic dwellers; dost thou flow,
Old Tiber! through a marble wilderness?
Rise with thy yellow waves, and mantle her distress.''
Childe Harold, IV. 79

An illustration of this story is a copy of a celebrated statue in the imperial gallery of Florence. It is the principal figure of a group supposed to have been originally arranged in the pediment of a temple. The figure of the mother clasped by the arm of her terrified child, is one of the most admired of the ancient statues. It ranks with the Laocoon and the Apollo among the masterpieces of art. The following is a translation of a Greek epigram supposed to relate to this statue:

"To stone the gods have changed her, but in vain;
  The sculptor's art has made her breathe again.''

Tragic as is the story of Niobe we cannot forbear to smile at the use Moore has made of it in "Rhymes on the Road":

" 'Twas in his carriage the sublime
  Sir Richard Blackmore used to rhyme,
    And, if the wits don't do him wrong,
  'Twixt death and epics passed his time,
    Scribbling and killing all day long;
      Like Phœbus in his car at ease,
    Now warbling forth a lofty song,
      Now murdering the young Niobes.''

Sir Richard Blackmore was a physician, and at the same time a very prolific and very tasteless poet, whose works are now forgotten, unless when recalled to mind by some wit like Moore for the sake of a joke.

·······
15

The Grææ and Gorgons—Perseus— Medusa—Atlas—Andromeda

The Grææ were three sisters who were gray-haired from their birth, whence their name. The Gorgons were monstrous females with huge teeth like those of swine, brazen claws, and snaky hair. None of these beings make much figure in mythology except Medusa, the Gorgon, whose story we shall next advert to. We mention them chiefly to introduce an ingenious theory of some modern writers, namely, that the Gorgons and Grææ were only personifications of the terrors of the sea, the former denoting the *strong* billows of the wide open main, and the latter the *white*-crested waves that dash against the rocks of the coast. Their names in Greek signify the above epithets.

Perseus and Medusa

Perseus was the son of Jupiter and Danae. His grandfather Acrisius, alarmed by an oracle which had told him that his daughter's child would be the instrument of his death, caused the mother and child to be shut up in a chest and set adrift on the sea. The chest floated towards Seriphus, where it was found by a fisherman who conveyed the mother and infant to Polydectes, king of the country, by whom they were treated with kindness. When Perseus was grown up Polydectes sent him to attempt the conquest of Medusa, a terrible monster who had laid waste the country. She was once a beautiful maiden whose hair was her chief glory, but as she dared to vie in beauty with Minerva, the goddess deprived her of her charms and changed her beautiful ringlets into hissing serpents. She became a cruel monster of so frightful an aspect that no living thing could behold her without being turned into stone. All around the cavern where she dwelt might be seen the stony figures of men and animals which had chanced to catch a glimpse of her and had been petrified with the sight. Perseus, favored by Minerva and Mercury, the former of whom lent him her shield and the latter his winged shoes, approached Medusa while she slept, and taking care not to look directly at her, but guided by her image reflected in the bright shield which he bore, he cut off her head, and gave it to Minerva, who fixed it in the middle of her Ægis.

Milton in his "Comus" thus alludes to the Ægis:

"What was that snaky-headed Gorgon-shield
    That wise Minerva wore, unconquered virgin,
    Wherewith she freezed her foes to congealed stone,
    But rigid looks of chaste austerity,
    And noble grace that dashed brute violence
    With sudden adoration and blank awe!"

Armstrong, the poet of the "Art of Preserving Health," thus describes the effect of frost upon the waters:

"Now blows the surly North and chills throughout
    The stiffening regions, while by stronger charms
    Than Circe e'er or fell Medea brewed,
    Each brook that wont to prattle to its banks
    Lies all bestilled and wedged betwixt its banks,
    Nor moves the withered reeds.   *   *   *
    The surges baited by the fierce North-east,
    Tossing with fretful spleen their angry heads,
    E'en in the foam of all their madness struck
    To monumental ice.
                *   *   *   *   *
                    Such execution,
    So stern, so sudden, wrought the grisly aspect
    Of terrible Medusa,
    When wandering through the woods she turned to stone

Their savage tenants; just as the foaming Lion
Sprang furious on his prey, her speedier power
Outran his haste,
And fixed in that fierce attitude he stands
Like Rage in marble!"

Imitations of Shakespeare

Perseus and Atlas

After the slaughter of Medusa, Perseus, bearing with him the head of
the Gorgon, flew far and wide, over land and sea. As night came on, he
reached the western limit of the earth, where the sun goes down. Here he
would gladly have rested till morning. It was the realm of King Atlas,
whose bulk surpassed that of all other men. He was rich in flocks and
herds and had no neighbor or rival to dispute his state. But his chief
pride was in his gardens, whose fruit was of gold, hanging from golden
branches, half hid with golden leaves. Perseus said to him, "I come as a
guest. If you honor illustrious descent, I claim Jupiter for my father; if
mighty deeds, I plead the conquest of the Gorgon. I seek rest and
food." But Atlas remembered that an ancient prophecy had warned
him that a son of Jove should one day rob him of his golden apples. So
he answered, "Begone! or neither your false claims of glory or parentage shall protect you"; and he attempted to thrust him out. Perseus,
finding the giant too strong for him, said, "Since you value my friendship so little, deign to accept a present"; and turning his face away, he
held up the Gorgon's head. Atlas, with all his bulk, was changed into
stone. His beard and hair became forests, his arms and shoulders cliffs,
his head a summit, and his bones rocks. Each part increased in bulk till
he became a mountain, and (such was the pleasure of the gods) heaven
with all its stars rests upon his shoulders.

Perseus, continuing his flight, arrived at the country of the Æthiopians, of which Cepheus was king. Cassiopeia his queen, proud of her
beauty, had dared to compare herself to the Sea-Nymphs, which roused
their indignation to such a degree that they sent a prodigious sea-
monster to ravage the coast. To appease the deities, Cepheus was directed by the oracle to expose his daughter Andromeda to be devoured by
the monster. As Perseus looked down from his aerial height he beheld
the virgin chained to a rock, and waiting the approach of the serpent.
She was so pale and motionless that if it had not been for her flowing
tears and her hair that moved in the breeze, he would have taken her for
a marble statue. He was so startled at the sight that he almost forgot to
wave his wings. As he hovered over her he said, "O virgin, undeserving
of those chains, but rather of such as bind fond lovers together, tell me, I
beseech you, your name, and the name of your country, and why you
are thus bound." At first she was silent from modesty, and, if she could,
would have hid her face with her hands; but when he repeated his questions, for fear she might be thought guilty of some fault which she dared
not tell, she disclosed her name and that of her country, and her

mother's pride of beauty. Before she had done speaking, a sound was heard off upon the water, and the sea-monster appeared, with his head raised above the surface, cleaving the waves with his broad breast. The virgin shrieked, the father and mother who had now arrived at the scene, wretched both, but the mother more justly so, stood by, not able to afford protection, but only to pour forth lamentations and to embrace the victim. Then spoke Perseus: "There will be time enough for tears; this hour is all we have for rescue. My rank as the son of Jove and my renown as the slayer of the Gorgon might make me acceptable as a suitor; but I will try to win her by services rendered, if the gods will only be propitious. If she be rescued by my valor, I demand that she be my reward." The parents consent (how could they hesitate?) and promise a royal dowry with her.

And now the monster was within the range of a stone thrown by a skillful slinger, when with a sudden bound the youth soared into the air. As an eagle, when from his lofty flight he sees a serpent basking in the sun, pounces upon him and seizes him by the neck to prevent him from turning his head round and using his fangs, so the youth darted down upon the back of the monster and plunged his sword into its shoulder. Irritated by the wound the monster raised himself into the air, then plunged into the depth; then, like a wild boar surrounded by a pack of barking dogs, turned swiftly from side to side, while the youth eluded its attacks by means of his wings. Wherever he can find a passage for his sword between the scales he makes a wound, piercing now the side, now the flank, as it slopes towards the tail. The brute spouts from his nostrils water mixed with blood. The wings of the hero are wet with it, and he dares no longer trust to them. Alighting on a rock which rose above the waves, and holding on by a projecting fragment, as the monster floated near he gave him a death stroke. The people who had gathered on the shore shouted so that the hills reechoed the sound. The parents, transported with joy, embraced their future son-in-law, calling him their deliverer and the savior of their house, and the virgin, both cause and reward of the contest, descended from the rock.

Cassiopeia was an Æthiopian, and consequently, in spite of her boasted beauty, black; at least so Milton seems to have thought, who alludes to this story in his "Penseroso," where he addresses Melancholy as the

> "——goddess, sage and holy,
> To hit the sense of human sight,
> And, therefore, to our weaker view
> O'erlaid with black, staid Wisdom's hue.
> Black, but such as in esteem,
> Prince Memnon's sister might beseem,
> Or that starred Æthiop queen that strove
> To set her beauty's praise above
> The sea-nymphs, and their powers offended."

Cassiopeia is called "the starred Æthiop queen" because after her death she was placed among the stars, forming the constellation of that name. Though she attained this honor, yet the Sea-Nymphs, her old enemies, prevailed so far as to cause her to be placed in that part of the heaven near the pole, where every night she is half the time held with her head downward, to give her a lesson of humility.

Memnon was an Æthiopian prince, of whom we shall tell in a future chapter.

Andromeda

The joyful parents, with Perseus and Andromeda, repaired to the palace, where a banquet was spread for them, and all was joy and festivity. But suddenly a noise was heard of warlike clamor, and Phineus, the betrothed of the virgin, with a party of his adherents, burst in, demanding the maiden as his own. It was in vain that Cepheus remonstrated—"You should have claimed her when she lay bound to the rock, the monster's victim. The sentence of the gods dooming her to such a fate dissolved all engagements, as death itself would have done." Phineus made no reply, but hurled his javelin at Perseus, but it missed its mark and fell harmless. Perseus would have thrown his in turn, but the cowardly assailant ran and took shelter behind the alter. But his act was a signal for an onset by his band upon the guests of Cepheus. They defended themselves and a general conflict ensued, the old king retreating from the scene after fruitless expostulations, calling the gods to witness that he was guiltless of this outrage on the rights of hospitality.

Perseus and his friends maintained for some time the unequal contest; but the numbers of the assailants were too great for them, and destruction seemed inevitable, when a sudden thought struck Perseus, "I will make my enemy defend me." Then with a loud voice he exclaimed, "If I have any friend here let him turn away his eyes!" and held aloft the Gorgon's head. "Seek not to frighten us with your jugglery," said Thescelus, and raised his javelin in the act to throw, and became stone in the very attitude. Ampyx was about to plunge his sword into the body of a prostrate foe, but his arm stiffened and he could neither thrust forward nor withdraw it. Another, in the midst of a vociferous challenge, stopped, his mouth open, but no sound issuing. One of Perseus's friends, Aconteus, caught sight of the Gorgon and stiffened like the rest. Astyages struck him with his sword, but instead of wounding, it recoiled with a ringing noise.

Phineus beheld this dreadful result of his unjust aggression, and felt confounded. He called aloud to his friends, but got no answer; he touched them and found them stone. Falling on his knees and stretching out his hands to Perseus, but turning his head away, he begged for mercy. "Take all," said he, "give me but my life." "Base coward," said Perseus, "this much I will grant you; no weapons shall touch you; moreover you shall be preserved in my house as a memorial of these events." So saying, he held the Gorgon's head to the side where Phineus was

looking, and in the very form in which he knelt, with his hands outstretched and face averted he became fixed immovably, a mass of stone!

The following allusion to Perseus is from Milman's "Samor":

"As 'mid the fabled Libyan bridal stood
 Perseus in stern tranquillity of wrath,
 Half stood, half floated on his ankle-plumes
 Out-swelling, while the bright face on his shield
 Looked into stone the raging fray; so rose,
 But with no magic arms, wearing alone
 Th' appalling and control of his firm look,
 The Briton Samor; at his rising awe
 Went abroad, and the riotous hall was mute."

. . . .

16

Monsters:
Giants—Sphinx—Pegasus and Chimæra—
Centaurs—Griffin—Pygmies

Monsters, in the language of mythology, were beings of unnatural
proportions or parts, usually regarded with terror, as possessing immense strength and ferocity, which they employed for the injury and
annoyance of men. Some of them were supposed to combine the members of different animals; such were the Sphinx and Chimæra; and to
these all the terrible qualities of wild beasts were attributed, together
with human sagacity and faculties. Others, as the giants, differed from
men chiefly in their size; and in this particular we must recognize a wide
distinction among them. The human giants, if so they may be called,
such as the Cyclopes, Antæus, Orion and others, must be supposed not
to be altogether disproportioned to human beings, for they mingled in
love and strife with them. But the superhuman giants, who warred with
the gods, were of vastly larger dimensions. Tityus, we are told, when
stretched on the plain, covered nine acres, and Enceladus required the
whole of Mount Ætna to be laid upon him to keep him down.

We have already spoken of the war which the giants waged against
the gods, and of its result. While this war lasted the giants proved a formidable enemy. Some of them, like Briareus, had a hundred arms; others,
like Typhon, breathed out fire. At one time they put the gods to
such fear that they fled into Egypt, and hid themselves under various
forms. Jupiter took the form of a ram, whence he was afterwards worshipped in Egypt as the god Ammon, with curved horns. Apollo
became a crow, Bacchus a goat, Diana a cat, Juno a cow, Venus a fish,
Mercury a bird. At another time the giants attempted to climb up into
heaven, and for that purpose took up the mountain Ossa and piled it on
Pelion.* They were at last subdued by thunderbolts, which Minerva in-

*See Proverbial Expressions, page 271.

vented, and taught Vulcan and his Cyclopes to make for Jupiter.

The Sphinx

Laius, king of Thebes, was warned by an oracle that there was danger to his throne and life if his new-born son should be suffered to grow up. He therefore committed the child to the care of a herdsman, with orders to destroy him; but the herdsman, moved with pity, yet not daring entirely to disobey, tied up the child by the feet, and left him hanging to the branch of a tree. In this condition the infant was found by a peasant, who carried him to his master and mistress, by whom he was adopted and called Œdipus, or Swollen-foot.

Many years afterwards Laius being on his way to Delphi, accompanied only by one attendant, met in a narrow road a young man also driving in a chariot. On his refusal to leave the way at their command, the attendant killed one of his horses, and the stranger, filled with rage, slew both Laius and his attendant. The young man was Œdipus, who thus unknowingly became the slayer of his own father.

Shortly after this event, the city of Thebes was afflicted with a monster which infested the high-road. It was called the Sphinx. It had the body of a lion, and the upper part of a woman. It lay crouched on the top of a rock, and arrested all travellers who came that way, proposing to them a riddle, with the condition that those who could solve it should pass safe, but those who failed should be killed. Not one had yet succeeded in solving it, and all had been slain. Œdipus was not daunted by these alarming accounts, but boldly advanced to the trial. The Sphinx asked him, "What animal is that which in the morning goes on four feet, at noon on two, and in the evening upon three?" Œdipus replied, "Man, who in childhood creeps on hands and knees, in manhood walks erect, and in old age with the aid of a staff." The Sphinx was so mortified at the solving of her riddle that she cast herself down from the rock and perished.

The gratitude of the people for their deliverance was so great that they made Œdipus their king, giving him in marriage their queen Jocasta. Œdipus, ignorant of his parentage, had already become the slayer of his father; in marrying the queen he became the husband of his mother. These horrors remained undiscovered, till at length Thebes was afflicted with famine and pestilence, and the oracle being consulted, the double crime of Œdipus came to light. Jocasta put an end to her own life, and Œdipus, seized with madness, tore out his eyes, and wandered away from Thebes, dreaded and abandoned by all, except his daughters, who faithfully adhered to him; till after a tedious period of miserable wandering, he found the termination of his wretched life.

Pegasus and The Chimæra

When Perseus cut of Medusa's head, the blood sinking into the earth produced the winged horse Pegasus. Minerva caught and tamed him, and presented him to the Muses. The fountain Hippocrene, on the Muses' mountain Helicon, was opened by a kick from his hoof.

The Chimæra was a fearful monster, breathing fire. The fore part of its body was a compound of the lion and the goat, and the hind part a dragon's. It made great havoc in Lycia, so that the king Iobates sought for some hero to destroy it. At that time there arrived at his court a gallant young warrior, whose name was Bellerophon. He brought letters from Prœtus, the son-in-law of Iobates, recommending Bellerophon in the warmest terms as an unconquerable hero, but added at the close a request to his father-in-law to put him to death. The reason was that Prœtus was jealous of him, suspecting that his wife Antea looked with too much admiration on the young warrior. From this instance of Bellerophon being unconsciously the bearer of his own death-warrant, the expression "Bellerophontic letters" arose, to describe any species of communication which a person is made the bearer of, containing matter prejudicial to himself.

Iobates, on perusing the letters, was puzzled what to do, not willing to violate the claims of hospitality, yet wishing to oblige his son-in-law. A lucky thought occurred to him, to send Bellerophon to combat with the Chimæra. Bellerophon accepted the proposal, but before proceeding to the combat consulted the soothsayer Polyidus, who advised him to procure if possible the horse Pegasus for the conflict. For this purpose he directed him to pass the night in the temple of Minerva. He did so, and as he slept Minerva came to him and gave him a golden bridle. When he awoke the bridle remained in his hand. Minerva also showed him Pegasus drinking at the well of Pirene, and at sight of the bridle, the winged steed came willingly and suffered himself to be taken. Bellerophon mounted him, rose with him into the air, soon found the Chimæra, and gained an easy victory over the monster.

After the conquest of the Chimæra, Bellerophon was exposed to further trials and labors by his unfriendly host, but by the aid of Pegasus he triumphed in them all; till at length Iobates, seeing that the hero was a special favorite of the gods, gave him his daughter in marriage and made him his successor on the throne. At last Bellerophon by his pride and presumption drew upon himself the anger of the gods; it is said he even attempted to fly up into heaven on his winged steed; but Jupiter sent a gadfly which stung Pegasus and made him throw his rider, who became lame and blind in consequence. After this Bellerophon wandered lonely through the Aleian field, avoiding the paths of men, and died miserably.

Milton alludes to Bellerophon in the beginning of the seventh book of "Paradise Lost":

"Descend from Heaven, Urania, by that name
   If rightly thou art called, whose voice divine
   Following above the Olympian hill I soar,
   Above the flight of Pegasean wing.

Upled by thee,
Into the Heaven of Heavens I have presumed,
An earthly guest, and drawn empyreal air,
(Thy tempering;) with like safety guided down
Return me to my native element;
Lest from this flying steed unreined, (as once
Bellerophon, though from a lower sphere,)
Dismounted on the Aleian field I fall,
Erroneous there to wander and forlorn.''

Young, in his "Night Thoughts," speaking of the sceptic, says,

"He whose blind thought futurity denies,
Unconscious beard, Bellerophon, like thee
His own indictment; he condemns himself.
Who reads his bosom reads immortal life,
Or nature there, imposing on her sons,
Has written fables; man was made a lie.''

Vol. II, p.12.

Pegasus, being the horse of the Muses, has always been at the service of the poets. Schiller tells a pretty story of his having been sold by a needy poet, and put to the cart and the plough. He was not fit for such service, and his clownish master could make nothing of him. But a youth stepped forth and asked leave to try him. As soon as he was seated on his back, the horse, which had appeared at first vicious, and afterwards spirit-broken, rose kingly, a spirit, a god, unfolded the splendor of his wings and soared towards heaven. Our own poet Longfellow also records an adventure of this famous steed in his "Pegasus in Pound."

Shakespeare alludes to Pegasus in "Henry IV," where Vernon describes Prince Henry:

"I saw young Harry, with his beaver on,
His cuishes on his thighs, gallantly armed,
Rise from the ground like feathered Mercury,
And vaulted with such case into his seat,
As if an angel dropped down from the clouds,
To turn and wind a fiery Pegasus,
And witch the world with noble horsemanship.''

The Centaurs

These monsters were represented as men from the head to the loins while the remainder of the body was that of a horse. The ancients were too fond of a horse to consider the union of his nature with man's as forming a very degraded compound, and accordingly the Centaur is the only one of the fancied monsters of antiquity to which any good traits are assigned. The Centaurs were admitted to the companionship of man, and at the marriage of Pirithous with Hippodamia, they were among the guests. At the feast, Eurytion, one of the Centaurs, becoming intoxicated with the wine, attempted to offer violence to the bride; the other Centaurs followed his example, and a dreadful conflict arose in which several of them were slain. This is the celebrated battle of the Lapithæ and Centaurs, a favorite subject with the sculptors and poets of antiquity.

But not all the Centaurs were like the rude guests of Pirithous. Chiron was instructed by Apollo and Diana, and was renowned for his skill in hunting, medicine, music, and the art of prophecy. The most distinguished heroes of Grecian story were his pupils. Among the rest the infant Æsculapius was intrusted to his charge, by Apollo, his father. When the sage returned to his home bearing the infant, his daughter Ocyroe came forth to meet him, and at sight of the child burst forth into a prophetic strain(for she was a prophetess), foretelling the glory that he was to achieve. Æsculapius when grown up became a renowned physician, and even in one instance succeeded in restoring the dead to life. Pluto resented this, and Jupiter, at his request, struck the bold physician with lightning, and killed him, but after his death received him into the number of the gods.

Chiron was the wisest and justest of all the Centaurs, and at his death Jupiter placed him among the stars as the constellation Sagittarius.

The Pygmies

The Pygmies were a nation of dwarfs, so called from a Greek word which means the cubit or measure of about thirteen inches, which was said to be the height of these people. They lived near the sources of the Nile, or according to others, in India. Homer tells us that the cranes used to migrate every winter to the Pygmies' country, and their appearance was the signal of bloody warfare to the puny inhabitants, who had to take up arms to defend their cornfields against the rapacious strangers. The Pygmies and their enemies the Cranes form the subject of several works of art.

Later writers tell of an army of Pygmies which finding Hercules asleep made preparations to attack him, as if they were about to attack a city. But the hero awaking laughed at the little warriors, wrapped some of them up in his lion's-skin, and carried them to Eurystheus.

Milton uses the Pygmies for a simile, "Paradise Lost," Book I:

"——like that Pygmæan race
Beyond the Indian mount, or fairy elves
Whose midnight revels by a forest side,
Or fountain, some belated peasant sees,
(Or dreams he sees,) while overhead the moon
Sits arbitress, and nearer to the earth
Wheels her pale course; they on their mirth and dance
Intent, with jocund music charm his ear.
At once with joy and fear his heart rebounds."

The Griffin, or Gryphon

The Griffin is a monster with the body of a lion, the head and wings of an eagle, and back covered with feathers. Like birds it builds its nest, and instead of an egg lays an agate therein. It has long claws and talons of such a size that the people of that country make them into drinking-cups. India was assigned as the native country of the Griffins. They found gold in the mountains and built their nests of it, for which reason their nests were very tempting to the hunters and they were forced to keep vigilant guard over them. Their instinct led them to know where buried treasures lay, and they did their best to keep plunderers at a distance. The Arimaspians, among whom the Griffins flourished, were a one-eyed people of Scythia.

Milton borrows a simile from the Griffins, "Paradise Lost," Book II:

"As when a Gryphon through the wilderness,
  With winged course, o'er hill and moory dale
  Pursues the Arimaspian who by stealth
  Hath from his wakeful custody purloined
  His guarded gold," etc.

. . . .

17

The Golden Fleece—Medea

In very ancient times there lived in Thessaly a king and queen named Athamas and Nephele. They had two children, a boy and a girl. After a time Athamas grew indifferent to his wife, put her away and took another. Nephele suspected danger to her children from the influence of the step-mother, and took measures to send them out of her reach. Mercury assisted her, and gave her a ram, with a *golden fleece,* on which she set the two children, trusting that the ram would convey them to a place of safety. The ram vaulted into the air with the children on his back, taking his course to the East, till when crossing the straight that divides Europe and Asia, the girl, whose name was Helle, fell from his back into the sea, which from her was called the Hellespont—now the Dardanelles. The ram continued his career till he reached the kingdom of Colchis, on the eastern shore of the Black Sea, where he safely landed the boy Phryxus, who was hospitably received by Æetes, the king of the country. Phryxus sacrificed the ram to Jupiter, and gave the *golden fleece* to Æetes, who placed it in a consecrated grove, under the care of a sleepless dragon.

There was another kingdom in Thessaly near to that of Athamus, and ruled over by a relative of his. The king Æson, being tired of the cares of government, surrendered his crown to his brother Pelias, on condition that he should hold it only during the minority of Jason, the son of

Æson. When Jason was grown up and came to demand the crown from his uncle, Pelias pretended to be willing to yield it, but at the same time suggested to the young man the glorious adventure of going in quest of the golden fleece, which it was well known was in the rightful property of their family. Jason was pleased with the thought, and forthwith made preparations for the expedition. At that time the only species of navigation known to the Greeks consisted of small boats or canoes hollowed out from trunks of trees, so that when Jason employed Argus to build him a vessel capable of containing fifty men, it was considered a gigantic undertaking. It was accomplished, however, and the vessel named Argo, from the name of the builder. Jason sent his invitation to all the adventurous young men of Greece, and soon found himself at the head of a band of bold youths, many of whom afterwards were renowned among the heroes and demigods of Greece. Hercules, Theseus, Orpheus, and Nestor were among them. They are called the Argonauts, from the name of their vessel.

The Argo with her crew of heroes left the shores of Thessaly and having touched at the Island of Lemnos, thence crossed to Mysia and thence to Thrace. Here they found the sage Phineus, and from him received instruction as to their future course. It seems the entrance of the Euxine Sea was impeded by two small rocky islands, which floated on the surface, and in their tossings and heavings occasionally came together, crushing and grinding to atoms any object that might be caught between them. They were called the Symplegades, or Clashing Islands. Phineus instructed the Argonauts how to pass this dangerous strait. When they reached the islands they let go a dove, which took her way between the rocks, and passed in safety, only losing some feathers of her tail. Jason and his men seized the favorable moment of the rebound, plied their oars with vigor, and passed safe through, though the islands closed behind them, and actually grazed their stern. They now rowed along the shore till they arrived at the eastern end of the sea, and landed at the kingdom of Colchis.

Jason made known his message to the Colchian king, Æetes, who consented to give up the golden fleece if Jason would yoke to the plough two fire-breathing bulls with brazen feet, and sow the teeth of the dragon, which Cadmus had slain, and from which it was well known that a crop of armed men would spring up, who would turn their weapons against their producer. Jason accepted the conditions, and a time was set for making the experiment. Previously, however, he found means to plead his cause to Medea, daughter of the king. He promised her marriage, and as they stood before the altar of Hecate, called the goddess to witness his oath. Medea yielded—and by her aid, for she was a potent sorceress, he was furnished with a charm, by which he could encounter safely the breath of the fire-breathing bulls and the weapons of the armed men.

At the time appointed, the people assembled at the grove of Mars, and the king assumed his royal seat, while the multitude covered the hill sides. The brazen-footed bulls rushed in, breathing fire from their nostrils, that burned up the herbage as they passed. The sound was like the roar of a furnace, and the smoke like that of water upon quick-lime. Jason advanced boldly to meet them. His friends, the chosen heroes of Greece, trembled to behold him. Regardless of the burning breath, he soothed their rage with his voice, patted their necks with fearless hand, and adroitly slipped over them the yoke, and compelled them to drag the plough. The Colchians were amazed; the Greeks trembled for their hero, and even she who had provided him a way of safety and taught him how to use it, Medea herself, grew pale with fear. Jason for a time kept his assailants at bay with his sword and shield, till finding their numbers overwhelming, he resorted to the charm which Medea had taught him, seized a stone and threw it in the midst of his foes. They immediately turned their arms against one another, and soon there was not one of the dragon's brood left alive. The Greeks embraced their hero, and Medea, if she dared, would have embraced him, too.

It remained to lull to sleep the dragon that guarded the fleece, and this was done by scattering over him a few drops of a preparation, which Medea had supplied. At the smell he relaxed his rage, stood for a moment motionless, then shut those great round eyes, that had never been known to shut before, and turned over on his side, fast asleep. Jason seized the fleece, and with his friends and Medea accompanying, hastened to their vessel, before Æetes, the king, could arrest their departure, and made the best of their way back to Thessaly, where they arrived safe, and Jason delivered the fleece to Pelias, and dedicated the Argo to Neptune. What became of the fleece afterwards we do not know, but perhaps it was found after all, like many other golden prizes, not worth the trouble it had cost to procure it.

This is one of those mythological tales, says a late writer, in which there is reason to believe that a substratum of truth exists, though overlaid by a mass of fiction. It probably was the first important maritime expedition, and like the first attempts of the kind of all nations, as we know from history, was probably of a half-piratical character. If rich spoils were the result, it was enough to give rise to the idea of the golden fleece.

Another suggestion of a learned mythologist, Bryant, is that it is a corrupt tradition of the story of Noah and the ark. The name Argo seems to countenance this, and the incident of the dove is another confirmation.

Pope, in his "Ode on St. Cecila's Day," thus celebrates the launching of the ship Argo, and the power of the music of Orpheus, whom he calls the Thracian:

"So when the first bold vessel dared the seas,
    High on the stern the Thracian raised his strain,
  While Argo saw her kindred trees
    Descend from Pelion to the main.

>   Transported demigods stood round,
>   And men grew heroes at the sound.''

In Dyer's poem of "The Fleece" there is an account of the ship Argo and her crew, which gives a good picture of this primitive maritime adventure:

>   "From every region of Ægea's shore
>   The brave assembled; those illustrious twins
>   Castor and Pollux; Orpheus, tuneful bard;
>   Zetes and Calais, as the wind in speed;
>   Strong Hercules and many a chief renowned.
>   On deep Iolcos' sandy shore they thronged,
>   Gleaming in armor, ardent of exploits;
>   And soon, the laurel cord and the huge stone
>   Uplifting to the deck, unmoored the bark;
>   Whose keel of wondrous length the skilful hand
>   On Argus fashioned for the proud attempt;
>   And in the extended keel a lofty mast
>   Upraised, and sails full swelling; to the chiefs
>   Unwonted objects. Now first, now they learned
>   Their bolder steerage over ocean wave,
>   Led by the golden stars, as Chiron's art
>   Had marked the sphere celestial," etc.

Hercules left the expedition at Mysia, for Hylas, a youth beloved by him, having gone for water, was laid hold of and kept by the nymphs of the spring, who were fascinated by his beauty. Hercules went in quest of the lad, and while he was absent the Argo put to sea and left him. Moore, in one of his songs, makes a beautiful allusion to this incident:

>   "When Hylas was sent with his urn to the fount,
>   Through fields full of light and with heart full of play,
>   Light rambled the boy over meadow and mount,
>   And neglected his task for the flowers in the way.

>   "Thus many like me, who in youth should have tasted
>   The fountain that runs by Philosophy's shrine,
>   Their time with the flowers on the margin have wasted,
>   And left their light urns all as empty as mine."

Medea and Æson

Amid the rejoicings for the recovery of the Golden Fleece, Jason felt that one thing was wanting, the presence of Æson, his father, who was prevented by his age and infirmities from taking part in them. Jason said to Medea, "My spouse, would that your arts, whose power I have seen so mighty for my aid, could do me one further service, take some years from my life and add them to my father's." Medea replied, "Not at such a cost shall it be done, but if my art avails me, his life shall be lengthened without abridging yours." The next full moon she issued forth alone, while all creatures slept; not a breath stirred the foliage, and all was still. To the stars she addressed her incantations, and to the moon; to Hecate,* the goddess of the underworld, and to Tellus the goddess of the earth, by whose power plants potent for enchantments are produced. She invoked the gods of the woods and caverns, of mountains and valleys, of lakes and rivers, of winds and vapors. While she spoke the stars shone brighter, and presently a chariot descended through the air, drawn by flying serpents. She ascended it, and borne aloft made her way to distant regions, where potent plants grew which she knew how to select for her purpose. Nine nights she employed in her search, and during that time came not within the doors of her palace nor under any roof, and shunned all intercourse with mortals.

She next erected two altars, the one to Hecate, the other to Hebe, the goddess of youth, and sacrificed a black sheep, pouring libations of milk and wine. She implored Pluto and his stolen bride that they would not hasten to take the old man's life. Then she directed that Æson should be led forth, and having thrown him into a deep sleep by a charm, had him laid on a bed of herbs, like one dead. Jason and all others were kept away from the place, that no profane eyes might look upon her mysteries. Then with streaming hair, she thrice moved round the altars, dipped flaming twigs in the blood, and laid them thereon to burn. Meanwhile the caldron with its contents was got ready. In it she put magic herbs, with seeds and flowers of acrid juice, stones from the distant east, and sand from the shore of all-surrounding ocean; hoar frost, gathered by moonlight, a screech owl's head and wings, and the entrails of a wolf. She added fragments of the shells of tortoises, and the liver of stags—animals tenacious of life—and the head and beak of a crow, that outlives nine generations of men. These with many things "without a name" she boiled together for her purposed work, stirring them up with a dry olive branch; and behold! the branch when taken out instantly became green, and before long was covered with leaves and a plentiful growth of young olives; and as the liquor boiled and bubbled, and sometimes ran over, the grass wherever the sprinklings fell shot forth with a verdure like that of spring.

Seeing that all was ready, Medea cut the throat of the old man and let out all his blood, and poured into his mouth and into his wound the juices of her caldron. As soon as he had completely imbibed them, his hair and beard laid by their whiteness and assumed the blackness of youth; his paleness and emaciation were gone; his veins were full of blood, his limbs of vigor and robustness Æson is amazed at himself, and remembers that such as he now is, he was in his youthful days, forty years before.

Medea used her arts here for a good purpose, but not so in another in-

*Hecate was a mysterious divinity sometimes identified with Diana and sometimes with Proserpine. As Diana represents the moonlight splendor of night, so Hecate represents its darkness and terrors. She was the goddess of sorcery and witchcraft, and was believed to wander by night along the earth, seen only by the dogs, whose barking told her approach.

stance where she made them the instruments of revenge. Pelias, our readers will recollect, was the usurping uncle of Jason, and had kept him out of his kingdom. Yet he must have had some good qualities, for his daughters loved him, and when they saw what Medea had done for Æson, they wished her to do the same for their father. Medea pretended to consent, and prepared her caldron as before. At her request an old sheep was brought and plunged into the caldron. Very soon a bleating was heard in the kettle, and when the cover was removed, a lamb jumped forth and ran frisking away into the meadow. The daughters of Pelias saw the experiment with delight, and appointed a time for their father to undergo the same operation. But Medea prepared her caldron for him in a very different way. She put in only water and a few simple herbs. In the night she with the sisters entered the bed chamber of the old king, while he and his guards slept soundly under the influence of a spell cast upon them by Medea. The daughters stood by the bedside with their weapons drawn, but hesitated to strike, till Medea chid their irresolution. Then, turning away their faces, and giving random blows, they smote him with their weapons. He starting from his sleep cried out, "My daughters, what are you doing? Will you kill your father?" Their hearts failed them and the weapons fell from their hands, but Medea struck him a fatal blow, and prevented his saying more.

Then they placed him in the caldron, and Medea hastened to depart in her serpent-drawn chariot before they discovered her treachery, or their vengeance would have been terrible. She escaped, however, but had little enjoyment of the fruits of her crime. Jason, for whom she had done so much, wishing to marry Creusa, princess of Corinth, put away Medea. She, enraged at his ingratitude, called on the gods for vengeance, sent a poisoned robe as a gift to the bride, and then killing her own children, and setting fire to the palace, mounted her serpent-drawn chariot and fled to Athens, where she married King Ægeus, the father of Theseus, and we shall meet her again when we come to the adventures of that hero.

The incantations of Medea will remind the reader of those of the witches in "Macbeth." The following lines are those which seem most strikingly to recall the ancient model:

> Round about the caldron go;
> In the poisoned entrails throw.

> *   *   *   *   *

> Fillet of a fenny snake
> In the caldron boil and bake;
> Eye of newt and toe of frog,
> Wool of bat and tongue of dog,
> Adder's fork and blind-worm's sting,
> Lizard's leg and howlet's wing:

> *   *   *   *   *

Maw of ravening salt-sea shark,
Root of hemlock digged in the dark," etc.

Macbeth, Act IV, Scene 1

And again:

"*Macbeth*—What is't you do?
Witches—A deed without a name."

There is another story of Medea almost too revolting for record even of a sorceress, a class of persons to whom both ancient and modern poets have been accustomed to attribute every degree of atrocity. In her flight from Colchis she had taken her young brother Absyrtus with her. Finding the pursuing vessels of Æetes gaining upon the Argonauts, she caused the lad to be killed and his limbs to be strewn over the sea. Æetes on reaching the place found these sorrowful traces of his murdered son; but while he tarried to collect the scattered fragments and bestow upon them an honorable interment, the Argonauts escaped.

In the poems of Campbell will be found a translation of one of the choruses of the tragedy of "Medea," where the poet Euripides has taken advantage of the occasion to pay a glowing tribute to Athens, his native city. It begins thus:

"O haggard queen! to Athens dost thou guide
    Thy glowing chariot, steeped in kindred gore;
Or seek to hide thy damned parricide
    Where Peace and Justice dwell for evermore?"

· · · · · · ·

18

Meleager and Atalanta

One of the heroes of the Argonautic expedition was Meleager, son of Œneus and Althea, king and queen of Calydon. Althea, when her son was born, beheld the three Destinies, who, as they spun their fatal thread, foretold that the life of the child should last no longer than a brand then burning upon the hearth. Althea seized and quenched the brand, and carefully preserved it for years, while Meleager grew to boyhood, youth, and manhood. It chanced, then, that Œneus, as he offered sacrifices to the gods, omitted to pay due honors to Diana; and she, indignant at the neglect, sent a wild boar of enormous size to lay waste the fields of Calydon. Its eyes shone with blood and fire, its bristles stood like threatening spears, its tusks were like those of Indian elephants. The growing corn was trampled, the vines and olive trees laid waste, the flocks and herds were driven in wild confusion by the slaughtering foe. All common aid seemed vain; but Meleager called on the heroes of Greece to join in a bold hunt for the ravenous monster. Theseus and his friend

Pirithous, Jason, Peleus, afterwards the father of Achilles, Telamon the father of Ajax, Nestor, then a youth, but who in his age bore arms with Achilles and Ajax in the Trojan war,—these and many more joined in the enterprise. With them came Atalanta, the daughter of Iasius, king of Arcadia. A buckle of polished gold confined her vest, an ivory quiver hung on her left shoulder, and her left hand bore the bow. Her face blent feminine beauty with the best graces of martial youth. Meleager saw and loved.

But now already they were near the monster's lair. They stretched strong nets from tree to tree; they uncoupled their dogs, they tried to find the footprints of their quarry in the grass. From the wood was a descent to marshy ground. Here the boar, as he lay among the reeds, heard the shouts of his pursuers, and rushed forth against them. One and another is thrown down and slain. Jason throws his spear, with a prayer to Diana for success; and the favoring goddess allows the weapon to touch, but not to wound, removing the steel point of the spear even in its flight. Nestor, assailed, seeks and finds safety in the branches of a tree. Telamon rushes on, but stumbling at a projecting root, falls prone. But an arrow from Atalanta at length for the first time tastes the monster's blood. It is a slight wound, but Meleager sees and joyfully proclaims it. Anceus, excited to envy by the praise given to a female, loudly proclaims his own valor, and defies alike the boar and the goddess who had sent it; but as he rushes on, the infuriated beast lays him low with a mortal wound. Theseus throws his lance, but it is turned aside by a projecting bough. The dart of Jason misses its object, and kills instead one of their own dogs. But Meleager, after one unsuccessful stroke, drives his spear into the monster's side, then rushes on and despatches him with repeated blows.

Then rose a shout from those around; they congratulated the conqueror, crowding to touch his hand. He, placing his foot upon the head of the slain boar, turned to Atalanta and bestowed on her the head and the rough hide which were the trophies of his success. But at this, envy excited the rest to strife. Plexippus and Toxeus, the brothers of Meleager's mother, beyond the rest opposed the gift, and snatched from the maiden the trophy she had received. Meleager, kindling with rage at the wrong done to himself, and still more at the insult offered to her whom he loved, forgot the claims of kindred, and plunged his sword into the offenders' hearts.

As Althea bore gifts of thankfulness to the temples for the victory of her son, the bodies of her murdered brothers met her sight. She shrieks, and beats her breast, and hastens to change the garments of rejoicing for those of mourning. But when the author of the deed is known, grief gives way to the stern desire of vengeance on her son. The fatal brand, which once she rescued from the flames, the brand which the Destinies had linked with Meleager's life, she brings forth, and commands a fire to be prepared. Then four times she essays to place the brand upon the pile; four times draws back, shuddering at the thought of bringing destruction on her son. The feelings of the mother and the sister contend within her. Now she is pale at the thought of the purposed deed, now flushed again with anger at the act of her son. As a vessel, driven in one direction by the wind, and in the opposite by the tide, the mind of Althea hangs suspended in uncertainty. But now the sister prevails above the mother, and she begins as she holds the fatal wood: "Turn, ye Furies, goddesses of punishment! turn to behold the sacrifice I bring! Crime must atone for crime. Shall Œneus rejoice in his victor son, while the house of Thestius is desolate? But, alas! to what deed am I borne along? Brothers, forgive a mother's weakness! my hand fails me. He deserves death, but not that I should destroy him. But shall he then live, and triumph, and reign over Calydon, while you, my brothers, wander unavenged among the shades? No! thou hast lived by my gift; die, now, for thine own crime. Return the life which twice I gave thee, first at thy birth, again when I snatched this brand from the flames. O that thou hadst then died! Alas! evil is the conquest; but, brothers, ye have conquered." And, turning away her face, she threw the fatal wood upon the burning pile.

It gave, or seemed to give, a deadly groan. Meleager, absent and unknowing of the cause, felt a sudden pang. He burns, and only by courageous pride conquers the pain which destroys him. He mourns only that he perishes by a bloodless and unhonored death. With his last breath he calls upon his aged father, his brother, and his fond sisters, upon his beloved Atalanta, and upon his mother, the unknown cause of his fate. The flames increase, and with them the pain of the hero. Now both subside; now both are quenched. The brand is ashes, and the life of Meleager is breathed forth to the wandering winds.

Althea, when the deed was done, laid violent hands upon herself. The sisters of Meleager mourned their brother with uncontrollable grief; till Diana, pitying the sorrows of the house that once had aroused her anger, turned them into birds.

Atalanta

The innocent cause of so much sorrow was a maiden whose face you might truly say was boyish for a girl, yet too girlish for a boy. Her fortune had been told, and it was to this effect: "Atalanta, do not marry; marriage will be your ruin." Terrified by this oracle, she fled the society of men, and devoted herself to the sports of the chase. To all suitors (for she had many) she imposed a condition which was generally effectual in relieving her of their persecutions—"I will be the prize of him who shall conquer me in the race; but death must be the penalty of all who try and fail." In spite of this hard condition some would try. Hippomenes was to be judge of the race. "Can it be possible that any will be so rash as to risk so much for a wife?" said he. But when he saw her lay aside her robe for the race, he changed his mind, and said, "Pardon me, youths, I knew not the prize you were competing for." As he surveyed them he wished them all to be beaten, and swelled with envy of any one that seemed at all likely to win. While such were his thoughts, the virgin darted forward. As she ran she looked more beautiful than ever. The breezes seemed to give wings to her feet; her hair flew over her shoulders, and the gay fringe of her garment fluttered behind her. A ruddy hue tinged the whiteness of her skin, such as a crimson curtain casts on a marble wall. All her competitors were distanced, and were to put to death without mercy. Hippomenes, not daunted by this result, fixing his eyes on the virgin, said, "Why boast of beating those laggards? I offer myself for the contest." Atalanta looked at him with a pitying countenance, and hardly knew whether she would rather conquer him or not. "What god can tempt one so young and handsome to throw himself away? I pity him, not for his beauty(yet he is beautiful), but for his youth. I wish he would give up the race, or if he will be so mad, I hope he may outrun me." While she hesitates, revolving these thoughts, the spectators grow impatient for the race, and her father prompts her to prepare. Then Hippomenes addressed a prayer to Venus: "Help me, Venus, for you have led me on." Venus heard, and was propitious.

In the garden of her temple, in her own island of Cyprus, is a tree with yellow branches, and golden fruit. Hence she gathered three golden apples, and, unseen by any one else, gave them to Hippomenes, and told him how to use them. The signal is given; each starts from the goal, and skims over the sand. So light their tread, you would almost have thought they might run over the river surface or over the waving grain without sinking. The cries of the spectators cheered Hippomenes— "Now, now do your best! haste, haste! you gain on her! relax not! one more effort!" It was doubtful whither the youth or the maiden heard these cries with the greater pleasure. But his breath began to fail him, his throat was dry, the goal yet far off. At that moment he threw down one of the golden apples. The virgin was all amazement. She stopped to pick it up. Hippomenes shot ahead. Shouts burst forth from all sides. She redoubled her efforts, and soon overtook him. Again he threw an apple. She stopped again, but again came up with him. The goal was near; one chance only remained "Now, goddess," said he, "prosper your gift!" and threw the last apple off at one side. She looked at it, and hesitated; Venus impelled her to turn aside for it. She did so, and was vanquished. The youth carried off his prize.

But the lovers were so full of their own happiness that they forgot to pay due honor to Venus; and the goddess was provoked at their ingratitude. She caused them to give offence to Cybele. That powerful goddess was not to be insulted with impunity. She took from them their human form and turned them into animals of characters resembling their own: of the huntress-heroine, triumphing in the blood of her lovers, she made a lioness, and of her lord and master a lion, and yoked them to her car, where they are still to be seen in all representations, in statuary or painting, of the goddess Cybele.

Cybele is the Latin name of the goddess called by the Greeks Rhea and Ops. She was the wife of Cronos and mother of Zeus. In works of art, she exhibits the matronly air which distinguishes Juno and Ceres. Sometimes she is veiled, and seated on a throne with lions at her side, at other times riding in a chariot drawn by lions. She wears a mural crown, that is, a crown whose rim is carved in the form of towers and battlements. Her priests were called Corybantes.

Byron in describing the city of Venice, which is built on a low island in the Adriatic Sea, borrows an illustration from Cybele:

"She looks a sea-Cybele fresh from ocean,
  Rising with her tiara of proud towers
  At airy distance, with majestic motion,
  A ruler of the waters and their powers.

Childe Harold, IV

In Moore's "Rhymes on the Road," the poet, speaking of Alpine scenery, alludes to the story of Atalanta and Hippomenes, thus:

"Even here, in this region of wonders, I find
  That light-footed Fancy leaves Truth far behind,
  Or at least, like Hippomenes, turns her astray
  By the golden illusions he flings in her way."

· · · · · · ·

19

Hercules—Hebe and Ganymede

Hercules was the son of Jupiter and Alemena. As Juno was always hostile to the offspring of her husband by mortal mothers, she declared war against Hercules from his birth. She sent two serpents to destroy him as he lay in his cradle, but the precocious infant strangled them with his own hands. He was however by the arts of Juno rendered subject to Eurystheus and compelled to perform all his commands. Eurystheus enjoined upon him a succession of desperate adventures, which are called the twelve "Labors of Hercules." The first was the fight with the Nemean lion. The valley of Nemea was infested by a terrible lion. Eurystheus ordered Hercules to bring him the skin of this monster. After using in vain his club and arrows against the lion, Hercules strangled the animal with his hands. He returned carrying the dead lion on his shoulders; but Eurystheus was so frightened at the sight of it and at this proof of the prodigious strength of the hero, that he ordered him to deliver the account of his exploits in future outside the town.

His next labor was the slaughter of the Hydra. This monster ravaged the country of Argos, and dwelt in a swamp near the well of Amymone. This well had been discovered by Amymone when the country was suffering from drought, and the story was, that Neptune, who loved her, had permitted her to touch the rock with his trident, and a spring of three outlets burst forth. Here the Hydra took up his position, and Hercules was sent to destroy him. The Hydra had nine heads, of which the middle one was immortal. Hercules struck off its heads with his club, but in the place of the head knocked off, two new ones grew forth each time. At length with the assistance of his faithful servant Iolaus, he burned away the heads of the Hydra, and buried the ninth or immortal one under a huge rock.

Another labor was the cleaning of the Augean stables. Augeas, king of Elis, had a herd of three thousand oxen, whose stalls had not been cleansed for thirty years. Hercules brought the rivers Alpheus and Peneus through them, and cleansed them thoroughly in one day.

His next labor was of a more delicate kind. Admeta, the daughter of Eurystheus, longed to obtain the girdle of the queen of the Amazons, and Eurystheus ordered Hercules to go and get it. The Amazons were a nation of women. They were very warlike and held several flourishing cities. It was their custom to bring up only the female children; the boys were either sent away to the neighboring nations or put to death. Hercules was accompanied by a number of volunteers, and after various adventures at last reached the country of the Amazons. Hippolyta, the queen, received him kindly, and consented to yield him her girdle, but Juno, taking the form of an Amazon, went and persuaded the rest that the strangers were carrying off their queen. They instantly armed and came in great numbers down to the ship. Hercules, thinking that Hippolyta had acted treacherously, slew her, and taking her girdle made sail homewards.

Another task enjoined him was to bring to Eurystheus the oxen of Geryon, a monster with three bodies, who dwelt in the island Erytheia (the red), so called because it lay at the west, under the rays of the setting sun. This description is thought to apply to Spain, of which Geryon was king. After traversing various countries, Hercules reached at length the frontiers of Libya and Europe, where he raised the two mountains of Calpe and Abyla, as monuments of his progress, or according to another account rent one mountain into two and left half on each side, forming the Straits of Gibraltar, the two mountains being called the Pillars of Hercules. The oxen were guarded by the giant Eurytion and his two-headed dog, but Hercules killed the giant and his dog and brought away the oxen in safety to Eurystheus.

The most difficult labor of all was getting the golden apples of the Hesperides, for Hercules did not know where to find them. These were the apples which Juno had received at her wedding from the goddess of the Earth, and which she had intrusted to the keeping of the daughters of Hesperis, assisted by a watchful dragon. After various adventures Hercules arrived at Mount Atlas in Africa. Atlas was one of the Titans who had warred against the gods, and after they were subdued, Atlas was condemned to bear on his shoulders the weight of the heavens. He was the father of the Hesperides, and Hercules thought, might, if any one could, find the apples and bring them to him. But how to send Atlas away from his post, or bear up the heavens while he was gone? Hercules took the burden on his own shoulders, and sent Atlas to seek the apples. He returned with them, and though somewhat reluctantly, took his burden upon his shoulders again, and let Hercules return with the apples to Eurystheus.

Milton, in his "Comus," makes the Hesperides the daughters of Hesperus, and nieces of Atlas:

> "——amidst the gardens fair
> Of Hesperus and his daughters three,
> That sing about the golden tree."

The poets, led by the analogy of the lovely appearance of the western sky at sunset, viewed the west as a region of brightness and glory. Hence they placed in it the Isles of the Blest, the ruddy isle Erytheia, on which the bright oxen of Geryon were pastured, and the isle of the Hesperides. The apples are supposed by some to be the oranges of Spain, of which the Greeks had heard some obscure accounts.

A celebrated exploit of Hercules was his victory over Antæus. Antæus, the son of Terra, the Earth, was a mighty giant and wrestler, whose strength was invincible as long as he remained in contact with his mother Earth. He compelled all strangers who came to his country to wrestle with him, on condition that if conquered (as they all were) they should be put to death. Hercules encountered him, and finding that it was of no avail to throw him, for he always rose with renewed strength from every fall, he lifted him up from the earth and strangled him in the air.

Cacus was a huge giant, who inhabited a cave on Mount Aventine, and plundered the surrounding country. When Hercules was driving home the oxen of Geryon, Cacus stole part of the cattle, while the hero slept. That their foot-prints might not serve to show where they had been driven, he dragged them backward by their tails to his cave; so their tracks all seemed to show that they had gone in the opposite direction. Hercules was deceived by this stratagem, and would have failed to find his oxen, if it had not happened that in driving the remainder of the herd past the cave where the stolen ones were concealed, those within began to low, and were thus discovered. Cacus was slain by Hercules.

The last exploit we shall record was bringing Cerberus from the lower world. Hercules descended into Hades, accompanied by Mercury and Minerva. He obtained permission from Pluto to carry Cerberus to the upper air provided he could do it without the use of weapons; and in spite of the monster's struggling, he seized him, held him fast, and carried him to Eurystheus, and afterwards brought him back again. When he was in Hades he obtained the liberty of Theseus, his admirer and imitator, who had been detained a prisoner there for an unsuccessful attempt to carry off Proserpine.

Hercules in a fit of madness killed his friend Iphitus, and was condemned for this offence to become the slave of Queen Omphale for three years. While in this service the hero's nature seemed changed. He lived effeminately, wearing at times the dress of a woman, and spinning wool with the hand-maidens of Omphale, while the queen wore his lion's skin. When this service was ended he married Dejanira and lived in peace with her three years. On one occasion as he was travelling with his wife, they came to a river, across which the Centaur Nessus carried travellers for a stated fee. Hercules himself forded the river, but gave Dejanira to Nessus to be carried across. Nessus attempted to run away with her, but Hercules heard her cries, and shot an arrow into the heart of Nessus. The dying Centaur told Dejanira to take a portion of his blood and keep it, as it might be used as a charm to preserve the love of her husband.

Dejanira did so, and before long fancied she had occasion to use it. Hercules in one of his conquests had taken prisoner a fair maiden, named Iole, of whom he seemed more fond than Dejanira approved. When Hercules was about to offer sacrifices to the gods in honor of his victory, he sent to his wife for a white robe to use on the occasion. Dejanira, thinking it a good opportunity to try her love-spell, steeped the garment in the blood of Nessus. We are to suppose she took care to wash out all traces of it, but the magic power remained, and as soon as the garment became warm on the body of Hercules, the poison penetrated into all his limbs and caused him the most intense agony. In his frenzy he seized Lichas, who had brought him the fatal robe, and hurled him into the sea. He wrenched off the garment, but it stuck to his flesh, and with it he tore away whole pieces of his body. In this state he embarked on board a ship and was conveyed home. Dejanira on seeing what she had unwittingly done, hung herself. Hercules, prepared to die, ascended Mount Œta, where he built a funeral pile of trees, gave his bow and arrows to Philoctetes, and laid himself down on the pile, his head resting on his club, and his lion's skin spread over him. With a countenance as serene as if he were taking his place at a festal board, he commanded Philoctetes to apply the torch. The flames spread apace and soon invested the whole mass.

Milton thus alludes to the frenzy of Hercules:

"As when Alcides,* from Œchalia crowned
   With conquest, felt the envenomed robe, and tore,
   Through pain, up by the roots Thessalian pines
   And Lichas from the top of Œta threw
   Into the Euboic Sea."

The gods themselves felt troubled at seeing the champion of the earth so brought to his end. But Jupiter with cheerful countenance thus ad-

*Alcides, a name of Hercules

dressed them: "I am pleased to see your concern, my princes, and am gratified to perceive that I am the ruler of a loyal people, and that my son enjoys your favor. For although your interest in him arises from his noble deeds, yet it is not the less gratifying to me. But now I say to you, Fear not. He who conquered all else is not to be conquered by those flames which you see blazing on Mount Œta. Only his mother's share in him can perish; what he derived from me is immortal. I shall take him, dead to earth, to the heavenly shores, and I require of you all to receive him kindly. If any of you feel grieved at his attaining this honor, yet no one can deny that he has deserved it." The gods all gave their assent; Juno only heard the closing words with some displeasure that she should be so particularly pointed at, yet not enough to make her regret the determination of her husband. So when the flames had consumed the mother's share of Hercules, the diviner part, instead of being injured thereby, seemed to start forth with new vigor, to assume a more lofty port and a more awful dignity. Jupiter enveloped him in a cloud, and took him up in a four-horse chariot to dwell among the stars. As he took his place in heaven, Atlas felt the added weight.

Juno, now reconciled to him, gave him her daughter Hebe in marriage.

The poet Schiller, in one of his pieces called the "Ideal and Life," illustrates the contrast between the practical and the imaginative in some beautiful stanzas, of which the last two may be thus translated:

"Deep degraded to a coward's slave,
Endless contests bore Alcides brave,
Through the thorny path of suffering led;
Slew the Hydra, crushed the lion's might,
Threw himself, to bring his friend to light,
Living, in the skiff that bears the dead.
All the torments, every toil of earth
Juno's hatred on him could impose,
Well he bore them, from his fated birth
To life's grandly mournful close.

"Till the god, the earthly part forsaken,
From the man in flames asunder taken,
Drank the heavenly ether's purer breath.
Joyous in the new unwonted lightness,
Soared he upwards to celestial brightness,
Earth's dark heavy burden lost in death.
High Olympus gives harmonious greeting
To the hall where reigns his sire adored;
Youth's bright goddess, with a blush at meeting,
Gives the nectar to her lord."

S. G. B.

Hebe and Ganymede

Hebe, the daughter of Juno, and goddess of youth, was cup-bearer
to the gods. The usual story is that she resigned her office on becoming
the wife of Hercules. But there is another statement which our countryman Crawford, the sculptor, has adopted in his group of Hebe and
Ganymede, not in the Athenæum gallery. According to this, Hebe was
dismissed from her office in consequence of a fall which she met with
one day when in attendance on the gods. Her successor was Ganymede,
a Trojan boy whom Jupiter, in the disguise of an eagle, seized and carried off from the midst of his playfellows on Mount Ida, bore up to
heaven, and installed in the vacant place.

Tennyson, in his "Palace of Art," describes among the decorations
on the walls, a picture representing this legend:

"There, too, flushed Ganymede, his rosy thigh
    Half buried in the eagle's down,
  Sole as a flying star shot through the sky
    Above the pillared town."

And in Shelley's "Prometheus," Jupiter calls to his cup-bearer thus:

"Pour forth heaven's wine, Idæan Ganymede,
  And let it fill the Dædal cups like fire."

The beautiful legend of the "Choice of Hercules" may be found in
the "Tatler," No. 97.

· · · · · · ·
20

Theseus—Dædalus—Castor and Pollux

Theseus was the son of Ægeus, king of Athens, and of Æthra, daughter of the king of Trœzen. He was brought up at Trœzen, and when arrived at manhood, was to proceed to Athens and present himself to his
father. Ægeus, on parting from Æthra, before the birth of his son,
placed his sword and shoes under a large stone, and directed her to send
his son to him when he became strong enough to roll away the stone and
take them from under it. When she thought the time had come, his
mother led Theseus to the stone, and he removed it with ease, and took
the sword and shoes. As the roads were infested with robbers, his grandfather pressed him earnestly to take the shorter and safer way to his
father's country, by sea; but the youth, feeling in himself the spirit and
the soul of a hero, and eager to signalize himself like Hercules, with
whose fame all Greece then rang, by destroying the evil-doers and monsters that oppressed the country, determined on the more perilous and
adventurous journey by land.

His first day's journey brought him to Epidaurus, where dwelt a man named Periphetes, a son of Vulcan. This ferocious savage always went armed with a club of iron, and all travellers stood in terror of his violence. When he saw Theseus approach, he assailed him, but speedily fell beneath the blows of the young hero, who took possession of his club, and bore it ever afterwards as a memorial of his first victory.

Several similar contests with the petty tyrants and marauders of the country followed, in all of which Theseus was victorious. One of these evil-doers was called Procrustes, or the Stretcher. He had an iron bedstead, on which he used to tie all travellers who fell into his hands. If they were shorter than the bed, he stretched their limbs to make them fit it; if they were longer than the bed, he lopped off a portion. Theseus served him as he had served others.

Having overcome all the perils of the road, Theseus at length reached Athens, where new dangers awaited him. Medea, the sorceress, who had fled from Corinth after her separation from Jason, had become the wife of Ægeus, the father of Theseus. Knowing by her arts who he was, and fearing the loss of her influence with her husband, if Theseus should be acknowledged as his son, she filled the mind of Ægeus with suspicions of the young stranger, and induced him to present him a cup of poison; but at the moment when Theseus stepped forward to take it, the sight of the sword which he wore discovered to his father who he was, and prevented the fatal draught. Medea, detected in her arts, fled once more from deserved punishment, and arrived in Asia, where the country afterwards called Media received its name from her. Theseus was acknowledged by his father, and declared his successor.

The Athenians were at that time in deep affliction, on account of the tribute which they were forced to pay to Minos, king of Crete. This tribute consisted of seven youths and seven maidens, who were sent every year to be devoured by the Minotaur, a monster with a bull's body and a human head. It was exceedingly strong and fierce, and was kept in a labyrinth constructed by Dædalus, so artfully contrived that whoever was enclosed in it could by no means find his way out unassisted. Here the Minotaur roamed, and was fed with human victims.

Theseus resolved to deliver his countrymen from this calamity, or to die in the attempt. Accordingly, when the time of sending off the tribute came, and the youths and maidens were, according to custom, drawn by lot to be sent, he offered himself as one of the victims, in spite of the entreaties of his father. The ship departed under black sails, as usual, which Theseus promised his father to change for white, in case of his returning victorious. When they arrived in Crete, the youths and maidens were exhibited before Minos; and Ariadne, the daughter of the king, being present, became deeply enamoured of Theseus, by whom her love was readily returned. She furnished him with a sword, with which to encounter the Minotaur, and with a clew of thread by which he might find his way out of the labyrinth. He was successful, slew the Minotaur, escaped from the labyrinth, and taking Ariadne as the companion of his way, with his rescued companions sailed for Athens. On their way they stopped at the island of Naxos, where Theseus abandoned Ariadne, leaving her asleep.* His excuse for this ungrateful treatment of his benefactress was that Minerva appeared to him in a dream and commanded him to do so.

On approaching the coast of Attica, Theseus forgot the signal appointed by his father, and neglected to raise the white sails, and the old king, thinking his son had perished, put an end to his own life. Theseus thus became king of Athens.

One of the most celebrated of the adventures of Theseus is his expedition against the Amazons. He assailed them before they had recovered from the attack of Hercules, and carried off their queen Antiope. The Amazons in their turn invaded the country of Athens and penetrated into the city itself; and the final battle in which Theseus overcame them was fought in the very midst of the city. This battle was one of the favorite subjects of the ancient sculptors, and is commemorated in several works of art that are still extant.

The friendship between Theseus and Pirithous was of a most intimate nature, yet it originated in the midst of arms. Pirithous had made an irruption into the plain of Marathon, and carried off the herds of the king of Athens. Theseus went to repel the plunderers. The moment Pirithous beheld him, he was seized with admiration; he stretched out his hand as a token of peace, and cried, "Be judge thyself—what satisfaction dost thou require?" "Thy friendship," replied the Athenian, and they swore inviolable fidelity. Their deeds corresponded to their professions, and they ever continued true brothers in arms. Each of them aspired to espouse a daughter of Jupiter. Theseus fixed his choice on Helen, then but a child, afterwards so celebrated as the cause of the Trojan war, and with the aid of his friend he carried her off. Pirithous aspired to the wife of the monarch of Erebus; and Theseus, though aware of the danger, accompanied the ambitious lover in his descent to the under world. But Pluto seized and set them on an enchanted rock at his palace gate, where they remained till Hercules arrived and liberated Theseus, leaving Pirithous to his fate.

After the death of Antiope, Theseus married Phædra, daughter of Minos, king of Crete. Phædra saw in Hippolytus, the son of Theseus, a youth endowed with all the graces and virtues of his father, and of an age corresponding to her own. She loved him, but he repulsed her advances, and her love was changed to hate. She used her influence over her infatuated husband to cause him to be jealous of his son, and he imprecated the vengeance of Neptune upon him. As Hippolytus was one day driving his chariot along the shore, a sea-monster raised himself above the waters, and frightened the horses so that they ran away and dashed the chariot to pieces. Hippolytus was killed, but by Diana's assistance Æsculapius restored him to life. Diana removed Hippolytus

*One of the finest pieces of sculpture in Italy, the recumbent "Ariadne of the Vatican," represents this incident. A copy is in the Athenæum gallery, Boston.

from the power of his deluded father and false step-mother, and placed him in Italy under the protection of the nymph Egeria.

Theseus at length lost the favor of his people, and retired to the court of Lycomedes, king of Scyros, who at first received him kindly, but afterwards treacherously slew him. In a later age the Athenian general Cimon discovered the place where his remains were laid, and caused them to be removed to Athens, where they were deposited in a temple called the Theseum, erected in honor of the hero.

The queen of the Amazons whom Theseus espoused is by some called Hippolyta. That is the name she bears in Shakespeare's "Midsummer Night's Dream"—the subject of which is the festivities attending the nuptials of Theseus and Hippolyta.

Mrs. Hemans has a poem on the ancient Greek tradition that the "Shade of Theseus" appeared strengthening his countrymen at the battle of Marathon.

Theseus is a semi-historical personage. It is recorded of him that he united the several tribes by whom the territory of Attica was then possessed into one state, of which Athens was the capital. In commemoration of this important event, he instituted the festival of Panathenæa, in honor of Minerva, the patron deity of Athens. This festival differed from the other Grecian games chiefly in two particulars. It was peculiar to the Athenians, and its chief feature was a solemn procession in which the Peplus or sacred robe of Minerva was carried to the Parthenon, and suspended before the statue of the goddess. The Peplus was covered with embroidery, worked by select virgins of the noblest families in Athens. The procession consisted of persons of all ages and both sexes. The old men carried olive branches in their hands, and the young men bore arms. The young women carried baskets on their heads, containing the sacred utensils, cakes, and all things necessary for the sacrifices. The procession formed the subject of the bas-reliefs which embellished the outside of the temple of the Parthenon. A considerable portion of these sculptures is now in the British Museum among those known as the "Elgin marbles."

Olympic and Other Games

It seems not inappropriate to mention here the other celebrated national games of the Greeks. The first and most distinguished were the Olympic, founded it was said by Jupiter himself. They were celebrated at Olympia in Elis. Vast numbers of spectators flocked to them from every part of Greece, and from Asia, Africa, and Sicily. They were repeated every fifth year in midsummer, and continued five days. They gave rise to the custom of reckoning time and dating events by Olympiads. The first Olympiad is generally considered as corresponding with the year 776 B.C. The Pythian games were celebrated in the vicinity of Delphi, the Isthmian on the Corinthian isthmus, the Nemean at Nemea, a city of Argolis.

The exercises in these games were of five sorts, running, leaping, wrestling, throwing the quoit, and hurling the javelin, or boxing. Besides these exercises of bodily strength and agility, there were contests in music, poetry, and eloquence. Thus the games furnished poets, musicians, and authors the best opportunities to present their productions to the public, and the fame of the victors was diffused far and wide.

Dædalus

The labyrinth from which Theseus escaped by means of the clew of Ariadne was built by Dædalus, a most skilful artificer. It was an edifice with numberless winding passages and turnings opening into one another, and seeming to have neither beginning nor end, like the river Mæander, which returns on itself, and flows now onward, now backward, in its course to the sea. Dædalus built the labyrinth for King Minos, but afterwards lost the favor of the king, and was shut up in a tower. He contrived to make his escape from his prison, but could not leave the island by sea, as the king kept strict watch on all the vessels, and permitted none to sail without being carefully searched. "Minos may control the land and sea," said Dædalus, "but not the regions of the air. I will try that way." So he set to work to fabricate wings for himself and his young son Icarus. He wrought feathers together, beginning with the smallest and adding larger, so as to form an increasing surface. The larger ones he secured with thread and the smaller with wax, and gave the whole a gentle curvature like the wings of a bird. Icarus, the boy, stood and looked on, sometimes running to gather up the feathers which the wind had blown away, and then handling the wax and working it over with his fingers, by his play impeding his father in his labors. When at last the work was done, the artist, waving his wings, found himself buoyed upwards and hung suspended, poising himself on the beaten air. He next equipped his son in the same manner, and taught him how to fly, as a bird tempts her young ones from the lofty nest into the air. When all was prepared for flight he said, "Icarus, my son, I charge you to keep at a moderate height, for if you fly too low the damp will clog your wings, and if too high the heat will melt them. Keep near me and you will be safe." While he gave him these instructions and fitted the wings to his shoulders, the face of the father was wet with tears, and his hands trembled. He kissed the boy, not knowing that it was for the last time. Then rising on his wings, he flew off, encouraging him to follow, and looked back from his own flight to see how his son managed his wings. As they flew the ploughman stopped his work to gaze, and the shepherd leaned on his staff and watched them, astonished at the sight, and thinking they were gods who could thus cleave the air.

They passed Samos and Delos on the left and Lebynthos on the right, when the boy, exulting in his career, began to leave the guidance of his companion and soar upward as if to reach heaven. The nearness of the blazing sun softened the wax which held the feathers together, and they came off. He fluttered with his arms, but no feathers remained to hold the air. While his mouth uttered cries to his father it was submerged in the blue waters of the sea, which thenceforth was called by his name. His father cried, "Icarus, Icarus, where are you?" At last he saw the feathers floating on the water, and bitterly lamenting his own arts, he buried the body and called the land Icaria in memory of his child. Dædalus arrived safe in Sicily, where he built a temple to Apollo, and hung up his wings, an offering to the god.

Dædalus was so proud of his achievements that he could not bear the idea of a rival. His sister had placed her son Perdix under his charge to be taught the mechanical arts. He was an apt scholar and gave striking evidences of ingenuity. Walking on the seashore he picked up the spine of a fish. Imitating it, he took a piece of iron and notched it on the edge, and thus invented the saw. He put two pieces of iron together, connecting them at one end with a rivet, and sharpening the other ends, and made a *pair of compasses*. Dædalus was so envious of his nephew's performances that he took an opportunity, when they were together one day on top of a high tower, to push him off. But Minerva, who favors ingenuity, saw him falling, and arrested his fate by changing him into a bird called after his name, the Partridge. This bird does not build his nest in the trees, nor take lofty flights, but nestles in the hedges, and mindful of his fall, avoids high places.

The death of Icarus is told in the following lines by Darwin:

"——with melting wax and loosened strings
Sunk hapless Icarus on unfaithful wings;
Headlong he rushed through the affrighted air,
With limbs distorted and dishevelled hair;
His scattered plumage danced upon the wave,
And sorrowing Nereids decked his watery grave;
O'er his pale corse their pearly sea-flowers shed,
And strewed with crimson moss his marble bed;
Struck in their coral towers the passing bell,
And wide in ocean tolled his echoing knell."

Castor and Pollux

Castor and Pollux were the offspring of Leda and the Swan, under which disguise Jupiter had concealed himself. Leda gave birth to an egg, from which sprang the twins. Helen, so famous afterwards as the cause of the Trojan war, was their sister.

When Theseus and his friend Pirithous had carried off Helen from Sparta, the youthful heroes Castor and Pollux, with their followers, hastened to her rescue. Theseus was absent from Attica and the brothers were successful in recovering their sister.

Castor was famous for taming and managing horses, and Pollux for skill in boxing. They were united by the warmest affection and inseparable in all their enterprises. They accompanied the Argonautic expedition. During the voyage a storm arose, and Orpheus prayed to the

Samothracian gods, and played on his harp, whereupon the storm ceased and stars appeared on the heads of the brothers. From this incident, Castor and Pollux came afterwards to be considered the patron deities of seamen and voyagers, and the lambent flames, which in certain states of the atmosphere play round the sails and masts of vessels, were called by their names.

After the Argonautic expedition, we find Castor and Pollux engaged in a war with Idas and Lynceus. Castor was slain, and Pollux, inconsolable for the loss of his brother, besought Jupiter to be permitted to give his own life as a ransom for him. Jupiter so far consented as to allow the two brothers to enjoy the boon of life alternately, passing one day under the earth and the next in the heavenly abodes. According to another form of the story Jupiter rewarded the attachment of the brothers by placing them among the stars as Gemini, the Twins.

They received divine honors under the name of Dioscuri (sons of Jove). They were believed to have appeared occasionally in later times, taking part with one side or the other, in hard-fought fields, and were said on such occasions to be mounted on magnificent white steeds. Thus in the early history of Rome they are said to have assisted the Romans at the battle of Lake Regillus, and after the victory a temple was erected in their honor on the spot where they appeared.

Macaulay, in his "Lays of Ancient Rome," thus alludes to the legend:

"So like they were, no mortal
　　Might one from other know;
White as snow their armor was,
　　Their steeds were white as snow.
Never on earthly anvil
　　Did such rare armor gleam,
And never did such gallant steeds
　　Drink of an earthly stream.
　　　*　　　*　　　*　　　*
"Back comes the chief in triumph
　　Who in the hour of fight
Hath seen the great Twin Brethren
　　In harness on his right.
Safe comes the ship to haven,
　　Through billows and through gales,
If once the great Twin Brethren
　　Sit shining on the sails."

Bacchus — Ariadne

Bacchus was the son of Jupiter and Semele. Juno, to gratify her resentment against Semele, contrived a plan for her destruction. Assuming the form of Beroe, her aged nurse, she insinuated doubts whether it was indeed Jove himself who came as a lover. Heaving a sigh, she said, "I hope it will turn out so, but I can't help being afraid. People are not always what they pretend to be. If he is indeed Jove, make him give some proof of it. Ask him to come arrayed in all his splendors, such as he wears in heaven. That will put the matter beyond a doubt." Semele was persuaded to try the experiment. She asks a favor, without naming what it is. Jove gives his promise, and confirms it with the irrevocable oath, attesting the river Styx, terrible to the gods themselves. Then she made known her request. The god would have stopped her as she spoke, but she was too quick for him. The words escaped, and he could neither unsay his promise nor her request. In deep distress he left her and returned to the upper regions. There he clothed himself in his splendors, not putting on all his terrors, as when he overthrew the giants, but what is known among the gods as his lesser panoply. Arrayed in this he entered the chamber of Semele. Her mortal frame could not endure the splendors of the immortal radiance. She was consumed to ashes.

Jove took the infant Bacchus and gave him in charge to the Nysæan nymphs, who nourished his infancy and childhood, and for their care were rewarded by Jupiter by being placed, as the Hyades, among the stars. When Bacchus grew up he discovered the culture of the vine and the mode of extracting its precious juice; but Juno struck him with madness, and drove him forth a wanderer through various parts of the earth. In Phrygia the goddess Rhea cured him and taught him her religious rites, and he set out on a progress through Asia teaching the people the cultivation of the vine. The most famous part of his wanderings is his expedition to India, which is said to have lasted several years. Returning in triumph he undertook to introduce his worship into Greece, but was opposed by some princess who dreaded its introduction on account of the disorders and madness it brought with it.

As he approached his native city Thebes, Pentheus the king, who had no respect for the new worship, forbade its rites to be performed. But when it was known that Bacchus was advancing, men and women, but chiefly the latter, young and old poured forth to meet him and to join his triumphal march.

Mr. Longfellow in his "Drinking Song" thus describes the march of Bacchus:

"Fauns with youthful Bacchus follow;
  Ivy crowns that brow, supernal
As the forehead of Apollo,
  And possessing youth eternal.

"Round about him fair Bacchantes,
  Bearing cymbals, flutes and thyrses,
Wild from Naxian groves or Zante's
  Vineyards, sing delirious verses."

It was in vain Pentheus remonstrated, commanded, and threatened. "Go," said he to his attendants, "seize this vagabond leader of the rout and bring him to me. I will soon make him confess his false claim of heavenly parentage and renounce his counterfeit worship." It was in vain his nearest friends and wisest counsellors remonstrated and begged him not to oppose the god. Their remonstrances only made him more violent.

But now the attendants returned whom he had despatched to seize Bacchus. They had been driven away by the Bacchanals, but had succeeded in taking one of them prisoner, whom, with his hands tied behind him, they brought before the king. Pentheus beholding him with wrathful countenance said, "Fellow! you shall speedily be put to death, that your fate may be a warning to others; but though I grudge the delay of your punishment, speak, tell us who you are, and what are these new rites you presume to celebrate."

The prisoner, unterrified, responded, "My name is Acetes; my country is Mæonia; my parents were poor people, who had no fields or flocks to leave me, but they left me their fishing rods and nets and their fisherman's trade. This I followed for some time, till growing weary of remaining in one place, I learned the pilot's art and how to guide my course by the stars. It happened as I was sailing for Delos, we touched at the island of Dia and went ashore. Next morning I sent the men for fresh water, and myself mounted the hill to observe the wind; when my men returned bringing with them a prize, as they thought, a boy of delicate appearance, whom they had found asleep. They judged he was a noble youth, perhaps a king's son, and they might get a liberal ransom for him. I observed his dress, his walk, his face. There was something in them which I felt sure was more than mortal. I said to my men, 'What god there is concealed in that form I know not, but some one there certainly is. Pardon us, gentle deity, for the violence we have done you, and give success to our undertakings.' Dictys, one of my best hands for climbing the mast and coming down by the ropes, and Melanthus my steersman, and Epopeus the leader of the sailors' cry, one and all exclaimed, 'Spare your prayers for us.' So blind is the lust of gain! When they proceeded to put him on board I resisted them. 'This ship shall not be profaned by such impiety,' said I. 'I have a greater share in her than any of you.' But Lycabas, a turbulent fellow, seized me by the throat and attempted to throw me overboard, and I scarcely saved myself by clinging to the ropes. The rest approved the deed.

"Then Bacchus (for it was indeed he) as if shaking off his drowsiness exclaimed, 'What are you doing with me? What is this fighting about? Who brought me here? Where are you going to carry me?' One of them replied, 'Fear nothing; tell us where you wish to go and we will take you there.' 'Naxos is my home,' said Bacchus; 'take me there and you shall be well rewarded.' They promised so to do, and told me to pilot the ship to Naxos. Naxos lay to the right, and I was trimming the sails to carry us there, when some by signs and others by whispers signified to me their will that I should sail in the opposite direction, and take the boy to Egypt to sell him for a slave. I was confounded and said, 'Let some one else pilot the ship'; withdrawing myself from any further agency in their wickedness. They cursed me, and one of them exclaiming, 'Don't flatter yourself that we depend on you for our safety,' took my place as pilot, and bore away from Naxos.

"Then the god, pretending that he had just become aware of their treachery, looked out over the sea and said in a voice of weeping, 'Sailors, these are not the shores you promised to take me to; yonder island is not my home. What have I done that you should treat me so? It is small glory you will gain by cheating a poor boy.' I wept to hear him, but the crew laughed at both of us, and sped the vessel fast over the sea. All at once—strange as it may seem, it is true—the vessel stopped, in the mid sea, as fast as if it was fixed on the ground. The men, astonished, pulled at their oars, and spread more sail, trying to make progress by the aid of both, but all in vain. Ivy twined round the oars and hindered their motion, and clung to the sails, with heavy clusters of berries. A vine, laden with grapes, ran up the mast, and along the sides of the vessel. The sound of flutes was heard and the odor of fragrant wine spread all around. The god himself had a chaplet of vine leaves, and bore in his hand a spear wreathed with ivy. Tigers crouched at his feet, and forms of lynxes and spotted panthers played around him. The men were seized with terror or madness; some leaped overboard; others preparing to do the same beheld their companions in the water undergoing a change, their bodies becoming flattened and ending in a crooked tail. One exclaimed, 'What miracle is this!' and as he spoke his mouth widened, his nostrils expanded, and scales covered all his body. Another endeavoring to pull the oar felt his hands shrink up and presently to be no longer hands but fins; another trying to raise his arms to a rope found he had no arms, and curving his mutilated body, jumped into the sea. What had been his legs became the two ends of a crescent-shaped tail. The whole crew became dolphins and swam about the ship, now upon the surface, now under it, scattering the spray, and spouting the water from their broad nostrils. Of twenty men I alone was left. Trembling with fear, the god cheered me. 'Fear not,' said he; 'steer towards Naxos.' I obeyed, and when we arrived there, I kindled the altars and celebrated the sacred rites of Bacchus.''

Pentheus here exclaimed, "We have wasted time enough on this silly story. Take him away and have him executed without delay." Acetes was led away by the attendants and shut up fast in prison; but while they were getting ready the instruments of execution, the prison doors came open of their own accord and the chains fell from his limbs, and when they looked for him he was nowhere to be found.

Pentheus would take no warning, but instead of sending others, determined to go himself to the scene of the solemnities. The mountain Citheron was all alive with worshippers, and the cries of the Bacchanals resounded on every side. The noise roused the anger of Pentheus as the sound of a trumpet does the fire of a war-horse. He penetrated through the wood and reached on open space where the chief scene of the orgies met his eyes. At the same moment the women saw him; and first among them his own mother, Agave, blinded by the god, cried out, "See there the wild boar, the hugest monster that prowls in these woods! Come on, sisters! I will be the first to strike the wild boar." The whole band rushed upon him, and while he now talks less arrogantly, now excuses himself, and now confesses his crime and implores pardon, they press upon and wound him. In vain he cries to his aunts to protect him from his mother. Autonoe seized one arm, Ino the other, and between them he was torn to pieces, while his mother shouted, "Victory! Victory! we have done it; the glory is ours!"

So the worship of Bacchus was established in Greece.

There is an allusion to the story of Bacchus and the mariners in Milton's "Comus," at line 46. The story of Circe will be found in Chapter 29.

> "Bacchus that first from out the purple grape
> Crushed the sweet poison of misused wine,
> After the Tuscan mariners transformed,
> Coasting the Tyrrhene shore as the winds listed
> On Circe's island fell; (who knows not Circe,
> The daughter of the Sun? whose charmed cup
> Whoever tasted lost his upright shape,
> And downward fell into a grovelling swine.)"

Ariadne

We have seen in the story of Theseus how Ariadne, the daughter of King Minos, after helping Theseus to escape from the labyrinth, was carried by him to the island of Naxos and was left there asleep, while the ungrateful Theseus pursued his way home without her. Ariadne on waking and finding herself deserted abandoned herself to grief. But Venus took pity on her, and consoled her with the promise that she should have an immortal lover, instead of the mortal one she had lost.

The island where Ariadne was left was the favorite island of Bacchus, the same that he wished the Tyrrhenian mariners to carry him to, when they so treacherously attempted to make prize of him. As Ariadne sat lamenting her fate, Bacchus found her, consoled her and made her his wife. As a marriage present he gave her a golden crown, enriched with gems, and when she died, he took her crown and threw it up into the sky. As it mounted the gems grew brighter and were turned into stars, and preserving its form Ariadne's crown remains fixed in the heavens as a constellation, between the kneeling Hercules and the man who holds the serpent.

Spenser alludes to Ariadne's crown, though he has made some mistakes in his mythology. It was at the wedding of Pirithous, and not Theseus, that the Centaurs and Lapithæ quarrelled.

"Look how the crown which Ariadne wore
  Upon her ivory forehead that same day
  That Theseus her unto his bridal bore,
  When the bold Centaurs made that bloody fray
  With the fierce Lapiths which did them dismay;
  Being now placed in the firmament,
  Through the bright heaven doth her beams display,
  And is unto the stars an ornament,
Which round about her move in order excellent."

· · · · · · ·

22

The Rural Deities — Erisichthon — Rhœcus — The Water Deities — Camenæ — Winds

P̲an, the god of woods and fields, of flocks and shepherds, dwelt in grottos, wandered on the mountains and in valleys, and amused himself with the chase or in leading the dances of the nymphs. He was fond of music, and, as we have seen, the inventor of the syrinx, or shepherd's pipe, which he himself played in a masterly manner. Pan, like other gods who dwelt in forests, was dreaded by those whose occupations caused them to pass through the woods by night, for the gloom and loneliness of such scenes dispose the mind to superstitious fears. Hence sudden fright without any visible cause was ascribed to Pan, and called a Panic terror.

As the name of the god signifies *all,* Pan came to be considered a symbol of the universe and personification of Nature; and later still to be regarded as a representative of all the gods and of heathenism itself.

Sylvanus and Faunus were Latin divinities, whose characteristics are so nearly the same as those of Pan that we may safely consider them as but different names of the same personage.

The wood-nymphs, Pan's partners in the dance, were but one class of nymphs. There were beside them the Naiads who presided over brooks and fountains, the Oreads, nymphs of mountains and grottos, and the Nereids, sea-nymphs. The three last named were immortal, but the wood-nymphs, called Dryads or Hamadryads, were believed to perish with the trees which had been their abode, and with which they had come into existence. It was therefore an impious act wantonly to destroy a tree, and in some aggravated cases was severely punished, as in the instance of Erisichthon, which we are about to record.

Milton, in his glowing description of early creation, thus alludes to Pan as the personification of Nature:

> "Universal Pan,
> Knit with the Graces and the Hours in dance,
> Led on the eternal spring."

And describing Eve's abode:

> "In shadier bower,
> More sacred or sequestered, though but feigned,
> Pan or Sylvanus never slept, nor Nymph
> Nor Faunus haunted."

Paradise Lost, Book IV

It was a pleasing trait in the old Paganism that it loved to trace in every operation of nature the agency of deity. The imagination of the Greeks peopled all the regions of earth and sea with divinities, to whose agency it attributed those phenomena which our philosophy ascribes to the operation of the laws of nature. Sometimes in our poetical moods we feel disposed to regret the change, and to think that the heart has lost as much as the head has gained by the substitution. The poet Wordsworth thus strongly expresses this sentiment:

> "Great God, I'd rather be
> A Pagan, suckled in a creed outworn,
> So might I, standing on this pleasant lea,
> Have glimpses that would make me less forlorn;
> Have sight of Proteus rising from the sea,
> And hear old Triton blow his wreathed horn."

Schiller, in his poem "Die Götter Griechenlands," expresses his regret for the overthrow of the beautiful mythology of ancient times in a way which has called forth an answer from a Christian poet, Mrs. E. Barrett Browning, in her poem called "The Dead Pan." The two following verses are a specimen:

> "By your beauty which confesses
> Some chief Beauty conquering you,
> By our grand heroic guesses
> Through your falsehood at the True,
> We will weep *not!* earth shall roll
> Heir to each god's aureole,
> And Pan is dead.

> "Earth outgrows the mythic fancies
> Sung beside her in her youth;
> And those debonaire romances
> Sound but dull beside the truth.

Phœbus' chariot course is run!
Look up, poets, to the sun!
                Pan, Pan is dead.''

These lines are founded on an early Christian tradition that when the heavenly host told the shepherds at Bethlehem of the birth of Christ, a deep groan, heard through all the isles of Greece, told that the great Pan was dead, and that all the royalty of Olympus was dethroned, and the several deities were sent wandering in cold and darkness. So Milton in his "Hymn to the Nativity":

"The lonely mountains o'er,
  And the resounding shore,
    A voice of weeping heard and loud lament;
  From haunted spring and dale,
  Edged with poplar pale,
    The parting Genius is with sighing sent;
  With flower-enwoven tresses torn,
  The nymphs in twilight shade of tangled thickets mourn."

Erisichthon

Erisichthon was a profane person and a despiser of the gods. On one occasion he presumed to violate with the axe a grove sacred to Ceres. There stood in this grove a venerable oak, so large that it seemed a wood in itself, its ancient trunk towering aloft, whereon votive garlands were often hung and inscriptions carved expressing the gratitude of suppliants to the nymph of the tree. Often had Dryads danced round it hand in hand. Its trunk measured fifteen cubits round, and it overtopped the other trees as they overtopped the shrubbery. But for all that, Erisichthon saw no reason why he should spare it, and he ordered his servants to cut it down. When he saw them hesitate, he snatched an axe from one, and thus impiously exclaimed: "I care not whether it be a tree beloved of the goddess or not; were it the goddess herself it should come down, if it stood in my way." So saying he lifted the axe, and the oak seemed to shudder and utter a groan. When the first blow fell upon the trunk, blood flowed from the wound. All the bystanders were horror-struck, and one of them ventured to remonstrate and hold back the fatal axe. Erisichthon, with a scornful look, said to him, "Receive the reward of your piety"; and turned against him the weapon which he had held aside from the tree, gashed his body with many wounds and cut off his head. Then from the midst of the oak came a voice, "I who dwell in this tree am a nymph beloved of Ceres, and dying by your hands, forewarn you that punishment awaits you." He desisted not from his crime, and at last the tree, sundered by repeated blows and drawn by ropes, fell with a crash, and prostrated a great part of the grove in its fall.

The Dryads in dismay at the loss of their companion, and at seeing the pride of the forest laid low, went in a body to Ceres, all clad in garments of mourning, and invoked punishment upon Erisichthon. She nodded her assent, and as she bowed her head the grain ripe for harvest in the laden fields bowed also. She planned a punishment so dire that one would pity him, if such a culprit as he could be pitied—to deliver him over to Famine. As Ceres herself could not approach Famine, for the Fates have ordained that these two goddesses shall never come together, she called on Oread from her mountain and spoke to her in these words: "There is a place in the farthest part of ice-clad Scythia, a sad and sterile region without trees and without crops. Cold dwells there, and Fear, and Shuddering, and Famine. Go and tell the last to take possession of the bowels of Erisichthon. Let not abundance subdue her, nor the power of my gifts drive her away. Be not alarmed at the distance" (for Famine dwells very far from Ceres), "but take my chariot. The dragons are fleet and obey the rein, and will take you through the air in a short time." So she gave her the reins, and she drove away and soon reached Scythia. On arriving at Mount Caucasus she stopped the dragons and found Famine in a stony field, pulling up with teeth and claws the scanty herbage. Her hair was rough, her eyes sunk, her face pale, her lips blanched, her jaws covered with dust, and her skin drawn tight, so as to show all her bones. As the Oread saw her afar off (for she did not dare to come near), she delivered the commands of Ceres; and, though she stopped as short a time as possible, and kept her distance as well as she could, yet she began to feel hungry, and turned the dragons' heads and drove back to Thessaly.

Famine obeyed the commands of Ceres and sped through the air to the dwelling of Erisichthon, entered the bed-chamber of the guilty man, and found him asleep. She enfolded him with her wings and breathed herself into him, infusing her poison into his veins. Having discharged her task, she hastened to leave the land of plenty and returned to her accustomed haunts. Erisichthon still slept, and in his dreams craved food, and moved his jaws as if eating. When he awoke his hunger was raging. Without a moment's delay he would have food set before him, of whatever kind earth, sea or air produces; and complained of hunger even while he ate. What would have sufficed for a city or a nation, was not enough for him. The more he ate the more he craved. His hunger was like the sea, which receives all the rivers, yet is never filled; or like fire that burns all the fuel that is heaped upon it, yet is still voracious for more.

His property rapidly diminished under the unceasing demands of his appetite, but his hunger continued unabated. At length he had spent all, and had only his daughter left, a daughter worthy of a better parent. *Her too he sold.* She scorned to be the slave of a purchaser, and as she stood by the sea side, raised her hands in prayer to Neptune. He heard her prayer, and, though her new master was not far off, and had his eye upon her a moment before, Neptune changed her form, and made her assume that of a fisherman busy at his occupation. Her master, looking for her and seeing her in her altered form, addressed her and said, "Good fisherman, whither went the maiden whom I saw just now, with hair dishevelled and in humble garb, standing about where you stand? Tell me truly; so may your luck be good, and not a fish nibble at your hook and get away.'' She perceived that her prayer was answered, and rejoiced inwardly at hearing herself inquired of about herself. She replied, ''Pardon me, stranger, but I have been so intent upon my line, that I have seen nothing else; but I wish I may never catch another fish if I believe any woman or other person except myself to have been hereabouts for some time.'' He was deceived and went his way, thinking his slave had escaped. Then she resumed her own form. Her father was well pleased to find her still with him, and the money too that he got by the sale of her; so he sold her again. But she was changed by the favor of Neptune as often as she was sold, now into a horse, now a bird, now an ox, and now a stag—got away from her purchasers and came home. By this base method the starving father procured food; but not enough for his wants, and at last hunger compelled him to devour his limbs, and he strove to nourish his body by eating his body, till death relieved him from the vengeance of Ceres.

Rhœcus

The Hamadryads could appreciate services as well as punish injuries. The story of Rhœcus proves this. Rhœcus, happening to see an oak just ready to fall, ordered his servants to prop it up. The nymph, who had been on the point of perishing with the tree, came and expressed her gratitude to him for having saved her life, and bade him ask what reward he would. Rhœcus boldly asked her love, and the nymph yielded to his desire. She at the same time charged him to be constant, and told him that a bee should be her messenger, and let him know when she would admit his society. One time the bee came to Rhœcus when he was playing at draughts, and he carelessly brushed it away. This so incensed the nymph that she deprived him of sight.

Our countryman J.R. Lowell has taken this story for the subject of one of his shorter poems. He introduces it thus:

"Hear now this fairy legend of old Greece,
    As full of freedom, youth and beauty still,
    As the immortal freshness of that grace
    Carved for all ages on some Attic frieze.''

The Water Deities

Oceanus and Tethys were the Titans who ruled over the watery element. When Jove and his brothers overthrew the Titans and assumed their power, Neptune and Amphitrite succeeded to the dominion of the waters in place of Oceanus and Tethys.

Neptune

Neptune was the chief of the water deities. The symbol of his power was the trident, or spear with three points, with which he used to shatter rocks, to call forth or subdue storms, to shake the shores, and the like. He created the horse and was the patron of horse races. His own horses had brazen hoofs and golden manes. They drew his chariot over the sea, which became smooth before him, while the monsters of the deep gambolled about his path.

Amphitrite

Amphitrite was the wife of Neptune. She was the daughter of Nereus and Doris, and the mother of Triton. Neptune, to pay his court to Amphitrite, came riding on a dolphin. Having won her, he rewarded the dolphin by placing him among the stars.

Nereus and Doris

Nereus and Doris were the parents of the Nereids, the most celebrated of whom were Amphitrite, Thetis, the mother of Achilles, and Galatea, who was loved by Cyclops Polyphemus. Nereus was distinguished for his knowledge and his love of truth and justice, whence he was termed an elder; the gift of prophecy was also assigned to him.

Triton and Proteus

Triton was the son of Neptune and Amphitrite, and the poets make him his father's trumpeter. Proteus was also a son of Neptune. He, like Nereus, is styled a sea-elder for his wisdom and knowledge of future events. His peculiar power was that of changing his shape at will.

Thetis

Thetis, the daughter of Nereus and Doris, was so beautiful that Jupiter himself sought her in marriage; but having learned from Prometheus the Titan that Thetis should bear a son who should be greater than his father, Jupiter desisted from his suit and decreed that Thetis should be the wife of a mortal. By the aid of Chiron the Centaur, Peleus succeeded in winning the goddess for his bride, and their son was the renowned Achilles. In our chapter on the Trojan war it will appear that Thetis was a faithful mother to him, aiding him in all difficulties, and watching over his interests from the first to the last.

Leucothea and Palæmon

Ino, the daughter of Cadmus and wife of Athamas, flying from her frantic husband with her little son Melicertes in her arms, sprang from a cliff into the sea. The gods, out of compassion, made her a goddess of the sea, under the name of Leucothea, and him a god under that of Palæmon. Both were held powerful to save from shipwreck and were invoked by sailors. Palæmon was usually represented riding on a dolphin. The Isthmian games were celebrated in his honor. He was called Portunus by the Romans, and believed to have jurisdiction of the ports and shores.

Milton alludes to all these deities in the song at the conclusion of "Comus."

> "Sabrina fair,
> Listen and appear to us,
> In the name of great Oceanus;
> By the earth-shaking Neptune's mace,
> And Tethys' grave, majestic pace,
> By hoary Nereus' wrinkled look,
> And the Carpathian wizard's hook,*
> By scaly Triton's winding shell,
> And old soothsaying Glaucus' spell,
> By Leucothea's lovely hands,
> And her son who rules the strands,
> By Thetis' tinsel-slippered feet,
> And the songs of Sirens sweet"; etc.

Armstrong, the poet of the "Art of Preserving Health," under the inspiration of Hygeia, the goddess of health, thus celebrates the Naiads. Pæon is a name both of Apollo and Æsculapius.

> "Come, ye Naiads" to the fountains lead!
> Propitious maids! the task remains to sing
> Your gifts, (so Pæon, so the powers of Health
> Command,) to praise your crystal element.
> O comfortable streams! with eager lips
> And trembling hands the languid thirsty quaff
> New life in you; fresh vigor fills their veins.
> No warmer cups the rural ages knew,
> None warmer sought the sires of humankind;
> Happy in temperate peace their equal days
> Felt not the alternate fits of feverish mirth
> And sick dejection; still serene and pleased,
> Blessed with divine immunity from ills,
> Long centuries they lived; their only fate
> Was ripe old age, and rather sleep that death."

The Camenæ

By this name the Latins designated the Muses, but included under it also some other deities, principally nymphs of fountains. Egeria was one of them, whose fountain and grotto are still shown. It was said that Numa, the second king of Rome, was favored by this nymph with secret interviews, in which she taught him those lessons of wisdom and of law

*Proteus

which he imbodied in the institutions of his rising nation. After the death of Numa the nymph pined away and was changed into a fountain.

Byron in "Childe Harold," Canto IV, thus alludes to Egeria and her grotto:

"Here didst thou dwell, in this enchanted cover,
Egeria! all thy heavenly bosom beating
For the far footsteps of thy mortal lover;
The purple midnight veiled that mystic meeting
With her most starry canopy"; etc.

Tennyson, also, in his "Palace of Art," gives us a glimpse of the royal lover expecting the interview.

"Holding one hand against his ear,
To list a footfall ere he saw
The wood-nymph, stayed the Tuscan king to hear
Of wisdom and of law."

The Winds

When so many less active agencies were personified, it is not to be supposed that the winds failed to be so. They were Boreas or Aquilo, the north wind, Zephyrus or Favonius, the west, Notus or Auster, the south and Eurus, the east. The first two have been chiefly celebrated by the poets, the former as the type of rudeness, the latter of gentleness. Boreas loved the nymph Orithyia, and tried to play the lover's part, but met with poor success. It was hard for him to breathe gently, and sighing was out of the question. Weary at last of fruitless endeavors, he acted out his true character, seized the maiden and carried her off. Their children were Zetes and Calais, winged warriors, who accompanied the Argonautic expedition, and did good service in an encounter with those monstrous birds the Harpies.

Zephyrus was the lover of Flora. Milton alludes to them in "Paradise Lost," where he describes Adam waking and contemplating Eve still asleep.

"He on his side
Leaning half raised, with looks of cordial love,
Hung over her enamored, and beheld
Beauty which, whether waking or asleep,
Shot forth peculiar graces; then with voice,
Mild as when Zephyrus on Flora breathes,
Her hand soft touching, whispered thus: 'Awake!
My fairest, my espoused, my latest found,
Heaven's last, best gift, my ever-new delight.' "

Dr. Young, the poet of the "Night Thoughts," addressing the idle and luxurious, says,

"Ye delicate! who nothing can support,
  (Yourselves most insupportable) for whom
  The winter rose must blow,   *   *
      *   *   *   *   and silky soft
  Favonius breathe still softer or be chid!"

. . . .
23

Achelous and Hercules—Admetus and Alcestis—Antigone—Penelope

The river-god Achelous told the story of Erisichthon to Theseus and his companions, whom he was entertaining at his hospitable board, while they were delayed on their journey by the overflow of his waters. Having finished his story he added, "But why should I tell of other persons' transformations, when I myself am an instance of the possession of this power. Sometimes I become a serpent, and sometimes a bull, with horns on my head. Or I should say, I once could do so; but now I have but one horn, having lost one." And here he groaned and was silent.

Theseus asked him the cause of his grief, and how he lost his horn. To which question the river-god replied as follows: "Who likes to tell of his defeats? Yet I will not hesitate to relate mine, comforting myself with the thought of the greatness of my conqueror, for it was Hercules. Perhaps you have heard of the fame of Dejanira, the fairest of maidens, whom a host of suitors strove to win. Hercules and myself were of the number, and the rest yielded to us two. He urged in his behalf his descent from Jove, and his labors by which he had exceeded the exactions of Juno, his stepmother. I, on the other hand, said to the father of the maiden, 'Behold me, the king of the waters that flow through your land. I am no stranger from a foreign shore, but belong to the country, a part of your realm. Let it not stand in my way that royal Juno owes me no enmity, nor punishes me with heavy tasks. As for this man, who boasts himself the son of Jove, it is either a false pretence, or disgraceful to him if true, for it cannot be true except by his mother's shame.' As I said this Hercules scowled upon me, and with difficulty restrained his rage. 'My hand will answer better than my tongue,' said he. 'I yield you the victory in words, but trust my cause to the strife of deeds.' With that he advanced towards me, and I was ashamed, after what I had said, to yield. I threw off my green vesture and presented myself for the struggle. He tried to throw me, now attacking my head, now my body. My bulk was my protection, and he assailed me in vain. For a time we stopped, then returned to the conflict. We each kept our position, determined not to yield, foot to foot, I bending over him, clinching his hands in mine, with my forehead almost touching his. Thrice Hercules tried to throw me off, and the fourth time he succeeded, brought me to the ground and himself upon my back. I tell you the truth, it was as if a mountain had fallen on me. I struggled to get my arms at liberty, panting and reeking with perspiration. He gave me no chance to recover, but seized my throat. My knees were on the earth and my mouth in the dust.

"Finding that I was no match for him in the warrior's art, I resorted to others, and glided away in the form of a serpent. I curled my body in a coil, and hissed at him with my forked tongue. He smiled scornfully at this, and said, 'It was the labor of my infancy to conquer snakes.' So saying he clasped my neck with his hands. I was almost choked, and struggled to get my neck out of his grasp. Vanquished in this form, I tried what alone remained to me, and assumed the form of a bull. He grasped my neck with his arm, and dragging my head down to the ground, overthrew me on the sand. Nor was this enough. His ruthless hand rent my horn from my head. The Naiades took it, consecrated it, and filled it with fragrant flowers. Plenty adopted my horn and made it her own, and called it Cornucopia."

The ancients were fond of finding a hidden meaning in their mythological tales. They explain this fight of Achelous with Hercules by saying Achelous was a river that in seasons of rain overflowed its banks. When the fable says that Achelous loved Dejanira, and sought a union with her, the meaning is, that the river in its windings flowed through part of Dejanira's kingdom. It was said to take the form of a snake because of its winding, and of a bull because it made a brawling or roaring in its course. When the river swelled, it made itself another channel. Thus its head was horned. Hercules prevented the return of these periodical overflows, by embankments and canals; and therefore he was said to have vanquished the river-god and cut off his horn. Finally, the lands formerly subject to overflow, but now redeemed, became very fertile, and this is meant by the horn of plenty.

There is another account of the origin of the Cornucopia. Jupiter at his birth was committed by his mother Rhea to the care of the daughters of Melisseus, a Cretan king. They fed the infant deity with the milk of the goat Amalthea. Jupiter broke off one of the horns of the goat and gave it to his nurses, and endowed it with the wonderful power of becoming filled with whatever the possessor might wish.

The name of Amalthea is also given by some writers to the mother of Bacchus. It is thus used by Milton, "Paradise Lost," Book IV:

> —That Nyseian isle,
> Girt with the river Triton, where old Cham,
> Whom Gentiles Ammon call, and Libyan Jove,
> Hid Amalthea and her florid son,
> Young Bacchus, from his stepdame Rhea's eye."

Admetus and Alcestis

Æsculapius, the son of Apollo, was endowed by his father with such skill in the healing art that he even restored the dead to life. At this Pluto took alarm, and prevailed on Jupiter to launch a thunderbolt at Æsculapius. Apollo was indignant at the destruction of his son, and wreaked his vengeance on the innocent workmen who had made the thunderbolt. These were the Cyclopes, who have their workshop under Mount Ætna, from which the smoke and flames of their furnaces are constantly issuing. Apollo shot his arrows at the Cyclopes, which so incensed Jupiter that he condemned him as a punishment to become the servant of a mortal for the space of one year. Accordingly Apollo went into the service of Admetus, king of Thessaly, and pastured his flocks for him on the verdant banks of the river Amphrysos.

Admetus was a suitor, with others, for the hand of Alcestis, the daughter of Pelias, who promised her to him who should come for her in a chariot drawn by lions and boars. This task Admetus performed by the assistance of his divine herdsman, and was made happy in the possession of Alcestis. But Admetus fell ill, and being near to death, Apollo prevailed on the Fates to spare him on condition that some one would consent to die in his stead. Admetus in his joy at this reprieve, thought little of the ransom, and perhaps remembering the declarations of attachment which he had often heard from his courtiers and dependents, fancied that it would be easy to find a substitute. But it was not so. Brave warriors, who would willingly have perilled their lives for their prince, shrunk from the thought of dying for him on the bed of sickness; and old servants who had experienced his bounty and that of his house from their childhood up, were not willing to lay down the scanty remnant of their days to show their gratitude. Men asked—"Why does not one of his parents do it? They cannot in the course of nature live much longer, and who can feel like them the call to rescue the life they gave, from an untimely end?" But the parents, distressed though they were at the thought of losing him, shrunk from the call. Then Alcestis, with a generous self-devotion, proffered herself as the substitute. Admetus, fond as he was of life, would not have submitted to receive it at such a cost; but there was no remedy. The condition imposed by the Fates had been met, and the decree was irrevocable. Alcestis sickened as Admetus revived, and she was rapidly sinking to the grave.

Just at this time Hercules arrived at the palace of Admetus, and found all the inmates in great distress for the impending loss of the devoted wife and beloved mistress. Hercules, to whom no labor was too arduous, resolved to attempt her rescue. He went and lay in wait at the door of the chamber of the dying queen, and when Death came for his prey, he seized him and forced him to resign his victim. Alcestis recovered, and was restored to her husband.

Milton alludes to the story of Alcestis in his Sonnet "on his deceased wife."

> "Methought I saw my late espoused saint
>   Brought to me like Alcestis from the grave,
>   Whom Jove's great son to her glad husband gave,
> Rescued from death by force, though pale and faint."

J.R. Lowell has chosen the "Shepherd of King Admetus" for the subject of a short poem. He makes that event the first introduction of poetry to men.

"Men called him but a shiftless youth,
    In whom no good they saw,
And yet unwittingly, in truth,
    They made his careless words their law.

"And day by day more holy grew
    Each spot where he had trod,
Till after-poets only knew
    Their first-born brother was a god."

Antigone

A large proportion both of the interesting persons and of the exalted acts of legendary Greece belongs to the female sex. Antigone was as bright an example of filial and sisterly fidelity as was Alcestis of connubial devotion. She was the daughter of Œdipus and Jocasta, who with all their descendants were the victims of an unrelenting fate, dooming them to destruction. Œdipus in his madness had torn out his eyes, and was driven forth from his kingdom Thebes, dreaded and abandoned by all men, as an object of divine vengeance. Antigone, his daughter, alone shared his wanderings and remained with him till he died, and then returned to Thebes.

Her brothers, Eteocles and Polynices, had agreed to share the kingdom between them, and reign alternately year by year. The first year fell to the lot of Eteocles, who, when his time expired, refused to surrender the kingdom to his brother. Polynices fled to Adrastus, king of Argos, who gave him his daughter in marriage, and aided him with an army to enforce his claim to the kingdom. This led to the celebrated expedition of the "Seven against Thebes," which furnished ample materials for the epic and tragic poets of Greece.

Amphiaraus, the brother-in-law of Adrastus, opposed the enterprise, for he was a soothsayer, and knew by his art that no one of the leaders except Adrastus would live to return. But Amphiaraus, on his marriage to Eriphyle, the king's sister, had agreed that whenever he and Adrastus should differ in opinion, the decision should be left to Eriphyle. Polynices, knowing this, gave Eriphyle the collar of Harmonia, and thereby gained her to his interest. This collar or necklace was a present which Vulcan had given to Harmonia on her marriage with Cadmus, and Polynices had taken it with him on his flight from Thebes. Eriphyle could not resist so tempting a bribe, and by her decision the war was resolved on, and Amphiaraus went to his certain fate. He bore his part bravely in the contest, but could not avert his destiny. Pursued by the enemy he fled along the river, when a thunderbolt launched by Jupiter opened the ground, and he, his chariot and his charioteer were swallowed up.

It would not be in place here to detail all the acts of heroism or atrocity which marked the contest; but we must not omit to record the fidelity of Evadne as an off-set to the weakness of Eriphyle. Capaneus, the husband of Evadne, in the ardor of the fight declared that he would force his way into the city in spite of Jove himself. Placing a ladder against the wall he mounted, but Jupiter, offended at his impious language struck him with a thunderbolt. When his obsequies were celebrated, Evadne cast herself on his funeral pile and perished.

Early in the contest Eteocles consulted the soothsayer Tiresias as to the issue. Tiresias in his youth had by chance seen Minerva bathing. The goddess in her wrath deprived him of his sight, but afterwards relenting gave him in compensation the knowledge of future events. When consulted by Eteocles, he declared that victory should fall to Thebes if Menœceus the son of Creon gave himself a voluntary victim. The heroic youth learning the response threw away his life in the first encounter.

The siege continued long, with various success. At length both hosts agreed that the brothers should decide their quarrel by single combat. They fought and fell by each other's hands. The armies then renewed the fight, and at last the invaders were forced to yield, and fled, leaving their dead unburied. Creon, the uncle of the fallen princes, now become king, caused Eteocles to be buried with distinguished honor, but suffered the body of Polynices to lie where it fell, forbidding every one on pain of death to give it burial.

Antigone, the sister of Polynices, heard with indignation the revolting edict which consigned her brother's body to the dogs and vultures, depriving it of those rites which were considered essential to the repose of the dead. Unmoved by the dissuading counsel of an affectionate but timid sister, and unable to procure assistance, she determined to brave the hazard and to bury the body with her own hands. She was detected in the act, and Creon gave orders that she should be buried alive, as having deliberately set at nought the solemn edict of the city. Her lover, Hæmon, the son of Creon, unable to avert her fate, would not survive her, and fell by his own hand.

Antigone forms the subject of two fine tragedies of the Grecian poet Sophocles. Mrs. Jameson, in her "Characteristics of Women," has compared her character with that of Cordelia, in Shakespeare's "King Lear." The perusal of her remarks cannot fail to gratify our readers.

The following is the lamentation of Antigone over Œdipus, when death has at last relieved him from his sufferings:

"Alas! I only wished I might have died
With my poor father; wherefore should I ask
For longer life?
O, I was fond of misery with him;
E'en what was most unlovely grew beloved
When he was with me. O my dearest father,
Beneath the earth now in deep darkness hid,

Worn as thou wert with age, to me thou still
Wast dear, and shalt be ever."

Francklin's Sophocles

Penelope

Penelope is another of those mythic heroines whose beauties were
rather those of character and conduct than of person. She was the
daughter of Icarius, a Spartan prince. Ulysses, king of Ithaca, sought
her in marriage, and won her, over all competitors. When the moment
came for the bride to leave her father's house, Icarius, unable to bear the
thoughts of parting with his daughter, tried to persuade her to remain
with him, and not accompany her husband to Ithaca. Ulysses gave
Penelope her choice, to stay or go with him. Penelope made no reply,
but dropped her veil over her face. Icarius urged her no further, but
when she was gone erected a statue to Modesty on the spot where they
parted.

Ulysses and Penelope had not enjoyed their union more than a year
when it was interrupted by the events which called Ulysses to the Trojan
war. During his long absence, and when it was doubtful whether he still
lived, and highly improbable that he would ever return, Penelope was
importuned by numerous suitors, from whom there seemed no refuge
but in choosing one of them for her husband. Penelope, however,
employed every art to gain time, still hoping for Ulysses' return. One of
her arts of delay was engaging in the preparation of a robe for the
funeral canopy of Laertes, her husband's father. She pledged herself to
make her choice among the suitors when the robe was finished. During
the day she worked at the robe, but in the night she undid the work of
the day. This is the famous Penelope's web, which is perpetually doing
but never done. The rest of Penelope's history will be told when we give
an account of her husband's adventures.

· · · · · · ·

24

Orpheus and Eurydice—Aristæus— Amphion—Linus—Thamyris—Marsyas— Melampus—Musæus

Orpheus was the son of Apollo and the Muse Calliope. He was
presented by his father with a Lyre and taught to play upon it, which he
did to such perfection that nothing could withstand the charm of his
music. Not only his fellow-mortals but wild beasts were softened by his
strains, and gathering round him laid by their fierceness, and stood en-
tranced with his lay. Nay, the very trees and rocks were sensible to the
charm. The former crowded round him and the latter relaxed somewhat
of their hardness, softened by his notes.

Hymen had been called to bless with his presence the nuptials of Orpheus with Eurydice; but though he attended, he brought no happy
omens with him. His very torch smoked and brought tears into their

eyes. In coincidence with such prognostics Eurydice, shortly after her marriage, while wandering with the nymphs, her companions, was seen by the shepherd Aristæus, who was struck with her beauty, and made advances to her. She fled, and in flying trod upon a snake in the grass, was bitten in the foot and died. Orpheus sang his grief to all who breathed the upper air, both gods and men, and finding it all unavailing resolved to seek his wife in the regions of the dead. He descended by a cave situated on the side of the promontory of Tænarus and arrived at the Stygian realm. He passed through crowds of ghosts and presented himself before the throne of Pluto and Proserpine. Accompanying the words with the lyre, he sung, "O deities of the under world, to whom all we who live must come, hear my words, for they are true. I come not to spy out the secrets of Tartarus, nor to try my strength against the three-headed dog with snaky hair who guards the entrance. I come to seek my wife, whose opening years the poisonous viper's fang had brought to an untimely end. Love has led me here, Love, a god all powerful with us who dwell on the earth, and, if old traditions say true, not less so here. I implore you by these abodes full of terror, these realms of silence and uncreated things, unite again the thread of Eurydice's life. We all are destined to you, and sooner or later must pass to your domain. She too, when she shall have filled her term of life, will rightly be yours. But till then grant her to me, I beseech you. If you deny me, I cannot return alone; you shall triumph in the death of us both."

As he sang these tender strains, the very ghosts shed tears. Tantalus, in spite of his thirst, stopped for a moment his efforts for water, Ixion's wheel stood still, the vulture ceased to tear the giant's liver, the daughters of Danaus rested from their task of drawing water in a sieve, and Sisyphus sat on his rock to listen. Then for the first time, it is said, the cheeks of the Furies were wet with tears. Proserpine could not resist, and Pluto himself gave way. Eurydice was called. She came from among the new-arrived ghosts, limping with her wounded foot. Orpheus was permitted to take her away with him on one condition, that he should not turn round to look at her till they should have reached the upper air. Under this condition they proceeded on their way, he leading, she following, through passages dark and steep, in total silence, till they had nearly reached the outlet into the cheerful upper world, when Orpheus, in a moment of forgetfulness, to assure himself that she was still following, cast a glance behind him, when instantly she was borne away. Stretching out their arms to embrace one another they grasped only the air! Dying now a second time she yet cannot reproach her husband, for how can she blame his impatience to behold her! "Farewell," she said, "a last farewell"—and was hurried away, so fast that the sound hardly reached his ears.

Orpheus endeavored to follow her, and besought permission to return and try once more for her release; but the stern ferryman repulsed him and refused passage. Seven days he lingered about the brink, without food or sleep; then bitterly accusing of cruelty the powers of

Erebus, he sang his complaints to the rocks and mountains, melting the hearts of tigers and moving the oaks from their stations. He held himself aloof from womankind, dwelling constantly on the recollection of his sad mischance. The Thracian maidens tried their best to captivate him, but he repulsed their advances. They bore with him as long as they could; but finding him insensible, one day, excited by the rites of Bacchus, one of them exclaimed, "See yonder our despiser!" and threw at him her javelin. The weapon, as soon as it came within the sound of his lyre, fell harmless at his feet. So did also the stones that they threw at him. But the women raised a scream and drowned the voice of the music, and then the missiles reached him and soon were stained with his blood. The maniacs tore him limb from limb, and threw his head and his lyre into the river Hebrus, down which they floated, murmuring sad music, to which the shores responded a plaintive symphony. The Muses gathered up the fragments of his body and buried them at Libethra, where the nightingale is said to sing over his grave more sweetly than in any other part of Greece. His lyre was placed by Jupiter among the stars. His shade passed a second time to Tartarus, where he sought out his Eurydice and embraced her, with eager arms. They roam the happy fields together now, sometimes he leading, sometimes she; and Orpheus gazes as much as he will upon her, no longer incurring a penalty for a thoughtless glance.

The story of Orpheus has furnished Pope with an illustration of the power of music, for his "Ode for St. Cecilia's Day." The following stanza relates the conclusion of the story:

"But soon, too soon the lover turns his eyes;
 Again she falls, again she dies, she dies!
 How wilt thou now the fatal sisters move?
 No crime was thine, if 'tis no crime to love.
  Now under hanging mountains,
  Beside the falls of fountains,
  Or where Hebrus wanders,
  Rolling in meanders,
   All alone,
   He makes his moan,
   And calls her ghost,
  Forever, ever, ever lost!
  Now with furies surrounded,
  Despairing, confounded,
  He trembles, he glows,
  Amidst Rhodope's snows.
See, wild as the winds o'er the desert he flies;
Hark! Hæmus resounds with the Bacchanals' cries.
  Ah, see, he dies!
Yet even in death Eurydice he sung,
Eurydice still trembled on his tongue:
Eurydice the woods
Eurydice the floods
Eurydice the rocks and hollow mountains rung."

The superior melody of the nightingale's song over the grave of Orpheus is alluded to by Southey in his "Thalaba":

"Then on his ear what sounds
Of harmony arose!
Far music and the distance-mellowed song
From bowers of merriment;
The waterfall remote;
The murmuring of the leafy groves;
The single nightingale
Perched in the rosier by, so richly toned,
That never from that most melodious bird
Singing a love song to his brooding mate,
Did Thracian shepherd by the grave
Of Orpheus hear a sweeter melody,
Though there the spirit of the sepulchre
All his own power infuse, to swell
The incense that he loves."

Aristæus, the Bee-Keeper

Man avails himself of the instincts of the inferior animals for his own advantage. Hence sprang the art of keeping bees. Honey must first have been known as a wild product, the bees building their structures in hollow trees or holes in the rocks, or any similar cavity that chance offered. Thus occasionally the carcass of a dead animal would be occupied by the bees for that purpose. It was no doubt from some such incident that the superstition arose that the bees were engendered by the decaying flesh of the animal; and Virgil, in the following story, shows how this supposed fact may be turned to account for renewing the swarm when it has been lost by disease or accident.

Aristæus, who first taught the management of bees, was the son of the water-nymph Cyrene. His bees had perished, and he resorted for aid to his mother. He stood at the river side and thus addressed her: "O mother, the pride of my life is taken from me! I have lost my precious bees. My care and skill have availed me nothing, and you my mother have not warded off from me the blow of misfortune." His mother heard these complaints as she sat in her palace at the bottom of the river, with her attendant nymphs around her. They were engaged in female occupations, spinning and weaving, while one told stories to amuse the rest. The sad voice of Aristæus interrupting their occupation, one of them put her head above the water and seeing him, returned and gave information to his mother, who ordered that he should be brought into her presence. The river at her command opened itself and let him pass in, while it stood curled like a mountain on either side. He descended to the region where the fountains of the great rivers lie; he saw the enormous receptacles of waters and was almost deafened with the roar, while he surveyed them hurrying off in various directions to water the face of the earth. Arriving at his mother's apartment he was hospitably received by Cyrene and her nymphs, who spread their table with the richest dainties. They first poured out libations to Neptune, then regaled themselves with the feast, and after that Cyrene thus addressed him: "There is an old prophet named Proteus, who dwells in the sea and is a favorite of Neptune, whose herd of sea-calves he pastures. We nymphs hold him in great respect, for he is a learned sage and knows all things, past, present, and to come. He can tell you, my son, the cause of the mortality among your bees, and how you may remedy it. But he will not do it voluntarily, however you may entreat him. You must compel him by force. If you seize him and chain him, he will answer your questions in order to get released, for he cannot by all his arts get away if you hold fast the chains. I will carry you to his cave, where he comes at noon to take his midday repose. Then you may easily secure him. But when he finds himself captured, his resort is to a power he possesses of changing himself into various forms. He will become a wild boar or a fierce tiger, a scaly dragon or lion with yellow mane. Or he will make a noise like the crackling of flames or the rush of water, so as to tempt you to let go the chain, when he will make his escape. But you have only to keep him fast bound, and at last when he finds all his arts unavailing, he will return to his own figure and obey your commands." So saying she sprinkled her son with fragrant nectar, the beverage of the gods, and immediately an unusual vigor filled his frame and courage his heart, while perfume breathed all around him.

The nymph led her son to the prophet's cave and concealed him among the recesses of the rocks, while she herself took her place behind the clouds. When noon came and the hour when men and herds retreat from the glaring sun to indulge in quiet slumber, Proteus issued from the water, followed by his herd of sea-calves which spread themselves along the shore. He sat on the rock and counted his herd; then stretched himself on the floor of the cave and went to sleep. Aristæus hardly allowed him to get fairly asleep before he fixed the fetters on him and shouted aloud. Proteus waking and finding himself captured immediately resorted to his arts, becoming first a fire, then a flood, then a horrible wild beast, in rapid succession. But finding all would not do, he at last resumed his own form and addressed the youth in angry accents: "Who are you, bold youth, who thus invade my abode, and what do you want with me?" Aristæus replied, "Proteus, you know already, for it is needless for any one to attempt to deceive you. And do you also cease your efforts to elude me. I am led hither by divine assistance, to know from you the cause of my misfortune and how to remedy it." At these words the prophet fixing on him his gray eyes, with a piercing look, thus spoke: "You received the merited reward of your deeds, by which Eurydice met her death, for in flying from you she trod upon a serpent, of whose bite she died. To avenge her death, the nymphs her companions have sent this destruction to your bees. You have to appease their anger, and thus it must be done: Select four bulls, of perfect form and size, and four cows of equal beauty, build four altars to the nymphs, and sacrifice the animals, leaving their carcasses in the leafy grove. To Orpheus and Eurydice you shall pay such funeral honors as may allay their resentment. Returning after nine days you will examine the bodies of the cattle slain and see what will befall." Aristæus faithfully obeyed these directions. He sacrificed the cattle, he left their bodies in the grove, he offered funeral honors to the shades of Orpheus and Eurydice; then returning on the ninth day he examined the bodies of the animals, and, wonderful to relate! a swarm of bees had taken possession of one of the carcasses and were pursuing their labors there as in a hive.

In the "Task," Cowper alludes to the story of Aristæus, when speaking of the ice-palace built by the Empress Anne of Russia. He has been describing the fantastic forms which ice assumes in connection with water-falls, etc.:

"Less worthy of applause though more admired
Because a novelty, the work of man,
Imperial mistress of the fur-clad Russ,
Thy most magnificent and mighty freak,
The wonder of the north. No forest fell
When thou wouldst build, no quarry sent its stores
T'enrich thy walls; but thou didst hew the floods
And make thy marble of the glassy wave.
In such a palace Aristæus found
Cyrene, when he bore the plaintive tale
Of his lost bees to her maternal ear."

Milton also appears to have had Cyrene and her domestic scene in his mind when he describes to us Sabrina, the nymph of the river Severn, in the Guardian-spirit's Song in "Comus":

"Sabrina fair!
Listen where thou art sitting
Under the glassy, cool, translucent wave
In twisted braids of lilies knitting
The loose train of thy amber-dropping hair;
Listen for dear honor's sake,
Goddess of the silver lake!
Listen and save."

The following are other celebrated mythical poets and musicians, some of whom were hardly inferior to Orpheus himself:

Amphion

Amphion was the son of Jupiter and Antiope, queen of Thebes. With his twin brother Zethus he was exposed at birth on Mount Cithæron, where they grew up among the shepherds, not knowing their parentage. Mercury gave Amphion a lyre and taught him to play upon it, and his brother occupied himself in hunting and tending the flocks. Meanwhile

Antiope, their mother, who had been treated with great cruelty by Lycus, the usurping king of Thebes, and by Dirce, his wife, found means to inform her children of their rights and to summon them to her assistance. With a band of their fellow-herdsmen they attacked and slew Lycus, and tying Dirce by the hair of her head to a bull, let him drag her till she was dead.* Amphion, having become king of Thebes, fortified the city with a wall. It is said that when he played on his lyre the stones moved of their own accord and took their places in the wall.

See Tennyson's poem of "Amphion" for an amusing use made of this story.

Linus

Linus was the instructor of Hercules in music, but having one day reproved his pupil rather harshly, he roused the anger of Hercules, who struck him with his lyre and killed him.

Thamyris

An ancient Thracian bard, who in his presumption challenged the Muses to a trial of skill, and being overcome in the contest was deprived by them of his sight. Milton alludes to him with other blind bards, when speaking of his own blindness, "Paradise Lost," Book III, 35.

Marsyas

Minerva invented the flute, and played upon it to the delight of all the celestial auditors; but the mischievous urchin Cupid having dared to laugh at the queer face which the goddess made while playing, Minerva threw the instrument indignantly away, and it fell down to earth, and was found by Marsyas. He blew upon it, and drew from it such ravishing sounds that he was tempted to challenge Apollo himself to a musical contest. The god of course triumphed, and punished Marsyas by flaying him alive.

Melampus

Melampus was the first mortal endowed with prophetic powers. Before his house there stood an oak tree containing a serpent's nest. The old serpents were killed by the servants, but Melampus took care of the young ones and fed them carefully. One day when he was asleep under the oak, the serpents licked his ears with their tongues. On awaking he was astonished to find that he now understood the language of birds and creeping things. This knowledge enabled him to foretell future events, and he became a renowned soothsayer. At one time his enemies took him captive and kept him strictly imprisoned. Melampus in the silence of the night heard the woodworms in the timbers talking

*The punishment of Dirce is the subject of a celebrated group of statuary now in the Museum at Naples.

together, and found out by what they said that the timbers were nearly eaten through and the roof would soon fall in. He told his captors and demanded to be let out, warning them also. They took his warning, and thus escaped destruction, and rewarded Melampus and held him in high honor.

Musæus

A semi-mythological personage who was represented by one tradition to be the son of Orpheus. He is said to have written sacred poems and oracles. Milton couples his name with that of Orpheus in his "Il Penseroso":

" But O, sad virgin, that thy power
   Might raise Musæus from his bower,
   Or bid the soul of Orpheus sing
   Such notes as warbled to the string,
   Drew iron tears down Pluto's cheek,
   And made Hell grant what love did seek."

• • • • • • •

25

Arion — Ibycus — Simonides — Sappho

The poets whose adventures compose this chapter were real persons some of whose works yet remain, and their influence on poets who succeeded them is yet more important than their poetical remains. The adventures recorded of them in the following stories rest on the same authority as other narratives of the Age of Fable, that is, of the poets who have told them. In their present form, the first two are translated from the German, Arion from Schlegel and Ibycus from Schiller.

Arion

Arion was a famous musician, and dwelt at the court of Periander, king of Corinth, with whom he was a great favorite. There was to be a musical contest in Sicily, and Arion longed to compete for the prize. He told his wish to Periander, who besought him like a brother to give up the thought. "Pray stay with me," he said, "and be contented. He who strives to win may lose." Arion answered, "A wandering life best suits the free heart of a poet. The talent which a god bestowed on me, I would fain make a source of pleasure to others. And if I win the prize, how will the enjoyment of it be increased by the consciousness of my widespread fame!" He went, won the prize, and embarked with his wealth in a Corinthian ship for home. On the second morning after setting sail, the wind breathed mild and fair. "O Periander," he exclaimed, "dismiss your fears! Soon shall you forget them in my embrace. With what lavish offerings will we display our gratitude to the gods, and how merry will we be at the festal board!'' The wind and sea continued propitious. Not a cloud dimmed the firmament. He had not trusted too much to the ocean—but he had to man. He overheard the seamen exchanging hints with one another, and found they were plotting to possess themselves of his treasure. Presently they surrounded him loud and mutinous, and said, "Arion, you must die! If you would have a grave on shore, yield yourself to die on this spot; but if otherwise, cast yourself into the sea." "Will nothing satisfy you but my life?" said he. "Take my gold, and welcome. I willingly buy my life at that price." "No, no; we cannot spare you. Your life would be too dangerous to us. Where could we go to escape from Periander, if he should know that you had been robbed by us? Your gold would be of little use to us, if, on returning home, we could never more be free from fear." "Grant me, then," said he, "a last request, since nought will avail to save my life, that I may die as I have lived, as becomes a bard. When I shall have sung my death song, and my harp-strings shall have ceased to vibrate, then I will bid farewell to life, and yield uncomplaining to my fate." This prayer, like the others, would have been unheeded—they thought only of their booty—but to hear so famous a musician, that moved their rude hearts. "Suffer me," he added, "to arrange my dress. Apollo will not favor me unless I be clad in my minstrel garb."

He clothed his well-proportioned limbs in gold and purple fair to see, his tunic fell around him in graceful folds, jewels adorned his arms, his brow was crowned with a golden wreath, and over his neck and shoulders flowed his hair perfumed with odors. His left hand held the lyre, his right the ivory wand with which he struck its chords. Like one inspired, he seemed to drink the morning air and glitter in the morning ray. The seamen gazed with admiration. He strode forward to the vessel's side and looked down into the blue sea. Addressing his lyre, he sang, "Companion of my voice, come with me to the realm of shades. Though Cerberus may growl, we know the power of song can tame his rage. Ye heroes of Elysium, who have passed the darkling flood—ye happy souls, soon shall I join your band. Yet can ye relieve my grief? Alas, I leave my friend behind me. Thou, who didst find thy Eurydice, and lose her again as soon as found; when she had vanished like a dream, how didst thou hate the cheerful light! I must away, but I will not fear. The gods look down upon us. Ye who slay me unoffending, when I am no more, your time of trembling shall come. Ye Nereids, receive your guest, who throws himself upon your mercy!" So saying, he sprang into the deep sea. The waves covered him, and the seamen held on their way, fancying themselves safe from all danger of detection.

But the strains of his music had drawn round him the inhabitants of the deep to listen, and Dolphins followed the ship as if chained by a spell. While he struggled in the waves, a Dolphin offered him his back, and carried him mounted thereon safe to shore. At the spot where he landed, a monument of brass was afterwards erected upon the rocky shore, to preserve the memory of the event.

When Arion and the Dolphin parted, each to his own element, Arion thus poured forth his thanks. "Farewell, thou faithful, friendly fish! Would that I could reward thee; but thou canst not wend with me, nor I with thee. Companionship we may not have. May Galatea, queen of the deep, accord thee her favor, and thou, proud of the burden, draw her chariot over the smooth mirror of the deep."

Arion hastened from the shore, and soon saw before him the towers of Corinth. He journeyed on, harp in hand, singing as he went, full of love and happiness, forgetting his losses, and mindful only of what remained, his friend and his lyre. He entered the hospitable halls, and was soon clasped in the embrace of Periander. "I come back to thee, my friend," he said. "The talent which a god bestowed has been the delight of thousands, but false knaves have stripped me of my well-earned treasure; yet I retain the consciousness of wide-spread fame." Then he told Periander all the wonderful events that had befallen him, who heard him with amazement. "Shall such wickedness triumph?" said he. "Then in vain is power lodged in my hands. That we may discover the criminals, you must remain here in concealment, and so they will approach without suspicion." When the ship arrived in the harbor, he summoned the mariners before him. "Have you heard any thing of Arion?" he inquired. "I anxiously look for his return." They replied, "We left him well and prosperous in Tarentum." As they said these words, Arion stepped forth and faced them. His well-proportioned limbs were arrayed in gold and purple fair to see, his tunic fell around him in graceful folds, jewels adorned his arms, his brow was crowned with a golden wreath, and over his neck and shoulders flowed his hair perfumed with odors; his left hand held the lyre, his right the ivory wand with which he struck its chords. They fell prostrate at his feet, as if a lightning bolt had struck them. "We meant to murder him, and he has become a god. O Earth, open and receive us!" Then Periander spoke. "He lives, the master of the lay! Kind Heaven protects the poet's life. As for you, I invoke not the spirit of vengeance; Arion wishes not your blood. Ye slaves of avarice, begone! Seek some barbarous land, and never may aught beautiful delight your souls!"

Spenser represents Arion, mounted on his dolphin, accompanying the train of Neptune and Amphitrite:

"Then was there heard a most celestial sound
   Of dainty music which did next ensue,
   And, on the floating waters as enthroned,
   Arion with his harp unto him drew
   The ears and hearts of all that goodly crew;
   Even when as yet the dolphin which him bore
   Through the Ægean Seas from pirates' view,

> Stood still, by him astonished at his lore,
> And all the raging seas for joy forgot to roar.''

Byron, in his ''Childe Harold,'' Canto II, alludes to the story of
Arion, when, describing his voyage, he represents one of the seamen
making music to entertain the rest:

> ''The moon is up; by Heaven a lovely eve!
> Long streams of light o'er dancing waves expand;
> Now lads on shore may sigh and maids believe;
> Such be our fate when we return to land!
> Meantime some rude Arion's restless hand
> Wakes the brisk harmony that sailors love;
> A circle there of merry listeners stand,
> Or to some well-known measure featly move,
> Thoughtless, as if on shore they still were free to rove.''

Ibycus

In order to understand the story of Ibycus which follows it is necessary to remember, first, that the theatres of the ancients were immense
fabrics capable of containing from ten to thirty thousand spectators,
and as they were used only on festal occasions, and admission was free
to all, they were usually filled. They were without roofs and open to the
sky, and the performances were in the daytime. Second, the appalling
representation of the Furies is not exaggerated in the story. It is recorded
that Æschylus, the tragic poet, having on one occasion represented the
Furies in a chorus of fifty performers, the terror of the spectators was
such that many fainted and were thrown into convulsions, and the
magistrates forbade a like representation for the future.

Ibycus, the pious poet, was on his way to the chariot races and
musical competitions held at the Isthmus of Corinth, which attracted all
of Grecian lineage. Apollo had bestowed on him the gift of song, the
honeyed lips of the poet, and he pursued his way with lightsome step,
full of the god. Already the towers of Corinth crowning the height appeared in view, and he had entered with pious awe the sacred grove of
Neptune. No living object was in sight, only a flock of cranes flew overhead taking the same course as himself in their migration to a southern
clime. ''Good luck to you, ye friendly squadrons,'' he exclaimed, ''my
companions from across the sea. I take your company for a good omen.
We come from far and fly in search of hospitality. May both of us meet
that kind reception which shields the stranger guest from harm!''

He paced briskly on, and soon was in the middle of the wood. There
suddenly, at a narrow pass, two robbers stepped forth and barred his
way. He must yield or fight. But his hand, accustomed to the lyre, and
not to the strife of arms, sank powerless. He called for help on men and
gods, but his cry reached no defender's ear. ''Then here must I die,''
said he, ''in a strange land, unlamented, cut off by the hand of outlaws,
and see none to avenge my cause.'' Sore wounded he sank to the earth,

when hoarse screamed the cranes overhead. "Take up my cause, ye cranes," he said, "since no voice but yours answers to my cry." So saying he closed his eyes in death.

The body, despoiled and mangled, was found, and though disfigured with wounds, was recognized by the friend in Corinth who had expected him as a guest. "Is it thus I find you restored to me?" he exclaimed; "I who hoped to entwine your temples with the wreath of triumph in the strife of song!"

The guests assembled at the festival heard the tidings with dismay. All Greece felt the wound, every heart owned its loss. They crowded round the tribunal of the magistrates, and demanded vengeance on the murderers and expiation with their blood.

But what trace or mark shall point out the perpetrator from amidst the vast multitude attracted by the splendor of the feast? Did he fall by the hands of robbers or did some private enemy slay him? The all-discerning sun alone can tell, for no other eye beheld it. Yet not improbably the murderer even now walks in the midst of the throng, and enjoys the fruits of his crime, while vengeance seeks for him in vain. Perhaps in their own temple's enclosure he defies the gods, mingling freely in this throng of men that now presses into the amphitheatre.

For now crowded together, row on row, the multitude fill the seats till it seems as if the very fabric would give way. The murmur of voices sounds like the roar of the sea, while the circles widening in their ascent rise, tier on tier, as if they would reach the sky.

And now the vast assemblage listens to the awful voice of the chorus personating the Furies, which in solemn guise advances with measured step, and moves around the circuit of the theatre. Can they be mortal women who compose that awful group, and can that vast concourse of silent forms be living beings!

The Choristers, clad in black, bore in their fleshless hands torches blazing with a pitchy flame. Their cheeks were bloodless, and in place of hair, writhing and swelling serpents curled around their brows. Forming a circle, these awful beings sang their hymn, rending the hearts of the guilty, and enchaining all their faculties. It rose and swelled, overpowering the sound of the instruments, stealing the judgment, palsying the heart, curdling the blood.

"Happy the man who keeps his heart pure from guilt and crime! Him we avengers touch not; he treads the path of life secure from us. But woe! woe! to him who has done the deed of secret murder. We the fearful family of Night fasten ourselves upon his whole being. Thinks he by flight to escape us? We fly still faster in pursuit, twine our snakes around his feet and bring him to the ground. Unwearied we pursue; no pity checks our course; still on and on to the end of life, we give him no peace nor rest." Thus the Eumenides sang, and moved in solemn cadence, while stillness like the stillness of death sat over the whole assembly as if in the presence of superhuman beings; and then in solemn march completing the circuit of the theatre, they passed out at the back of the stage.

Every heart fluttered between illusion and reality, and every breast panted with undefined terror, quailing before the awful power that watches secret crimes and winds unseen the skein of destiny. At that moment a cry burst forth from one of the uppermost benches—"Look! look! comrade, yonder are the cranes of Ibycus!" And suddenly there appeared sailing across the sky a dark object which a moment's inspection showed to be a flock of cranes flying directly over the theatre. "Of Ibycus! did he say?" The beloved name revived the sorrow in every breast. As wave follows wave over the face of the sea, so ran from mouth to mouth the words, "Of Ibycus! him whom we all lament, whom some murderer's hand laid low! What have the cranes to do with him?" And louder grew the swell of voices, while like a lightning's flash the thought sped through every heart, "Observe the power of the Eumenides! The pious poet shall be avenged! the murderer has informed against himself. Seize the man who uttered that cry and the other to whom he spoke!"

The culprit would gladly have recalled his words, but it was too late. The faces of the murderers pale with terror betrayed their guilt. The people took them before the judge, they confessed their crime and suffered the punishment that they deserved.

Simonides

Simonides was one of the most prolific of the early poets of Greece, but only a few fragments of his compositions have descended to us. He wrote hymns, triumphal odes, and elegies. In the last species of composition he particularly excelled. His genius was inclined to the pathetic, and none could touch with truer effect the chords of human sympathy. The "Lamentation of Danae," the most important of the fragments which remain of his poetry, is based upon the tradition that Danae and her infant son were confined by order of her father Acrisius in a chest and set adrift on the sea. The chest floated towards the island of Seriphus, where both were rescued by Dictys, a fisherman, and carried to Polydectes, king of the country, who received and protected them. The child Perseus when grown up became a famous hero, whose adventures have been recorded in a previous chapter.

Simonides passed much of his life at the courts of princes and often employed his talents in panegyric and festal odes, receiving his reward from the munificence of those whose exploits he celebrated. This employment was not derogatory, but closely resembles that of the earliest bards, such as Demodocus, described by Homer, or of Homer himself as recorded by tradition.

On one occasion when residing at the court of Scopas, king of Thessaly, the prince desired him to prepare a poem in celebration of his exploits, to be recited at a banquet. In order to diversify his theme, Simonides who was celebrated for his piety introduced into his poem the exploits of Castor and Pollux. Such digressions were not unusual with the poets on similar occasions, and one might suppose an ordinary mortal might have been content to share the praises of the sons of Leda. But vanity is exacting; and as Scopas sat at his festal board among his courtiers and sycophants, he grudged every verse that did not rehearse his own praises. When Simonides approached to receive the promised reward Scopas bestowed but half the expected sum, saying, "Here is payment for my portion of thy performance, Castor and Pollux will doubtless compensate thee for so much as relates to them." The disconcerted poet returned to his seat amidst the laughter which followed the great man's jest. In a little time he received a message that two young men on horseback were waiting without and anxious to see him. Simonides hastened to the door, but looked in vain for the visitors. Scarcely however had he left the banquetting hall when the roof fell in with a loud crash, burying Scopas and all his guests beneath the ruins. On inquiring as to the appearance of the young men who had sent for him, Simonides was satisfied that they were no other than Castor and Pollux themselves.

Sappho

Sappho was a poetess who flourished in a very early age of Greek literature. Of her works few fragments remain, but they are enough to establish her claim to eminent poetical genius. The story of Sappho commonly alluded to is that she was passionately in love with a beautiful youth named Phaon, and failing to obtain a return of affection she threw herself from the promontory of Leucadia into the sea, under a superstition that those who should take that 'Lover's-leap' would, if not destroyed, be cured of their love.

Byron alludes to the story of Sappho in "Childe Harold," Canto II:

"Childe Harold sailed and passed the barren spot
   Where sad Penelope o'erlooked the wave,
   And onward viewed the mount, not yet forgot,
   The lover's refuge and the Lesbian's grave.
   Dark Sappho! could not verse immortal save
   That breast imbued with such immortal fire?

" 'Twas on a Grecian autumn's gentle eve
   Childe Harold hailed Leucadia's cape afar"; etc.

Those who wish to know more of Sappho and her 'leap' are referred to the "Spectator," Nos. 223 and 229. See also Moore's "Evenings in Greece."

Endymion—Orion—Aurora and Tithonus—Acis and Galatea

Endymion was a beautiful youth who fed his flock on Mount Latmos. One calm, clear night, Diana, the Moon, looked down and saw him sleeping. The cold heart of the virgin goddess was warmed by his surpassing beauty, and she came down to him, kissed him, and watched over him while he slept.

Another story was that Jupiter bestowed on him the gift of perpetual youth united with perpetual sleep. Of one so gifted we can have but few adventures to record. Diana it was said took care that his fortunes should not suffer by his inactive life, for she made his flock increase, and guarded his sheep and lambs from the wild beasts.

The story of Endymion has a peculiar charm from the human meaning which it so thinly veils. We see in Endymion the young poet, his fancy and his heart seeking in vain for that which can satisfy them, finding his favorite hour in the quiet moonlight, and nursing there beneath the beams of the bright and silent witness the melancholy and the ardor which consumes him. The story suggests aspiring and poetic love, a life spent more in dreams than in reality, and an early and welcome death.

S.G.B.

The "Endymion" of Keats is a wild and fanciful poem, containing some exquisite poetry, as this, to the moon:

> "The sleeping kine
> Couched in thy brightness dream of fields divine.
> Innumerable mountains rise, and rise,
> Ambitious for the hallowing of thine eyes,
> And yet thy benediction passeth not
> One obscure hiding-place, one little spot
> Where pleasure may be sent; the nested wren
> Has thy fair face within its tranquil ken;" etc., etc.

Dr. Young in the "Night Thoughts" alludes to Endymion thus:

> "These thoughts, O Night, are thine;
> From thee they came like lovers' secret sighs,
> While others slept. So Cynthia, poets feign,
> In shadows veiled, soft, sliding from her sphere,
> Her shepherd cheered, of her enamoured less
> Than I of thee."

Fletcher, in the "Faithful Shepherdess," tells,

"How the pale Phœbe, hunting in a grove,
 First saw the boy Endymion, from whose eyes
 She took eternal fire that never dies;
 How she conveyed him softly in a sleep,
 His temples bound with poppy, to the steep
 Head of old Latmos, where she stoops each night,
 Gilding the mountain with her brother's light,
 To kiss her sweetest."

Orion

Orion was the son of Neptune. He was a handsome giant and a mighty hunter. His father gave him the power of wading through the depths of the sea, or as others say of walking on its surface.

Orion loved Merope, the daughter of Œnopion, king of Chios, and sought her in marriage. He cleared the island of wild beasts, and brought the spoils of the chase as presents to his beloved; but as Œnopion constantly deferred his consent, Orion attempted to gain possession of the maiden by violence. Her father, incensed at this conduct, having made Orion drunk, deprived him of his sight and cast him out on the sea shore. The blinded hero followed the sound of a Cyclops' hammer till he reached Lemnos, and came to the forge of Vulcan, who, taking pity on him, gave him Kedalion, one of his men, to be his guide to the abode of the sun. Placing Kedalion on his shoulders, Orion proceeded to the east, and there meeting the sun-god, was restored to sight by his beam.

After this he dwelt as a hunter with Diana, with whom he was a favorite, and it is even said she was about to marry him. Her brother was highly displeased and often chid her, but to no purpose. One day, observing Orion wading through the sea with his head just above the water, Apollo pointed it out to his sister and maintained that she could not hit that black thing on the sea. The archer goddess discharged a shaft with fatal aim. The waves rolled the dead body of Orion to the land, and bewailing her fatal error with many tears, Diana placed him among the stars, where he appears as a giant, with a girdle, sword, lion's skin, and club. Sirius, his dog, follows him, and the Pleiads fly before him.

The Pleiads were daughters of Atlas, and nymphs of Diana's train. One day Orion saw them and became enamoured and pursued them. In their distress they prayed to the gods to change their form, and Jupiter in pity turned them into pigeons, and then made them a constellation in the sky. Though their number was seven, only six stars are visible, for Electra, one of them, it is said left her place that she might not behold the ruin of Troy, for that city was founded by her son Dardanus. The sight had such an effect on her sisters that they have looked pale ever since.

Mr. Longfellow has a poem on the "Occultation of Orion." The following lines are those in which he alludes to the mythic story. We must premise that on the celestial globe Orion is represented as robed in a lion's skin, and wielding a club. At the moment the stars of the constellation one by one were quenched in the light of the moon, the poet tells us—

"Down fell the red skin of the lion
Into the river at his feet.
His mighty club no longer beat
The forehead of the bull; but he
Reeled as of yore beside the sea,
When blinded by Œnopion
    He sought the blacksmith at his forge,
    And climbing up the narrow gorge,
Fixed his blank eyes upon the sun."

Tennyson has a different theory of the Pleiads.

"Many a night I saw the Pleiads, rising through the mellow shade,
Glitter like a swarm of fire-flies tangled in a silver braid."
Locksley Hall

Byron alludes to the lost Pleiad.

"Like the lost Pleiad seen no more below."

See also Mrs. Hemans's verses on the same subject.

Aurora and Tithonus

The goddess of the Dawn, like her sister the Moon, was at times inspired with the love of mortals. Her greatest favorite was Tithonus, son of Laomedon, king of Troy. She stole him away, and prevailed on Jupiter to grant him immortality; but forgetting to have youth joined in the gift, after some time she began to discern, to her great mortification, that he was growing old. When his hair was quite white she left his society; but he still had the range of her palace, lived on ambrosial food and was clad in celestial raiment. At length he lost the power of using his limbs, and then she shut him up in his chamber, whence his feeble voice might at times be heard. Finally she turned him into a grasshopper.

Memnon was the son of Aurora and Tithonus. He was king of the Æthiopians and dwelt in the extreme east, on the shore of Ocean. He came with his warriors to assist the kindred of his father in the war of Troy. King Priam received him with great honors, and listened with admiration to his narrative of the wonders of the ocean shore.

The very day after his arrival, Memnon, impatient of repose, led his troops to the field. Antilochus, the brave son of Nestor, fell by his hand, and the Greeks were put to flight, when Achilles appeared and restored the battle. A long and doubtful contest ensued between him and the son of Aurora; at length, victory declared for Achilles, Memnon fell, and the Trojans fled in dismay.

Aurora, who from her station in the sky had viewed with apprehension the danger of her son, when she saw him fall directed his brothers the Winds to convey his body to the banks of the river Esepus in Paphlagonia. In the evening, Aurora came, accompanied by the Hours and the Pleiads, and wept and lamented over her son. Night, in sympathy with her grief, spread the heaven with clouds; all nature mourned for the offspring of the Dawn. The Æthiopians raised his tomb on the banks of the stream in the grove of the Nymphs, and Jupiter caused the sparks and cinders of his funeral pile to be turned into birds, which, dividing into two flocks, fought over the pile till they fell into the flame. Every year at the anniversary of his death they return and celebrate his obsequies in like manner. Aurora remains inconsolable for the loss of her son. Her tears still flow, and may be seen at early morning in the form of dew-drops on the grass.

Unlike most of the marvels of ancient mythology, there still exist some memorials of this. On the banks of the river Nile, in Egypt, are two colossal statues, one of which is said to be the statue of Memnon. Ancient writers record that when the first rays of the rising sun fall upon this statue, a sound is heard to issue from it which they compare to the snapping of a harpstring. There is some doubt about the identification of the existing statue with the one described by the ancients, and the mysterious sounds are still more doubtful. Yet there are not wanting some modern testimonies to their being still audible. It has been suggested that sounds produced by confined air making its escape from crevices or caverns in the rocks may have given some ground for the story. Sir Gardner Wilkinson, a late traveller, of the highest authority, examined the statue itself, and discovered that it was hollow, and that "in the lap of the statue is a stone, which on being struck emits a metallic sound, that might still be made use of to deceive a visitor who was predisposed to believe its powers."

The vocal statue of Memnon is a favorite subject of allusion with the poets. Darwin in his "Botanic Garden" says—

> "So to the sacred Sun in Memnon's fane
> Spontaneous concords choired the matin strain;
> Touched by his orient beam responsive rings
> The living lyre and vibrates all its strings;
> Accordant aisles the tender tones prolong,
> And holy echoes swell the adoring song."

Book I., 1, 182

Acis and Galatea

Scylla was a fair virgin of Sicily, a favorite of the Sea-Nymphs. She had many suitors, but repelled them all, and would go to the grotto of Galatea, and tell her how she was persecuted. One day the goddess, while Scylla dressed her hair, listened to the story, and then replied, "Yet, maiden, your persecutors are of the not ungentle race of men, whom if you will you can repel; but I, the daughter of Nereus, and protected by such a band of sisters, found no escape from the passion of the Cyclops but in the depths of the sea;'' and tears stopped her utterance, which when the pitying maiden had wiped away with her delicate finger, and soothed the goddess, "Tell me, dearest," said she, "the cause of your grief." Galatea then said, "Acis was the son of Faunus and a Naiad. His father and mother loved him dearly, but their love was not equal to mine. For the beautiful youth attached himself to me alone, and he was just sixteen years old, the down just beginning to darken his cheeks. As much as I sought his society, so much did the Cyclops seek mine; and if you ask me whether my love for Acis or my hatred of Polyphemus was the stronger, I cannot tell you; they were in equal measure. O Venus, how great is thy power! this fierce giant, the terror of the woods, whom no hapless stranger escaped unharmed, who defied even Jove himself, learned to feel what love was, and, touched with a passion for me, forgot his flocks and his well-stored caverns. Then for the first time he began to take some care of his appearance, and to try to make himself agreeable; he harrowed those coarse locks of his with a comb, and mowed his beard with a sickle, looked at his harsh features in the water and composed his countenance. His love of slaughter, his fierceness and thirst of blood prevailed no more, and ships that touched at his island went away in safety. He paced up and down the sea shore, imprinting huge tracks with his heavy tread, and, when weary, lay tranquilly in his cave.

"There is a cliff which projects into the sea, which washes it on either side. Thither one day the huge Cyclops ascended, and sat down while his flocks spread themselves around. Laying down his staff which would have served for a mast to hold a vessel's sail, and taking his instrument compacted of numerous pipes, he made the hills and the waters echo the music of his song. I lay hid under a rock by the side of my beloved Acis, and listened to the distant strain. It was full of extravagant praises of my beauty, mingled with passionate reproaches of my coldness and cruelty.

"When he had finished, he rose up and like a raging bull, that cannot stand still, wandered off into the woods. Acis and I thought no more of him, till on a sudden he came to a spot which gave him a view of us as we sat. 'I see you,' he exclaimed, 'and I will make this the last of your love-meetings.' His voice was a roar such as an angry Cyclops alone could utter. Ætna trembled at the sound. I, overcome with terror, plunged into the water. Acis turned and fled, crying, 'Save me, Galatea, save me, my parents!' The Cyclops pursued him, and tearing a rock from the side of the mountain hurled it at him. Though only a corner of it touched him it overwhelmed him."

"All that fate left in my power I did for Acis. I endowed him with the honors of his grandfather the river-god. The purple blood flowed out from under the rock, but by degrees grew paler and looked like the stream of a river rendered turbid by rains, and in time it became clear. The rock cleaved open, and the water, as it gushed from the chasm, uttered a pleasing murmur."

Thus Acis was changed into a river, and the river retains the name of Acis.

Dryden, in his "Cymon and Iphigenia," has told the story of a clown converted into a gentleman by the power of love, in a way that shows traces of kindred to the old story of Galatea and the Cyclops.

> "What not his father's care nor tutor's art
>   Could plant with pains in his unpolished heart,
>   The best instructor, Love, at once inspired,
>   As barren grounds to fruitfulness are fired.
>   Love taught him shame, and shame with love at strife
>   Soon taught the sweet civilities of life."
>
> . . . .

27

The Trojan War

Minerva was the goddess of wisdom, but on one occasion she did a very foolish thing; she entered into competition with Juno and Venus for the prize of beauty. It happened thus: At the nuptials of Peleus and Thetis all the gods were invited with the exception of Eris, or Discord. Enraged at her exclusion, the goddess threw a golden apple among the guests, with the inscription, "For the fairest." Thereupon Juno, Venus, and Minerva each claimed the apple. Jupiter, not willing to decide in so delicate a matter, sent the goddesses to Mount Ida, where the beautiful shepherd Paris was tending his flocks, and to him was committed the decision. The goddesses accordingly appeared before him. Juno promised him power and riches, Minerva glory and renown in war, and Venus the fairest of women for his wife, each attempting to bias his decision in her own favor. Paris decided in favor of Venus and gave her the golden apple, thus making the two other goddesses his enemies. Under the protection of Venus, Paris sailed to Greece, and was hospitably received by Menelaus, king of Sparta. Now Helen, the wife of Menelaus, was the very woman whom Venus had destined for Paris, the fairest of her sex. She had been sought as a bride by numerous suitors, and before her decision was made known, they all, at the suggestion of Ulysses, one of their number, took an oath that they would defend her from all injury and avenge her cause if necessary. She chose Menelaus, and was living with him happily when Paris became their guest. Paris, aided by Venus, persuaded her to elope with him, and carried her to Troy, whence arose the famous Trojan war, the theme of the greatest poems of antiquity, those of Homer and Virgil.

Menelaus called upon his brother chieftains of Greece to fulfil their pledge, and join him in his efforts to recover his wife. They generally came forward, but Ulysses, who had married Penelope and was very happy in his wife and child, had no disposition to embark in such a troublesome affair. He therefore hung back and Palamedes was sent to urge him. When Palamedes arrived at Ithaca, Ulysses pretended to be mad. He yoked an ass and an ox together to the plough and began to sow salt. Palamedes, to try him, placed the infant Telemachus before the plough, whereupon the father turned the plough aside, showing plainly that he was no madman, and after that could no longer refuse to fulfil his promise. Being now himself gained for the undertaking he lent his aid to bring in other reluctant chiefs, especially Achilles. This hero was the son of that Thetis at whose marriage the apple of Discord had been thrown among the goddesses. Thetis was herself one of the immortals, a sea-nymph, and knowing that her son was fated to perish before Troy if he went on the expedition, she endeavored to prevent his going. She sent him away to the court of King Lycomedes, and induced him to conceal himself in the disguise of a maiden among the daughters of the king. Ulysses, hearing he was there, went disguised as a merchant to the palace and offered for sale female ornaments, among which he had placed some arms. While the king's daughters were engrossed with the other contents of the merchant's pack, Achilles handled the weapons and thereby betrayed himself to the keen eye of Ulysses, who found no great difficulty in persuading him to disregard his mother's prudent counsels and join his countrymen in the war.

Priam was king of Troy, and Paris, the shepherd and seducer of Helen, was his son. Paris had been brought up in obscurity, because there were certain ominous forebodings connected with him from his infancy that he would be the ruin of the state. These forebodings seemed at length likely to be realized, for the Grecian armament now in preparation was the greatest that had ever been fitted out. Agamemnon, king of Mycenæ, and brother of the injured Menelaus, was chosen commander-in-chief. Achilles was their most illustrious warrior. After him ranked Ajax, gigantic in size and of great courage, but dull of intellect, Diomede, second only to Achilles in all the qualities of a hero, Ulysses, famous for his sagacity, and Nestor, the oldest of the Grecian chiefs, and one to whom they all looked up for counsel. But Troy was no feeble enemy. Priam the king was now old, but he had been a wise prince and had strengthened his state by good government at home and numerous alliances with his neighbors. But the principal stay and support of his throne was his son Hector, one of the noblest characters painted by heathen antiquity. He felt, from the first, a presentiment of the fall of his country, but still persevered in his heroic resistance, yet by no means justified the wrong which brought this danger upon her. He was united in marriage with Andromache, and as a husband and father his character was not less admirable than as a warrior. The principal leaders on the side of the Trojans, besides Hector, were Æneas and Deiphobus, Glaucus and Sarpetlon.

After two years of preparation the Greek fleet and army assembled in the port of Aulis in Boeotia. Here Agamemnon in hunting killed a stag which was sacred to Diana, and the goddess in return visited the army with pestilence, and produced a calm which prevented the ships from leaving the port. Calchas the soothsayer thereupon announced that the wrath of the virgin goddess could only be appeased by the sacrifice of a virgin on her altar, and that none other but the daughter of the offender would be acceptable. Agamemnon, however reluctant, yielded his consent, and the maiden Iphigenia was sent for under the pretence that she was to be married to Achilles. When she was about to be sacrificed the goddess relented and snatched her away, leaving a hind in her place, and Iphigenia enveloped in a cloud was carried to Tauris, where Diana made her priestess of her temple.

Tennyson, in his "Dream of Fair Women," makes Iphigenia thus describe her feelings at the moment of sacrifice; the moment represented in our engraving:

"I was cut off from hope in that sad place,
    Which yet to name my spirit loathes and fears;
My father held his hand upon his face;
        I, blinded by my tears,

"Still strove to speak; my voice was thick with sighs,
    As in a dream. Dimly I could descry
The stern black-bearded kings, with wolfish eyes,
        Waiting to see me die.

"The tall masts quivered as they lay afloat,
    The temples and the people and the shore;
One drew a sharp knife through my tender throat
        Slowly—and—nothing more."

The wind now proving fair the fleet made sail and brought the forces to the coast of Troy. The Trojans came to oppose their landing, and at the first onset Protesilaus fell by the hand of Hector. Protesilaus had left at home his wife Laodamia, who was most tenderly attached to him. When the news of his death reached her she implored the gods to be allowed to converse with him only three hours. The request was granted. Mercury led Protesilaus back to the upper world, and when he died a second time Laodamia died with him. There was a story that the nymphs planted elm trees round his grave which grew very well till they were high enough to command a view of Troy, and then withered away, while fresh branches sprang from the roots.

Wordsworth has taken the story of Protesilaus and Laodamia for the subject of a poem. It seems the oracle had declared that victory should be the lot of that party from which should fall the first victim to the war. The poet represents Protesilaus, on his brief return to earth, as relating to Laodamia the story of his fate:

"The wished-for wind was given; I then revolved
    The oracle, upon the silent sea;
And if no worthier led the way, resolved
    That of a thousand vessels mine should be

The foremost prow impressing to the strand,—
Mine the first blood that tinged the Trojan sand.

"Yet bitter, ofttimes bitter was the pang
    When of thy loss I thought, beloved wife!
On thee too fondly did my memory hang,
    And on the joys we shared in mortal life,
The paths which we had trod,—these fountains, flowers;
My new planned cities and unfinished towers.

"But should suspense permit the foe to cry,
    'Behold thy tremble! haughty their array,
Yet of their number no one dares to die?'
    In soul I swept the indignity away:
Old frailties then recurred: but lofty thought
In act imbodied my deliverance wrought.

*   *   *   *   *

                              "——upon the side
    Of Hellespont (such faith was entertained
A knot of spiry trees for ages grew
    From out the tomb of him for whom she died;
    And ever when such stature they had gained
That Ilium's walls were subject to their view,
The trees' tall summits withered at the sight,
A constant interchange of growth and blight!"

The Iliad

The war continued without decisive results for nine years. Then an event occurred which seemed likely to be fatal to the cause of the Greeks, and that was a quarrel between Achilles and Agamemnon. It is at this point that the great poem of Homer, the *Iliad,* begins. The Greeks, though unsuccessful against Troy, had taken the neighboring and allied cities, and in the division of the spoil a female captive, by name Chryseis, daughter of Chryses, priest of Apollo, had fallen to the share of Agamemnon. Chryses came bearing the sacred emblems of his office, and begged the release of his daughter. Agamemnon refused. Thereupon Chryses implored Apollo to afflict the Greeks till they should be forced to yield their prey. Apollo granted the prayer of his priest, and sent pestilence into the Grecian camp. Then a council was called to deliberate how to allay the wrath of the gods and avert the plague. Achilles boldly charged their misfortunes upon Agamemnon as caused by his witholding Chryseis. Agamemnon, enraged, consented to relinquish his captive, but demanded that Achilles should yield to him in her stead Briseis, a maiden who had fallen to Achilles' share in the division of the spoil. Achilles submitted, but forthwith declared that he would take no further part in the war. He withdrew his forces from the general camp and openly avowed his intention of returning home to Greece.

The gods and goddesses interested themselves as much in this famous war as the parties themselves. It was well known to them that fate had decreed that Troy should fall, at last, if her enemies should persevere and not voluntarily abandon the enterprise. Yet there was room enough left for chance to excite by turns the hopes and fears of the powers above who took part with either side. Juno and Minerva, in consequence of the slight put upon their charms by Paris, were hostile to the Trojans; Venus for the opposite cause favored them. Venus enlisted her admirer Mars on the same side, but Neptune favored the Greeks. Apollo was neutral, sometimes taking one side, sometimes the other, and Jove himself, though he loved the good King Priam, yet exercised a degree of impartiality; not however without exceptions.

Thetis, the mother of Achilles, warmly resented the injury done to her son. She repaired immediately to Jove's palace and besought him to make the Greeks repent of their injustice to Achilles by granting success to the Trojan arms. Jupiter consented; and in the battle which ensued the Trojans were completely successful. The Greeks were driven from the field and took refuge in their ships.

Then Agamemnon called a council of his wisest and bravest chiefs. Nestor advised that an embassy should be sent to Achilles to persuade him to return to the field; that Agamemnon should yield the maiden, the cause of the dispute, with ample gifts to atone for the wrong he had done. Agamemnon consented, and Ulysses, Ajax, and Phœnix were sent to carry to Achilles the penitent message. They performed that duty, but Achilles was deaf to their entreaties. He positively refused to return to the field, and persisted in his resolution to embark for Greece without delay.

The Greeks had constructed a rampart around their ships, and now instead of besieging Troy they were in a manner besieged themselves, within their rampart. The next day after the unsuccessful embassy to Achilles, a battle was fought, and the Trojans, favored by Jove, were successful, and succeeded in forcing a passage through the Grecian rampart, and were about to set fire to the ships. Neptune, seeing the Greeks so pressed, came to their rescue. He appeared in the form of Calchas the prophet, encouraged the warriors with his shouts and appealed to each individually till he raised their ardor to such a pitch that they forced the Trojans to give way. Ajax performed prodigies of valor, and at length encountered Hector. Ajax shouted defiance, to which Hector replied, and hurled his lance at the huge warrior. It was well aimed and struck Ajax where the belts that bore his sword and shield crossed each other on the breast. The double guard prevented its penetrating and it fell harmless. Then Ajax seizing a huge stone, one of those that served to prop the ships, hurled it at Hector. It struck him in the neck and stretched him on the plain. His followers instantly seized him and bore him off stunned and wounded.

While Neptune was thus aiding the Greeks and driving back the Trojans, Jupiter saw nothing of what was going on, for his attention had been drawn from the field by the wiles of Juno. That goddess had arrayed herself in all her charms, and to crown all had borrowed of Venus her girdle called Cestus, which had the effect to heighten the wearer's charms to such a degree that they were quite irresistible. So prepared,

Juno went to join her husband, who sat on Olympus watching the battle. When he beheld her she looked so charming that the fondness of his early love revived, and, forgetting the contending armies and all other affairs of state, he thought only of her and let the battle go as it would.

But this absorption did not continue long, and when, upon turning his eyes downward, he beheld Hector stretched on the plain almost lifeless from pain and bruises, he dismissed Juno in a rage, commanding her to send Iris and Apollo to him. When Iris came he sent her with a stern message to Neptune, ordering him instantly to quit the field. Apollo was despatched to heal Hector's bruises and to inspirit his heart. These orders were obeyed with such speed that while the battle still raged, Hector returned to the field and Neptune betook himself to his own dominions.

An arrow from Paris's bow wounded Machaon, son of Æsculapius, who inherited his father's art of healing, and was therefore of great value to the Greeks as their surgeon, besides being one of their bravest warriors. Nestor took Machaon in his chariot and conveyed him from the field. As they passed the ships of Achilles, that hero, looking out over the field, saw the chariot of Nestor and recognized the old chief, but could not discern who the wounded chief was. So calling Patroclus, his companion and dearest friend, he sent him to Nestor's tent to inquire.

Patroclus, arriving at Nestor's tent, saw Machaon wounded, and having told the cause of his coming would have hastened away, but Nestor detained him, to tell him the extent of the Grecian calamities. He reminded him also how, at the time of departing for Troy, Achilles and himself had been charged by their respective fathers with different advice; Achilles to aspire to the highest pitch of glory, Patroclus, as the elder, to keep watch over his friend, and to guide his inexperience. "Now," said Nestor, "is the time for such influence. If the gods so please, thou mayest win him back to the common cause; but if not let him at least send his soldiers to the field, and come thou Patroclus clad in his armor, and perhaps the very sight of it may drive back the Trojans."

Patroclus was strongly moved with this address, and hastened back to Achilles revolving in his mind all he had seen and heard. He told the prince the sad condition of affairs at the camp of their late associates; Diomede, Ulysses, Agamemnon, Machaon, all wounded, the rampart broken down, the enemy among the ships preparing to burn them, and thus to cut off all means of return to Greece. While they spoke the flames burst forth from one of the ships. Achilles, at the sight, relented so far as to grant Patroclus his request to lead the Myrmidons (for so were Achilles' soldiers called) to the field, and to lend him his armor that he might thereby strike more terror into the minds of the Trojans. Without delay the soldiers were marshalled, Patroclus put on the radiant armor and mounted the chariot of Achilles, and led forth the men ardent for battle. But before he went, Achilles strictly charged him that he should be content with repelling the foe. "Seek not," said he, "to press the Trojans without me, lest thou add still more to the disgrace already mine." Then exhorting the troops to do their best he dismissed them full of ardor to the fight.

Patroclus and his Myrmidons at once plunged into the contest where it raged hottest; at the sight of which the joyful Grecians shouted and the ships reechoed the acclaim. The Trojans, at the sight of the well-known armor, struck with terror, looked everywhere for refuge. First those who had got possession of the ship and set it on fire left and allowed the Grecians to retake it and extinguish the flames. Then the rest of the Trojans fled in dismay. Ajax, Menelaus, and the two sons of Nestor performed prodigies of valor. Hector was forced to turn his horses' heads and retire from the enclosure, leaving his men entangled in the fosse to escape as they could. Patroclus drove them before him, slaying many, none daring to make a stand against him.

At last Sarpedon, son of Jove, ventured to oppose himself in fight to Patroclus. Jupiter looked down upon him and would have snatched him from the fate which awaited him, but Juno hinted that if he did so it would induce all others of the inhabitants of heaven to interpose in like manner whenever any of their offspring were endangered; to which reason Jove yielded. Sarpedon threw his spear but missed Patroclus, but Patroclus threw his with better success. It pierced Sarpedon's breast and he fell, and, calling to his friends to save his body from the foe, expired. Then a furious contest arose for the possession of the corpse. The Greeks succeeded and stripped Sarpedon of his armor; but Jove would not allow the remains of his son to be dishonored, and by his command Apollo snatched from the midst of the combatants the body of Sarpedon and committed it to the care of the twin brothers Death and Sleep, by whom it was transported to Lycia, the native land of Sarpedon, where it received due funeral rites.

Thus far Patroclus had succeeded to his utmost wish in repelling the Trojans and relieving his countrymen, but now came a change of fortune. Hector, borne in his chariot, confronted him. Patroclus threw a vast stone at Hector, which missed its aim, but smote Cebriones, the charioteer, and knocked him from the car. Hector leaped from the chariot to rescue his friend, and Patroclus also descended to complete his victory. Thus the two heroes met face to face. At this decisive moment the poet, as if reluctant to give Hector the glory, records that Phœbus took part against Patroclus. He struck the helmet from his head and the lance from his hand. At the same moment an obscure Trojan wounded him in the back, and Hector pressing forward pierced him with his spear. He fell mortally wounded.

Then arose a tremendous conflict for the body of Patroclus, but his armor was at once taken possession by Hector, who retiring a short distance divested himself of his own armor and put on that of Achilles, then returned to the fight. Ajax and Menelaus defended the body, and Hector and his bravest warriors struggled to capture it. The battle raged with equal fortunes, when Jove enveloped the whole face of heaven with a dark cloud. The lightning flashed, the thunder roared, and Ajax, looking round for someone whom he might despatch to Achilles to tell him of the death of his friend and of the imminent danger that his remains would fall into the hands of the enemy, could see no suitable messenger. It was then that he exclaimed in those famous lines so often quoted,

> "Father of heaven and earth! deliver thou
> Achaia's host from darkness; clear the skies;
> Give day; and, since thy sovereign will is such,
> Destruction with it; but, O, give us day."
>
> *Cowper*

Or, as rendered by Pope,

> "Lord of earth and air!
> O king! O father! hear my humble prayer!
> Dispel this cloud, the light of heaven restore;
> Give me to see and Ajax asks no more;
> If Greece must perish we thy will obey,
> But let us perish in the face of day."

Jupiter heard the prayer and dispersed the clouds. Then Ajax sent Antilochus to Achilles with the intelligence of Patroclus's death, and of the conflict raging for his remains. The Greeks at last succeeded in bearing off the body to the ships, closely pursued by Hector and Æneas and the rest of the Trojans.

Achilles heard the fate of his friend with such distress that Antilochus feared for a while that he would destroy himself. His groans reached the ears of his mother Thetis, far down in the deeps of ocean where she abode, and she hastened to him to inquire the cause. She found him overwhelmed with self-reproach that he had indulged his resentment so far, and suffered his friend to fall a victim to it. But his only consolation was the hope of revenge. He would fly instantly in search of Hector. But his mother reminded him that he was now without armor, and promised him, if he would but wait till the morrow, she would procure for him a suit of armor from Vulcan more than equal to that he had lost. He consented, and Thetis immediately repaired to Vulcan's palace. She found him busy at his forge making tripods for his own use, so artfully constructed that they moved forward of their own accord when wanted, and retired again when dismissed. On hearing the request of Thetis, Vulcan immediately laid aside his work and hastened to comply with her wishes. He fabricated a splendid suit of armor for Achilles, first a shield adorned with elaborate devices, then a helmet crested with gold, then a corselet and greaves of impenetrable temper, all perfectly adapted to his form and of consummate workmanship. It was all done in one night, and Thetis, receiving it, descended with it to earth and laid it down at Achilles' feet at the dawn of day.

The first glow of pleasure that Achilles had felt since the death of

Patroclus was at the sight of this splendid armor. And now arrayed in it, he went forth into the camp calling all the chiefs to council. When they were assembled he addressed them. Renouncing his displeasure against Agamemnon and bitterly lamenting the miseries that had resulted from it, he called on them to proceed at once to the field. Agamemnon made a suitable reply, laying all the blame on Ate, the goddess of discord; and thereupon complete reconcilement took place between the heroes.

Then Achilles went forth to battle inspired with a rage and thirst for vengeance that made him irresistible. The bravest warriors fled before him or fell by his lance. Hector, cautioned by Apollo, kept aloof; but the god, assuming the form of one of Priam's sons, Lycaon, urged Æneas to encounter the terrible warrior. Æneas, though he felt himself unequal, did not decline the combat. He hurled his spear with all his force against the shield, the work of Vulcan. It was formed of five metal plates; two were of brass, two of tin, and one of gold. The spear pierced two thicknesses, but was stopped in the third. Achilles threw his with better success. It pierced through the shield of Æneas, but glanced near his shoulder and made no wound. Then Æneas siezed a stone, such as two men of modern times could hardly lift, and was about to throw it, and Achilles, with sword drawn, was about to rush upon him, when Neptune, who looked out upon the contest, moved with pity for Æneas, who he saw would surely fall a victim if not speedily rescued, spread a cloud between the combatants, and lifting Æneas from the ground, bore him over the heads of warriors and steeds to the rear of the battle. Achilles, when the mist cleared away, looked round in vain for his adversary, and acknowledging the prodigy, turned his arms against other champions. But none dared stand before him, and Priam looking down from his city walls beheld his whole army in full flight towards the city. He gave command to open wide the gates to receive the fugitives, and to shut them as soon as the Trojans should have passed, lest the enemy should enter likewise. But Achilles was so close in pursuit that that would have been impossible if Apollo had not, in the form of Agenor, Priam's son, encountered Achilles for a while, then turned to fly, and taken the way apart from the city. Achilles pursued and had chased his supposed victim far from the walls, when Apollo disclosed himself, and Achilles, perceiving how he had been deluded, gave up the chase.

But when the rest had escaped into the town Hector stood without determined to await the combat. His old father called to him from the walls and begged him to retire nor tempt the encounter. His mother, Hecuba, also besought him to the same effect, but all in vain. "How can I," said he to himself, "by whose command the people went to this day's contest, where so many have fallen, seek safety for myself against a single foe? But what if I offer him to yield up Helen and all her treasures and ample of our own beside? Ah no! it is too late. He would not even hear me through, but slay me while I spoke." While he thus rumi-

nated, Achilles approached, terrible as Mars, his armor flashing lightning as he moved. At that sight Hector's heart failed him and he fled.
Achilles swiftly pursued. They ran, still keeping near the walls, till they
had thrice encircled the city. As often as Hector approached the walls
Achilles intercepted him and forced him to keep out in a wider circle.
But Apollo sustained Hector's strength and would not let him sink in
weariness. Then Pallas, assuming the form of Deiphobus, Hector's
bravest brother, appeared suddenly at his side. Hector saw him with
delight, and thus strengthened stopped his flight and turned to meet
Achilles. Hector threw his spear, which struck the shield of Achilles and
bounded back. He turned to receive another from the hand of Deiphobus, but Deiphobus was gone. Then Hector understood his doom
and said, "Alas! it is plain this is my hour to die! I thought Deiphobus at
hand, but Pallas deceived me, and he is still in Troy. But I will not fall inglorious." So saying he drew his falchion from his side and rushed at
once to combat. Achilles, secured behind his shield, waited the approach of Hector. When he came within reach of his spear, Achilles
choosing with his eye a vulnerable part where the armor leaves the neck
uncovered, aimed his spear at that part, and Hector fell, death-
wounded, and feebly said, "Spare my body! Let my parents ransom it,
and let me receive funeral rites from the sons and daughters of Troy."
To which Achilles replied, "Dog, name not ransom nor pity to me, on
whom you have brought such dire distress. No! trust me, nought shall
save thy carcass from the dogs. Though twenty ransoms and thy weight
in gold were offered, I would refuse it all."

So saying he stripped the body of its armor, and fastening cords to the
feet tied them behind his chariot, leaving the body to trail along the
ground. Then mounting the chariot he lashed the steeds and so dragged
the body three times round the city. What words can tell the grief of
King Priam and Queen Hecuba at this sight! His people could scarce
restrain the old king from rushing forth. He threw himself in the dust
and besought them each by name to give him way. Hecuba's distress
was not less violent. The citizens stood round them weeping. The sound
of the mourning reached the ears of Andromache, the wife of Hector, as
she sat among her maidens at work, and anticipating evil she went forth
to the wall. When she saw the sight there presented, she would have
thrown herself headlong from the wall, but fainted and fell into the
arms of her maidens. Recovering she bewailed her fate, picturing to herself her country ruined, herself a captive, and her son dependent for his
bread on the charity of strangers.

When Achilles and the Greeks had taken their revenge on the killer of
Patroclus they busied themselves in paying due funeral rites to their
friend. A pile was erected, and the body burned with due solemnity; and
then ensued games of strength and skill, chariot races, wrestling, boxing, and archery. Then the chiefs sat down to the funeral banquet and
after that retired to rest. But Achilles neither partook of the feast nor of
sleep. The recollection of his lost friend kept him awake, remembering

their companionship in toil and dangers, in battle or on the perilous deep. Before the earliest dawn he left his tent, and joining to his chariot his swift steeds, he fastened Hector's body to be dragged behind. Twice he dragged him round the tomb of Patroclus, leaving him at length stretched in the dust. But Apollo would not permit the body to be torn or disfigured with all this abuse, but preserved it free from all taint or defilement.

While Achilles indulged his wrath in thus disgracing brave Hector, Jupiter in pity summoned Thetis to his presence. He told her to go to her son and prevail on him to restore the body of Hector to his friends. Then Jupiter sent Iris to King Priam to encourage him to go to Achilles and beg the body of his son. Iris delivered her message, and Priam immediately prepared to obey. He opened his treasuries and took out rich garments and cloths, with ten talents in gold and two splendid tripods and a golden cup of matchless workmanship. Then he called to his sons and bade them draw forth his litter and place in it the various articles designed for a ransom to Achilles. When all was ready, the old king with a single companion as aged as himself, the herald Idæus, drove forth from the gates, parting there with Hecuba his queen and all his friends, who lamented him going to certain death.

But Jupiter, beholding with compassion the venerable king, sent Mercury to be his guide and protector. Mercury, assuming the form of a young warrior, presented himself to the aged couple, and while at the sight of him they hesitated whether to fly or yield, the god approached, and grasping Priam's hand, offered to be their guide to Achilles' tent. Priam gladly accepted his offered service, and he mounting the cariage assumed the reins and soon conveyed them to the tent of Achilles. Mercury's wand put to sleep all the guards, and without hinderance he introduced Priam into the tent where Achilles sat, attended by two of his warriors. The old king threw himself at the feet of Achilles and kissed those terrible hands which had destroyed so many of his sons. "Think, O Achilles," he said, "of they own father, full of days like me, and trembling on the gloomy verge of life. Perhaps even now some neighbor chief oppresses him and there is none at hand to succor him in his distress. Yet doubtless knowing that Achilles lives he still rejoices, hoping that one day he shall see thy face again. But no comfort cheers me, whose bravest sons, so late the flower of Ilium, all have fallen. Yet one I had, one more than all the rest the strength of my age whom fighting for his country thou hast slain. I come to redeem his body, bringing inestimable ransom with me. Achilles! reverence the gods! recollect thy father! for his sake show compassion to me!" These words moved Achilles and he wept; remembering by turns his absent father and his lost friend. Moved with pity of Priam's silver locks and beard, he raised him from the earth and thus spake: "Priam, I know that thou hast reached this place conducted by some god, for without aid divine no mortal even in his prime of youth and dared the attempt. I grant thy request, moved thereto by the evident will of Jove." So saying he arose, and went forth with his two friends, and unloaded of its charge the litter, leaving two mantles and a robe for the covering of the body, which they placed on the litter, and spread the garments over it, that not unveiled it should be borne back to Troy. Then Achilles dismissed the old king with his attendants, having first pledged himself to allow a truce of twelve days for the funeral solemnities.

As the litter approached the city and was descried from the walls, the people poured forth to gaze once more on the face of their hero. Foremost of all, the mother and the wife of Hector came, and at the sight of the lifeless body renewed their lamentations. The people all wept with them, and to the going down of the sun there was no pause or abatement of their grief.

The next day, preparations were made for the funeral solemnities. For nine days the people brought wood and built the pile, and on the tenth they placed the body on the summit and applied the torch; while all Troy thronging forth encompassed the pile. When it had completely burned, they quenched the cinders with wine, collected the bones and placed them in a golden urn, which they buried in the earth, and reared a pile of stones over the spot.

> "Such honors Ilium to her hero paid,
>   And peaceful slept the mighty Hector's shade.
>
>   *Pope*

. . . .
28

The Fall of Troy—Return of the Greeks—Orestes and Electra

T he story of the *Iliad* ends with the death of Hector, and it is from the *Odyssey* and later poems that we learn the fate of the other heroes. After the death of Hector, Troy did not immediately fall, but receiving aid from new allies still continued its resistance. One of these allies was Memnon, the Æthiopian prince, whose story we have already told. Another was Penthesilea, queen of the Amazons, who came with a band of female warriors. All the authorities attest their valor and the fearful effect of their war cry. Penthesilea slew many of the bravest warriors, but was at last slain by Achilles. But when the hero bent over his fallen foe, and contemplated her beauty, youth and valor, he bitterly regretted his victory. Thersites, an insolent brawler and demagogue, ridiculed his grief, and was in consequence slain by the hero.

Achilles by chance had seen Polyxena, daughter of King Priam, perhaps on occasion of the truce which was allowed the Trojans for the burial of Hector. He was captivated with her charms, and to win her in marriage agreed to use his influence with the Greeks to grant peace to Troy. While in the temple of Apollo, negotiating the marriage, Paris discharged at him a poisoned arrow, which, guided by Apollo, wounded Achilles in the heel, the only vulnerable part about him. For Thetis his mother had dipped him when an infant in the river Styx, which made every part of him invulnerable except the heel by which she held him.*

The body of Achilles so treacherously slain was rescued by Ajax and Ulysses. Thetis directed the Greeks to bestow her son's armor on the hero who of all the survivors should be judged most deserving of it. Ajax and Ulysses were the only claimants; a select number of the other chiefs were appointed to award the prize. It was awarded to Ulysses, thus placing wisdom before valor; whereupon Ajax slew himself. On the spot where his blood sank into the earth a flower sprang up, called the hyacinth, bearing on its leaves the first two letters of the name of Ajax, Ai, the Greek for "woe." Thus Ajax is a claimant with the boy Hyacinthus for the honor of giving birth to this flower. There is a species of Larkspur which represents the hyacinth of the poets in preserving the memory of this event, the Delphinium Ajacis—Ajax's Larkspur.

It was now discovered that Troy could not be taken but by the aid of the arrows of Hercules. They were in possession of Philoctetes, the friend who had been with Hercules at the last and lighted his funeral pyre. Philoctetes had joined the Grecian expedition against Troy, but had accidentally wounded his foot with one of the poisoned arrows, and the smell from his wound proved so offensive that his companions carried him to the isle of Lemnos and left him there. Diomed was now sent to induce him to rejoin the army. He succeeded. Philoctetes was cured of his wound by Machaon, and Paris was the first victim of the fatal arrows. In his distress Paris bethought him of one whom in his prosperity he had forgotten. This was the nymph Œnone, whom he had married when a youth, and had abandoned for the fatal beauty of Helen. Œnone remembering the wrongs she had suffered, refused to heal the wound, and Paris went back to Troy and died. Œnone quickly repented, and hastened after him with remedies, but came too late, and in her grief hung herself.**

There was in Troy a celebrated statue of Minerva called the Palladium. It was said to have fallen from heaven, and the belief was that the city could not be taken so long as this statue remained within it. Ulysses and Diomed entered the city in disguise and succeeded in obtaining the Palladium, which they carried off to the Grecian camp.

But Troy still held out, and the Greeks began to despair of ever subduing it by force, and by advice of Ulysses resolved to resort to stratagem. They pretended to be making preparations to abandon the siege, and a portion of the ships were withdrawn and lay hid behind a neighboring island. The Greeks then constructed an immense *wooden horse,* which they gave out was intended as a propitiatory offering to

*The story of the invulnerability of Achilles is not found in Homer, and is inconsistent with his account. For how could Achilles require the aid of celestial armor if he were invulnerable?

**Tennyson has chosen Œnone as the subject of a short poem; but he has omitted the most poetical part of the story, the return of Paris wounded, her cruelty and subsequent repentance.

178   BULFINCH'S MYTHOLOGY

Minerva, but in fact was filled with armed men. The remaining Greeks then betook themselves to their ships and sailed away, as if for a final departure. The Trojans seeing the encampment broken up, and the fleet gone, concluded the enemy to have abandoned the siege. The gates were thrown open, and the whole population issued forth rejoicing at the long-prohibited liberty of passing freely over the scene of the late encampment. The great *horse* was the chief object of curiosity. All wondered what it could be for. Some recommended to take it into the city as a trophy; others felt afraid of it.

While they hesitate, Laocoön, the priest of Neptune, exclaims, "What madness citizens, is this! Have you not learned enough of Grecian fraud to be on your guard against it? For my part I fear the Greeks even when they offer gifts."* So saying he threw his lance at the horse's side. It struck, and a hollow sound reverberated like a groan. Then perhaps the people might have taken his advice and destroyed the fatal horse and all its contents; but just at that moment a group of people appeared dragging forward one who seemed a prisoner and a Greek. Stupefied with terror he was brought before the chiefs, who reassured him, promising that his life should be spared on condition of his returning true answers to the questions asked him. He informed them that he was a Greek, Sinon by name, and that in consequence of the malice of Ulysses he had been left behind by his countrymen at their departure. With regard to the wooden horse, he told them that it was a propitiatory offering to Minerva, and made so huge for the express purpose of preventing its being carried within the city; for Calchas the prophet had told them that if the Trojans took possession of it, they would assuredly triumph over the Greeks. This language turned the tide of the people's feelings and they began to think how they might best secure the monstrous horse and the favorable auguries connected with it, when suddenly a prodigy occurred which left no room to doubt. There appeared advancing over the sea two immense serpents. They came upon the land, and the crowd fled in all directions. The serpents advanced directly to the spot where Laocoön stood with his two sons. They first attacked the children, winding round their bodies and breathing their pestilential breath in their faces. The father attempting to rescue them is next seized and involved in the serpents' coils. He struggles to tear them away, but they overpower all his efforts and strangle him and the children in their poisonous folds. This event was regarded as a clear indication of the displeasure of the gods at Laocoön's irreverent treatment of the wooden horse, which they no longer hesitated to regard as a sacred object and prepared to introduce with due solemnity into the city. This was done with songs and triumphal acclamations, and the day closed with festivity. In the night the armed men who were enclosed in the body of the horse, being let out by the traitor Sinon, opened the gates of the city to their friends who had returned under cover of the night. The city

*See Proverbial Expressions, page 271.

was set on fire; the people, overcome with feasting and sleep, put to the sword, and Troy completely subdued.

One of the most celebrated groups of statuary in existence is that of Laocoön and his children in the embrace of the serpents. There is a cast of it in the Boston Athenaeum; the original is in the Vatican at Rome. The following lines are from the "Childe Harold" of Byron:

> "Now turning to the Vatican go see
> Laocoön's torture dignifying pain;
> A father's love and mortal's agony
> With an immortal's patience blending;—vain
> The struggle! vain against the coiling strain
> And gripe and deepening of the dragon's grasp
> The old man's clinch; the long evenomed chain
> Rivets the living links; the enormous asp
> Enforces pang on pang and stifles gasp on gasp."

The comic poets will also occasionally borrow a classical allusion. The following is from Swift's "Description of a City Shower":

> "Boxed in a chair the beau impatient sits,
> While spouts run clattering o'er the roof by fits,
> And ever and anon with frightful din
> The leather sounds; he trembles from within.
> So when Troy chairmen bore the wooden steed
> Pregnant with Greeks impatient to be freed,
> (Those bully Greeks, who, as the moderns do,
> Instead of paying chairmen, run them through;)
> Laocoön struck the outside with a spear,
> And each imprisoned champion quaked with fear."

King Priam lived to see the downfall of his kingdom, and was slain at last on the fatal night when the Greeks took the city. He had armed himself and was about to mingle with the combatants, but was prevailed on by Hecuba, his aged queen, to take refuge with herself and his daughters as a suppliant at the altar of Jupiter. While there, his youngest son Polites, pursued by Pyrrhus, the son of Achilles, rushed in wounded, and expired at the feet of his father; whereupon Priam, overcome with indignation, hurled his spear with feeble hand against Pyrrhus,* and was forthwith slain by him.

Queen Hecuba and her daughter Cassandra were carried captives to Greece. Cassandra had been loved by Apollo, and he gave her the gift of prophecy; but afterwards offended with her, he rendered the gift unavailing by ordaining that her predictions should never be believed. Polyxena, another daughter, who had been loved by Achilles, was demanded by the ghost of that warrior, and was sacrificed by the Greeks upon his tomb.

---

*Pyrrhus's exclamation, "Not such aid nor such defenders does the time require," has become proverbial. See Proverbial Expressions, page 271.

Menelaus and Helen

Our readers will be anxious to know the fate of Helen, the fair but guilty occasion of so much slaughter. On the fall of Troy Menelaus recovered possession of his wife, who had not ceased to love him, though she had yielded to the might of Venus and deserted him for another. After the death of Paris she aided the Greeks secretly on several occasions, and in particular when Ulysses and Diomed entered the city in disguise to carry off the Palladium. She saw and recognized Ulysses, but kept the secret, and even assisted them in obtaining the image. Thus she became reconciled to her husband, and they were among the first to leave the shores of Troy for their native land. But having incurred the displeasure of the gods they were driven by storms from shore to shore of the Mediterranean, visiting Cyprus, Phœnicia and Egypt. In Egypt they were kindly treated and presented with rich gifts, of which Helen's share was a golden spindle and basket on wheels. The basket was to hold the wool and spools for the queen's work.

Dyer, in his poem of the "Fleece," thus alludes to this incident:

"——many yet adhere
To the ancient distaff, at the bosom fixed,
Casting the whirling spindle as they walk.
　　　*　*　*　*　*
This was of old, in no inglorious days,
The mode of spinning, when the Egyptian prince
A golden distaff gave that beauteous nymph,
Too beauteous Helen; no uncourtly gift."

Milton also alludes to a famous recipe for an invigorating draught, called Nepenthe, which the Egyptian queen gave to Helen:

"Not that Nepenthes which the wife of Thone
In Egypt gave to Jove-born Helena,
Is of such power to stir up joy as this,
To life so friendly or so cool to thirst."
　　　　　　　　　　　　　　　　Comus

Menelaus and Helen at length arrived in safety at Sparta, resumed their royal dignity and lived and reigned in splendor; and when Telemachus, the son of Ulysses, in search of his father, arrived at Sparta, he found Menelaus and Helen celebrating the marriage of their daughter Hermione to Neoptolemus, son of Achilles.

Agamemnon, Orestes, and Electra

Agamemnon, the general-in-chief of the Greeks, the brother of Menelaus, and who had been drawn into the quarrel to avenge his brother's wrongs, not his own, was not so fortunate in the issue. During his absence his wife Clytemnestra had been false to him, and when his return was expected, she with her paramour, Ægisthus, laid a plan for his destruction, and at the banquet given to celebrate his return, murdered him.

It was intended by the conspirators to slay his son Orestes also, a lad not yet old enough to be an object of apprehension, but from whom, if he should be suffered to grow up, there might be danger. Electra, the sister of Orestes, saved her brother's life by sending him secretly away to his uncle Strophius, King of Phocis. In the palace of Strophius Orestes grew up with the king's son Pylades, and formed with him that ardent friendship which has become proverbial. Electra frequently reminded her brother by messengers of the duty of avenging his father's death, and when grown up he consulted the oracle of Delphi, which confirmed him in his design.He therefore repaired in disguise to Argos, pretending to be a messenger from Strophius, who had come to announce the death of Orestes, and brought the ashes of the deceased in a funeral urn. After visiting his father's tomb and sacrificing upon it, according to the rites of the ancients, he made himself known to his sister Electra, and soon after slew both Ægisthus and Clytemnestra.

This revolting act, the slaughter of a mother by her son, though alleviated by the guilt of the victim and the express command of the gods, did not fail to awaken in the breasts of the ancients the same abhorrence that it does in ours. The Eumenides, avenging deities, seized upon Orestes, and drove him frantic from land to land. Pylades accompanied him in his wanderings and watched over him. At length in answer to a second appeal to the oracle, he was directed to go to Tauris in Scythia, and to bring thence a statue of Diana which was believed to have fallen from heaven. Accordingly Orestes and Pylades went to Tauris, where the barbarous people were accustomed to sacrifice to the goddess all strangers who fell into their hands. The two friends were seized and carried bound to the temple to be made victims. But the priestess of Diana was no other than Iphigenia, the sister of Orestes, who, our readers will remember, was snatched away by Diana, at the moment when she was about to be sacrificed. Ascertaining from the prisoners who they were, Iphigenia disclosed herself to them, and the three made their escape with the statue of the goddess, and returned to Mycenæ.

But Orestes was not yet relieved from the vengeance of the Erinyes. At length he took refuge with Minerva at Athens. The goddess afforded him protection, and appointed the court of Areopagus to decide his fate. The Erinyes brought forward their accusation, and Orestes made the command of the Delphic oracle his excuse. When the court voted and the voices were equally divided, Orestes was acquitted by the command of Minerva.

Byron, in "Childe Harold," Canto IV, alludes to the story of Orestes:

"O thou who never yet of human wrong
   Left the unbalanced scale, great Nemesis!
   Thou who didst call the Furies from the abyss,
   And round Orestes bade them howl and hiss,
   For that unnatural retribution,—just,
   Had it but been from hands less near,—in this,
   Thy former realm, I call thee from the dust!''

One of the most pathetic scenes in the ancient drama is that in which Sophocles represents the meeting of Orestes and Electra, on his return from Phocis. Orestes mistaking Electra for one of the domestics, and desirous of keeping his arrival a secret till the hour of vengeance should arrive, produces the urn in which his ashes are supposed to rest. Electra, believing him to be really dead, takes the urn and embracing it, pours forth her grief in language full of tenderness and despair.

Milton, in one of his sonnets, says,

           "The repeated air
Of sad Electra's poet had the power
To save the Athenian walls from ruin bare.''

This alludes to the story that when, on one occasion, the city of Athens was at the mercy of her Spartan foes, and it was proposed to destroy it, the thought was rejected upon the accidental quotation, by some one, of a chorus of Euripides.

Troy

After hearing so much about the city of Troy and its heroes, the reader will perhaps be surprised to learn that the exact site of that famous city is still a matter of dispute. There are some vestiges of tombs on the plain which most nearly answers to the description given by Homer and the ancient geographers, but no other evidence of the former existence of a great city. Byron thus describes the present appearance of the scene:

"The winds are high, and Helle's tide
   Rolls darkly heaving to the main;
And night's descending shadows hide
   That field with blood bedewed in vain,
The desert of old Priam's pride,
   The tombs, sole relics of his reign,
All—save immortal dreams that could beguile
The blind old man of Scio's rocky isle.''

Bride of Abydos

Adventures of Ulysses — The Lotus-Eaters — Cyclopes — Circe — Sirens — Scylla and Charybdis — Calypso

The romantic poem of the *Odyssey* is now to engage our attention. It narrates the wanderings of Ulysses (Odysseus in the Greek language) in his return from Troy to his own kingdom Ithaca.

From Troy the vessels first made land at Ismarus, city of the Ciconians, where, in a skirmish with the inhabitants, Ulysses lost six men from each ship. Sailing thence they were overtaken by a storm which drove them for nine days along the sea till they reached the country of the Lotus-eaters. Here, after watering, Ulysses sent three of his men to discover who the inhabitants were. These men on coming among the Lotus-eaters were kindly entertained by them, and were given some of their own food, the lotus-plant, to eat. The effect of this food was such that those who partook of it lost all thoughts of home and wished to remain in that country. It was by main force that Ulysses dragged these men away, and he was even obliged to tie them under the benches of his ship.*

They next arrived at the country of the Cyclopes. The Cyclopes were giants, who inhabited an island of which they were the only possessors. the name means "round eye," and these giants were so called because they had but one eye, and that placed in the middle of the forehead. They dwelt in caves and fed on the wild productions of the island and on what their flocks yielded, for they were shepherds. Ulysses left the main body of his ships at anchor, and with one vessel went to the Cyclopes' island to explore for supplies. He landed with his companions, carrying with them a jar of wine for a present, and coming to a large cave they entered it, and finding no one within examined its contents. They found it stored with the riches of the flock, quantities of cheese, pails and

---

*Tennyson in the "Lotus-eaters" has charmingly expressed the dreamy, languid feeling which the lotus-food is said to have produced.

"How sweet it were, hearing the downward stream
　With half-shut eyes ever to seem
　Falling asleep in a half-dream!
　To dream and dream, like yonder amber light
　Which will not leave the myrrh-bush on the height;
　To hear each others' whispered speech;
　Eating the Lotos, day by day,
　To watch the crisping ripples on the beach,
　And tender curving lines of creamy spray:
　To lend our hearts and spirits wholly
　To the influence of mild-minded melancholy;
　To muse and brood and live again in memory,
　With those old faces of our infancy
　Heaped over with a mound of grass,
　Two handfuls of white dust, shut in an urn of brass."

bowls of milk, lambs and kids in their pens, all in nice order. Presently arrived the master of the cave, Polyphemus, bearing an immense bundle of firewood, which he threw down before the cavern's mouth. He then drove into the cave the sheep and goats to be milked, and entering, rolled to the cave's mouth an enormous rock, that twenty oxen could not draw. Next he sat down and milked his ewes, preparing a part for cheese, and setting the rest aside for his customary drink. Then turning round his great eye he discerned the strangers, and growled out to them, demanding who they were, and where from. Ulysses replied most humbly, stating that they were Greeks, from the great expedition that had lately won so much glory in the conquest of Troy; that they were now on their way home, and finished by imploring his hospitality in the name of the gods. Polyphemus deigned no answer, but reaching out his hand seized two of the Greeks, whom he hurled against the side of the cave, and dashed out their brains. He proceeded to devour them with great relish, and having made a hearty meal, stretched himself out on the floor to sleep. Ulysses was tempted to seize the opportunity and plunge his sword into him as he slept, but recollected that it would only expose them all to certain destruction, as the rock with which the giant had closed up the door was far beyond their power to remove, and they would therefore be in hopeless imprisonment. Next morning the giant seized two more of the Greeks, and despatched them in the same manner as their companions, feasting on their flesh till no fragment was left. He then moved away the rock from the door, dove out his flocks, and went out, carefully replacing the barrier after him. When he was gone Ulysses planned how he might take vengeance for his murdered friends, and effect his escape with his surviving companions. He made his men prepare a massive bar of wood cut by the Cyclops for a staff, which they found in the cave. They sharpened the end of it and seasoned it in the fire, and hid it under the straw on the cavern floor. Then four of the boldest were selected, with whom Ulysses joined himself as a fifth. The Cyclops came home at evening, rolled away the stone and drove in his flock as usual. After milking them and making his arrangements as before, he seized two more of Ulysses' companions and dashed their brains out, and made his evening meal upon them as he had on the others. After he had supped, Ulysses approaching him handed him a bowl of wine, saying, "Cyclops, this is wine; taste and drink after thy meal of man's flesh." He took and drank it, and was hugely delighted with it, and called for more. Ulysses supplied him once and again, which pleased the giant so much that he promised him as a favor that he should be the last of the party devoured. He asked his name, to which Ulysses replied, "My name is Noman."

After his supper the giant lay down to repose, and was soon sound asleep. Then Ulysses with his four select friends thrust the end of the stake into the fire till it was all one burning coal, then poising it exactly above the giant's only eye, they buried it deeply into the socket, twirling it round as a carpenter does his auger. The howling monster with his outcry filled the cavern, and Ulysses with his aids nimbly got out of his way and concealed themselves in the cave. He, bellowing, called aloud on all the Cyclopes dwelling in the caves around him, far and near. They on his cry flocked round the den, and inquired what grievous hurt had caused him to sound such an alarm and break their slumbers. He replied, "O friends, I die, and Noman gives the blow." They answered, "If no man hurts thee it is the stroke of Jove, and thou must bear it." So saying, they left him groaning.

Next morning the Cyclops rolled away the stone to let his flock out to pasture, but planted himself in the door of the cave to feel of all as they went out, that Ulysses and his men should not escape with them. But Ulysses had made his men harness the rams of the flock three abreast, with osiers which they found on the floor of the cave. To the middle ram of the three one of the Greeks suspended himself, so protected by the exterior rams on either side. As they passed, the giant felt of the animals' backs and sides, but never thought of their bellies; so the men all passed safe, Ulysses himself being on the last one that passed. When they had got a few paces from the cavern, Ulysses and his friends released themselves from the rams, and drove a good part of the flock down to the shore to their boat. They put them aboard with all haste, then pushed off from the shore, and when at a safe distance Ulysses shouted out, "Cyclops, the gods have well requited thee for they atrocious deeds. Know it is Ulysses to whom thou owest thy shameful loss of sight." The Cyclops, hearing this, seized a rock that projected from the side of mountain, and rending it from its bed he lifted it high in the air, then exerting all his force, hurled it in the direction of the voice. Down came the mass, just clearing the vessel's stern. The ocean, at the plunge of the huge rock, heaved the ship towards the land, so that it barely escaped being swamped by the waves. When they had with the utmost difficulty pulled off shore, Ulysses was about to hail the giant again, but his friends besought him not to do so. He could not forbear, however, letting the giant know that they had escaped his missile, but waited till they had reached a safer distance than before. The giant answered them with curses, but Ulysses and his friends plied their oars vigorously, and soon regained their companions.

Ulysses next arrived at the island of Æolus. To this monarch Jupiter had intrusted the government of the winds, to send them forth or retain them at his will. He treated Ulysses hospitably, and at his departure gave him, tied up in a leathern bag with a silver string, such winds as might be hurtful and dangerous, commanding fair winds to blow the barks towards their country. Nine days they sped before the wind, and all that time Ulysses had stood at the helm, without sleep. At last quite exhausted he lay down to sleep. While he slept, the crew conferred together about the mysterious bag, and concluded it must contain treasures given by the hospitable King Æolus to their commander. Tempted to secure some portion for themselves they loosed the string, when immediately the winds rushed forth. The ships were driven far from their course, and back again to the island they had just left. Æolus was so indignant at their folly that he refused to assist them further, and they were obliged to labor over their course once more by means of their oars.

The Læstrygonians

Their next adventure was with the barbarous tribe of Læstrygonians. The vessels all pushed into the harbor, tempted by the secure appearance of the cove, completely land-locked; only Ulysses moored his vessel without. As soon as the Læstrygonians found the ships completely in their power they attacked them, heaving huge stones which broke and overturned them, and with their spears despatched the seamen as they struggled in the water. All the vessels with their crews were destroyed, except Ulysses' own ship which had remained outside, and finding no safety but in flight, he exhorted his men to ply their oars vigorously, and they escaped.

With grief for their slain companions mixed with joy at their own escape, they pursued their way till they arrived at the Æaean isle, where Circe dwelt, the daughter of the sun. Landing here Ulysses climbed a hill, and gazing round saw no signs of habitation except in one spot at the centre of the island, where he perceived a palace embowered with trees. He sent forward one half of his crew, under the command of Eurylochus, to see what prospect of hospitality they might find. As they approached the palace, they found themselves surrounded by lions, tigers and wolves, not fierce, but tamed by Circe's art, for she was a powerful magician. These dreadful animals fawned upon them, wagging their tails and rising on their hinder feet, playful as dogs. The sounds of soft music were heard from within, and a sweet female voice singing. Eurylochus called aloud and the goddess came forth and invited them in; they all gladly entered except Eurylochus, who suspected danger. The goddess conducted her guests to a seat, and had them served with wine and other delicacies. When they had feasted heartily, she touched them one by one with her wand, and they became immediately changed into *swine*, in "head, body, voice and bristles," yet with their intellects as before. She shut them in her sties and supplied them with acorns and such other things as swine love.

Eurylochus hurried back to the ship and told the tale. Ulysses thereupon determined to go himself, and try if by any means he might deliver his companions. As he strode onward alone, he met a youth who addressed him familiarly, appearing to be acquainted with his adventures. He announced himself as Mercury, and informed Ulysses of the arts of Circe, and of the danger of approaching her. As Ulysses was not to be dissuaded from his attempt, Mercury provided him with a sprig of the plant Moly, of wonderful power to resist sorceries, and instructed him how to act. Ulysses proceeded, and reaching the palace was courteously received by Circe, who entertained him as she had done his companions, and after he had eaten and drank, touched him with her wand, saying "Hence, seek the sty and wallow with thy friends." But he, in-

stead of obeying, drew his sword and rushed upon her with fury in his
countenance. She fell on her knees and begged for mercy. He dictated a
solemn oath that she would release his companions and practise no further harm against him or them; and she repeated it, at the same time
promising to dismiss them all in safety after hospitably entertaining
them. She was as good as her word. The men were restored to their
shapes, the rest of the crew summoned from the shore, and the whole
magnificently entertained day after day, till Ulysses seemed to have forgotten his native land, and to have reconciled himself to an inglorious
life of ease and pleasure.

At length his companions recalled him to nobler sentiments, and he
received their admonition gratefully. Circe aided their departure, and
instructed them how to pass safely by the coast of the Sirens. The Sirens
were sea-nymphs who had the power of charming by their song all who
heard them, so that the unhappy mariners were irresistibly impelled to
cast themselves into the se to their destruction. Circe directed Ulysses
to fill the ears of his seamen with wax, so that they should not hear the
strain, and to cause himself to be bound to the mast, and his people to be
strictly enjoined, whatever he might say or do, by no means to release
him till they should have passed the Sirens' island. Ulysses obeyed these
directions. He filled the ears of his people with wax, and suffered them
to bind him with cords firmly to the mast. As they approached the
Sirens' island, the sea was calm, and over the waters came the notes of
music so ravishing and attractive, that Ulysses struggled to get loose,
and by cries and signs to his people begged to be released; but they, obedient to his previous orders, sprang forward and bound him still faster.
They held on heir course, and the music grew fainter till it ceased to be
heard, when with job Ulysses gave his companions the signal to unseal
their ears, and they relieved him from his bonds.

The imagination of a modern poet, Keats, has discovered for us the
thoughts that passed through the brains of the victims of Circe, after
their transformation. In his "Endymion" he represents one of them, a
monarch in the guise of an elephant, addressing the sorceress in human
language thus:

> "I sue not for my happy crown again;
> I sue not for my phalanx on the plain;
> I sue not for my lone, my widowed wife;
> I sue not for my ruddy drops of life,
> My children fair, my lovely girls and boys;
> I will forget them; I will pass these joys,
> Ask nought so heavenward; so too-too high;
> Only I pray, as fairest boon, to die;
> To be delivered from this cumbrous flesh,
> From this gross, detestable, filthy mesh,
> and merely given to the cold, bleak air.
> Have mercy, goddess! Circe, feel my prayer!"

Scylla and Charybdis

Ulysses had been warned by Circe of the two monsters Scylla and Charybdis. We have already met with Scylla in the story of Glaucus, and remember that she was once a beautiful maiden and was changed into a snaky monster by Circe. She dwelt in a cave high up on the cliff, from whence she was accustomed to thrust forth her long necks (for she had six heads), and in each of her mouths to seize one of the crew of every vessel passing within reach. The other terror, Charybdis, was a gulf, nearly on a level with the water. Thrice each day the water rushed into a frightful chasm, and thrice was disgorged. Any vessel coming near the whirlpool when the tide was rushing in must inevitably be ingulphed; not Neptune himself could save it.

On approaching the haunt of the dread monsters, Ulysses kept strict watch to discover them. The roar of the waters as Charybdis ingulphed them, gave warning at a distance, but Scylla could nowhere be discerned. While Ulysses and his men watched with anxious eyes the dreadful whirlpool, they were not equally on their guard from the attack of Scylla, and the monster darting forth her snaky heads, sought six of his men, and bore them away shrieking to her den. It was the saddest sight Ulysses had yet seen; to behold his friends thus sacrificed and hear their cries, unable to afford them any assistance.

Circe had warned him of another danger. After passing Scylla and Charybdis the next land he would make was Thrinakia, an island whereon were pastured the cattle of Hyperion, the Sun, tended by his daughters Lampetia and Phaethusa. These flocks must not be violated, whatever the wants of the voyagers might be. If this injunction were transgressed, destruction was sure to fall on the offenders.

Ulysses would willingly have passed the island of the Sun without stopping, but his companions so urgently pleaded for the rest and refreshment that would be derived from anchoring and passing the night on shore, that Ulysses yielded. He bound them however with an oath that they would not touch one of the animals of the sacred flocks and herds, but content themselves with what provision they yet had left of the supply which Circe had put on board. So long as this supply lasted the people kept their oath, but contrary winds detained them at the island for a month, and after consuming all their stock of provisions, they were forced to rely upon the birds and fishes they could catch. Famine pressed them, and at length one day, in the absence of Ulysses, they slew some of the cattle, vainly attempting to make amends for the deed by offering from them a portion to the offended powers. Ulysses, on his return to the shore, was horror-struck at perceiving what they had done, and the more so on account of the portentous signs which followed. The skins crept on the ground, and the joints of meat lowed on the spits while roasting.

The wind becoming fair they sailed from the island. They had not gone far when the weather changed, and a storm of thunder and lightning ensued. A stroke of lightning shattered their mast, which in its fall killed the pilot. At last the vessel itself came to pieces. The keel and mast floating side by side, Ulysses formed of them a raft, to which he clung, and, the wind changing, the waves bore him to Calypso's island. All the rest of the crew perished.

The following allusion to the topics we have just been considering is from Milton's "Comus," line 252.

> "I have often heard
> My mother Circe and the Sirens three
> Amidst the flowery-kirtled Naiades,
> Culling their potent herbs and baneful drugs,
> Who as they sung would take the prisoned soul
> And lap it in Elysium. Scylla wept,
> And chid her barking waves into attention,
> And fell Charybdis murmured soft applause."

Scylla and Charybdis have become proverbial, to denote opposite dangers which beset one's course. (See Proverbial Expressions, p. 272.)

Calypso

Calypso was a sea-nymph, which name denotes a numerous class of female divinities of lower rank, yet sharing many of the attributes of the gods. Calypso received Ulysses hospitably, entertained him magnificently, became enamoured of him, and wished to retain him forever, conferring on him immortality. But he persisted in his resolution to return to his country and his wife and son. Calypso at last received the command of Jove to dismiss him. Mercury brought the message to her, and found her in her grotto, which is thus described by Homer:

> "A garden vine, luxuriant on all sides,
> Mantled the spacious cavern, cluster-hung
> Profuse; four fountains of serenest lymph,
> Their sinuous course pursuing side by side,
> Strayed all around, and every where appeared
> Meadows of softest verdure, purpled o'er
> With violets; it was a scene to fill
> A god from heaven with wonder and delight."

Calypso with much reluctance proceeded to obey the commands of Jupiter. She supplied Ulysses with the means of constructing a raft, provisioned it well for him, and gave him a favoring gale. He sped on his course prosperously for many days, till at length, when in sight of land, a storm arose that broke his mast and threatened to rend the raft asunder. In this crisis he was seen by a compassionate sea-nymph, who in the form of a cormorant alighted on the raft, and presented him a girdle, directing him to bind it beneath his breast, and if he should be compelled to trust himself to the waves, it would buoy him up and enable him by swimming to reach the land.

Fenelon, in his romance of "Telemachus," has given us the adventures of the son of Ulysses in search of his father. Among other places at which he arrived, following on his father's footsteps, was Calypso's isle, and, as in the former case, the goddess tried every art to keep him with her, and offered to share her immortality with him. But Minerva, who in the shape of Mentor accompanied him and governed all his movements, made him repel her allurements, and when no other means of escape could be found, the two friends leaped from a cliff into the sea, and swam to a vessel which lay becalmed off shore. Byron alludes to this leap of Telemachus and Mentor in the following stanza:

"But not in silence pass Calypso's isles,
   The sister tenants of the middle deep;
   There for the weary still a haven smiles,
   Though the fair goddess long has ceased to weep,
   And o'er her cliffs a fruitless watch to keep
   For him who dared prefer a mortal bride.
   Here too his boy essayed the dreadful leap,
   Stern Mentor urged from high to yonder tide;
While thus of both bereft the nymph-queen doubly sighed."

30

The Phæacians—Fate of the Suitors

Ulysses clung to the raft while any of its timbers kept together, and when it no longer yielded him support, binding the girdle around him, he swam. Minerva smoothed the billows before him and sent him a wind that rolled the waves towards the shore. The surf beat high on the rocks and seemed to forbid approach; but at length finding calm water at the mouth of a gentle stream, he landed, spent with toil, breathless and speechless and almost dead. After some time reviving he kissed the soil, rejoicing, yet at a loss what course to take. At a short distance he perceived a wood, to which he turned his steps. There finding a covert sheltered by intermingling branches alike from the sun and the rain, he collected a pile of leaves and formed a bed, on which he stretched himself, and heaping the leaves over him, fell asleep.

The land where he was thrown was Scheria, the country of the Phæacians. These people dwelt originally near the Cyclopes; but being oppressed by that savage race, they migrated to the isle of Scheria, under the conduct of Nausithous their king. They were, the poet tells us, a people akin to the gods, who appeared manifestly and feasted among them when they offered sacrifices, and did not conceal themselves from solitary wayfarers when they met them. They had abundance of wealth and lived in the enjoyment of it undisturbed by the alarms of war, for as they dwelt remote from gain-seeking man, no enemy ever approached their shores, and they did not even require to make use of bows and quivers.

Their chief employment was navigation. Their ships, which went with the velocity of birds, were endued with intelligence; they knew every port and needed no pilot. Alcinous, the son of Nausithous, was now their king, a wise and just sovereign, beloved by his people.

Now it happened that the very night on which Ulysses was cast ashore on the Phæacian island, and while he lay sleeping on his bed of leaves, Nausicaa, the daughter of the king, had a dream sent by Minerva, reminding her that her wedding day was not far distant, and that it would be but a prudent preparation for that event to have a general washing of the clothes of the family. This was no slight affair, for the fountains were at some distance and the garments must be carried thither. On awaking, the princess hastened to her parents to tell them what was on her mind; not alluding to her wedding day, but finding other reasons equally good. Her father readily assented and ordered the grooms to furnish forth a wagon for the purpose. The clothes were put therein, and the queen mother placed in the wagon likewise an abundant supply of food and wine. The princess took her seat and plied the lash, her attendant virgins following her on foot. Arrived at the river side they turned out the mules to graze, and unlading the carriage, bore the garments down to the water, and working with cheerfulness and alacrity soon despatched their labor. Then having spread the garments on the shore to dry, and having themselves bathed, they sat down to enjoy their meal; after which they rose and amused themselves with a game of ball, the princess singing to them while they played. But when they had refolded the apparel and were about to resume their way to the town, Minerva caused the ball thrown by the princess to fall into the water, whereat they all screamed and Ulysses awaked at the sound.

Now we must picture to ourselves Ulysses, a shipwrecked mariner, but a few hours escaped from the waves, and utterly destitute of clothing, awaking and discovering that only a few bushes were interposed between him and a group of young maidens whom by their deportment and attire he discovered to be not mere peasant girls, but of a higher class. Sadly needing help, how could he yet venture naked as he was to discover himself and make his wants known? It certainly was a case worthy of the interposition of his patron goddess Minerva, who never failed him at a crisis. Breaking off a leafy branch from a tree he held it before him and stepped out from the thicket. The virgins at sight of him fled in all directions, Nausicaa alone excepted, for *her* Minerva aided and endowed with courage and discernment. Ulysses, standing respectfully aloof, told his sad case, and besought the fair object (whether queen or goddess he professed he knew not) for food and clothing. The princess replied courteously, promising present relief and her father's hospitality when he should become acquainted with the facts. She called back her scattered maidens, chiding their alarm, and reminding them that the Phæacians had no enemies to fear. This man, she told them, was an unhappy wanderer, whom it was a duty to cherish, for the poor and stranger are from Jove. She bade them bring food and clothing, for some of her brothers' garments were among the contents of the wagon. When this was done, and Ulysses retiring to a sheltered place had washed his body free from the sea-foam, clothed and refreshed himself with food, Pallas dilated his form and diffused grace over his ample chest and manly brows.

The princess seeing him was filled with admiration, and scrupled not to say to her damsels that she wished the gods would send her such a husband. To Ulysses she recommended that he should repair to the city, following herself and train so far as the way lay through the fields; but when they should approach the city she desired that he would no longer be seen in her company, for she feared the remarks which rude and vulgar people might make on seeing her return accompanied by such a gallant stranger. To avoid which she directed him to stop at a grove adjoining the city, in which were a farm and garden belonging to the king. After allowing time for the princess and her companions to reach the city, he was then to pursue his way thither, and would be easily guided by any he might meet to the royal abode.

Ulysses obeyed the directions and in due time proceeded to the city, on approaching which he met a young woman bearing a pitcher forth for water. It was Minerva who had assumed that form. Ulysses accosted her and desired to be directed to the palace of Aleinous the king. The maiden replied respectfully, offering to be his guide; for the palace she informed him stood near her father's dwelling. Under the guidance of the goddess and by her power enveloped in a cloud which shielded him from observation, Ulysses passed among the busy crowd, and with wonder observed their harbor, their ships, their forum (the resort of heroes), and their battlements, till they came to the palace, where the goddess, having first given him some information of the country, king, and people he was about to meet, left him. Ulysses, before entering the court-yard of the palace, stood and surveyed the scene. Its splendor astonished him. Brazen walls stretched from the entrance to the interior house, of which the doors were gold, the door-posts silver, standing in rows as if to guard the approach. Along the walls were seats spread through all their length with mantles of finest texture, the work of Phæacian maidens. On these seats the princes sat and feasted, while golden statues of graceful youths held in their hands lighted torches which shed radiance over the scene. Full fifty female menials served in household offices, some employed to grind the corn, others to wind off the purple wool or ply the loom. For the Phæacian women as far exceeded all other women in household arts as the mariners of that country did the rest of mankind in the management of ships. Without the court a spacious garden lay, four acres in extent. In it grew many a lofty tree, pomegranate, pear, apple, fig, and olive. Neither winter's cold nor summer's drought arrested their growth, but they flourished in constant succession, some budding while others were maturing. The vineyard was equally prolific. In one quarter you might see the vines, some in blossom, some loaded with ripe grapes, and in another observe the vintagers treading the wine press. On the garden's borders flowers of all hues bloomed all the year round, arranged with neatest art. In the midst two fountains poured forth their waters, one flowing by artificial channels over all the garden, the other conducted through the court-yard of the palace, whence every citizen might draw his supplies.

Ulysses stood gazing in admiration, unobserved himself, for the cloud which Minerva spread around him still shielded him. At length having sufficiently observed the scene, he advanced with rapid step into the hall where the chiefs and senators were assembled, pouring libation to Mercury, whose worship followed the evening meal. Just then Minerva dissolved the cloud and disclosed him to the assembled chiefs. Advancing to the place where the queen sat, he knelt at her feet and implored her favor and assistance to enable him to return to his native country. Then withdrawing, he seated himself in the manner of suppliants, at the hearth side.

For a time none spoke. At last an aged statesman, addressing the king, said, "It is not fit that a stranger who asks our hospitality should be kept waiting in suppliant guise, none welcoming him. Let him therefore be led to a seat among us and supplied with food and wine." At these words the king rising gave his hand to Ulysses and led him to a seat, displacing thence his own son to make room for the stranger. Food and wine were set before him and he ate and refreshed himself.

The king then dismissed his guests, notifying them that the next day he would call them to council to consider what had best be done for the stranger.

When the guests had departed and Ulysses was left alone with the king and queen, the queen asked him who he was and whence he came, and (recognizing the clothes which he wore as those which her maidens and herself had made) from whom he received those garments. He told them of his residence in Calypso's isle and his departure thence; of the wreck of his raft, his escape by swimming, and of the relief afforded by the princess. The parents heard approvingly, and the king promised to furnish a ship in which his guest might return to his own land.

The next day the assembled chiefs confirmed the promise of the king. A bark was prepared and a crew of stout rowers selected, and all betook themselves to the palace, where a bounteous repast was provided. After the feast the king proposed that the young men should show their guest their proficiency in manly sports, and all went forth to the arena for games of running, wrestling, and other exercises. After all had done their best, Ulysses being challenged to show what he could do, at first declined, but being taunted by one of the youths, seized a quoit of weight far heavier than any the Phæacians had thrown, and sent it farther than the utmost throw of theirs. All were astonished, and viewed their guest with greatly increased respect.

After the games they returned to the hall, and the herald led in Demodocus, the blind bard,

> "Dear to the Muse,
> Who yet appointed him both good and ill,
> Took from his sight, but gave him strains divine."

He took for his theme the Wooden Horse, by means of which the Greeks found entrance into Troy. Apollo inspired him, and he sang so feelingly the terrors and the exploits of that eventful time that all were delighted, but Ulysses was moved to tears. Observing which, Alcinous, when the song was done, demanded of him why at the mention of Troy his sorrows awaked. Had he lost there a father, or brother, or any dear friend? Ulysses replied by announcing himself by his true name, and at their request, recounted the adventures which had befallen him since his departure from Troy. This narrative raised the sympathy and admiration of the Phæacians for their guest to the highest pitch. The king proposed that all the chiefs should present him with a gift, himself setting the example. They obeyed, and vied with one another in loading the illustrious stranger with costly gifts.

The next day Ulysses set sail in the Phæacian vessel, and in a short time arrived safe at Ithaca, his own island. When the vessel touched the strand he was asleep. The mariners, with waking him, carried him on shore, and landed with him he chest containing his presents, and then sailed away.

Neptune was so displeased at the conduct of the Phæacians in thus rescuing Ulysses from his hands that on the return of the vessel to port he transformed it into a rock right opposite the mouth of the harbor.

Homer's description of the ships of the Phæacians has been thought to look like an anticipation of the wonders of modern steam navigation. Alcinous says to Ulysses,

> "Say from what city, from what regions tossed,
> And what inhabitants those regions boast?
> So shalt thou quickly reach the realm assigned,
> In wondrous ships, self-moved, instinct with mind;
> No helm secures their course, no pilot guides;
> Like man intelligent they plough the tides,
> Conscious of every coast and every bay
> That lies beneath the sun's all-seeing ray."

Odyssey, Book VIII

Lord Carlisle, in his "Diary in the Turkish and Greek Waters," thus speaks of Corfu, which he considers to be the ancient Phæacian island—

"The sites explain the *Odyssey.* The temple of the sea-god could not have been more fitly placed, upon a grassy platform of the most elastic turf, on the brow of a crag commanding harbor, and channel, and ocean. Just at the entrance of the inner harbor there is a picturesque rock with a small covent perched upon it, which by one legend is the transformed pinnace of Ulysses.

"Almost the only river in the island is just at the proper distance from the probable site of the city and palace of the king, to justify the princess Nausicaa having had resort to her chariot and to luncheon when she went with the maidens of the court to wash their garments."

Fate of the Suitors

Ulysses had now been away from Ithaca for twenty years, and when he awoke he did not recognize his native land. Minerva appeared to him in the form of a young shepherd, informed him where he was, and told him the state of things at his palace. More than a hundred nobles of Ithaca and of the neighboring islands had been for years suing for the hand of Penelope, his wife, imagining him dead, and lording it over his palace and people, as if they were owners of both. That he might be able to take vengeance upon them, it was important that he should not be recognized. Minerva accordingly metamorphosed him into an unsightly beggar, and as such he was kindly received by Eumæus, the swine-herd, a faithful servant of his house.

Telemachus, his son, was absent in quest of his father. He had gone to the courts of other kings, who had returned from the Trojan expedition. While on the search, he received counsel from Minerva to return home. He arrived and sought Eumæus to learn something of the state of affairs at the palace before presenting himself among the suitors. Finding a stranger with Eumæus, he treated him courteously, though in garb of a beggar, and promised him assistance. Eumæus was sent to the palace to inform Penelope privately of her son's arrival, for caution was necessary with regard to the suitors, who, as Telemachus had learned, were plotting to intercept and kill him. When Eumæus was gone, Minerva presented herself to Ulysses, and directed him to make himself known to his son. At the same time she touched him, removed at once from him the appearance of age and penury, and gave him the aspect of vigorous manhood that belonged to him. Telemachus viewed him with astonishment, and at first thought he must be more than mortal. But Ulysses announced himself as his father, and accounted for the change of appearance, by explaining that it was Minerva's doing.

> "Then threw Telemachus
> His arms around his father's neck and wept.
> Desire intense of lamentation seized
> On both; soft murmurs uttering, each indulged
> His grief."

The father and son took counsel together how they should get the better of the suitors and punish them for their outrages. It was arranged that Telemachus should proceed to the palace and mingle with the suitors as formerly; that Ulysses should also go as a beggar, a character which in the rude old times had different privileges from what we concede to it now. As traveller and story-teller, the beggar was admitted in the halls of chieftains, and often treated like a guest; though sometimes, also, no doubt, with contumely. Ulysses charged his son not to betray, by any display of unusual interest in him, that he knew him to be other than he seemed, and even if he saw him insulted, or beaten, not to interpose otherwise than he might do for any stranger. At the palace they found the usual scene of feasting and riot going on. The suitors pretended to receive Telemachus with job at his return, though secretly mortified at the failure of their plots to take his life. The old beggar was permitted to enter, and provided with a portion from the table. A touching incident occurred as Ulysses entered the court-yard of the palace. An old dog lay in yard almost dead with age, and seeing a stranger enter, raised his head, with ears erect. It was Argus, Ulysses' own dog, that he had in other days often led to the chase.

> "Soon as he perceived
> Long-lost Ulysses nigh, down fell his ears
> Clapped close, and with his tail glad sign he gave
> Of gratulation, impotent to rise,
> And to approach his master as of old.
> Ulysses, noting him, wiped off a tear
> Unmarked.
> * * * Then his destiny released
> Old Argus, soon as he had lived to see
> Ulysses in the twentieth year restored."

As Ulysses sat eating his portion in the hall, the suitors soon began to exhibit their insolence to him. When he mildly remonstrated, one of them raised a stool and with it gave him a blow. Telemachus had hard work to restrain his indignation at seeing his father so treated in his own hall, but remembering his father's injunctions, said no more than what became him as master of the house, though young, and protector of his guests.

Penelope had protracted her decision in favor of either of her suitors so long, that there seemed to be no further pretence for delay. The continued absence of her husband seemed to prove that his return was no longer to be expected. Meanwhile her son had grown up, and was able to manage his own affairs. She therefore consented to submit the question of her choice to a trial of skill among the suitors. The test selected was shooting with the bow. Twelve rings were arranged in a line, and he whole arrow was sent through the whole twelve, was to have the queen for his prize. A bow that one of his brother heroes had given to Ulysses in former times, was brought from the armory, and with its quiver full of arrows was laid in the hall. Telemachus had taken care that all other weapons should be removed, under pretence that in the heat of competition, there was danger, in some rash moment, of putting them to an improper use.

All things being prepared for the trial, the first thing to be done was to bend the bow in order to attach the string. Telemachus endeavored to do it, but found all his efforts fruitless; and modestly confessing that he had attempted a task beyond his strength, he yielded the bow to another. *He* tried it with no better success, and, amidst the laughter and jeers of the companions, gave it up. Another tried it and another; they rubbed the bow with tallow, but all to no purpose; it would not bend. Then spoke Ulysses, humbly suggesting that he should be permitted to try; for, said he, "beggar as I am, I was once a soldier, and there is still some strength in these old limbs of mine." The suitors hooted with derision, and commanded to turn him out of the hall for his insolence. But Telemachus spoke up for him, and merely to gratify the old man, bade him try. Ulysses took the bow, and handled it with the hand of a master. With ease he adjusted the cord to its notch, then fitting an arrow to the bow he drew the string and sped the arrow unerring through the rings.

Without allowing them time to express their astonishment, he said, "Now for another mark!" and aimed direct at the most insolent one of the suitors. The arrow pierced through his throat and he fell dead. Telemachus, Eumæus, and another faithful follower, well armed, now sprang to the side of Ulysses. The suitors, in amazement, looked round for arms, but found none, neither was there any way of escape, for Eumæus had secured the door. Ulysses left them not long in uncertainty; he announced himself as the long-lost chief, whose house they had invaded, whose substance they had squandered, whose wife and son they had persecuted for ten long years; and told them he meant to have ample vengeance. All were slain, and Ulysses was left master of his palace and possessor of his kingdom and his wife.

Tennyson's poem of *Ulysses* represents the old hero, after his dangers past and nothing left but to stay at home and be happy, growing tired on inaction and resolving to set forth in quest of new adventures.

> "Come, my friends,
> 'Tis not too late to seek a newer world.
> Push off, and sitting well in smite
> The sounding furrows; for my purpose holds
> To sail beyond the sunset, and the baths
> Oft all the western stars, until I die.
> It may be that the gulfs will wash us down;
> It may be we shall touch the Happy Isles,
> And see the great Achilles whom we knew;" etc.

· · · · · · ·

31

Adventures of Æneas—The Harpies— Dido—Palinurus

We have followed one of the Grecian heroes, Ulysses, in his wanderings, on his return home from Troy, and now we propose to share the fortunes of the remnant of the *conquered* people, under their chief Æneas, in their search for a new home, after the ruin of their native city. On that fatal night when the wooden horse disgorged its contents of armed men, and the capture and conflagration of the city were the result, Æneas made his escape from the scene of destruction, with his father, and his wife, and young son. The father, Anchises, was too old to walk with the speed required, and Æneas took him upon his shoulders. Thus burdened, leading his son and followed by his wife, he made the best of his way out of the burning city; but, in the confusion, his wife was swept away and lost.

On arriving at the place of rendezvous, numerous fugitives, of both sexes, were found, who put themselves under the guidance of Æneas. Some months were spent in preparation, and at length they embarked. They first landed on the neighboring shores of Thrace, and were preparing to build a city, but Æneas was deterred by a prodigy. Preparing to offer sacrifice, he tore some twigs from one of the bushes. To his dismay the wounded part dropped blood. When he repeated the act, a voice from the ground cried out to him, "Spare me, Æneas; I am your kinsman, Polydore, here murdered with many arrows, from which a bush has grown, nourished with my blood." These words recalled to the recollection of Æneas that Polydore was a young prince of Troy, whom his father had sent with ample treasures to the neighboring land of Thrace, to be there brought up, at a distance from the horrors of war. The king to whom he was sent had murdered him, and seized his treasure. Æneas and his companions, considering the land accursed by the stain of such a crime, hastened away.

They next landed on the island of Delos, which was once a floating island, till Jupiter fastened it by adamantine chains to the bottom of the sea. Apollo and Diana were born there, and the island was sacred to Apollo. Here Æneas consulted the oracle of Apollo, and received an answer, ambiguous as usual—"Seek your ancient mother; there the race of Æneas shall dwell, and reduce all other nations to their sway." The Trojans heard with joy, and immediately began to ask one another, "Where is the spot intended by the oracle?" Anchises remembered that there was a tradition that their forefathers came from Crete, and thither they resolved to steer. They arrived at Crete, and began to build their city, but sickness broke out among them, and the fields that they had planted, failed to yield a crop. In this gloomy aspect of affairs, Æneas was warned in a dream to leave the country, and seek a western land, called Hesperia, whence Dardanus, the true founder of the Trojan race, had originally migrated. To Hesperia, now called Italy, therefore, they directed their future course, and not till after many adventures and the lapse of time sufficient to carry a modern navigator several times round the world, did they arrive there.

Their first landing was at the island of the Harpies. These were disgusting birds, with the heads of maidens, with long claws and faces pale with hunger. They were sent by the gods to torment a certain Phineus, whom Jupiter had deprived of his sight, in punishment of his cruelty; and whenever a meal was placed before him, the Harpies darted down from the air and carried it off. They were driven away from Phineus by the heroes of the Argonautic expedition, and took refuge in the island where Æneas now found them.

When they entered the port the Trojans saw herds of cattle roaming over the plain. They slew as many as they wished, and prepared for a feast. But no sooner had they seated themselves at the table, than a horrible clamor was heard in the air, and a flock of these odious harpies came rushing down upon them, seizing in their talons the meat from the dishes, and flying away with it. Æneas and his companions drew their swords and dealt vigorous blows among the monsters, but to no purpose, for they were so nimble it was almost impossible to hit them, and their feathers were like armor impenetrable to steel. One of them, perched on a neighboring cliff, screamed out, "Is it thus, Trojans, you treat us innocent birds, first slaughter our cattle, and then make war on ourselves?" She then predicted dire sufferings to them in their future course, and having vented her wrath flew away. The Trojans made haste to leave the country, and next found themselves coasting along the shore of Epirus. Here they landed, and to their astonishment learned that certain Trojan exiles, who had been carried there as prisoners, had become rulers of the country. Andromache, the widow of Hector, became the wife of one of the victorious Grecian chiefs, to whom she bore a son. Her husband dying, she was left regent of the country, as guardian of her son, and had married a fellow-captive, Helenus, of the royal race of Troy. Helenus and Andromache treated the exiles with the utmost hospitality, and dismissed them loaded with gifts.

From hence Æneas coasted along the shore of Sicily, and passed the country of the Cyclopes. Here they were hailed from the shore by a miserable object, whom by his garments, tattered as they were, they perceived to be a Greek. He told them he was one of Ulysses' companions, left behind by that chief in his hurried departure. He related the story of Ulysses' adventure with Polyphemus, and besought them to take him off with them, as he had no means of sustaining his existence where he was, but wild berries and roots, and lived in constant fear of the Cyclopes. While he spoke Polyphemus made his appearance; a terrible monster, shapeless, vast, whose only eye had been put out.* He walked with cautious steps, feeling his way with a staff, down to the sea-side, to wash his eye-socket in the waves. When he reached the water, he waded out towards them, and his immense height enabled him to advance far into the sea, so that the Trojans, in terror, took to their oars to get out of his way. Hearing the oars, Polyphemus shouted after them, so that the shores resounded, and at the noise the other Cyclopes came forth from their caves and woods, and lined the shore, like a row of lofty pine trees. The Trojans plied their oars, and soon left them out of sight.

Æneas had been cautioned by Helenus to avoid the strait guarded by the monsters Scylla and Charybdis. There Ulysses, the reader will remember, had lost six of his men, seized by Scylla, while the navigators

*See Proverbial Expressions, page 272.

were wholly intent upon avoiding Charybdis. Æneas following the advice of Helenus shunned the dangerous pass and coasted along the island of Sicily.

Juno, seeing the Trojans speeding their way prosperously towards their destined shore, felt her old grudge against them revive, for she could not forget the slight that Paris had put upon her, in awarding the prize of beauty to another. In heavenly minds can such resentments dwell!* Accordingly she hastened to Æolus, the ruler of the winds—the same who supplied Ulysses with favoring gales, giving him the contrary ones tied up in a bag. Æolus obeyed the goddess and sent forth his sons, Boreas, Typhon and the other winds, to toss the ocean. A terrible storm ensued, and the Trojan ships were driven out of their course towards the coast of Africa. They were in imminent danger of being wrecked, and were seperated, so that Æneas thought that all were lost except his own.

At this crisis, Neptune, hearing the storm raging, and knowing that he had given no orders for one, raised his head above the waves, and saw the fleet of Æneas driving before the gale. Knowing the hostility of Juno, he was at no loss to account for it, but his anger was not the less at this interference in his province. He called the winds, soothed the waves, and brushed away the clouds from before the face of the sun. Some of the ships which had got on the rocks, he pried off with his own trident, while Triton and a sea-nymph, putting their shoulders under others, set them afloat again. The Trojans, when the sea became calm, sought the nearest shore, which was the coast of Carthage, where Æneas was so happy as to find that one by one the ships all arrived safe, though badly shaken.

Waller, in his "Panegyric to the Lord Protector" (Cromwell), alludes to this stilling of the storm by Neptune:

"Above the waves, as Neptune showed his face,
  To chide the winds and save the Trojan race,
  So has your Highness, raised above the rest,
  Storms of ambition tossing us repressed."

Dido

Carthage, where the exiles had now arrived, was a spot on the coast of Africa opposite Sicily, where at that time a Tyrian colony under Dido their queen, were laying the foundations of a state destined in later ages to be the rival of Rome itself. Dido was the daughter of Belus, king of Tyre, and sister of Pygmalion who succeeded his father on the throne. Her husband was Sichæus, a man of immense wealth, but Pygmalion, who coveted his treasures, caused him to be put to death. Dido, with a numerous body of friends and followers, both men and women, suc-

*See Proverbial Expressions, page 272.

ceeded in effecting their escape from Tyre, in several vessels, carrying with them the treasures of Sichæus. On arriving at the spot which they selected as the seat of their future home, they asked of the natives only so much land as they could enclose with a bull's hide. When this was readily granted, she caused the hide to be cut into strips, and with them enclosed a spot on which she built a citadel, and called it Byrsa (a hide). Around this fort the city of Carthage rose, and soon became a powerful and flourishing place.

Such was the state of affairs when Æneas with his Trojans arrived there. Dido received the illustrious exiles with friendliness and hospitality. "Not unacquainted with distress," she said, "I have learned to succor the unfortunate."* The queen's hospitality displayed itself in festivities at which games of strength and skill were exhibited. The strangers contended for the palm with her own subjects, on equal terms, the queen declaring that whether the victor were "Trojan or Tyrian should make no difference to her."* At the feast which followed the games, Æneas gave at her request a recital of the closing events of the Trojan history and his own adventures after the fall of the city. Dido was charmed with his discourse and filled with admiration of his exploits. She conceived an ardent passion for him, and he for his part seemed well content to accept the fortunate chance which appeared to offer him at once a happy termination of his wanderings, a home, a kingdom, and a bride. Months rolled away in the enjoyment of pleasant intercourse, and it seemed as if Italy and the empire destined to be founded on its shores were alike forgotten. Seeing which, Jupiter despatched Mercury with a message to Æneas recalling him to a sense of his high destiny, and commanding him to resume his voyage.

Æneas parted from Dido, though she tried every allurement and persuasion to detain him. The blow to her affection and her pride was too much for her to endure, and when she found that he was gone, she mounted a funeral pile which she had caused to be prepared, and having stabbed herself was consumed with the pile. The flames rising over the city were seen by the departing Trojans, and though the cause was unknown, gave to Æneas some intimation of the fatal event.

The following epigram we find in "Elegant Extracts":

FROM THE LATIN

"Unhappy, Dido, was thy fate
  In first and second married state!
  One husband caused thy flight by dying,
  Thy death the other caused by flying."

Palinurus

After touching at the island of Sicily, where Acestes, a prince of Trojan lineage, bore sway, who gave them a hospitable reception, the

*See Proverbial Expressions, page 272.

Trojans reembarked, and held on their course for Italy. Venus now interceded with Neptune to allow her son at last to attain the wished-for goal and find an end of his perils on the deep. Neptune consented, stipulating only for one life as a ransom for the rest. The victim was Palinurus, the pilot. As he sat watching the stars, with his hand on the helm, Somnus sent by Neptune approached in the guise of Phorbas and said, "Palinurus, the breeze is fair, the water smooth, and the ship sails steadily on her course. Lie down a while and take needful rest. I will stand at the helm in your place." Palinurus replied, "Tell me not of smooth seas or favoring winds—me who have seen so much of their treachery. Shall I trust Æneas to the chances of the weather and the winds?" And he continued to grasp the helm and to keep his eyes fixed on the stars. But Somnus waved over him a branch moistened with Lethæan dew, and his eyes closed in spite of all his efforts. Then Somnus pushed him overboard and he fell; but keeping his hold upon the helm, it came away with him. Neptune was mindful of his promise and kept the ship on her track without helm or pilot, till Æneas discovered his loss, and sorrowing deeply for his faithful steersman took charge of the ship himself.

There is a beautiful allusion to the story of Palinurus in Scott's "Marmion," Introduction to Canto I, where the poet, speaking of the recent death of William Pitt, says,

"O, think now, to his latest day,
   When death just hovering claimed his prey,
   With Palinure's unaltered mood,
   Firm at his dangerous post he stood;
   Each call for needful rest repelled,
   With dying hand the rudder held,
   Till in his fall, with fateful sway,
   The steerage of the realm gave way."

The ships at last reached the shores of Italy, and joyfully did the adventurers leap to land. While his people were employed in making their encampment Æneas sought the abode of the Sibyl. It was a cave connected with a temple and grove, sacred to Apollo and Diana. While Æneas contemplated the scene, the Sibyl accosted him. She seemed to know his errand, and under the influence of the deity of the place, burst forth in a prophetic strain, giving dark intimations of labors and perils through which he was destined to make his way to final success. She closed with the encouraging words which have become proverbial: "Yield not to disasters, but press onward the more bravely."* Æneas replied that he had prepared himself for whatever might await him. He had but one request to make. Having been directed in a dream to seek the abode of the dead in order to confer with his father Anchises to receive from him a revelation of his future fortunes and those of his

*See Proverbial Expressions, page 272.

race, he asked her assistance to enable him to accomplish the task. The Sibyl replied, "The descent to Avernus is easy; the gate of Pluto stands open night and day; but to retrace one's steps and return to the upper air, that is the toil, that the difficulty.* She instructed him to seek in the forest a tree on which grew a golden branch. This branch was to be plucked off and borne as a gift to Proserpine, and if fate was propitious it would yield to the hand and quit its parent trunk, but otherwise no force could rend it away. If torn away another would succeed.*

Æ neas followed the directions of the Sibyl. His mother Venus sent two of her doves to fly before him and show him the way, and by their assistance he found the tree, plucked the branch, and hastened back with it to the Sibyl.

· · · · · · · ·

32

The Infernal Regions – The Sibyl

As at the commencement of our series we have given the pagan account of the creation of the world, so as we approach its conclusion, we present a view of the regions of the dead, depicted by one of their most enlightened poets, who drew his doctrines from their most esteemed philosophers. The region where Virgil locates the entrance into this abode, is perhaps the most strikingly adapted to excite ideas of the terrific and preternatural of any on the face of the earth. It is the volcanic region near Vesuvius, where the whole country is cleft with chasms from which sulphurous flames arise, while the ground is shaken with pent-up vapors, and mysterious sounds issue from the bowels of the earth. The lake Avernus is supposed to fill the crater of an extinct volcano. It is circular, half a mile wide, and very deep, surrounded by high banks, which in Virgil's time were covered with a gloomy forest. Mephitic vapors rise from its waters, so that no life is found on its banks, and no birds fly over it. Here, according to the poet, was the cave which afforded access to the infernal regions, and here Æneas offered sacrifices to the infernal deities, Proserpine, Hecate, and the Furies. Then a roaring was heard in the earth, the woods on the hill-tops were shaken, and the howling of dogs announced the approach of the deities. "Now," said the Sibyl, "summon up your courage, for you will need it." She descended into the cave, and Æneas followed. Before the threshold of hell they passed through a group of beings who are enumerated as Griefs and avenging Cares, pale Diseases and melancholy Age, Fear and Hunger that tempt to crime, Toil, Poverty, and Death, forms horrible to view. The Furies spread their couches there, and Discord, whose hair was of vipers tied up with a bloody fillet. Here also were the monsters, Briareus with his hundred arms, Hydras hissing, and Chimæras breathing fire. Æneas

*See Proverbial Expressions, page 272.

shuddered at the sight, drew his sword and would have struck, but the Sibyl restrained him. They then came to the black river Cocytus, where they found the ferryman, Charon, old and squalid, but strong and vigorous, who was receiving passengers of all kinds into his boat, magnanimous heroes, boys and unmarried girls, as numerous as the leaves that fall at autumn, or the flocks that fly southward at the approach of winter. They stood pressing for a passage and longing to touch the opposite shore. But the stern ferryman took in only such as he chose, driving the rest back. Æneas, wondering at the sight, asked the Sibyl, "Why this discrimination?" She answered, "Those who are taken on board the bark are the souls of those who have received due burial rites; the host of others who have remained unburied, are not permitted to pass the flood, but wander a hundred years, and flit to and fro about the shore, till at last they are taken over." Æneas grieved at recollecting some of his own companions who had perished in the storm. At that moment he beheld Palinurus, his pilot, who fell overboard and was drowned. He addressed him and asked him the cause of his misfortune. Palinurus replied that the rudder was carried away, and he clinging to it was swept away with it. He besought Æneas most urgently to extend to him his hand and take him in company to the opposite shore. But the Sibyl rebuked him for the wish thus to transgress the laws of Pluto; but consoled him by informing him that the people of the shore where his body had been wafted by the waves, should be stirred up by prodigies to give it due burial, and that the promontory should bear the name of Cape Palinurus, which it does to this day. Leaving Palinurus consoled by these words, they approached the boat. Charon, fixing his eyes sternly upon the advancing warrior, demanded by what right he, living and armed, approached that shore. To which the Sibyl replied that they would commit no violence, that Æneas's only object was to see his father, and finally exhibited the golden branch, at sight of which Charon's wrath relaxed, and he made haste to turn his bark to the shore, and receive them on board. The boat, adapted only to the light freight of bodiless spirits, groaned under the weight of the hero. They were soon conveyed to the opposite shore. There they were encountered by the three-headed dog Cerberus, with his necks bristling with snakes. He barked with all his three throats till the Sibyl threw him a medicated cake, which he eagerly devoured, and then stretched himself out in his den and fell asleep. Æneas and the Sibyl sprang to land. The first sound that struck their ears was the wailing of young children, who had died on the threshold of life, and near to these were they who had perished under false charges. Minos presides over them as judge, and examines the deeds of each. The next class was of those who had died by their own hand, hating life and seeking refuge in death. O, how willingly would they now endure poverty, labor, and any other infliction, if they might but return to life! Next were situated the regions of sadness, divided off into retired paths, leading through groves of myrtle. Here roamed those who had fallen victims to unrequited love, not freed from pain even by death itself. Among these, Æneas thought he descried the form of Dido, with a wound still recent. In the dim light he was for a moment uncertain, but approaching, perceived it was indeed herself. Tears fell from his eyes, and he addressed her in the accents of love. "Unhappy Dido! was then the rumor true that you had perished? and was I, alas! the cause? I call the gods to witness that my departure from you was reluctant, and in obedience to the commands of Jove; nor could I believe that my absence would have cost you so dear. Stop, I beseech you, and refuse me not a last farewell." She stood for a moment with averted countenance, and eyes fixed on the ground, and then silently passed on, as insensible to his pleadings as a rock. Æneas followed for some distance; then, with a heavy heart, rejoined his companion and resumed his route.

They next entered the fields where roam the heroes who have fallen in battle. Here they saw many shades of Grecian and Trojan warriors. The Trojans thronged around him, and could not be satisfied with the sight. They asked the case of his coming, and plied him with innumerable questions. But the Greeks, at the sight of his armor glittering through the murky atmosphere, recognized the hero, and filled with terror turned their backs and fled, as they used to do on the plains of Troy.

Æneas would have lingered long with his Trojan friends, but the Sibyl hurried him away. They next came to a place where the road divided, the one leading to Elysium, the other to the regions of the condemned. Æneas beheld on one side the walls of a mighty city, around which Phlegethon rolled its fiery waters. Before him was the gate of adamant that neither gods nor men can break through. An iron tower stood by the gate, on which Tisiphone, the avenging Fury, kept guard. From the city were heard groans, and the sound of the scourge, the creaking of iron, and the clanking of chains. Æneas, horror-struck, inquired of his guide what crimes were those whose punishments produced the sounds he heard? The Sibyl answered, "Here is the judgment hall of Rhadamanthus, who brings to light crimes done in life, which the perpetrator vainly thought impenetrably hid. Tisiphone applies her whip of scorpions, and delivers the offender over to her sister Furies. At this moment with horrid clang the brazen gates unfolded, and Æneas saw within, a Hydra with fifty heads, guarding the entrance. The Sibyl told him that the gulf of Tartarus descended deep, so that its recesses were as far beneath their feet as heaven was high above their heads. In the bottom of this pit, the Titan race, who warred against the gods, lie prostrate; Salmoneus, also, who presumed to vie with Jupiter, and built a bridge of brass over which he drove his chariot that the sound might resemble thunder, launching flaming brands at his people in imitation of lightning, till Jupiter struck him with a real thunderbolt, and taught him the difference between mortal weapons and divine. Here, also, is Tityus, the giant, whose form is so immense that as he lies, he stretches over nine acres, while a vulture preys upon his liver, which as fast as it is devoured grows again, so that his punishment will have no end.

Æneas saw groups seated at tables loaded with dainties, while nearby stood a Fury who snatched away the viands from their lips, as fast as they prepared to taste them. Others beheld suspended over their heads huge rocks, threatening to fall, keeping them in a state of constant alarm. These were they who had hated their brothers, or struck their parents, or defrauded the friends who trusted them, or who, having grown rich, kept their money to themselves, and gave no share to others; the last being the most numerous class. Here also were those who had violated the marriage vow, or fought in a bad cause, or failed in fidelity to their employers. Here was one who had sold his country for gold, another who perverted the laws, making them say one thing to-day and another to-morrow.

Ixion was there, fastened to the circumference of a wheel ceaselessly revolving; and Sisyphus, whose task was to roll a huge stone up to a hill-top, but when the steep was well-nigh gained, the rock, repulsed by some sudden force, rushed again headlong down to the plain. Again he toiled at it, while the sweat bathed all his weary limbs, but all to no effect. There was Tantalus, who stood in a pool, his chin level with the water, yet he was parched with thirst, and found nothing to assuage it; for when he bowed his hoary head, eager to quaff, the water fled away, leaving the ground at his feet all dry. Tall trees laden with fruit stooped their heads to him, pears, pomegranates, apples, and luscious figs; but when with a sudden grasp he tried to seize them, winds whirled them high above his reach.

The Sibyl now warned Æneas that it was time to turn from these melancholy regions and seek the city of the blessed. They passed through a middle tract of darkness, and came upon the Elysian fields, the groves where the happy reside. They breathed a freer air, and saw all objects clothed in a purple light. The region has a sun and stars of its own. The inhabitants were enjoying themselves in various ways, some in sports on the grassy turf, in games of strength or skill, others dancing or singing. Orpheus struck the chords of his lyre, and called forth ravishing sounds. Here Æneas saw the founders of the Trojan state, magnamimous heroes who lived in happier times. He gazed with admiration on the war chariots and glittering arms now reposing in disuse. Spears stood fixed in the ground, and the horses, unharnessed, roamed over the plain. The same pride in splendid armor and generous steeds which the old heroes felt in life, accompanied them here. He saw another group feasting, and listening to the strains of music. They were in a laurel grove, whence the great river Po has its origin, and flows out among men. Here dwelt those who fell by wounds received in their country's cause, holy priests also, and poets who have uttered thoughts worthy of Apollo, and others who have contributed to cheer and adorn life by their discoveries in the useful arts, and have made their memory blessed by rendering service to mankind. They wore snow-white fillets about their brows. The Sibyl addressed a group of these, and inquired where Anchises was to be found. They were directed where to seek him, and soon found him in a verdant valley, where he was contemplating the ranks of his posterity, their destinies and worthy deeds to be achieved in coming times. When he recognized Æneas approaching, he stretched out both hands to him, while tears flowed freely. "Have you come at last," said he, "long expected, and do I behold you after such perils past? O my son, how have I trembled for you as I have watched your career!" To which Æneas replied, "O father! your image was always before me to guide and guard me." Then he endeavored to enfold his father in his embrace, but his arms enclosed only an unsubstantial image.

Æneas perceived before him a spacious valley, with trees gently waving to the wind, a tranquil landscape, through which the river Lethe flowed. Along the banks of the stream wandered a countless multitude, numerous as insects in summer air. Æneas, with surprise, inquired who were these. Anchises answered, "They are souls to which bodies are to be given in due time. Meanwhile they dwell on Lethe's bank, and drink oblivion of their former lives." "O, father!" said Æneas, "is it possible that any can be so in love with life, as to wish to leave these tranquil seats for the upper world?" Anchises replied by explaining the plan of creation. The Creator, he told him, originally made the material of which souls are composed, of the four elements, fire, air, earth, and water, all which when united took the form of the most excellent part, fire, and became *flame*. This material was scattered like seed among the heavenly bodies, the sun, moon, and stars. Of this seed the inferior gods created man and all other animals, mingling it with various proportions of earth, by which its purity was alloyed and reduced. Thus the more earth predominates in the composition, the less pure is the individual; and we see men and women with their full-grown bodies have not the purity of childhood. So in proportion to the time which the union of body and soul has lasted, is the impurity contracted by the spiritual part. This impurity must be purged away after death, which is done by ventilating the souls in the current of winds, or merging them in water, or burning out their impurities by fire. Some few, of whom Anchises intimates that he is one, are admitted at once to Elysium, there to remain. But the rest, after the impurities of earth are purged away, are sent back to life endowed with new bodies, having had the remembrance of their former lives effectually washed away by the waters of Lethe. Some, however, there still are, so thoroughly corrupted, that they are not fit to be intrusted with human bodies, and these are made into brute animals, lions, tigers, cats, dogs, monkeys, etc. This is what the ancients called Metempsychosis, or the transmigration of souls; a doctrine which is still held by the natives of India, who scruple to destroy the life, even of the most insignificant animal, not knowing but it may be one of their relations in an altered form.

Anchises, having explained so much, proceeded to point out to Æneas individuals of his race, who were hereafter to be born, and to relate to him the exploits they should perform in the world. After this he reverted to the present, and told his son of the events that remained to him to be accomplished before the complete establishment of himself and his followers in Italy. Wars were to be waged, battles fought, a bride to be won, and in the result a Trojan state founded, from which should rise the Roman power, to be in time the sovereign of the world.

Æneas and the Sibyl then took leave of Anchises, and returned by some short cut, which the poet does not explain, to the upper world.

Elysium

Virgil, we have seen, places his Elysium under the earth, and assigns it for a residence to the spirits of the blessed. But in Homer Elysium forms no part of the realms of the dead. He places it on the west of the earth, near Ocean, and describes it as a happy land, where there is neither snow, nor cold, nor rain, and is always fanned by the delightful breezes of Zephyrus. Hither favored heroes pass without dying and live happy under the rule of Rhadamanthus. The Elysium of Hesiod and Pindar is in the Isles of the Blessed, or Fortunate Islands, in the Western Ocean. From these sprang the legend of the happy island Atlantis. This blissful region may have been wholly imaginary, but possibly may have sprung from the reports of some storm-driven mariners who had caught a glimpse of the coast of America.

J.R. Lowell, in one of his shorter poems, claims for the present age some of the privileges of that happy realm. Addressing the Past, he says,

> "Whatever of true life there was in thee,
>   Leaps in our age's veins.
>   *   *   *   *   *
> "Here, 'mid the bleak waves of our strife and care,
>   Float the green Fortunate Isles,
>   Where all thy hero-spirits dwell and share
>   Our martyrdoms and toils.
>   The present moves attended
>   With all of brave and excellent and fair
>   That made the old time splendid."

Milton also alludes to the same fable in "Paradise Lost," Book III, 1, 568.

> "Like those Hesperian gardens famed of old,
>   Fortunate fields and groves and flowery vales,
>   Thrice happy isles."

And in Book II he characterizes the rivers of Erebus according to the meaning of their names in the Greek language:

> "Abhorred Styx, the flood of deadly hate,
>   Sad Acheron of sorrow black and deep;
>   Cocytus named of lamentation loud

Heard on the rueful stream; fierce Phlegethon
Whose waves of torrent fire inflame with rage.
Far off from these a slow and silent stream,
Lethe, the river of oblivion, rolls
Her watery labyrinth, whereof who drinks
Forthwith his former state and being forgets,
Forgets both joy and grief, pleasure and pain."

The Sibyl

As Æneas and the Sibyl pursued their way back to earth, he said to her, "Whether thou be a goddess or a mortal beloved of the gods, by me thou shalt always be held in reverence. When I reach the upper air, I will cause a temple to be built to thy honor, and will myself bring offerings." "I am no goddess," said the Sibyl; "I have no claim to sacrifice or offering. I am mortal; yet if I could have accepted the love of Apollo, I might have been immortal. He promised me the fulfilment of my wish, if I would consent to be his. I took a handful of sand, and holding it forth, said, 'Grant me to see as many birthdays as there are sand grains in my hand.' Unluckily I forgot to ask for enduring youth. This also he would have granted, could I have accepted his love, but offended at my refusal, he allowed me to grow old. My youth and youthful strength fled long ago. I have lived seven hundred years, and to equal the number of the sand-grains, I have still to see three hundred springs and three hundred harvests. My body shrinks up as years increase, and in time, I shall be lost to sight, but my voice will remain, and future ages will respect my sayings."

These concluding words of the Sibyl alluded to her prophetic power. In her cave she was accustomed to inscribe on leaves gathered from the trees the names and fates of individuals. The leaves thus inscribed were arranged in order within the cave, and might be consulted by her votaries. But if perchance at the opening of the door the wind rushed in and dispersed the leaves, the Sibyl gave no aid to restoring them again, and the oracle was irreparably lost.

The following legend of the Sibyl is fixed at a later date. In the reign of one of the Tarquins there appeared before the king a woman who offered him nine books for sale. The king refused to purchase them, whereupon the woman went away and burned three of the books, and returning offered the remaining books for the same price she had asked for the nine. The king again rejected them; but when the woman, after burning three books more, returned and asked for the three remaining the same price which she had before asked for the nine, his curiosity was excited, and he purchased the books. They were found to contain the destinies of the Roman state. They were kept in the temple of Jupiter Capitolinus, preserved in a stone chest, and allowed to be inspected only by especial officers appointed for that duty, who on great occasions consulted them and interpreted their oracles to the people.

There were various Sibyls; but the Cumæan Sibyl, of whom Ovid and

Virgil write, is the most celebrated of them. Ovid's story of her life protracted to one thousand years may be intended to represent the various Sibyls as being only reappearances of one and the same individual.

Young, in the "Night Thoughts," alludes to the Sibyl. Speaking of Worldly Wisdom, he says,

> "If future fate she plans 'tis all in leaves,
> Like Sibyl, unsubstantial, fleeting bliss;
> At the first blast it vanishes in air.
>   *   *   *   *
> As worldly schemes resemble Sibyl's leaves,
> The good man's days to Sibyl's books compare,
> The price still rising as in number less."
>   · · · · · · ·

33

Camilla – Evander – Nisus and Euryalus – Mezentius – Turnus

Æneas, having parted from the Sibyl and rejoined his fleet, coasted along the shores of Italy and cast anchor in the mouth of the Tiber. The poet, having brought his hero to this spot, the destined termination of his wanderings, invokes his Muse to tell him the situation of things at that eventful moment. Latinus, third in descent from Saturn, ruled the country. He was now old and had no male descendant, but had one charming daughter, Lavinia, who was sought in marriage by many neighboring chiefs, one of whom, Turnus, king of the Rutulians, was favored by the wishes of her parents. But Latinus had been warned in a dream by his father Faunus, that the destined husband of Lavinia should come from a foreign land. From that union should spring a race destined to subdue the world.

Our readers will remember that in the conflict with the Harpies, one of those half-human birds had threatened the Trojans with dire sufferings. In particular she predicted that before their wanderings ceased they should be pressed by hunger to devour their tables. This portent now came true; for as they took their scanty meal, seated on the grass, the men placed their hard biscuit on their laps, and put thereon whatever their gleanings in the woods supplied. Having despatched the latter they finished by eating the crusts. Seeing which, the boy Iulus said playfully, "See, we are eating our tables." Æneas caught the words and accepted the omen. "All hail, promised land!" he exclaimed, "this is our home, this our country!" He then took measures to find out who were the present inhabitants of the land, and who their rulers. A hundred chosen men were sent to the village of Latinus, bearing presents and a request for friendship and alliance. They went and were favorably received. Latinus immediately concluded that the Trojan hero was no other than the promised son-in-law announced by the oracle. He cheerfully granted his alliance and sent back the messengers mounted on steeds from his stables, and loaded with gifts and friendly messages.

Juno, seeing things go thus prosperously for the Trojans, felt her old animosity revive, summoned Alecto from Erebus, and sent her to stir up discord. The Fury first took possession of the queen, Amata, and roused her to oppose in every way the new alliance. Alecto then speeded to the city of Turnus, and assuming the form of an old priestess, informed him of the arrival of the foreigners and of the attempts of their prince to rob him of his bride. Next she turned her attention to the camp of the Trojans. There she saw the boy Iulus and his companions amusing themselves with hunting. She sharpened the scent of the dogs, and led them to rouse up from the thicket a tame stag, the favorite of Silvia, the daughter of Tyrrheus, the king's herdsman. A javelin from the hand of Iulus wounded the animal, and he had only strength left to run homewards, and died at his mistress's feet. Her cries and tears roused her brothers and herdsmen, and they, seizing whatever weapons came to hand, furiously assaulted the hunting party. These were protected by their friends, and the herdsmen were finally driven back with the loss of two of their number.

These things were enough to rouse the storm of war, and the queen, Turnus, and the peasants all urged the old king to drive the strangers from the country. He resisted as long as he could, but finding his opposition unavailing, finally gave way and retreated to his retirement.

Opening the Gates of Janus

It was the custom of the country, when war was to be undertaken, for the chief magistrate, clad in his robes of office, with solemn pomp to open the gates of the temple of Janus, which were kept shut as long as peace endured. His people now urged the old king to perform that solemn office, but he refused to do so. While they contested, Juno herself, descending from the skies, smote the doors with irresistible force, and burst them open. Immediately the whole country was in a flame. The people rushed from every side breathing nothing but war.

Turnus was recognized by all as leader; others joined as allies, chief of whom was Mezentius, a brave and able soldier, but of detestable cruelty. He had been the chief of one of the neighboring cities, but his people drove him out. With him was joined his son Lausus, a generous youth worthy of a better sire.

Camilla

Camilla, the favorite of Diana, a huntress and warrior, after the fashion of the Amazons, came with her band of mounted followers, including a select number of her own sex, and ranged herself on the side of Turnus. This maiden had never accustomed her fingers to the distaff or the loom, but had learned to endure the toils of war, and in speed to outstrip the wind. It seemed as if she might run over the standing corn without crushing it, or over the surface of the water without dipping her feet. Camilla's history had been singular from the beginning. Her father, Metabus, driven from his city by civil discord, carried with him in his flight his infant daughter. As he fled through the woods, his enemies in hot pursuit, he reached the bank of the river Amazenus, which, swelled by rains, seemed to debar a passage. He paused for a moment, then decided what to do. He tied the infant to his lance with wrappers of bark, and poising the weapon in his upraised hand, thus addressed Diana: "Goddess of the woods! I consecrate this maid to you"; then hurled the weapon with its burden to the opposite bank. The spear flew across the roaring water. His pursuers were already upon him, but he plunged into the river and swam across, and found the spear, with the infant safe on the other side. Thenceforth he lived among the shepherds and brought up his daughter in woodland arts. While a child she was taught to use the bow and throw the javelin. With her sling she could bring down the crane or the wild swan. Her dress was a tiger's skin. Many mothers sought her for a daughter-in-law, but she continued faithful to Diana and repelled the thought of marriage.

Evander

Such were the formidable allies that ranged themselves against Æneas. It was night and he lay stretched in sleep on the bank of the river, under the open heavens. The god of the stream, Father River, seemed to raise his head above the willows and to say, "O goddess-born, destined possessor of the Latin realms, this is the promised land, here is to be your home, here shall terminate the hostility of the heavenly powers, if only you faithfully persevere. There are friends not far distant. Prepare your boats and row up my stream; I will lead you to Evander the Arcadian chief. He has long been at strife with Turnus and the Rutulians, and is prepared to become an ally of yours. Rise! offer your vows to Juno, and deprecate her anger. When you have achieved your victory then think of me." Æneas woke and paid immediate obedience to the friendly vision. He sacrificed to Juno, and invoked the god of the river and all his tributary fountains to lend their aid. Then for the first time a vessel filled with armed warriors floated on the stream of the Tiber. The river smoothed its waves, and bade its current flow gently, while, impelled by the vigorous strokes of the rowers, the vessel shot rapidly up the stream.

About the middle of the day they came in sight of the scattered buildings of the infant town where in after times the proud city of Rome grew, whose glory reached the skies. By chance the old king, Evander, was that day celebrating annual solemnities in honor of Hercules and all the gods. Pallas, his son, and all the chiefs of the little commonwealth stood by. When they saw the tall ship gliding onward through the wood, they were alarmed at the sight, and rose from the tables. But Pallas forbade the solemnities to be interrupted, and seizing a weapon, stepped forward to the river's bank. He called aloud, demanding who they were, and what their object. Æneas, holding forth an olive-branch, replied, "We are Trojans, friends to you and enemies to the Rutulians. We seek Evander, and offer to join our arms with yours." Pallas, in amaze at the sound of so great a name, invited them to land, and when Æneas touched the shore he seized his hand, and held it long in friendly grasp. Proceeding through the wood they joined the king and his party and were most favorably received. Seats were provided for them at the tables, and the repast proceeded.

Infant Rome

When the solemnities were ended all moved towards the city. The king, bending with age, walked between his son and Æneas, taking the arm of one or the other of them, and with much variety of pleasing talk shortening the way. Æneas with delight looked and listened, observing all the beauties of the scene, and learning much of heroes renowned in ancient times. Evander said, "These extensive groves were once inhabited by fauns and nymphs, and a rude race of men who sprang from the trees themselves, and had neither laws nor social culture. They knew not how to yoke the cattle nor raise a harvest, nor provide from present abundance for future want; but browsed like beasts upon the leafy boughs, or fed voraciously on their hunted prey. Such were they when Saturn, expelled from Olympus by his sons, came among them and drew together the fierce savages, formed them into society, and gave them laws. Such peace and plenty ensued that men ever since have called his reign the golden age; but by degrees far other times succeeded, and the thirst of gold and the thirst of blood prevailed. The land was a prey to successive tyrants, till fortune and resistless destiny brought me hither, an exile from my native land, Arcadia."

Having thus said, he showed him the Tarpeian rock, and the rude spot then overgrown with bushes where in after times the Capitol rose in all its magnificence. He next pointed to some dismantled walls, and said, "Here stood Janiculum, built by Janus, and there Saturnia, the town of Saturn." Such discourse brought them to the cottage of poor Evander, whence they saw the lowing herds roaming over the plain where now the proud and stately Forum stands. They entered, and a couch was spread for Æneas, well stuffed with leaves and covered with the skin of a Libyan bear.

Next morning, awakened by the dawn and the shrill song of birds beneath the eaves of his low mansion, old Evander rose. Clad in a tunic, and a panther's skin thrown over his shoulders, with sandals on his feet, and his good sword girded to his side, he went forth to seek his guest. Two mastiffs followed him, his whole retinue and body guard. He found the hero attended by his faithful Achates, and, Pallas soon joining them, the old king spoke thus:

"Illustrious Trojan, it is but little we can do in so great a cause. Our state is feeble, hemmed in on one side by the river, on the other by the Rutulians. But I propose to ally you with a people numerous and rich, to whom fate has brought you at the propitious moment. The Etruscans hold the country beyond the river. Mezentius was their king, a monster of cruelty, who invented unheard-of torments to gratify his vengeance. He would fasten the dead to the living, hand to hand and face to face, and leave the wretched victims to die in that dreadful embrace. At length the people cast him out, him and his house. They burned his palace and slew his friends. He escaped and took refuge with Turnus, who protects him with arms. The Etruscans demand that he shall be given up to deserved punishment, and would ere now have attempted to enforce their demand; but their priests restrain them, telling them that it is the will of heaven that no native of the land shall guide them to victory, and that their destined leader must come from across the sea. They have offered the crown to me, but I am too old to undertake such great affairs, and my son is native-born, which precludes him from the choice. You, equally by birth and time of life, and fame in arms, pointed out by the gods, have but to appear to be hailed at once as their leader. With you I will join Pallas, my son, my only hope and comfort. Under you he shall learn the art of war, and strive to emulate your great exploits.''

Then the king ordered horses to be furnished for the Trojan chiefs, and Æneas, with a chosen band of followers and Pallas accompanying, mounted and took the way to the Etruscan city,* having sent back the rest of his party in the ships. Æneas and his band safely arrived at the Etruscan camp and were received with open arms by Tarchon and his countrymen.

Nisus and Euryalus

In the meanwhile Turnus had collected his bands and made all necessary preparations for the war. Juno sent Iris to him with a message inciting him to take advantage of the absence of Æneas and surprise the Trojan camp. Accordingly the attempt was made, but the Trojans were found on their guard, and having received strict orders from Æneas not to fight in his absence, they lay still in their intrenchments, and resisted all the efforts of the Rutulians to draw them into the field. Night coming on, the army of Turnus, in high spirits at their fancied superiority, feasted and enjoyed themselves, and finally stretched themselves on the field and slept secure.

In the camp of the Trojans things were far otherwise. There all was watchfulness and anxiety, and impatience for Æneas's return. Nisus stood guard at the entrance of the camp, and Euryalus, a youth distinguished above all in the army for graces of person and fine qualitites, was with him. These two were friends and brothers in arms. Nisus said to his friend, ''Do you perceive what confidence and carelessness the enemy display? Their lights are few and dim, and the

---

*The poet here inserts a famous line which is thought to imitate in its sound the galloping of horses. It may be thus translated: ''Then struck the hoofs of the steeds on the ground with a four-footed trampling.'' See Proverbial Expressions, page 273.

men seem all oppressed with wine or sleep. You know how anxiously our chiefs wish to send to Æneas, and to get intelligence from him. Now I am strongly moved to make my way through the enemy's camp and to go in search of our chief. If I succeed, the glory of the deed will be reward enough for me, and if they judge the service deserves any thing more, let them pay it to you.''

Euryalus, all on fire with the love of adventure, replied, ''Would you then, Nisus, refuse to share your enterprise with me? And shall I let you go into such danger alone? Not so my brave father brought me up, nor so have I planned for myself when I joined the standard of Æneas, and resolved to hold my life cheap in comparison with honor.'' Nisus replied, ''I doubt it not, my friend; but you know the uncertain event of such an undertaking, and whatever may happen to me, I wish you to be safe. You are younger than I and have more of life in prospect. Nor can I be the cause of such grief to your mother, who has chosen to be here in the camp with you rather than stay and live in peace with the other matrons in Acestes' city.'' Euryalus replied, ''Say no more. In vain you seek arguments to dissuade me. I am fixed in the resolution to go with you. Let us lose no time.'' They called the guard, and committing the watch to them, sought the general's tent. They found the chief officers in consultation, deliberating how they should send notice to Æneas of their situation. The offer of the two friends was gladly accepted, themselves loaded with praises and promised the most liberal rewards in case of success. Iulus especially addressed Euryalus, assuring him of his lasting friendship. Euryalus replied, ''I have but one boon to ask. My aged mother is with me in the camp. For me she left the Trojan soil, and would not stay behind with the other matrons at the city of Acestes. I go now without taking leave of her. I could not bear her tears nor set at nought her entreaties. But do thou, I beseech you, comfort her in her distress. Promise me that and I shall go more boldly into whatever dangers may present themselves.'' Iulus and the other chiefs were moved to tears, and promised to do all his request. ''Your mother shall be mine,'' said Iulus, ''and all that I have promised to you shall be made good to her, if you do not return to receive it.''

The two friends left the camp and plunged at once into the midst of the enemy. They found no watch, no sentinels posted, but all about, the sleeping soldiers strewn on the grass and among the wagons. The laws of war at that early day did not forbid a brave man to slay a sleeping foe, and the two Trojans slew, as they passed, such of the enemy as they could without exciting alarm. In one tent Euryalus made prize of a helmet brilliant with gold and plumes. They had passed through the enemy's ranks without being discovered, but now suddenly appeared a troop directly in front of them, which under Volscens, their leader, were approaching the camp. The glittering helmet of Euryalus caught their attention, and Volscens hailed the two, and demanded who and whence they were. They made no answer, but plunged into the wood. The horsemen scattered in all directions to intercept their flight. Nisus had eluded pursuit and was out of danger, but Euryalus being missing he turned back to seek him. He again entered the wood and soon came within sound of voices. Looking through the thicket he saw the whole band surrounding Euryalus with noisy questions. What should he do! How extricate the youth! Or would it be better to die with him?

Raising his eyes to the moon which now shone clear, he said, "Goddess! favor my effort!" and aiming his javelin at one of the leaders of the troop, struck him in the back and stretched him on the plain with a death-blow. In the midst of their amazement another weapon flew and another of the party fell dead. Volscens, the leader, ignorant whence the darts came, rushed sword in hand upon Euryalus. "You shall pay the penalty of both," he said, and would have plunged the sword into his bosom, when Nisus, who from his concealment saw the peril of his friend, rushed forward exclaiming, " 'Twas I, 'twas I; turn your swords against me, Rutulians; I did it; he only followed me as a friend." While he spoke the sword fell, and pierced the comely bosom of Euryalus. His head fell over his shoulder, like a flower cut down by the plough. Nisus rushed upon Volscens and plunged his sword into his body, and was himself slain on the instant by numberless blows.

Mezentius

Æneas, with his Etrurian allies, arrived on the scene of action on time to rescue his beleaguered camp; and now the two armies being nearly equal in strength, the war began in good earnest. We cannot find space for all the details, but must simply record the fate of the principal characters whom we have introduced to our readers. The tyrant Mezentius, finding himself engaged against his revolted subjects, raged like a wild beast. He slew all who dared to withstand him, and put the multitude to flight wherever he appeared. At last he encountered Æneas, and the armies stood still to see the issue. Mezentius threw his spear, which striking Æneas's shield glanced off and hit Anthor. He was a Grecian by birth, who had left Argos, his native city, and followed Evander into Italy. The poet says of him with simple pathos which has made the words proverbial, "He fell, unhappy, by a wound intended for another, looked up to the skies, and dying remembered sweet Argos."* Æneas now in turn hurled his lance. It pierced the shield of Mezentius, and wounded him in the thigh. Lausus, his son, could not bear the sight, but rushed forward and interposed himself, while the followers pressed round Mezentius and bore him away. Æneas held his sword suspended over Lausus and delayed to strike, but the furious youth pressed on and he was compelled to deal the fatal blow. Lausus fell, and Æneas bent over him in pity. "Hapless youth," he said, "what can I do for you worthy of your praise? Keep those arms in which you glory, and fear not but that your body shall be restored to your friends, and have due funeral honors."

See Proverbial Expressions, page 273.

So saying, he called the timid followers and delivered the body into their hands.

Mezentius meanwhile had been borne to the river-side, and washed his wound. Soon the news reached him of Lausus's death, and rage and despair supplied the place of strength. He mounted his horse and dashed into the thickest of the fight, seeking Æneas. Having found him, he rode round him in a circle, throwing one javelin after another, while Æneas stood fenced with his shield, turning every way to meet them. At last, after Mezentius had three times made the circuit, Æneas threw his lance directly at the horse's head. It pierced his temples and he fell, while a shout from both armies rent the skies. Mezentius asked no mercy, but only that his body might be spared the insults of his revolted subjects, and be buried in the same grave with his son. He received the fatal stroke not unprepared, and poured out his life and his blood together.

Pallas, Camilla, Turnus

While these things were doing in one part of the field, in another Turnus encountered the youthful Pallas. The contest between champions so unequally matched could not be doubtful. Pallas bore himself bravely, but fell by the lance of Turnus. The victor almost relented when he saw the brave youth lying dead at his feet, and spared to use the privilege of a conqueror in despoiling him of his arms. The belt only, adorned with studs and carvings of gold, he took and clasped round his own body. The rest he remitted to the friends of the slain.

After the battle there was a cessation of arms for some days to allow both armies to bury their dead. In this interval Æneas challenged Turnus to decide the contest by single combat, but Turnus evaded the challenge. Another battle ensued, in which Camilla, the virgin warrior, was chiefly conspicuous. Her deeds of valor surpassed those of the bravest warriors, and many Trojans and Etruscans fell pierced with her darts or struck down by her battle-axe. At last an Etruscan named Aruns, who had watched her long, seeking for some advantage, observed her pursuing a flying enemy whose splendid armor offered a tempting prize. Intent on the chase she observed not her danger, and the javelin of Aruns struck her and inflicted a fatal wound. She fell and breathed her last in the arms of her attendant maidens. But Diana, who beheld her fate, suffered not her slaughter to be unavenged. Aruns, as he stole away, glad but frightened, was struck by a secret arrow, launched by one of the nymphs of Diana's train, and died ignobly and unknown.

At length the final conflict took place between Æneas and Turnus. Turnus had avoided the contest as long as he could, but at last impelled by the ill success of his arms, and by the murmurs of his followers, he braced himself to the conflict. It could not be doubtful. On the side of Æneas were the expressed decree of destiny, the aid of his goddess-mother at every emergency, and impenetrable armor fabricated by

Vulcan, at her request, for her son. Turnus, on the other hand, was deserted by his celestial allies, Juno having been expressly forbidden by Jupiter to assist him any longer. Turnus threw his lance, but it recoiled harmless from the shield of Æneas. The Trojan hero then threw his, which penetrated the shield of Turnus, and pierced his thigh. Then Turnus's fortitude forsook him and he begged for mercy; and Æneas would have given him his life, but at the instant his eye fell on the belt of Pallas, which Turnus had taken from the slaughtered youth. Instantly his rage revived, and exclaiming, "Pallas immolates thee with this blow," he thrust him through with his sword.

Here the poem of the Æneid closes, and we are left to infer that Æneas, having triumphed over his foes, obtained Lavinia for his bride. Tradition adds that he founded his city, and called it after her name, Lavinium. His son Iulus founded Alba Longa, which was the birthplace of Romulus and Remus, and the cradle of Rome itself.

There is an allusion to Camilla in those well-known lines of Pope, in which, illustrating the rule that "the sound should be an echo to the sense," he says,

> "When Ajax strives some rock's vast weight to throw,
>   The line too labors and the words move slow.
> Not so when swift Camilla scours the plain,
> Flies o'er th' unbending corn or skims along the main."
>
> *Essay on Criticism*

· · · · · · ·

34

Pythagoras — Egyptian Deities — Oracles

The teachings of Anchises to Æneas, respecting the nature of the human soul, were in conformity with the doctrines of the Pythagoreans. Pythagoras (born five hundred and forty years B.C.) was a native of the island of Samos, but passed the chief portion of his life at Crotona in Italy. He is therefore sometimes called "the Samian," and sometimes "the philosopher of Crotona." When young he travelled extensively, and it is said visited Egypt, where he was instructed by priests in all their learning, and afterwards journeyed to the East, and visited the Persian and Chaldean Magi, and the Brahmins of India.

At Crotona, where he finally established himself, his extraordinary qualities collected round him a great number of disciples. The inhabitants were notorious for luxury and licentiousness, but the good effects of his influence were soon visible. Sobriety and temperance succeeded. Six hundred of the inhabitants became his disciples and enrolled themselves in a society to aid each other in the pursuit of wisdom; uniting their property in one common stock, for the benefit of the whole. They were required to practise the greatest purity and simplicity of manners.

The first lesson they learned was *silence;* for a time they were required to be only hearers. "He [Pythagoras] said so" (*Ipse dixit*),was to be held by them as sufficient, without any proof. It was only the advanced pupils, after years of patient submission, who were allowed to ask questions and to state objections.

Pythagoras considered *numbers* as the essence and principle of all things, and attributed to them a real and distinct existence; so that in his view, they were the elements out of which the universe was constructed. How he conceived this process has never been satisfactorily explained. He traced the various forms and phenomena of the world to numbers as their basis and essence. The "Monad" or *unit* he regarded as the source of all numbers. The number *Two* was imperfect, and the cause of increase and division. *Three* was called the number of the whole because it had a beginning, middle, and end; *Four,* representing the square, is in the highest degree perfect; and *Ten,* as it contains the sum of the four prime numbers, comprehends all musical and arithmetical proportions, and denotes the system of the world.

As the numbers proceed from the monad, so he regarded the pure and simple essence of the Deity as the source of all the forms of nature. Gods, demons and heroes are emanations of the Supreme, and there is a fourth emanation, the human soul. This is immortal, and when freed from the fetters of the body, passes to the habitation of the dead, where it remains till it returns to the world, to dwell in some other human or animal body, and at last when sufficiently purified, it returns to the source from which it proceeded. This doctrine of the transmigration of souls (metempsychosis), which was originally Egyptian and connected with the doctrine of reward and punishment of human actions, was the chief cause why the Pythagoreans killed no animals. Ovid represents Pythagoras addressing his disciples in these words: "Souls never die, but always on quitting one abode, pass to another. I myself can remember that in the time of the Trojan war I was Euphorbus, the son of Panthus, and fell by the spear of Menelaus. Lately being in the temple of Juno, at Argos, I recognized my shield hung up there among the trophies. All things change, nothing perishes. The soul passes hither and thither, occupying now this body, now that, passing from the body of a beast into that of a man, and thence to a beast's again. As wax is stamped with certain figures, then melted, then stamped anew with others, yet is always the same wax, so the soul, being always the same, yet wears, at different times, different forms. Therefore, if the love of kindred is not extinct in your bosoms, forbear, I entreat you, to violate the life of those who may haply be your own relatives."

Shakespeare, in the "Merchant of Venice," makes Gratiano allude to the metempsychosis, where he says to Shylock,

"Thou almost mak'st me waver in my faith,
    To hold opinion with Pythagoras,
    That souls of animals infuse themselves

> Into the trunks of men; thy currish spirit
> Governed a wolf; who hanged for human slaughter
> Infused his soul in thee; for thy desires
> Are wolfish, bloody, starved and ravenous."

The relation of the notes of the musical scale to numbers, whereby harmony results from vibrations in equal times, and discord from the reverse, led Pythagoras to apply the word "harmony" to the visible creation, meaning by it the just adaptation of parts to each other. This is the idea which Dryden expresses in the beginning of his "Song for St. Cecilia's Day":

> "From harmony, from heavenly harmony
> This everlasting frame began;
> From harmony to harmony
> Through all the compass of the notes it ran,
> The Diapason closing full in Man."

In the centre of the universe (he taught) there was a central fire, the principle of life. The central fire was surrounded by the earth, the moon, the sun, and the five planets. The distances of the various heavenly bodies from one another were conceived to correspond to the proportions of the musical scale. The heavenly bodies, with the gods who inhabited them, were supposed to perform a choral dance round the central fire, "not without song." It is this doctrine which Shakespeare alludes to when he makes Lorenzo teach astronomy to Jessica in this fashion:

> "Look, Jessica, see how the floor of heaven
> Is thick inlaid with patterns of bright gold!
> There's not the smallest orb that thou behold'st
> But in his motion like an angel sings,
> Still quiring to the young-eyed cherubim;
> Such harmony is in immortal souls!
> But whilst this muddy vesture of decay
> Doth grossly close it in we cannot hear it."
>
> *Merchant of Venice*

The spheres were conceived to be crystalline or glassy fabrics arranged over one another like a nest of bowls reversed. In the substance of each sphere one or more of the heavenly bodies was supposed to be fixed, so as to move with it. As the spheres are transparent we look through them and see the heavenly bodies which they contain and carry round with them. But as these spheres cannot move on one another without friction, a sound is thereby produced which is of exquisite harmony, too fine for mortal ears to recognize. Milton, in his "Hymn to the Nativity," thus alludes to the music of the spheres:

> "Ring out, ye crystal spheres!
> Once bless our human ears;
>   (If ye have power to charm our senses so;)

And let your silver chime
Move in melodious time,
    And let the base of Heaven's deep organ blow;
And with your ninefold harmony
Make up full concert with the angelic symphony.''

Pythagoras is said to have invented the lyre. Our own poet Longfellow, in "Verses to a Child," thus relates the story:

"As great Pythagoras of yore,
Standing beside the blacksmith's door,
And hearing the hammers as they smote
The anvils with a different note,
Stole from the varying tones that hung
Vibrant on every iron tongue,
The secret of the sounding wire,
And formed the seven-chorded lyre.''

See also the same poet's "Occultation of Orion."

"The Samian's great Æolian lyre.''

Sybaris and Crotona

Sybaris, a neighboring city to Crotona, was as celebrated for luxury and effeminacy as Crotona for the reverse. The name has become proverbial. J.R. Lowell uses it in this sense in his charming little poem, "To the Dandelion":

"Not in mid June the golden-cuirassed bee
Feels a more summer-like, warm ravishment
    In the white lily's breezy tent,
(His conquered Sybaris) than I when first
From the dark green thy yellow circles burst.''

A war arose between the two cities, and Sybaris was conquered and destroyed. Milo the celebrated athlete led the army of Crotona. Many stories are told of Milo's vast strength, such as his carrying a heifer of four years old upon his shoulders and afterwards eating the whole of it in a single day. The mode of his death is thus related. As he was passing through a forest he saw the trunk of a tree which had been partially split open by wood-cutters, and attempted to rend it further; but the wood closed upon his hands and held him fast, in which state he was attacked and devoured by wolves.

Byron, in his "Ode to Napoleon Bonaparte," alludes to the story of Milo:

"He who of old would rend the oak
    Deemed not of the rebound;
Chained by the trunk he vainly broke,
    Alone, how looked he round!''

Egyptian Deities

The Egyptians acknowledged as the highest deity Amun, afterwards called Zeus, or Jupiter Ammon. Amun manifested himself in his word or will, which created Kneph and Athor, of different sexes. From Kneph and Athor proceeded Osiris and Isis. Osiris was worshipped as the god of the sun, the source of warmth, life, and fruitfulness, in addition to which he was also regarded as the god of the Nile, who annually visited his wife, Isis (the Earth), by means of an inundation. Serapis or Hermes is sometimes represented as identical with Osiris, and sometimes as a distinct divinity, the ruler of Tartarus and god of medicine. Anubis is the guardian god, represented with a dog's head, emblematic of his character of fidelity and watchfulness. Horus or Harpocrates was the son of Osiris. He is represented seated on a Lotus flower, with his finger on his lips, as the god of Silence.

In one of Moore's "Irish Melodies" is an allusion to Harpocrates:

> "Thyself shall, under some rosy bower,
>   Sit mute, with thy finger on thy lip;
> Like him, the boy, who born among
>   The flowers that on the Nile-stream blush,
> Sits ever thus,—his only song
>   To Earth and Heaven, "Hush all, hush!""

Myth of Osiris and Isis

Osiris and Isis were at one time induced to descend to the earth to bestow gifts and blessings on its inhabitants. Isis showed them first the use of wheat and barley, and Osiris made the instruments of agriculture and taught men the use of them, as well as how to harness the ox to the plough. He then gave men laws, the institution of marriage, a civil organization, and taught them how to worship the gods. After he had thus made the valley of the Nile a happy country, he assembled a host with which he went to bestow his blessings upon the rest of the world. He conquered the nations every where, but not with weapons, only with music and eloquence. His brother Typhon saw this, and filled with envy and malice sought during his absence to usurp his throne. But Isis, who held the reins of government, frustrated his plans. Still more embittered, he now resolved to kill his brother. This he did in the following manner. Having organized a conspiracy of seventy-two members he went with them to the feast which was celebrated in honor of the king's return. He then caused a box or chest to be brought in, which had been made to fit exactly the size of Osiris, and declared that he would give that chest of precious wood to whosoever could get into it. The rest tried in vain, but no sooner was Osiris in it than Typhon and his companions closed the lid and flung the chest into the Nile. When Isis heard of the cruel murder she wept and mourned, and then with her hair shorn, clothed in black and beating her breast, she sought diligently for the body of her husband. In this search she was materially assisted by Anubis, the son of Osiris and Nephthys. They sought in vain for some time; for when the chest, carried by the waves to the shores of Byblos, had become entangled in the reeds that grew at the edge of the water, the divine power that dwelt in the body of Osiris imparted such strength to the shrub that it grew into a mighty tree, enclosing in its trunk the coffin of the god. This tree with its sacred deposit was shortly after felled, and erected as a column in the palace of the king of Phœnicia. But at length by the aid of Anubis and the sacred birds, Isis ascertained these facts, and then went to the royal city. There she offered herself at the palace as a servant, and being admitted, threw off her disguise and appeared as the goddess, surrounded with thunder and lightning. Striking the column with her wand she caused it to split open and give up the sacred coffin. This she seized and returned with it, and concealed it in the depth of a forest, but Typhon discovered it, and cutting the body into fourteen pieces scattered them hither and thither. After a tedious search, Isis found thirteen pieces, the fishes of the Nile having eaten the other. This she replaced by an imitation of sycamore wood, and buried the body at Philoe, which became ever after the great burying place of the nation, and the spot to which pilgrimages were made from all parts of the country. A temple of surpassing magnificence was also erected there in honor of the god, and at every place where one of his limbs had been found, minor temples and tombs were built to commemorate the event. Osiris became after that the tutelar deity of the Egyptians. His soul was supposed always to inhabit the body of the bull Apis, and at his death to transfer itself to his successor.

Apis, the Bull of Memphis, was worshipped with the greatest reverence by the Egyptians. The individual animal who was held to be Apis was recognized by certain signs. It was requisite that he should be quite black, have a white square mark on the forehead, another, in the form of an eagle, on his back, and under his tongue a lump somewhat in the shape of a scarabæus or beetle. As soon as a bull thus marked was found by those sent in search of him, he was placed in a building facing the east, and was fed with milk for four months. At the expiration of this term the priests repaired at new moon, with great pomp, to his habitation and saluted him Apis. He was placed in a vessel magnificently decorated and conveyed down the Nile to Memphis, where a temple, with two chapels and a court for exercise, was assigned to him. Sacrifices were made to him, and once every year, about the time when the Nile began to rise, a golden cup was thrown into the river, and a grand festival was held to celebrate his birthday. The people believed that during this festival the crocodiles forgot their natural ferocity and became harmless. There was however one drawback to his happy lot; he was not permitted to live beyond a certain period; and if when he had attained the age of twenty-five years, he still survived, the priests drowned him in the sacred cistern, and then buried him in the temple of Serapis.

On the death of this bull, whether it occurred in the course of nature or by violence, the whole land was filled with sorrow and lamentations, which lasted until his successor was found.

We find the following item in one of the newspapers of the day:

The Tomb of Apis—The excavations going on at Memphis bid fair to make that buried city as interesting as Pompeii. The monster tomb of Apis is now open after having lain unknown for centuries.

Milton, in his "Hymn of the Nativity," alludes to the Egyptian deities, not as imaginary beings, but as real demons, put to flight by the coming of Christ:

> "The brutish gods of Nile as fast,
>   Isis and Horus and the dog Anubis haste.
>   Nor is Osiris seen
>   In Memphian grove or green
>   Trampling the unshowered* grass with lowings loud;
>   Nor can he be at rest
>   Within his sacred chest;
>   Nought but profoundest hell can be his shroud
>   In vain with timbrel'd anthems dark
>   The sable-stoled sorcerers bear his worshipped ark."

Isis was represented in statuary with the head veiled, a symbol of mystery. It is this which Tennyson alludes to in "Maud," IV, 8:

> "For the drift of the Maker is dark, an
>   Isis hid by the veil," etc.

Oracles

Oracle was the name used to denote the place where answers were supposed to be given by any of the divinities to those who consulted them respecting the future. The word was also used to signify the response which was given.

The most ancient Grecian oracle was that of Jupiter at Dodona. According to one account it was established in the following manner. Two black doves took their flight from Thebes in Egypt. One flew to Dodona in Epirus, and alighting in a grove of oaks, it proclaimed in human language to the inhabitants of the district that they must establish there an oracle of Jupiter. The other dove flew to the temple of Jupiter Ammon in the Libyan oasis, and delivered a similar command there. Another account is, that they were not doves, but priestesses, who were carried off from Thebes in Egypt by the Phoenicians, and set up oracle at the Oasis and Dodona. The responses of the oracle were given

---

*There being no rain in Egypt, the grass is "unshowered," and the country depends for its fertility upon the overflowings of the Nile. The ark alluded to in the last line is shown by pictures still remaining on the walls of the Egyptian temples to have been borne by the priests in their religious processions. It probably represented the chest in which Osiris was placed.

from the trees, by the branches rustling in the wind, the sounds being interpreted by the priests.

But the most celebrated of the Grecian oracles was that of Apollo at Delphi, a city built on the slopes of Parnassus in Phocis.

It had been observed at a very early period that the goats feeding of Parnassus were thrown into convulsions when they approached a certain long deep cleft in the side of the mountain. This was owing to a peculiar vapor arising out of the cavern, and one of the goatherds was induced to try its effects upon himself. Inhaling the intoxicating air he was affected in the same manner as the cattle had been, and the inhabitants of the surrounding country, unable to explain the circumstance, imputed the convulsive ravings to which he gave utterance while under the power of the exhalations to a divine inspiration. The fact was speedily circulated widely, and a temple was erected on the spot. The prophetic influence was at first variously attributed to the goddess Earth, to Neptune, Themis, and others, but it was at length assigned to Apollo, and to him alone. A priestess was appointed whose office it was to inhale the hallowed air, and who was named the Pythia. She was prepared for this duty by previous ablution at the fountain of Castalia, and being crowned with laurel was seated upon a tripod similarly adorned, which was placed over the chasm whence the divine afflatus proceeded. Her inspired words while thus situated were interpreted by the priests.

Oracle of Trophonius

Besides the oracles of Jupiter and Apollo, at Dodona and Delphi, that of Trophonius in Bœotia was held in high estimation. Trophonius and Agamedes were brothers. They were distinguished architects, and built the temple of Apollo at Delphi, and a treasury for King Hyrieus. In the wall of the treasury they placed a stone, in such a manner that it could be taken out; and by this means from time to time purloined the treasure. This amazed Hyrieus, for his locks and seals were untouched, and yet his wealth continually diminished. At length he set a trap for the thief and Agamedes was caught. Trophonius, unable to extricate him, and fearing that when found he would be compelled by torture to discover his accomplice, cut off his head. Trophonius himself is said to have been shortly afterwards swallowed up by the earth.

The oracle of Trophonius was at Lebadea in Bœotia. During a great drought the Bœotians, it is said, were directed by the god at Delphi to seek aid of Trophonius at Lebadea. They came thither, but could find no oracle. One of them however, happening to see a swarm of bees, followed them to a chasm in the earth, which proved to be the place sought.

Peculiar ceremonies were to be performed by the person who came to consult the oracle. After these preliminaries, he descended into the cave by a narrow passage. This place could be entered only in the night. The person returned from the cave by the same narrow passage, but walking backwards. He appeared melancholy and dejected; and hence the proverb which was applied to a person low-spirited and gloomy, "He had been consulting the oracle of Trophonius."

Oracle of Æsculapius

There were numerous oracles of Æsculapius, but the most celebrated one was at Epidaurus. Here the sick sought responses and the recovery of their health by sleeping in the temple. It has been inferred from the accounts that have come down to us that the treatment of the sick resembled what is now called Animal Magnetism or Mesmerism.

Serpents were sacred to Æsculapius, probably because of a superstition that those animals have a faculty of renewing their youth by a change of skin. The worship of Æsculapius was introduced into Rome in a time of great sickness, and an embassy sent to the temple of Epidaurus to entreat the aid of the god. Æsculapius was propitious, and on the return of the ship accompanied it in the form of a serpent. Arriving in the river Tiber, the serpent glided from the vessel and took possession of an island in the river, and a temple was there erected to his honor.

Oracle of Apis

At Memphis the sacred bull Apis gave answer to those who consulted him, by the manner in which he received or rejected what was presented to him. If the bull refused food from the hand of the inquirer it was considered an unfavorable sign, and the contrary when he received it.

It has been a question whether oracular responses ought to be ascribed to mere human contrivance or to the agency of evil spirits. The latter opinion has been most general in past ages. A third theory has been advanced since the phenomena of Mesmerism have attracted attention, that something like the mesmeric trance was induced in the Pythoness, and the faculty of clairvoyance really called into action.

Another question is as to the time when the Pagan oracles ceased to give responses. Ancient Christian writers assert that they became silent at the birth of Christ, and were heard no more after that date. Milton adopts this view in his "Hymn of the Nativity," and in lines of solemn and elevated beauty pictures the consternation of the heathen idols at the advent of the Savior.

> "The oracles are dumb;
>   No voice or hideous hum
>   Rings through the arched roof in words deceiving.
>   Apollo from his shrine
>   Can no more divine,
>   With hollow shriek the steep of Delphos leaving.
>   No nightly trance or breathed spell
>   Inspires the pale-eyed priest from the prophetic cell."

In Cowper's poem of "Yardley Oak" there are some beautiful mythological allusions. The former of the two following is to the fable of Castor and Pollux; the latter is more appropriate to our present subject. Addressing the acorn he says,

"Thou fell'st mature; and in the loamy clod,
  Swelling with vegetative force instinct,
  Didst burst thine egg, as theirs the fabled Twins
  Now stars; two lobes protruding, paired exact;
  A leaf succeeded and another leaf,
  And, all the elements thy puny growth
  Fostering propitious, then becam'st a twig.
  Who lived when thou wast such?   O, couldst thou speak,
  As in Dodona once thy kindred trees
  Oracular, I would not curious ask
  The future, best unknown, but at thy mouth
  Inquisitive, the less ambiguous past."

Tennyson in his "Talking Oak" alludes to the oaks of Dodona in these lines:

"And I will work in prose and rhyme,
    And praise thee more in both
  Than bard has honored beech or lime,
    On that Thessalian growth
  In which the swarthy ring-dove sat
    And mystic sentence spoke;" etc.

Byron alludes to the oracle of Delphi where, speaking of Rousseau, whose writings he conceives did much to bring on the French revolution, he says,

"For then he was inspired, and from him came,
    As from the Pythian's mystic cave of yore,
  Those oracles which set the world in flame,
    Nor ceased to burn till kingdoms were no more."

• • • • • • •
35

Origin of Mythology—Statues of Gods and Goddesses—Poets of Mythology

Having reached the close of our series of stories of Pagan mythology, an inquiry suggests itself. "Whence came these stories? Have they a foundation in truth, or are they simply dreams of the imagination?" Philosophers have suggested various theories on the subject; and

1. The Scriptural theory; according to which all mythological legends are derived from the narratives of Scripture, though the real facts have been disguised and altered. Thus Deucalion is only another name for Noah, Hercules for Samson, Arion for Jonah, etc. Sir Walter Raleigh, in his "History of the World," says, "Jubal, Tubal, and Tubal-Cain were Mercury, Vulcan, and Apollo, inventors of Pasturage, Smithing, and Music. The Dragon which kept the golden apples was the serpent

that beguiled Eve. Nimrod's tower was the attempt of the Giants against Heaven.'' There are doubtless many curious coincidences like these, but the theory cannot without extravagance be pushed so far as to account for any great proportion of the stories.

2. The Historical theory; according to which all the persons mentioned in mythology were once real human beings, and the legends and fabulous traditions relating to them are merely the additions and embellishments of later times. Thus the story of Æolus, the king and god of the winds, is supposed to have risen from the fact that Æolus was the ruler of some islands in the Tyrrhenian Sea, where he reigned as a just and pious king, and taught the natives the use of sails for ships, and how to tell from the signs of the atmosphere the changes of the weather and the winds. Cadmus, who, the legend says, sowed the earth with dragon's teeth, from which sprang a crop of armed men, was in fact an emigrant from Phœnicia, and brought him into Geece the knowledge of the letters of the alphabet, which he taught to the natives. From these rudiments of learning sprung civilization, which the poets have always been prone to describe as a deterioration of man's first estate, the Golden Age of innocence and simplicity.

3. The Allegorical theory supposes that all the myths of the ancients were allegorical and symbolical, and contained some moral, religious, or philosophical truth or historical fact, under the form of an allegory, but came in process of time to be understood literally. Thus Saturn, who devours his own children, is the same power whom the Greeks called Cronos (Time), which may truly be said to destroy whatever it has brought into existence. The story of Io is interpreted in a similar manner. Io is the moon, and Argus the starry sky, which, as it were, keeps sleepless watch over her. The fabulous wanderings of Io represent the continual revolutions of the moon, which also suggested to Milton the same idea.

> "To behold the wandering moon
>   Riding near her highest noon,
>   Like one that had been led astray
>   In the heaven's wide, pathless way."
>   *Il Penseroso*

4. The Physical theory; according to which the elements of air, fire, and water were originally the objects of religious adoration, and the principal deities were personifications of the powers of nature. The transition was easy from a personification of the elements to the notion of supernatural beings presiding over and governing the different objects of nature. The Greeks, whose imagination was lively, peopled all nature with invisible beings, and supposed that every object, from the sun and sea to the smallest fountain and rivulet, was under the care of some particular divinity. Wordsworth, in his "Excursion," has beautifully developed this view of Grecian mythology.

"In that fair clime the lonely herdsman, stretched
On the soft grass through half a summer's day,
With music lulled his indolent repose;
And, in some fit of weariness, if he,
When his own breath was silent, chanced to hear
A distant strain far sweeter than the sounds
Which his poor skill could make, his fancy fetched
Even from the blazing chariot of the Sun
A beardless youth who touched a golden lute,
And filled the illumined groves with ravishment.
The mighty hunter, lifting up his eyes
Toward the crescent Moon, with grateful heart
Called on the lovely Wanderer who bestowed
That timely light to share his joyous sport;
And hence a beaming goddess with her nymphs
Across the lawn and through the darksome grove
(Not unaccompanied with tuneful notes
By echo multiplied from rock or cave)
Swept in the storm of chase, as moon and stars
Glance rapidly along the clouded heaven
When winds are blowing strong. The Traveller slaked
His thirst from rill or gushing fount, and thanked
The Naiad. Sunbeams upon distant hills
Gliding apace with shadows in their train,
Might with small help from fancy, be transformed
Into fleet Oreads sporting visibly.
The Zephyrs, fanning, as they passed, their wings,
Lacked not for love fair objects whom they wooed
With gentle whisper. Withered boughs grotesque,
Stripped of their leaves and twigs by hoary age.
From depth of shaggy covert peeping forth
In the low vale, or on steep mountain side;
And sometimes intermixed with stirring horns
Of the live deer, or goat's depending beard;
These were the lurking Satyrs, a wild brood
Of gamesome deities; or Pan himself,
The simple shepherd's awe-inspiring god."

All the theories which have been mentioned are true to a certain extent. It would therefore be more correct to say that the mythology of a nation has sprung from all these sources combined than from any one in particular. We may add also that there are many myths which have arisen from the desire of man to account for those natural phenomena which he cannot understand; and not a few have had their rise from a similar desire of giving a reason for the names of places and persons.

Statues of the Gods and Goddesses

To adequately represent to the eye the ideas intended to be conveyed to the mind under the several names of deities, was a task which called into exercise the highest powers of genius and art. Of the many attempts *four* have been most celebrated, the first two known to us only by the descriptions of the ancients, the others still extant and the acknowledged masterpieces of the sculptor's art.

The Olympian Jupiter

The statue of the Olympian Jupiter by Phidias was considered the highest achievement of this department of Grecian art. It was of colossal dimensions, and was what the ancients called "chryselephantine"; that is, composed of ivory and gold; the parts representing flesh being of ivory laid on a core of wood or stone, while the drapery and other ornaments were of gold. The height of the figure was forty feet, on a pedestal twelve feet high. The god was represented seated on his throne. His brows were crowned with a wreath of olive, and he held in his right hand a sceptre, and in his left a statue of Victory. The throne was of cedar, adorned with gold and precious stones.

The idea which the artist essayed to imbody was that of the supreme deity of the Hellenic (Grecian) nation, enthroned as a conqueror, in perfect majesty and repose, and ruling with a nod the subject world. Phidias avowed that he took his idea from the representation which Homer gives in the first book of the *Iliad*, in the passage thus translated by Pope:

> "He spoke and awful bends his sable brows,
> Shakes his ambrosial curls and gives the nod,
> The stamp of fate and sanction of the god.
> High heaven with reverence the dread signal took,
> And all Olympus to the centre shook."*

The Minerva of the Parthenon

This was also the work of Phidias. It stood in the Parthenon, or temple of Minerva at Athens. The goddess was represented standing. In one hand she held a spear, in the other a statue of Victory. Her helmet, highly decorated, was surmounted by a Sphinx. The statue was forty feet in height, and, like the Jupiter, composed of ivory and gold. The

---

*Cowper's version is less elegant, but truer to the original.

> "He ceased, and under his dark brows the nod
> Vouchsafed of confirmation. All around
> The sovereign's everlasting head his curls
> Ambrosial shook, and the huge mountain reeled."

It may interest our readers to see how this passage appears in another famous version, that which was issued under the name of Tickell, contemporaneously with Pope's, and which, being by many attributed to Addison, led to the quarrel which ensued between Addison and Pope.

> "This said, his kingly brow the sire inclined;
> The large black curls fell awful from behind,
> Thick shadowing the stern forehead of the god;
> Olympus trembled at the almighty nod."

eyes were of marble, and probably painted to represent the iris and pupil. The Parthenon in which this statue stood was also constructed under the direction and superintendence of Phidias. Its exterior was enriched with sculptures, many of them from the hand of Phidias. The Elgin marbles now in the British Museum are a part of them.

Both the Jupiter and Minerva of Phidias are lost, but there is good ground to believe that we have, in several extant statues and busts, the artist's conceptions of the countenances of both. They are characterized by grave and dignified beauty, and freedom from any transient expression, which in the language of art is called *repose*.

The Venus de' Medici

The Venus of the Medici is so called from its having been in the possession of the princes of that name in Rome when it first attracted attention, about two hundred years ago. An inscription on the base records it to be the work of Cleomenes, an Athenian sculptor of 200 B.C., but the authenticity of the inscription is doubtful. There is a story that the artist was employed by public authority to make a statue exhibiting the perfection of female beauty, and to aid him in his task, the most perfect forms the city could supply were furnished him for models. It is this which Thomson alludes to in his "Summer."

> "So stands the statue that enchants the world;
>   So bending tries to veil the matchless boast,
>   The mingled beauties of exulting Greece."

Byron also alludes to this statue. Speaking of the Florence Museum, he says,

> "There too the goddess loves in stone, and fills
>   The air around with beauty;" etc.

And in the next stanza,

> "Blood, pulse, and breast confirm the Dardan shepherd's prize."

See this last allusion explained in Chapter 27.

The Apollo Belvedere

The most highly esteemed of all the remains of ancient sculpture is the statue of Apollo, called the Belvedere, from the name of the apartment of the Pope's palace at Rome in which it is placed. The artist is unknown. It is supposed to be a work of Roman art, of about the first century of our era. It is a standing figure, in marble, more than seven feet high, naked except for the cloak which is fastened around the neck and hangs over the extended left arm. It is supposed to represent the god in the moment when he has shot the arrow to destroy the monster Python. (See Chapter 3.) The victorious divinity is in the act of stepping forward. The left arm which seems to have held the bow is outstretched, and the head is turned in the same direction. In attitude and proportion the graceful majesty of the figure is unsurpassed. The effect is completed by the countenance, where, on the perfection of youthful godlike beauty there dwells the consciousness of triumphant power.

The Diana á la Biche

The Diana of the Hind, in the palace of the Louvre, may be considered the counterpart to Apollo Belvedere. The attitude much resembles that of the Apollo, the sizes correspond and also the style of execution. It is a work of the highest order, though by no means equal to the Apollo. The attitude is that of hurried and eager motion, the face that of a huntress in the excitement of the chase. The left hand is extended over the forehead of the Hind which runs by her side, the right arm reaches backward over the shoulder to draw an arrow from the quiver.

The Poets of Mythology

Homer, from whose poems of the *Iliad* and *Odyssey* we have taken the chief part of our chapters of the Trojan war and the return of the Grecians, is almost as mythical a personage as the heroes he celebrates. The traditionary story is that he was a wandering minstrel, blind and old, who travelled from place to place singing his lays to the music of his harp, in the courts of princes or the cottages of peasants, and dependent upon the voluntary offerings of his hearers for support. Byron calls him "The blind old man of Scio's rocky isle," and a well-known epigram, alluding to the uncertainty of the fact of his birthplace, says,

> "Seven wealthy towns contend for Homer dead,
>   Through which the living Homer begged his bread."

These seven were Smyrna, Scio, Rhodes, Colophon, Salamis, Argos, and Athens.

Modern scholars have doubted whether the Homeric poems are the work of any single mind. This arises from the difficulty of believing that poems of such length could have been committed to writing at so early an age as that usually assigned to these, an age earlier than the date of any remaining inscriptions or coins, and when no materials capable of containing such long productions were yet introduced into use. On the other hand it is asked how poems of such length could have been handed down from age to age by means of the memory alone. This is answered by the statement that there was a professional body of men, called Rhapsodists, who recited the poems of others, and whose business it was to commit to memory and rehearse for pay the national and patriotic legends.

The prevailing opinion of the learned, at this time, seems to be that the framework and much of the structure of the poems belongs to Homer, but that there are numerous interpolations and additions by other hands.

The date assigned to Homer, on the authority of Herodotus, is 850 B.C.

Virgil

Virgil, called also by his surname Maro, from whose poem of the
Æneid we have taken the story of Æneas, was one of the great poets
who made the reign of the Roman emperor Augustus so celebrated,
under the name of the Augustan age. Virgil was born in Mantua in the
year 70 B.C. His great poem is ranked next to those of Homer, in the
highest class of poetical composition, the Epic. Virgil is far inferior to
Homer in originality and invention, but superior to him in correctness
and elegance. To critics of English lineage Milton alone of modern poets
seems worthy to be classed with these illustrious ancients. His poem of
"Paradise Lost," from which we have borrowed so many illustrations,
is in many respects equal, in some superior, to either of the great works
of antiquity. The following epigram of Dryden characterizes the three
poets with as much truth as it is usual to find in such pointed criticism:

ON MILTON

"Three poets in three different ages born,
   Greece, Italy, and England did adorn.
   The first in loftiness of soul surpassed,
   The next in majesty, in both the last.
   The force of nature could no further go;
   To make a third she joined the other two."

From Cowper's "Table Talk":

"Ages elapsed ere Homer's lamp appeared,
   And ages ere the Mantuan swan was heard.
   To carry nature lengths unknown before,
   To give a Milton birth, asked ages more.
   Thus genius rose and set at ordered times,
   And shot a dayspring into distant climes,
   Ennobling every region that he chose;
   He sunk in Greece, in Italy he rose,
   And, tedious years of Gothic darkness past,
   Emerged all splendor in our isle at last.
   Thus lovely Halcyons dive into the main,
   Then show far off their shining plumes again."

Ovid

Often alluded to in poetry by his other name of Naso, was born in the
year 43 B.C. He was educated for public life and held some offices of
considerable dignity, but poetry was his delight, and he early resolved
to devote himself to it. He accordingly sought the society of the contemporary poets, and was acquainted with Horace and saw Virgil, though the
latter died when Ovid was yet too young and undistinguished to have
formed his acquaintance. Ovid spent an easy life at Rome in the enjoyment of a competent income. He was intimate with the family of
Augustus, the emperor, and it is supposed that some serious offence
given to some member of that family was the cause of an event which

reversed the poet's happy circumstances and clouded all the latter portion of his life. At the age of fifty he was banished from Rome, and ordered to betake himself to Tomi, on the borders of the Black Sea. Here, among the barbarous people and in a severe climate, the poet, who had been accustomed to all the pleasures of a luxurious capital and the society of his most distinguished contemporaries, spent the last ten years of his life, worn out with grief and anxiety. His only consolation in exile was to address his wife and absent friends, and his letters were all poetical. Though these poems (the "Tristia" and "Letters from Pontus") have no other topic than the poet's sorrows, his exquisite taste and fruitful invention have redeemed them from the charge of being tedious, and they are read with pleasure and even with sympathy.

The two great works of Ovid are his "Metamorphoses" and his "Fasti." They are both mythological poems, and from the former we have taken most of our stories of Grecian and Roman mythology. A late writer thus characterizes these poems:

"The rich mythology of Greece furnished Ovid, as it may still furnish the poet, the painter, and the sculptor, with materials for his art. With exquisite taste, simplicity, and pathos he has narrated the fabulous traditions of early ages, and given to them that appearance of reality which only a master-hand could impart. His pictures of nature are striking and true; he selects with care that which is appropriate; he rejects the superfluous; and when he has completed his work, it is neither defective nor redundant. The "Metamorphoses" are read with pleasure by youth, and are re-read in more advanced age with still greater delight. The poet ventured to predict that his poem would survive him, and be read wherever the Roman name was known."

The prediction above alluded to is contained in the closing lines of the "Metamorphoses," of which we give a literal translation below:

"And now I close my work, which not the ire
Of Jove, nor tooth of time, nor sword, nor fire
Shall bring to nought. Come when it will that day
Which o'er the body, not the mind, has sway,
And snatch the remnant of my life away,
My better part above the stars shall soar,
And my renown endure forevermore.
Where'er the Roman arms and arts shall spread,
There by the people shall my book be read;
And, if aught true in poet's visions be,
My name and fame have immortality."

36

Modern Monsters— The Phœnix— Basilisk— Unicorn—Salamander

There is a set of imaginary beings which seem to have been the successors of the "Gorgons, Hydras, and Chimeras dire" of the old superstitions, and, having no connection with the false gods of Paganism, to have continued to enjoy an existence in the popular belief after Paganism was superseded by Christianity. They are mentioned perhaps by the classical writers, but their chief popularity and currency seem to have been in more modern times. We seek our accounts of them not so much in the poetry of the ancients, as in the old natural history books and narrations of travellers. The accounts which we are about to give are taken chiefly from the Penny Cyclopedia.

The Phœnix

Ovid tells the story of the Phœnix as follows. "Most beings spring from other individuals; but there is a certain kind which reproduces itself. The Assyrians call it the Phœnix. It does not live on fruit or flowers, but on frankincense and odoriferous gums. When it has lived five hundred years, it builds itself a nest in the branches of an oak, or on the top of a palm tree. In this it collects cinnamon, and spikenard, and myrrh, and of these materials builds a pile on which it deposits itself, and dying, breathes out its last breath amidst odors. From the body of the parent bird, a young Phœnix issues forth, destined to live as long a life as its predecessor. When this has grown up and gained sufficient strength, it lifts its nest from the tree (its own cradle and its parent's sepulchre), and carries it to the city of Heliopolis in Egypt, and deposits it in the temple of the Sun."

Such is the account given by a poet. Now let us see that of a philosophic historian. Tacitus says, "In the consulship of Paulus Fabius (A.D. 34) the miraculous bird known to the world by the name of the Phœnix, after disappearing for a series of ages, revisited Egypt. It was attended in its flight by a group of various birds, all attracted by the novelty, and gazing with wonder at so beautiful an appearance." He then gives an account of the bird, not varying materially from the preceding, but adding some details. "The first care of the young bird as soon as fledged, and able to trust to his wings, is to perform the obsequies of his father. But this duty is not undertaken rashly. He collects a quantity of myrrh, and to try his strength makes frequent excursions with a load on his back. When he has gained sufficient confidence in his own vigor, he takes up the body of his father and flies with it to the altar of the Sun, where he leaves it to be consumed in flames of fragrance." Other writers add a few particulars. The myrrh is compacted in the form of an egg, in which the dead Phœnix is enclosed. From the mouldering flesh of the dead bird a worm springs, and this worm, when grown large, is transformed into a bird. Herodotus *describes* the bird, though he says, "I have not seen it myself, except in a picture. Part of his plumage is gold-colored, and part crimson; and he is for the most part very much like an eagle in outline and bulk."

The first writer who disclaimed a belief in the existence of the Phœnix, was Sir Thomas Browne, in his "Vulgar Errors," published in 1646. He was replied to a few years later by Alexander Ross, who says, in answer to the objection of the Phœnix so seldom making his appearance, "His instinct teaches him to keep out of the way of the tyrant of the creation, *man,* for if he were to be got at, some wealthy glutton would surely devour him, though there were no more in the world."

Dryden in one of his early poems has this allusion to the Phœnix:

"So when the new-born Phœnix first is seen
  Her feathered subjects all adore their queen,
  And while she makes her progress through the East,
  From every grove her numerous train's increased;
  Each poet of the air her glory sings,
  And round him the pleased audience clap their wings."

Milton, in "Paradise Lost," Book V, compares the angel Raphael descending to earth to a Phœnix:

"Down thither, prone in flight
  He speeds, and through the vast ethereal sky
  Sails between worlds and worlds, with steady wing,
  Now on the polar winds, then with quick fan
  Winnows the buxom air; till within soar
  Of towering eagles, to all the fowls he seems
  A Phœnix, gazed by all; as that sole bird
  When, to enshrine his relics in the sun's
  Bright temple, to Egyptian Thebes he flies."

The Cockatrice, or Basilisk

This animal was called the king of the serpents. In confirmation of his royalty, he was said to be endowed with a crest, or comb upon the head, constituting a crown. He was supposed to be produced from the egg of a cock hatched under toads or serpents. There were several species of this animal. One species burned up whatever they approached; a second were a kind of wandering Medusa's heads, and their look caused an instant horror which was immediately followed by death. In Shakespeare's play of "Richard the Third," Lady Anne, in answer to Richard's compliment on her eyes, says, "Would they were basilisk's, to strike thee dead!"

The basilisks were called kings of serpents because all other serpents and snakes, behaving like good subjects, and wisely not wishing to be burned up or struck dead, fled, the moment they heard the distant hiss of their king, although they might be in full feed upon the most delicious prey, leaving the sole enjoyment of the banquet to the royal monster.

The Roman naturalist Pliny thus describes him. "He does not impel his body, like other serpents, by a multiplied flexion, but advances lofty and upright. He kills the shrubs, not only by contact but by breathing on them, and splits the rocks, such power of evil is there in him." It was formerly believed that if killed by a spear from on horseback the power of the poison conducted through the weapon killed not only the rider, but the horse also. To this Lucan alludes in these lines:

"What though the Moor the basilisk hath slain,
  And pinned him lifeless to the sandy plain,
  Up through the spear the subtle venom flies,
  The hand imbibes it, and the victor dies."

Such a prodigy was not likely to be passed over in the legends of the saints. Accordingly we find it recorded that a certain holy man going to a fountain in the desert suddenly beheld a basilisk. He immediately raised his eyes to heaven, and with a pious appeal to the Deity, laid the monster dead at his feet.

These wonderful powers of the basilisk are attested by a host of learned persons, such as Galen, Avicenna, Scaliger, and others. Occasionally one would demur to some part of the tale while he admitted the rest. Jonston, a learned physician, sagely remarks, "I would scarcely believe that it kills with its look, for who could have seen it and lived to tell the story?" The worthy sage was not aware that those who went to hunt the basilisk of this sort took with them a mirror, which reflected back the deadly glare upon its author, and by a kind of poetical justice slew the basilisk with his own weapon.

But what was to attack this terrible and unapproachable monster? There is an old saying that "every thing has its enemy"—and the cockatrice quailed before the weasel. The basilisk might look daggers, the weasel cared not, but advanced boldly to the conflict. When bitten, the weasel retired for a moment to eat some rue, which was the only plant the basilisks could not wither, returned with renewed strength and soundness to the charge, and never left the enemy till he was stretched dead on the plain. The monster, too, as if conscious of the irregular way in which he came into the world, was supposed to have a great antipathy to a cock; and well he might, for as soon as he heard the cock crow he expired.

The basilisk was of some use after death. Thus we read that its carcass was suspended in the temple of Apollo, and in private houses, as a sovereign remedy against spiders, and that it was also hung up in the temple of Diana, for which reason no swallow ever dared enter the sacred place.

The reader will, we apprehend, by this time have had enough of absurdities, but still we can imagine his anxiety to know what a cockatrice was like. The following is from Aldrovandus, a celebrated naturalist of the sixteenth century, whose work on natural history, in thirteen folio volumes, contains with much that is valuable a large proportion of fables and inutilities. In particular he is so ample on the subject of the cock and the bull, that from his practice, all rambling, gossiping tales of doubtful credibility are called *cock and bull stories.*

Shelley, in his "Ode to Naples," full of the enthusiasm excited by the intelligence of the proclamation of a Constitutional Government at Naples, in 1820, thus uses an allusion to the basilisk—

"What though Cimmerian anarchs dare blaspheme
Freedom and thee? a new Actæon's error
Shall theirs have been,—devoured by their own hounds!
　Be thou like the imperial basilisk,
Killing thy foe with unapparent wounds!
　　Gaze on oppression, till at that dread risk,
　　Aghast she pass from the earth's disk.
Fear not, but gaze,—for freemen mightier grow,
And slaves more feeble, gazing on their foe."

The Unicorn

Pliny, the Roman naturalist, out of whose account of the unicorn most of the modern unicorns have been described and figured, records it as "a very ferocious beast, similar in the rest of its body to a horse, with the head of a deer, the feet of an elephant, the tail of a boar, a deep bellowing voice, and a single black horn, two cubits in length, standing out in the middle of its forehead." He adds that "it cannot be taken alive"; and some such excuse may have been necessary in those days for not producing the living animal upon the arena of the amphitheatre.

The unicorn seems to have been a sad puzzle to the hunters, who hardly knew how to come at so valuable a piece of game. Some described the horn as movable at the will of the animal, a kind of small sword in short, with which no hunter who was not exceedingly cunning in fence could have a chance. Others maintained that all the animal's strength lay in its horn, and that when hard pressed in pursuit, it would throw itself from the pinnacle of the highest rocks horn foremost, so as to pitch upon it, and then quietly march off not a whit the worse for its fall.

But it seems they found out how to circumvent the poor unicorn at last. They discovered that it was a great lover of purity and innocence, so they took the field with a young *virgin,* who was placed in the unsuspecting admirer's way. When the unicorn spied her, he approached with all reverence, couched beside her, and laying his head in her lap, fell asleep. The treacherous virgin then gave a signal, and the hunters made in and captured the simple beast.

Modern zoologists, disgusted as they well may be with such fables as these, disbelieve generally the existence of the unicorn. Yet there are animals bearing on their heads a bony protuberance more or less like a horn, which may have given rise to the story. The rhinoceros horn, as it is called, is such a protuberance, though it does not exceed a few inches in height, and is far from agreeing with the descriptions of the horn of the unicorn. The nearest approach to a horn in the middle of the forehead is exhibited in the bony protuberance on the forehead of the giraffe; but this also is short and blunt, and is not the only horn of the animal, but a third horn, standing in front of the two others. In fine, though it would be presumptuous to deny the existence of a one-horned quadruped other than the rhinoceros, it may be safely stated that the insertion of a long and solid horn in the living forehead of a horse-like or deer-like animal, is as near an impossibility as any thing can be.

The Salamander

The following is from the "Life of Benvenuto Cellini," an Italian artist of the sixteenth century, written by himself. "When I was about five years of age, my father, happening to be in a little room in which they had been washing, and where there was a good fire of oak burning, looked into the flames and saw a little animal resembling a lizard, which could live in the hottest part of that element. Instantly perceiving what it was he called for my sister and me, and after he had shown us the creature, he gave me a box on the ear. I fell a-crying, while he, soothing me with caresses, spoke these words: 'My dear child, I do not give you that blow for any fault you have committed, but that you may recollect that the little creature you see in the fire is a salamander; such a one as never was beheld before to my knowledge.' So saying he embraced me, and gave me some money."

It seems unreasonable to doubt a story of which Signor Cellini was both an eye and ear witness. Add to which the authority of numerous sage philosophers, at the head of whom are Aristotle and Pliny, affirms this power of the salamander. According to them, the animal not only resists fire, but extinguishes it, and when he sees the flame charges it as an enemy which he well knows how to vanquish.

That the skin of an animal which could resist the action of fire should be considered proof against that element, is not to be wondered at. We accordingly find that a cloth made of the skins of salamanders (for there really is such an animal, a kind of lizard) was incombustible, and very valuable for wrapping up such articles as were too precious to be intrusted to any other envelopes. These fireproof cloths were actually produced, said to be made of salamander's wool, though the knowing ones detected that the substance of which they were composed was asbestos, a mineral, which is in fine filaments capable of being woven into a flexible cloth.

The foundation of the above fables is supposed to be the fact that the salamander really does secrete from the pores of his body a milky juice, which when he is irritated is produced in considerable quantity, and would doubtless, for a few moments, defend the body from fire. Then it is a hibernating animal, and in winter retires to some hollow tree or other cavity, where it coils itself up and remains in a torpid state till the spring again calls it forth. It may therefore sometimes be carried with the fuel to the fire, and wake up only time enough to put forth all its faculties for its defence. Its viscous juice would do good service, and all who profess to have seen it, acknowledge that it got out of the fire as fast as its legs could carry it; indeed too fast for them ever to make prize of one, except in one instance, and in that one, the animal's feet and some parts of its body were badly burned.

Dr. Young, in the "Night Thoughts," with more quaintness than good taste, compares the sceptic who can remain unmoved in the contemplation of the starry heavens, to a salamander unwarmed in the fire:

"An undevout astronomer is mad!
            *   *   *
"O, what a genius must inform the skies!
  And is Lorenzo's salamander-heart
  Cold and untouched amid these sacred fires?"
                  . . . .

37

Eastern Mythology—Zoroaster— Hindu Mythology—Castes—Buddha— Grand Lama—Prester John

Our knowledge of the religion of the ancient Persians is principally derived from the Zendavesta, or sacred books of that people. Zoroaster was the founder of their religion, or rather the reformer of the religion which preceded him. The time when he lived is doubtful, but it is certain that his system became the dominant religion of Western Asia from the time of Cyrus (550 B.C.) to the conquest of Persia by Alexander the Great. Under the Macedonian monarchy the doctrines of Zoroaster appear to have been considerably corrupted by the introduction of foreign opinions, but they afterwards recovered their ascendency.

Zoroaster taught the existence of a supreme being, who created two other mighty beings and imparted to them as much of his own nature as seemed good to him. Of these, Ormuzd (called by the Greeks Oromasdes) remained faithful to his creator, and was regarded as the source of all good, while Ahriman (Arimanes) rebelled, and became the author of all evil upon the earth. Ormuzd created man and supplied him with all the materials of happiness; but Ahriman marred this happiness by introducing evil into the world, and creating savage beasts and poisonous reptiles and plants. In consequence of this, evil and good are now mingled together in every part of the world, and the followers of good and evil—the adherents of Ormuzd and Ahriman—carry on incessant war. But this state of things will not last forever. The time will come when the adherents of Ormuzd shall every where be victorious, and Ahriman and his followers be consigned to darkness forever.

The religious rites of the ancient Persians were exceedingly simple. They used neither temples, altars, nor statues, and performed their sacrifices on the tops of mountains. They adored fire, light, and the sun as emblems of Ormuzd, the source of all light and purity, but did not regard them as independent deities. The religious rites and ceremonies were regulated by the priests, who were called Magi. The learning of the Magi was connected with astrology and enchantment, in which they were so celebrated that their name was applied to all orders of magicians and enchanters.

Wordsworth thus alludes to the worship of the Persians—

"—the Persian,—zealous to reject
Altar and Image, and the inclusive walls
And roofs of temples built by human hands,—
The loftiest heights ascending, from their tops,
With myrtle-wreathed Tiara on his brows,
Presented sacrifice to Moon and Stars,
And to the Winds and mother Elements,
And the whole circle of the Heavens, for him
A sensitive existence and a God."

Excursion, Book IV

In "Childe Harold," Byron speaks thus of the Persian worship—

"Not vainly did the early Persian make
His altar the high places and the peak
Of earth-o'er-gazing mountains, and thus take
A fit and unwalled temple, there to seek
The Spirit, in whose honor shrines are weak,
Upreared of human hands. Come and compare
Columns and idol-dwellings, Goth or Greek,
With Nature's realms of worship, earth and air,
Nor fix on fond abodes to circumscribe thy prayer."

III, 91

The religion of Zoroaster continued to flourish even after the introduction of Christianity, and in the third century was the dominant faith of the East, till the rise of the Mahometan power and the conquest of Persia by the Arabs in the seventh century, who compelled the greater number of the Persians to renounce their ancient faith. Those who refused to abandon the religion of their ancestors fled to the deserts of Kerman and to Hindustan, where they still exist under the name of Parsees, a name derived from Pars, the ancient name of Persia. The Arabs call them Guebers, from an Arabic word signifying unbelievers. At Bombay the Parsees are at this day a very active, intelligent, and wealthy class. For purity of life, honesty, and conciliatory manners, they are favorably distinguished. They have numerous temples to fire, which they adore as the symbol of the divinity.

The Persian religion makes the subject of the finest tale in Moore's "Lalla Rookh, the Fire Worshippers." The Gueber chief says,

> "Yes! I am of that impious race,
>   Those slaves of fire, that morn and even
> Hail their creator's dwelling-place
>   Among the living lights of heaven;
> Yes! I am of that outcast crew
> To Iran and to vengeance true,
> Who curse the hour your Arabs came
> To desecrate our shrines of flame,
> And swear before God's burning eye,
> To break our country's chains or die."

Hindu Mythology

The religion of the Hindus is professedly founded on the Vedas. To these books of their scripture they attach the greatest sanctity, and state that Brahma himself composed them at the creation. But the present arrangement of the Vedas is attributed to the sage Vyasa, about five thousand years ago.

The Vedas undoubtedly teach the belief of one supreme God. The name of this deity is Brahma. His attributes are represented by the three personified powers of *creation, preservation,* and *destruction,* which under the respective names Brahma, Vishnu, and Siva form the *Trimurti* or triad of principal Hindu gods. Of the inferior gods the most important are,   1. Indra, the god of heaven, of thunder, lightning, storm, and rain;   2. Agni, the god of fire;   3. Yama, the god of the infernal regions;   4. Surya, the god of the sun.

Brahma is the creator of the universe, and the source from which all the individual deities have sprung, and into which all will ultimately be absorbed. "As milk changes to curd, and water to ice, so is Brahma variously transformed and diversified, without aid of exterior means of any sort." The human soul, according to the Vedas, is a portion of the supreme ruler as a spark is of the fire.

Vishnu

Vishnu occupies the second place in the triad of the Hindus, and is the personification of the preserving principle. To protect the world in various epochs of danger, Vishnu descended to the earth in different incarnations, or bodily forms, which descents are called Avatars. They are very numerous, but ten are more particularly specified. The first Avatar was as Matsya, the Fish, under which form Vishnu preserved Manu, the ancestor of the human race, during a universal deluge. The second Avatar was in the form of a Tortoise, which form he assumed to support the earth when the gods were churning the sea for the beverage of immortality, Amrita.

We may omit the other Avatars, which were of the same general character, that is, interpositions to protect the right or to punish wrong-doers, and come to the ninth, which is the most celebrated of the Avatars of Vishnu, in which he appeared in the human form of Krishna, an invincible warrior, who by his exploits relieved the earth from the tyrants who oppressed it.

Buddha is by the followers of the Brahmanical religion regarded as a delusive incarnation of Vishnu, assumed by him in order to induce the Asuras, opponents of the gods, to abandon the sacred ordinances of the Vedas, by which means they lost their strength and supremacy.

Kalki is the name of the *tenth* Avatar, in which Vishnu will appear at the end of the present age of the world to destroy all vice and wickedness, and to restore mankind to virtue and purity.

Siva

Siva is the third person of the Hindu triad. He is the personification of the destroying principle. Though the third name, he is, in respect to the number of his worshippers and the extension of his worship, before either of the others. In the Puranas (the scriptures of the modern Hindu religion) no allusion is made to the original power of this god as a destroyer; that power not being to be called into exercise till after the expiration of twelve millions of years, or when the universe will come to an end; and Mahadeva (another name for Siva) is rather the representative of regeneration than of destruction.

The worshippers of Vishnu and Siva form two sects, each of which proclaims the superiority of its favorite deity, denying the claims of the other, and Brahma, the creator, having finished his work, seems to be regarded as no longer active, and has now only one temple in India, while Mahadeva and Vishnu have many. The worshippers of Vishnu are generally distinguished by a greater tenderness for life and consequent abstinence from animal food, and a worship less cruel than that of the followers of Siva.

Juggernaut

Whether the worshippers of Juggernaut are to be reckoned among the followers of Vishnu or Siva, our authorities differ. The temple stands near the shore, about three hundred miles south-west of Calcutta. The idol is a carved block of wood, with a hideous face, painted black, and a distended blood-red mouth. On festival days the throne of the image is placed on a tower sixty feet high, moving on wheels. Six long ropes are attached to the tower, by which the people draw it along. The priests and their attendants stand round the throne on the tower, and occasionally turn to the worshippers with songs and gestures. While the tower moves along numbers of the devout worshippers throw themselves on the ground, in order to be crushed by the wheels, and the multitude shout in approbation of the act, as a pleasing sacrifice to the idol. Every year, particularly at two great festivals in March and July, pilgrims flock in crowds to the temple. Not less than seventy or eighty thousand people are said to visit the place on these occasions, when all castes eat together.

Castes

The division of the Hindus into classes or castes, with fixed occupations, existed from the earliest times. It is supposed by some to have been founded upon conquest, the first three castes being composed of a foreign race, who subdued the natives of the country and reduced them to an inferior caste. Others trace it to the fondness of perpetuating, by descent from father to son, certain offices or occupations.

The Hindu tradition gives the following account of the origin of the various castes. At the creation Brahma resolved to give the earth inhabitants who should be direct emanations from his own body. Accordingly from his mouth came forth the eldest born, Brahma (the priest), to whom he confided the four Vedas; from his right arm issued Shatriya (the warrior), and from his left, the warrior's wife. His thighs produced Vaissyas, male and female (agriculturists and traders), and lastly from his feet sprang Sudras (mechanics and laborers).

The four sons of Brahma, so significantly brought into the world, became the fathers of the human race, and heads of their respective castes. They were commanded to regard the four Vedas as containing all the rules of their faith, and all that was necessary to guide them in their religious ceremonies. They were also commanded to take rank in the order of their birth, the Brahmans uppermost, as having sprung from the head of Brahma.

A strong line of demarcation is drawn between the first three castes and the Sudras. The former are allowed to receive instruction from the Vedas, which is not permitted to the Sudras. The Brahmans possess the privilege of teaching the Vedas, and were in former times in exclusive possession of all knowledge. Though the sovereign of the country was chosen from the Shatriya class, also called Rajputs, the Brahmans possessed the real power, and were the royal counsellors, the judges and magistrates of the country; their persons and property were inviolable; and though they committed the greatest crimes, they could only be banished from the kingdom. They were to be treated by sovereigns with the greatest respect, for "a Brahman, whether learned or ignorant, is a powerful divinity."

When the Brahman arrives at years of maturity it becomes his duty to marry. He ought to be supported by the contributions of the rich, and not to be obliged to gain his subsistence by any laborious or productive occupation. But as all the Brahmans could not be maintained by the working classes of the community, it was found necessary to allow them to engage in productive employments.

We need say little of the two intermediate classes, whose rank and privileges may be readily inferred from their occupations. The Sudras or fourth class are bound to servile attendance on the higher classes, especially the Brahmans, but they may follow mechanical occupations and practical arts, as painting and writing, or become traders or husbandmen. Consequently they sometimes grow rich, and it will also sometimes happen that Brahmans become poor. That fact works its usual consequence, and rich Sudras sometimes employ poor Brahmans in menial occupations.

There is another class lower even than the Sudras, for it is not one of the original pure classes, but springs from an unauthorized union of individuals of different castes. These are the Pariahs, who are employed in the lowest services and treated with the utmost severity. They are compelled to do what no one else can do without pollution. They are not only considered unclean themselves, but they render unclean every thing they touch. They are deprived of all civil rights, and stigmatized by particular laws, regulating their mode of life, their houses and their furniture. They are not allowed to visit the pagodas, or temples of the other castes, but have their own pagodas and religious exercises. They are not suffered to enter the houses of the other castes; if it is done incautiously or from necessity, the place must be purified by religious ceremonies. They must not appear at public markets, and are confined to use of particular wells, which they are obliged to surround with bones of animals, to warn others against using them. They dwell in miserable hovels, distant from cities and villages, and are under no restrictions in regard to food, which last is not a privilege, but a mark of ignominy, as if they were so degraded that nothing could pollute them. The three higher castes are prohibited entirely the use of flesh. The fourth is allowed to eat all kinds except beef, but only the lowest caste is allowed every kind of food without restriction.

Buddha

Buddha, whom the Vedas represent as a delusive incarnation of Vishnu, is said by his followers to have been a mortal sage, whose name was Gautama, called also by the complimentary epithets of Sakyasinha, the Lion, and Buddha, the Sage.

By a comparison of the various epochs assigned to his birth, it is inferred that he lived about one thousand years before Christ.

He was the son of a king; and when in conformity to the usage of the country he was, a few days after his birth, presented before the altar of a deity, the image is said to have inclined its head, as a presage of the future greatness of the new-born prophet. The child soon developed faculties of the first order, and became equally distinguished by the uncommon beauty of his person. No sooner had he grown to years of

maturity than he began to reflect deeply on the depravity and misery of
mankind, and he conceived the idea of retiring from society and
devoting himself to meditation. His father in vain opposed this design.
Buddha escaped the vigilance of his guards, and having found a secure
retreat, lived for six years undisturbed in his devout contemplations. At
the expiration of that period he came forward at Benares as a religious
teacher. At first some who heard him doubted of the soundness of his
mind; but his doctrines soon gained credit, and were propagated so
rapidly that Buddha himself lived to see them spread all over India. He
died at the age of eighty years.

The Buddhists reject entirely the authority of the Vedas, and the
religious observances prescribed in them and kept by the Hindus. They
also reject the distinction of castes, and prohibit all bloody sacrifices,
and allow animal food. Their priests are chosen from all classes; they
are expected to procure their maintenance by perambulation and begging, and among other things it is their duty to endeavor to turn to some
use things thrown aside as useless by others, and to discover the
medicinal power of plants. But in Ceylon three orders of priests are
recognized; those of the highest order are usually men of high birth and
learning, and are supported at the principal temples, most of which
have been richly endowed by the former monarchs of the country.

For several centuries after the appearance of Buddha, his sect seems
to have been tolerated by the Brahmans, and Buddhism appears to have
penetrated the peninsula of Hindustan in every direction, and to have
been carried to Ceylon, and to the eastern peninsula. But afterwards it
had to endure in India a long continued persecution, which ultimately
had the effect of entirely abolishing it, in the country where it had originated, but to scatter it widely over adjacent countries. Buddhism appears to have been introduced into China about the year 65 of our era.
From China it was subsequently extended to Corea, Japan, and Java.

Grand Lama

It is a doctrine alike of the Brahminical Hindus and of the Buddhist
sect that the confinement of the human soul, an emanation of the divine
spirit, in a human body, is a state of misery, and the consequence of
frailties and sins committed during former existences. But they hold
that some few individuals have appeared on the earth from time to time,
not under the necessity of terrestrial existence, but who voluntarily
descended to the earth to promote the welfare of mankind. These individuals have gradually assumed the character of reappearances of Buddha himself, in which capacity the line is continued till the present day,
in the several Lamas of Thibet, China, and other countries where Buddhism prevails. In consequence of the victories of Gengis Khan and his
successors, the Lama residing in Thibet was raised to the dignity of chief
pontiff of the sect. A separate province was assigned to him as his own
territory, and besides his spiritual dignity he became to a limited extent a
temporal monarch. He is styled the Dalai Lama.

The first Christian missionaries who proceeded to Thibet were surprised to find there in the heart of Asia a pontifical court and several other ecclesiastical institutions resembling those of the Roman Catholic church. They found convents for priests and nuns; also, processions and forms of religious worship, attended with much pomp and splendor; and many were induced by these similarities to consider Lamaism as a sort of degenerated Christianity. It is not improbable that the Lamas derived some of these practices from the Nestorian Christians, who were settled in Tartary when Buddhism was introduced into Thibet.

Prester John

An early account, communicated probably by travelling merchants, of a Lama or spiritual chief among the Tartars, seems to have occasioned in Europe the report of a Presbyter or Prester John, a Christian pontiff, resident in Upper Asia. The Pope sent a mission in search of him, as did also Louis IX of France, some years later, but both missions were unsuccessful, though the small communities of Nestorian Christians, which they did find, served to keep up the belief in Europe that such a personage did exist somewhere in the East. At last in the fifteenth century, a Portuguese traveller, Pedro Covilham, happening to hear that there was a Christian prince in the country of the Abessines (Abyssinia), not far from the Red Sea, concluded that this must be the true Prester John. He accordingly went thither, and penetrated to the court of the king, whom he calls Negus. Milton alludes to him in "Paradise Lost," Book XI, where, describing Adam's vision of his descendants in their various nations and cities, scattered over the face of the earth, he says,

> "Nor did his eyes not ken
> Th' empire of Negus, to his utmost port,
> Ercoco, and the less maritime kings,
> Mombaza and Quiloa and Melind."

. . . .

38

Northern Mythology—Valhalla— The Valkyrior

The stories which have engaged our attention thus far relate to the mythology of southern regions. But there is another branch of ancient superstitions which ought not to be entirely overlooked, especially as it belongs to the nations from which we, through our English ancestors, derive our origin. It is that of the northern nations called Scandinavians, who inhabited the countries now known as Sweden, Denmark, Norway, and Iceland. These mythological records are contained in two collections called the Eddas, of which the oldest is in poetry and dates back to the year 1056, the more modern or prose Edda being of the date of 1640.

According to the Eddas there was once no heaven above nor earth beneath, but only a bottomless deep, and a world of mist in which flowed a fountain. Twelve rivers issued from this fountain, and when they had flowed far from their source, they froze into ice, and one layer accumulating over another, the great deep was filled up.

Southward from the world of mist was the world of light. From this flowed a warm wind upon the ice and melted it. The vapors rose in the air and formed clouds, from which sprang Ymir, the Frost giant and his progeny, and the cow Audhumbla, whose milk afforded nourishment and food to the giant. The cow got nourishment by licking the hoar frost and salt from the ice. While she was one day licking the salt stones there appeared at first the hair of a man, on the second day the whole head, and on the third the entire form endowed with beauty, agility, and power. This new being was a god, from whom and his wife, a daughter of the giant race, sprang the three brothers Odin, Vili, and Ve. They slew the giant Ymir, and out of his body formed the earth, of his blood the seas, of his bones the mountains, of his hair the trees, of his skull the heavens, and of his brain clouds, charged with hail and snow. Of Ymir's eyebrows the gods formed Midgard (mid earth), destined to become the abode of man.

Odin then regulated the periods of day and night and the seasons by placing in the heavens the sun and moon, and appointing to them their respective courses. As soon as the sun began to shed its rays upon the earth, it caused the vegetable world to bud and sprout. Shortly after the gods had created the world they walked by the side of the sea, pleased with their new work, but found that it was still incomplete, for it was without human beings. They therefore took an ash tree and made a man out of it, and they made a woman out of an alder, and called the man Aske and the woman Embla. Odin then gave them life and soul, Vili reason and motion, and Ve bestowed upon them senses, expressive features, and speech. Midgard was then given them as their residence, and they became the progenitors of the human race.

The mighty ash tree Ygdrasill was supposed to support the whole universe. It sprang from the body of Ymir, and had three immense roots, extending one into Asgard (the dwelling of the gods), the other into Jotunheim (the abode of the giants), and the third to Niffleheim (the regions of darkness and cold). By the side of each of these roots is a spring, from which it is watered. The root that extends into Asgard is carefully tended by the three Norns, goddesses, who are regarded as the dispensers of fate. They are Urdur (the past), Verdandi (the present), Skuld (the future). The spring at the Jotunheim side is Ymir's well, in which wisdom and wit lie hidden, but that of Niffleheim feeds the adder, Nidhogge (darkness), which perpetually gnaws at the root. Four harts run across the branches of the tree and bite the buds; they represent the four winds. Under the tree lies Ymir, and when he tries to shake off its weight the earth quakes.

Asgard is the name of the abode of the gods, access to which is only gained by crossing the bridge, Bifrost (the rainbow). Asgard consists of golden and silver palaces, the dwellings of the gods, but the most beautiful of these is Valhalla, the residence of Odin. When seated on his throne he overlooks all heaven and earth. Upon his shoulders are the ravens Hugin and Munin, who fly every day over the whole world, and on their return report to him all they have seen and heard. At his feet lie his two wolves, Geri and Freki, to whom Odin gives all the meat that is set before him, for he himself stands in no need of food. Mead is for him both food and drink. He invented the Runic characters, and it is the business of the Norns to engrave the runes of fate upon a metal shield. From Odin's name, spelt Woden, as it sometimes is, came Wednesday, the name of the fourth day of the week.

Odin is frequently called Alfadur (All-father), but this name is sometimes used in a way that shows that the Scandinavians had an idea of a deity superior to Odin, uncreated and eternal.

Of the Joys of Valhalla

Valhalla is the great hall of Odin, wherein he feasts with his chosen heroes, all those who have fallen bravely in battle, for all who die a peaceful death are excluded. The flesh of the boar Schrimnir is served up to them, and is abundant for all. For although this boar is cooked every morning, he becomes whole again every night. For drink the heroes are supplied abundantly with mead from the she-goat Heidrun. When the heroes are not feasting they amuse themselves with fighting. Every day they ride out into the court or field and fight until they cut each other in pieces. This is their pastime; but when meal time comes, they recover from their wounds and return to feast in Valhalla.

The Valkyrior

The Valkyrior are warlike virgins, mounted upon horses and armed with helmets, shields, and spears. Odin, who is desirous to collect a great many heroes in Valhalla, to be able to meet the giants in a day when the final contest must come, sends down to every battle-field to make choice of those who shall be slain. The Valkyrior are his messengers, and their name means "Choosers of the slain." When they ride forth on their errand, their armor sheds a strange flickering light, which flashes up over the northern skies, making what men call the "Aurora Borealis," or "Northern Lights."*

---

*Gray's ode, "The Fatal Sisters," is founded on this superstition.

Of Thor and the Other Gods

Thor, the thunderer, Odin's eldest son, is the strongest of gods and men, and possesses three very precious things. The first is a hammer, which both the Frost and the Mountain giants know to their cost, when they see it hurled against them in the air, for it has split many a skull of their fathers and kindred. When thrown, it returns to his hand of its own accord. The second rare thing he possesses is called the belt of strength. When he girds it about him his divine might is doubled. The third, also very precious, is his iron gloves, which he puts on whenever he would use his mallet efficiently. From Thor's name is derived our word Thursday.

Frey is one of the most celebrated of the gods. He presides over rain and sunshine and all the fruits of the earth. His sister Freya is the most propitious of the goddesses. She loves music, spring, and flowers, and is particularly fond of the Elves (fairies). She is very fond of love ditties, and all lovers would do well to invoke her.

Bragi is the god of poetry, and his song records the deeds of warriors. His wife, Iduna, keeps in a box the apples which the gods, when they feel old age approaching, have only to taste of to become young again.

Heimdall is the watchman of the gods, and is therefore placed on the borders of heaven to prevent the giants from forcing their way over the bridge Bifrost (the rainbow). He requires less sleep than a bird, and sees by night as well as by day a hundred miles around him. So acute is his ear that no sound escapes him, for he can even hear the grass grow and the wool on a sheep's back.

Of Loki and His Progeny

There is another deity who is described as the calumniator of the gods and the contriver of all fraud and mischief. His name is Loki. He is handsome and well made, but of a very fickle mood and most evil disposition. He is of the giant race, but forces himself into the company of the gods, and seems to take pleasure in bringing them into difficulties, and in extricating them out of the danger by his cunning, wit, and skill. Loki has three children. The first is the wolf Fenris, the second the Midgard serpent, the third Hela (Death). The gods were not ignorant that these monsters were growing up, and that they would one day bring much evil upon gods and men. So Odin deemed it advisable to send one to bring them to him. When they came he threw the serpent into that deep ocean by which the earth is surrounded. But the monster has grown to such an enormous size that holding his tail in his mouth he encircles the whole earth. Hela he cast into Niffleheim, and gave her power over nine worlds or regions, into which she distributes those who are sent to her; that is, all who die of sickness or old age. Her hall is called Elvidnir. Hunger is her tale, Starvation her knife, Delay her man, Slowness her maid, Precipice her threshold, Care her bed, and Burning-anguish forms the hangings of her apartments. She may easily be recognized, for her body is half flesh color and half blue, and she has a dreadfully stern and forbidding countenance.

The wolf Fenris gave the gods a great deal of trouble before they succeeded in chaining him. He broke the strongest fetters as if they were made of cobwebs. Finally the gods sent a messenger to the mountain spirits, who made for them the chain called Gleipnir. It is fashioned of six things, viz., the noise made by the footfall of a cat, the beards of women, the roots of stones, the breath of fishes, the nerves (sensibilities) of bears, and the spittle of birds. When finished it was as smooth and soft as a silken string. But when the gods asked the wolf to suffer himself to be bound with this apparently slight ribbon, he suspected their design, fearing that it was made by enchantment. He therefore only consented to be bound with it upon condition that one of the gods put his hand in his (Fenris's) mouth as a pledge that the band was to be removed again. Tyr (the god of battles) alone had courage enough to do this. But when the wolf found that he could not break his fetters, and that the gods would not release him, he bit off Tyr's hand, and he has ever since remained one-handed.

How Thor Paid the Mountain Giant His Wages

Once on a time, when the gods were constructing their abodes and had already finished Midgard and Valhalla, a certain artificer came and offered to build them a residence so well fortified that they should be perfectly safe from the incursions of the Frost giants and the giants of the mountains. But he demanded for his reward the goddess Freya, together with the sun and moon. The gods yielded to his terms, provided he would finish the whole work himself without any one's assistance, and all within the space of one winter. But if any thing remained unfinished on the first day of summer he should forfeit the recompense agreed on. On being told these terms the artificer stipulated that he should be allowed the use of his horse Svadilfari, and this by the advice of Loki was granted to him. He accordingly set to work on the first day of winter, and during the night let his horse draw stone for the building. The enormous size of the stones struck the gods with astonishment, and they saw clearly that the horse did one half more of the toilsome work that his master. Their bargain however had been concluded, and confirmed by solemn oaths, for without these precautions a giant would not have thought himself safe among the gods, especially when Thor should return from an expedition he had then undertaken against the evil demons.

As the winter drew to a close, the building was far advanced, and the bulwarks were sufficiently high and massive to render the place impregnable. In short when it wanted but three days to summer the only part that remained to be finished was the gateway. Then sat the gods on their seats of justice and entered into consultation, inquiring of one another who among them could have advised to give Freya away, or to plunge the heavens in darkness by permitting the giant to carry away the sun and the moon.

They all agreed that no one but Loki, the author of so many evil deeds, could have given such bad counsel, and that he should be put to a cruel death if he did not contrive some way to prevent the artificer from completing his task and obtaining the stipulated recompense. They proceeded to lay hands on Loki, who in his fright promised upon oath that, let it cost him what it would, he would so manage matters that the man should lose his reward. That very night when the man went with Svadilfari for building stone, a mare suddenly ran out of a forest and began to neigh. The horse thereat broke loose and ran after the mare into the forest, which obliged the man also to run after his horse, and thus between one and another the whole night was lost, so that at dawn the work had not made the usual progress. The man seeing that he must fail of completing his task, resumed his own gigantic stature, and the gods now clearly perceived that it was in reality a mountain giant who had come amongst them. Feeling no longer bound by their oaths, they called on Thor, who immediately ran to their assistance, and lifting up his mallet, paid the workman his wages, not with the sun and moon, and not even by sending him back to Jotunheim, for with the first blow he shattered the giant's skull to pieces and hurled him headlong into Niffleheim.

The Recovery of the Hammer

Once upon a time it happened that Thor's hammer fell into the possession of the giant Thrym, who buried it eight fathoms deep under the rocks of Jotunheim. Thor sent Loki to negotiate with Thrym, but he could only prevail so far as to get the giant's promise to restore the weapon if Freya would consent to be his bride. Loki returned and reported the result of his mission, but the goddess of love was quite horrified at the idea of bestowing her charms on the king of the Frost giants. In this emergency Loki persuaded Thor to dress himself in Freya's clothes and accompany him to Jotunheim. Thrym received his veiled bride with due courtesy, but was greatly surprised at seeing her eat for her supper eight salmons and a full grown ox besides other delicacies, washing the whole down with three tuns of mead. Loki however assured him that she had not tasted any thing for eight long nights, so great was her desire to see her lover, the renowned ruler of Jotunheim. Thrym had at length the curiosity to peep under his bride's veil, but started back in affright and demanded why Freya's eyeballs glistened with fire. Loki repeated the same excuse and the giant was satisfied. He ordered the hammer to be brought in and laid on the maiden's lap. Thereupon Thor threw off his disguise, grasped his redoubted weapon and slaughtered Thrym and all his followers.

Frey also possessed a wonderful weapon, a sword which would of itself spread a field with carnage whenever the owner desired it. Frey parted with this sword, but was less fortunate than Thor and never recovered it. It happened in this way: Frey once mounted Odin's throne, from whence one can see over the whole universe, and looking round saw far off in the giant's kingdom a beautiful maid, at the sight of whom he was struck with sudden sadness, insomuch that from that moment he could neither sleep, nor drink, nor speak. At last Skirnir, his messenger, drew his secret from him, and undertook to get him the maiden for his bride, if he would give him his sword as a reward. Frey consented and gave him the sword, and Skirnir set off on his journey and obtained the maiden's promise that within nine nights she would come to a certain place and there wed Frey. Skirnir having reported the success of his errand, Frey exclaimed,

> "Long is one night,
>   Long are two nights,
>   But how shall I hold out three?
>   Shorter hath seemed
>   A month to me oft
>   Than of this longing time the half."

So Frey obtained Gerda, the most beautiful of all women, for his wife, but he lost his sword.

This story, entitled "Skirnir For," and the one immediately preceeding it, "Thrym's Quida," will be found poetically told in Longfellow's "Poets and Poetry of Europe."

· · · · · · ·

39

Thor's Visit to Jotunheim, The Giant's Country

One day the god Thor, with his servant Thialfi, and accompanied by Loki, set out on a journey to the giant's country. Thialfi was of all men the swiftest of foot. He bore Thor's wallet, containing their provisions. When night came on they found themselves in an immense forest, and searched on all sides for a place where they might pass the night, and at last came to a very large hall, with an entrance that took the whole breadth of one end of the building. Here they lay down to sleep, but towards midnight were alarmed by an earthquake which shook the whole edifice. Thor rising up called on his companions to seek with him a place of safety. On the right they found an adjoining chamber, into which the others entered, but Thor remained at the doorway with his mallet in his hand, prepared to defend himself, whatever might happen. A terrible groaning was heard during the night, and at dawn of day Thor went out and found lying near him a huge giant, who slept and snored in the way that had alarmed them so. It is said that for once Thor was afraid to use his mallet, and as the giant soon waked up, Thor contented himself with simply asking his name.

"My name is Skrymir," said the giant, "but I need not ask thy name, for I know that thou art the god Thor. But what has become of my glove?'' Thor then perceived that what they had taken overnight for a hall was the giant's glove, and the chamber where his two companions had sought refuge was the thumb. Skrymir then proposed that they should travel in company, and Thor consenting, they sat down to eat their breakfast, and when they had done, Skrymir packed all the provisions into one wallet, threw it over his shoulder, and strode on before them, taking such tremendous strides that they were hard put to it to keep up with him. So they travelled the whole day, and at dusk, Skrymir chose a place for them to pass the night under a large oak tree. Skrymir then told them he would lie down to sleep. ''But take ye the wallet,'' he added, ''and prepare your supper.''

Skrymir soon fell asleep and began to snore strongly; but when Thor tried to open the wallet, he found the giant had tied it up so tight he could not untie a single knot. At last Thor became wroth, and grasping his mallet with both hands he struck a furious blow on the giant's head. Skrymir awakening merely asked whether a leaf had not fallen on his head, and whether they had supped and were ready to go to sleep. Thor answered that they were just going to sleep, and so saying went and laid himself down under another tree. But sleep came not that night to Thor, and when Skrymir snored again so loud that the forest re-echoed with the noise, he arose, and grasping his mallet launched it with such force at the giant's skull that it made a deep dint in it. Skrymir awakening cried out, ''What's the matter? are there any birds perched on this tree? I felt some moss from the branches fall on my head. How fares it with thee, Thor?'' But Thor went away hastily, saying that he had just then awoke, and that as it was only midnight, there was still time for sleep. He however resolved that if he had an opportunity of striking a third blow, it should settle all matters between them. A little before daybreak he perceived that Skrymir was again fast asleep, and again grasping his mallet, he dashed it with such violence that it forced its way into the giant's skull up to the handle. But Skrymir sat up, and stroking his cheek said, ''An acorn fell on my head. What! Art thou awake, Thor? Methinks it is time for us to get up and dress ourselves; but you have not now a long way before you to the city called Utgard. I have heard you whispering to one another that I am not a man of small dimensions; but if you come to Utgard you will see there many men much taller than I. Wherefore I advise you, when you come there, not to make too much of yourselves, for the followers of Utgard-Loki will not brook the boasting of such little fellows as you are. You must take the road that leads eastward, mine lies northward, so we must part here.''

Hereupon he threw his wallet over his shoulders, and turned away from them into the forest, and Thor had no wish to stop him or to ask for any more of his company.

Thor and his companions proceeded on their way, and towards noon descried a city standing in the middle of a plain. It was so lofty that they were obliged to bend their necks quite back on their shoulders in order to see to the top of it. On arriving they entered the city, and seeing a large palace before them with the door wide open, they went in, and found a number of men of prodigious stature, sitting on benches in the hall. Going further, they came before the king Utgard-Loki, whom they saluted with great respect. The king, regarding them with a scornful smile, said, "If I do not mistake me, that stripling yonder must be the god Thor." Then addressing himself to Thor, he said, "Perhaps thou mayst be more than thou appearest to be. What are the feats that thou and thy fellows deem yourselves skilled in, for no one is permitted to remain here who does not, in some feat or other, excell all other men?"

"The feat that I know," said Loki, "is to eat quicker than any one else, and in this I am ready to give a proof against any one here who may choose to compete with me."

"That will indeed be a feat," said Utgard-Loki, "if thou performest what thou promisest, and it shall be tried forthwith."

He then ordered one of his men who was sitting at the farther end of the bench, and whose name was Logi, to come forward and try his skill with Loki. A trough filled with meat having been set on the hall floor, Loki placed himself at one end, and Logi at the other, and each of them began to eat as fast as he could, until they met in the middle of the trough. But it was found that Loki had only eaten the flesh, while his adversary had devoured both flesh and bone, and the trough to boot. All the company therefore adjudged that Loki was vanquished.

Utgard-Loki then asked what feat the young man who accompanied Thor could perform. Thialfi answered that he would run a race with any one who might be matched against him. The king observed that skill in running was something to boast of, but if the youth would win the match he must display great agility. He then arose and went with all who were present to a plain where there was good ground for running on, and calling a young man named Hugi, bade him run a match with Thialfi. In the first course Hugi so much outstripped his competitor that he turned back and met him not far from the starting place. Then they ran a second and a third time, but Thialfi met with no better success.

Utgard-Loki then asked Thor in what feats he would choose to give proofs of that prowess for which he was so famous. Thor answered that he would try a drinking match with any one; Utgard-Loki bade his cupbearer bring the large horn which his followers were obliged to empty when they had trespassed in any way against the law of the feast. The cupbearer having presented it to Thor, Utgard-Loki said, "Whoever is a good drinker will empty that horn at a single draught, though most men make two of it, but the most puny drinker can do it in three."

Thor looked at the horn, which seemed of no extraordinary size though somewhat long; however, as he was very thirsty, he set it to his lips, and without drawing breath, pulled as long and as deeply as he could, that he might not be obliged to make a second draught of it; but when he set the horn down and looked in, he could scarcely perceive that the liquor was diminished.

After taking breath, Thor went to it again with all his might, but when he took the horn from his mouth, it seemed to him that he had drank rather less than before, although the horn could now be carried without spilling.

"How now, Thor," said Utgard-Loki, "thou must not spare thyself; if thou meanest to drain the horn at the third draught thou must pull deeply; and I must needs say that thou wilt not be called so mighty a man here as thou art at home if thou showest no greater prowess in other feats than methinks will be shown in this."

Thor, full of wrath, again set the horn to his lips, and did his best to empty it; but on looking in found the liquor was only a little lower, so he resolved to make no further attempt, but gave back the horn to the cupbearer.

"I now see plainly," said Utgard-Loki, "that thou art not quite so stout as we thought thee; but wilt thou try any other feat, though methinks thou art not likely to bear any prize away with thee hence."

"What new trial hast thou to propose?" said Thor.

"We have a very trifling game here," answered Utgard-Loki, "in which we exercise none but children. It consists in merely lifting my cat from the ground; nor should I have dared to mention such a feat to the great Thor if I had not already observed that thou art by no means what we took thee for."

As he finished speaking, a large gray cat sprang on the hall floor. Thor put his hand under the cat's belly and did his utmost to raise him from the floor, but the cat, bending his back, had, notwithstanding all Thor's efforts, only one of his feet lifted up, seeing which Thor made no further attempt.

"This trial has turned out," said Utgard-Loki, "just as I imagined it would. The cat is large, but Thor is little in comparison to our men."

"Little as ye call me," answered Thor, "let me see who among you will come hither now I am in wrath and wrestle with me."

"I see no one here," said Utgard-Loki, looking at the men sitting on the benches, "who would not think it beneath him to wrestle with thee; let somebody, however, call hither that old crone, my nurse Elli, and let Thor wrestle with her if he will. She has thrown to the ground many a man not less strong than this Thor is.

A toothless old woman then entered the hall, and was told by Utgard-Loki to take hold of Thor. The tale is shortly told. The more Thor tightened his hold on the crone the firmer she stood. At length after a very violent struggle, Thor began to lose his footing, and was finally brought down upon one knee. Utgard-Loki then told them to desist, adding that Thor had now no occasion to ask any one else in the hall to wrestle with him, and it was getting late; so he showed Thor and his companions to their seats, and they passed the night there in good cheer.

The next morning at break of day, Thor and his companions dressed themselves and prepared for their departure. Utgard-Loki ordered a table to be set for them, on which there was no lack of victuals or drink.

After the repast Utgard-Loki led them to the gate of the city, and on parting asked Thor how he thought his journey had turned out, and whether he had met with any men stronger than himself. Thor told him that he could not deny but that he had brought great shame on himself. "And what grieves me most," he added, "is that ye will call me a person of little worth."

"Nay," said Utgard-Loki, "it behooves me to tell thee the truth, now thou art out of the city, which so long as I live and have my way thou shalt never enter again. And, by my troth, had I known beforehand, that thou hadst so much strength in thee, and wouldst have brought me so near to a great mishap, I would not have suffered thee to enter this time. Know then that I have all along deceived thee by my illusions; first in the forest, where I tied up the wallet with iron wire so that thou couldst not untie it. After this thou gavest me three blows with thy mallet; the first, though the least, would have ended my days had it fallen on me, but I slipped aside and thy blows fell on the mountain where thou wilt find three glens, one of them remarkably deep. These are the dints made by thy mallet. I have made use of similar illusions in the contests you have had with my followers. In the first, Loki, like hunger itself, devoured all that was set before him, but Logi was in reality nothing else than Fire, and therefore consumed not only the meat, but the trough which held it. Hugi, with whom Thialfi contended in running, was Thought, and it was impossible for Thialfi to keep pace with that. When thou in thy turn didst attempt to empty the horn, thou didst perform, by my troth, a deed so marvellous, that had I not seen it myself, I should never have believed it. For one end of that horn reached the sea, which thou wast not aware of, but when thou comest to the shore thou wilt perceive how much the sea has sunk by thy draughts. Thou didst perform a feat no less wonderful by lifting up the cat, and to tell thee the truth, when we saw that one of his paws was off the floor, we were all of us terror-stricken, for what thou tookest for a cat was in reality the Midgard serpent that encompasseth the earth, and he was so stretched by thee, that he was barely long enough to enclose it between his head and tail. Thy wrestling with Elli was also a most astonishing feat, for there was never yet a man, nor ever will be, whom Old Age, for such in fact was Elli, will not sooner or later lay low. But now, as we are going to part, let me tell thee that it will be better for both of us if thou never come near me again, for shouldst thou do so, I shall again defend myself by other illusions, so that thou wilt only lose thy labor and get no fame from the contest with me."

On hearing these words Thor in a rage laid hold of his mallet and would have launched it at him, but Utgard-Loki had disappeared, and when Thor would have returned to the city to destroy it, he found nothing around him but a verdant plain.

The Death of Baldur—The Elves—
Runic Letters—Skalds—Iceland

Baldur the Good, having been tormented with terrible dreams
indicating that his life was in peril, told them to the assembled gods, who
resolved to conjure all things to avert from him the threatened danger.
Then Frigga, the wife of Odin, exacted an oath from fire and water,
from iron and all other metals, from stones, trees, diseases, beasts,
birds, poisons, and creeping things, that none of them would do any
harm to Baldur. Odin, not satisfied with all this, and feeling alarmed for
the fate of his son, determined to consult the prophetess Angerbode, a
giantess, mother of Fenris, Hela, and the Midgard serpent. She was
dead, and Odin was forced to seek her in Hela's dominions. This Descent of Odin forms the subject of Gray's fine ode beginning,

> "Uprose the king of men with speed
> And saddled straight his coal-black steed."

But the other gods, feeling that what Frigga had done was quite sufficient, amused themselves with using Baldur as a mark, some hurling
darts at him, some stone, while others hewed at him with their swords
and battle-axes; for do what they would none of them could harm him.
And this became a favorite pastime with them and was regarded as an
honor shown to Baldur. But when Loki beheld the scene he was sorely
vexed that Baldur was not hurt. Assuming, therefore, the shape of a
woman, he went to Fensalir, the mansion of Frigga. That goddess,
when she saw the pretended woman, inquired of her if she knew what
the gods were doing at their meetings. She replied that they were throwing darts and stones at Baldur, without being able to hurt him. "Ay,"
said Frigga, "neither stones, nor sticks, nor any thing else can hurt
Baldur, for I have exacted an oath from all of them." "What," exclaimed the woman, "have all things sworn to spare Baldur?" "All
things," replied Frigga, "except one little shrub that grows on the eastern side of Valhalla, and is called Mistletoe, and which I thought too
young and feeble to crave an oath from."

As soon as Loki heard this he went away, and resuming his natural
shape, cut off the mistletoe, and repaired to the place where the gods
were assembled. There he found Hodur standing apart, without partak-
ing of the sports, on account of his blindness, and going up to him, said,
"Why dost thou not also throw something at Baldur?"

"Because I am blind," answered Hodur, "and see not where Baldur
is, and have moreover nothing to throw."

"Come, then," said Loki, "do like the rest, and show honor to

Baldur by throwing this twig at him, and I will direct thy arm towards the place where he stands.''

Hodur then took the mistletoe, and under the guidance of Loki, darted it at Baldur, who pierced through and through, fell down lifeless. Surely never was there witnessed, either among gods or men, a more atrocious deed than this. When Baldur fell, the gods were struck speechless with horror, and then they looked at each other, and all were of one mind to lay hands on him who had done the deed, but they were obliged to delay their vengeance out of respect for the sacred place where they were assembled. They gave vent to their grief by loud lamentations. When the gods came to themselves, Frigga asked who among them wished to gain all her love and good will. ''For this,'' said she, ''shall he have who will ride to Hel and offer Hela a ransom if she will let Baldur return to Asgard.'' Whereupon Hermod, surnamed the Nimble, the son of Odin, offered to undertake the journey. Odin's horse, Sleipnir, which has eight legs, and can outrun the wind, was then led forth, on which Hermod mounted and galloped away on his mission. For the space of nine days and as many nights he rode through deep glens so dark that he could not discern any thing, until he arrived at the river Gyoll, which he passed over on a bridge covered with glittering gold. The maiden who kept the bridge asked him his name and lineage, telling him that the day before five bands of dead persons had ridden over the bridge, and did not shake it as much as he alone. ''But,'' she added, ''thou hast not death's hue on thee; why then ridest thou here on the way to Hel?''

''I ride to Hel,'' answered Hermod, ''to seek Baldur. Hast thou perchance seen him pass this way?''

She replied, ''Baldur hath ridden over Gyoll's bridge, and yonder lieth the way he took to the abodes of death.''

Hermod pursued his journey until he came to the barred gates of Hel. Here he alighted, girthed his saddle tighter, and remounting, clapped both spurs to his horse, who cleared the gate by a tremendous leap without touching it. Hermod then rode on to the palace, where he found his brother Baldur occupying the most distinguished seat in the hall, and passed the night in his company. The next morning he besought Hela to let Baldur ride home with him, assuring her that nothing but lamentations were to be heard among the gods. Hela answered that it should now be tried whether Baldur was so beloved as he was said to be. ''If, therefore,'' she added, ''all things in the world, both living and lifeless, weep for him, then shall he return to life; but if any one thing speak against him or refuse to weep, he shall be kept in Hel.''

Hermod then rode back to Asgard and gave an account of all he had heard and witnessed.

The gods upon this despatched messengers throughout the world to beg every thing to weep in order that Baldur might be delivered from Hel. All things very willingly complied with this request, both men and every other living being, as well as earths, and stones, and trees, and metals, just as we have all seen these things weep when they are brought from a cold place into a hot one. As the messengers were returning, they found an old hag named Thaukt sitting in a cavern, and begged her to weep Baldur out of Hel. But she answered,

"Thaukt will wail
With dry tears
Baldur's bale-fire.
Let Hela keep her own."

It was strongly suspected that this hag was no other than Loki himself, who never ceased to work evil among gods and men. So Baldur was prevented from coming back to Asgard.*

The Funeral of Baldur

The gods took up the dead body and bore it to the sea-shore where stood Baldur's ship Hringham, which passed for the largest in the world. Baldur's dead body was put on the funeral pile, on board the ship, and his wife Nanna was so struck with grief at the sight that she broke her heart, and her body was burned on the same pile with her husband's. There was a vast concourse of various kinds of people at Baldur's obsequies. First came Odin accompanied by Frigga, the Valkyrior, and his ravens; then Frey in his car drawn by Gullinbursti, the boar; Heimdall rode his horse Gulltopp, and Freya drove in her chariot drawn by cats. There were also a great many Frost giants and giants of the mountain present. Baldur's horse was led to the pile fully caparisoned and consumed in the same flames with his master.

But Loki did not escape his deserved punishment. When he saw how angry the gods were, he fled to the mountain, and there built himself a hut with four doors, so that he could see every approaching danger. He invented a net to catch the fishes, such as fishermen have used since his time. But Odin found out his hiding-place and the gods assembled to take him. He, seeing this, changed himself into a salmon, and lay hid among the stones of the brook. But the gods took his net and dragged the brook, and Loki finding he must be caught, tried to leap over the net; but Thor caught him by the tail and compressed it so, that salmons ever since have had that part remarkably fine and thin. They bound him with chains and suspended a serpent over his head, whose venom falls upon his face drop by drop. His wife Siguna sits by his side and catches the drops as they fall, in a cup; but when she carries it away to empty it, the venom falls upon Loki, which makes him howl with horror, and twist his body about so violently that the whole earth shakes, and this produces what men call earthquakes.

*In Longfellow's "Poems," vol. II, will be found a poem entitled "Tegner's Drapa," upon the subject of Baldur's death.

The Elves

The Edda mentions another class of beings, inferior to the gods, but still possessed of great power; these were called Elves. The white spirits, or Elves of Light, were exceedingly fair, more brilliant that the sun, and clad in garments of a delicate and transparent texture. They loved the light, were kindly disposed to mankind, and generally appeared as fair and lovely children. Their country was called Alfheim, and was the domain of Freyr, the god of the sun, in whose light they were always sporting.

The black or Night Elves were a different kind of creatures. Ugly, long-nosed dwarfs, of a dirty brown color, they appeared only at night, for they avoided the sun as their most deadly enemy, because whenever his beams fell upon any of them they changed them immediately into stones. Their language was the echo of solitudes, and their dwelling-places subterranean caves and clefts. They were supposed to have come into existence as maggots produced by the decaying flesh of Ymir's body, and were afterwards endowed by the gods with a human form and great understanding. They were particularly distinguished for a knowledge of the mysterious powers of nature, and for the runes which they carved and explained. They were the most skilful artificers of all created beings, and worked in metals and in wood. Among their most noted works were Thor's hammer, and the ship Skidbladnir, which they gave to Freyr, and which was so large that it could contain all the deities with their war and household implements, but so skilfully was it wrought that when folded together it could be put into a side pocket.

Ragnarok, The Twilight of the Gods

It was a firm belief of the northern nations that a time would come when all the visible creation, the gods of Valhalla and Niffleheim, the inhabitants of Jotunheim, Alfheim, and Midgard, together with their habitations, would be destroyed. The fearful day of destruction will not however be without its forerunners. First will come a triple winter, during which snow will fall from the four corners of the heavens, the frost be very severe, the wind piercing, the weather tempestuous, and the sun impart no gladness. Three such winters will pass away without being tempered by a single summer. Three other similar winters will then follow, during which war and discord will spread over the universe. The earth itself will be frightened and begin to tremble, the sea leave its basin, the heavens tear asunder, and men perish in great numbers, and the eagles of the air feast upon their still quivering bodies. The wolf Fenris will now break his bands, the Midgard serpent rise out of her bed in the sea, and Loki, released from his bonds, will join the enemies of the gods. Amidst the general devastation the sons of Muspelheim will rush forth under their leader Surtur, before and behind whom are flames and burning fire. Onward they ride over Bifrost, the rainbow bridge, which breaks under the horses' hoofs. But they, disregarding its fall, direct their course to the battle-field called Vigrid. Thither also repair the wolf Fenris, the Midgard serpent, Loki with all the followers of Hela, and the Frost giants.

Heimdall now stands up and sounds the Giallar horn to assemble the gods and heroes for the contest. The gods advance led on by Odin, who engages the wolf Fenris, but falls a victim to the monster, who is however slain by Vidar, Odin's son. Thor gains great renown by killing the Midgard serpent, but recoils and falls dead, suffocated with the venom which the dying monster vomits over him. Loki and Heimdall meet and fight till they are both slain. The gods and their enemies having fallen in battle, Surtur, who has killed Freyr, darts fire and flames over the world, and the whole universe is burned up. The sun becomes dim, the earth sinks into the ocean, the stars fall from heaven, and time is no more.

After this Alfadur (the Almighty) will cause a new heaven and a new earth to arise out of the sea. The new earth filled with abundant supplies will spontaneously produce its fruits without labor or care. Wickedness and misery will no more be known, but the gods and men will live happily together.

Runic Letters

One cannot travel far in Denmark, Norway, or Sweden without meeting with great stones, of different forms, engraven with characters called Runic, which appear at first sight very different from all we know. The letters consist almost invariably of straight lines, in the shape of little sticks either singly or put together. Such sticks were in early times used by the northern nations for the purpose of ascertaining future events. The sticks were shaken up, and from the figures that they formed a kind of divination was derived.

The Runic characters were of various kinds. They were chiefly used for magical purposes. The noxious,or, as they called them, the *bitter* runes, were employed to bring various evils on their enemies; the favorable averted misfortune. Some were medicinal, others employed to win love, etc. In later times they were frequently used for inscriptions, of which more than a thousand have been found. The language is a dialect of the Gothic, called Norse, still in use in Iceland. The inscriptions may therefore be read with certainty, but hitherto very few have been found which throw the least light on history. They are mostly epitaphs on tombstones.

Gray's ode on the "Descent of Odin" contains an allusion to the use of Runic letters for incantation:

"Facing to the northern clime,
   Thrice he traced the Runic rhyme;
   Thrice pronounced, in accents dread,

The thrilling verse that wakes the dead,
Till from out the hollow ground
Slowly breathed a sullen sound."

The Skalds

The Skalds were the bards and poets of the nation, a very important class of men in all communities in an early stage of civilization. They are the depositaries of whatever historic lore there is, and it is their office to mingle something of intellectual gratification with the rude feasts of the warriors, by rehearsing, with such accompaniments of poetry and music as their skill can afford, the exploits of their heroes living or dead. The compositions of the Skalds were called Sagas, many of which have come down to us, and contain valuable materials of history, and a faithful picture of the state of society at the time to which they relate.

Iceland

The Eddas and Sagas have come to us from Iceland. The following extract from Carlyle's lectures on "Heroes and Hero Worship" gives an animated account of the region where the strange stories we have been reading had their origin. Let the reader contrast it for a moment with Greece, the parent of classical mythology.

"In that strange island, Iceland—burst up, the geologists say, by fire from the bottom of the sea, a wild land of barrenness and lava, swallowed many months of every year in black tempests, yet with a wild, gleaming beauty in summer time, towering up there stern and grim in the North Ocean, with its snow yokuls [mountains], roaring geysers [boiling springs], sulphur pools, and horrid volcanic chasms, like the waste, chaotic battle-field of Frost and Fire—where, of all places, we least looked for literature or written memorials—the record of these things was written down. On the seaboard of this wild land is a rim of grassy country, where cattle can subsist, and men by means of them and of what the sea yields; and it seems they were poetic men these, men who had deep thoughts in them and uttered musically their thoughts. Much would be lost had Iceland not been burst up from the sea, not been discovered by the Northmen!"

. . . .

41

The Druids—Iona

The Druids were the priests or ministers of religion among the ancient Celtic nations in Gaul, Britain, and Germany. Our information respecting them is borrowed from notices in the Greek and Roman writers, compared with the remains of Welsh and Gaelic poetry still extant.

The Druids combined the functions of the priest, the magistrate, the scholar, and the physician. They stood to the people of the Celtic tribes in a relation closely analogous to that in which the Brahmans of India, the Magi of Persia, and the priests of the Egyptians stood to the people respectively by whom they were revered.

The Druids taught the existence of one god, to whom they gave a name "Be' al," which Celtic antiquaries tell us means "the life of every thing," or "the source of all beings," and which seems to have affinity with the Phœnician Baal. What renders this affinity more striking is that the Druids as well as the Phœnicians identified this, their supreme deity, with the *Sun*. Fire was regarded as a symbol of the divinity. The Latin writers assert that the Druids also worshipped numerous inferior gods.

They used no images to represent the object of their worship, nor did they meet in temples or buildings of any kind for the performance of their sacred rites. A circle of stones (each stone generally of vast size) enclosing an area of from twenty feet to thirty yards in diameter, constituted their sacred place. The most celebrated of these now remaining is Stonehenge, on Salisbury Plain, England.

These sacred circles were generally situated near some stream, or under the shadow of a grove or wide-spreading oak. In the centre of the circle stood the Cromlech or altar, which was a large stone, placed in the manner of a table upon other stones set up on end. The Druids had also their high places, which were large stones or piles of stones on the summits of hills. These were called Cairns, and were used in the worship of the deity under the symbol of the sun.

That the Druids offered sacrifices to their deity there can be no doubt. But there is some uncertainty as to what they offered, and of the ceremonies connected with their religious services we know almost nothing. The classical (Roman) writers affirm that they offered on great occasions human sacrifices; as for success in war or for relief from dangerous diseases. Cæsar has given a detailed account of the manner in which this was done. "They have images of immense size, the limbs of which are framed with twisted twigs and filled with living persons. These being set on fire, those within are encompassed by the flames." Many attempts have been made by Celtic writers to shake the testimony of the Roman historians to this fact, but without success.

The Druids observed two festivals in each year. The former took place in the beginning of May, and was called Beltane or "fire of God." On this occasion a large fire was kindled on some elevated spot, in honor of the sun, whose returning beneficence they thus welcomed after the gloom and desolation of winter. Of this custom a trace remains in the name given to Whitsunday in parts of Scotland to this day. Sir Walter Scott uses the word in the "Boat Song" in the "Lady of the Lake":

> "Ours is no sapling, chance sown by the fountain,
> Blooming at Beltane in winter to fade"; etc.

The other great festival of the Druids was called "Samh'in," or "fire of peace," and was held on Hallow-eve (first of November), which still retains this designation in the Highlands of Scotland. On this occasion the Druids assembled in solemn conclave, in the most central part of the district, to discharge the judicial functions of their order. All questions, whether public or private, all crimes against person or property, were at this time brought before them for adjudication. With these judicial acts were combined certain superstitious usages, especially the kindling of the sacred fire, from which all the fires in the district, which had been beforehand scrupulously extinguished, might be relighted. This usage of kindling fires on Hallow-eve lingered in the British islands long after the establishment of Christianity.

Besides these two great annual festivals, the Druids were in the habit of observing the full moon, and especially the sixth day of the moon. On the latter they sought the Mistletoe, which grew on their favorite oaks, and to which, as well as to the oak itself, they ascribed a peculiar virtue and sacredness. The discovery of it was an occasion of rejoicing and solemn worship. "They call it," says Pliny, "by a word in their language which means 'heal-all,' and having made solemn preparation for feasting and sacrifice under the tree, they drive thither two milk-white bulls, whose horns are then for the first time bound. The priest then, robed in white, ascends the tree, and cuts off the mistletoe with a golden sickle. It is caught in a white mantle, after which they proceed to slay the victims, at the same time praying that God would render his gift prosperous to those to whom he had given it." They drink the water in which it has been infused, and think it a remedy for all diseases. The mistletoe is a parasitic plant, and is not always nor often found on the oak, so that when it is found it is the more precious.

The Druids were the teachers of morality as well as of religion. Of their ethical teaching a valuable specimen is preserved in the Triads of the Welsh Bards, and from this we may gather that their views of moral rectitude were on the whole just, and that they held and inculcated many very noble and valuable principles of conduct. They were also the men of science and learning of their age and people. Whether they were acquainted with letters or not has been disputed, though the probability is strong that they committed nothing of their doctrine, their history, or their poetry to writing. Their teaching was oral, and their literature (if such a word may be used in such a case) was preserved solely by tradition. But the Roman writers admit that "they paid much attention to the order and laws of nature, and investigated and taught to the youth under their charge many things concerning the stars and their motions, the size of the world and the lands, and concerning the might and power of the immortal gods."

Their history consisted in traditional tales, in which the heroic deeds of their forefathers were celebrated. These were apparently in verse, and thus constituted part of the poetry as well as the history of the Druids. In the poems of Ossian we have, if not the actual productions of Druidical times, what may be considered faithful representations of the songs of the Bards.

The Bards were an essential part of the Druidical hierarchy. One author, Pennant, says, "The Bards were supposed to be endowed with powers equal to inspiration. They were the oral historians of all past transactions, public and private. They were also accomplished genealogists," etc.

Pennant gives a minute account of the Eisteddfods or sessions of the Bards and minstrels, which were held in Wales for many centuries, long after the Druidical priesthood in its other departments became extinct. At these meetings none but Bards of merit were suffered to rehearse their pieces, and minstrels of skill to perform. Judges were appointed to decide on their respective abilities, and suitable degrees were conferred. In the earlier period the judges were appointed by the Welsh princes, and after the conquest of Wales, by commission from the kings of England. Yet the tradition is that Edward I, in revenge for the influence of the Bards, in animating the resistance of the people to his sway, persecuted them with great cruelty. This tradition has furnished the poet Gray with the subject of his celebrated ode, the "Bard."

There are still occasional meetings of the lovers of Welsh poetry and music, held under the ancient name. Among Mrs. Hemans's poems is one written for an Eisteddfod, or meeting of Welsh Bards, held in London, May 22, 1822. It begins with a description of the ancient meeting, of which the following lines are a part:

> "—midst the eternal cliffs, whose strength defied
> The crested Roman in his hour of pride;
> And where the Druid's ancient cromlech frowned,
> And the oaks breathed mysterious murmurs round,
> There thronged the inspired of yore! on plain or height,
> In the sun's face, beneath the eye of light,
> And baring unto heaven each noble head,
> Stood in the circle, where none else might tread."

The Druidical system was at its height at the time of the Roman invasion under Julius Caesar. Against the Druids, as their chief enemies, these conquerors of the world directed their unsparing fury. The Druids, harassed at all points on the main land, retreated to Anglesey and Iona, where for a season they found shelter and continued their now-dishonored rites.

The Druids retained their predominance in Iona and over the adjacent islands and mainland until they were supplanted and their superstitions overturned by the arrival of St. Columba, the apostle of the Highlands, by whom the inhabitants of that district were first led to profess Christianity.

Iona

One of the smallest of the British Isles, situated near a rugged and barren coast, surrounded by dangerous seas, and possessing no sources of internal wealth, Iona has obtained an imperishable place in history as the seat of civilization and religion at a time when the darkness of heathenism hung over almost the whole of Northern Europe. Iona or Icolmkill is situated at the extremity of the island of Mull, from which it is separated by a strait of half a mile in breadth, its distance from the main land of Scotland being thirty-six miles.

Columba was a native of Ireland, and connected by birth with the princes of the land. Ireland was at that time a land of gospel light, while the western and northern parts of Scotland were still immersed in the darkness of heathenism. Columba with twelve friends landed on the island of Iona in the year of our Lord 563, having made the passage in a wicker boat covered with hides. The Druids who occupied the island endeavored to prevent his settling there, and the savage nations on the adjoining shores incommoded him with their hostility, and on several occasions endangered his life by their attacks. Yet by his perseverance and zeal he surmounted all opposition, procured from the king a gift of the island, and established there a monastery of which he was the abbot. He was unwearied in his labors to disseminate a knowledge of the Scriptures throughout the Highlands and islands of Scotland, and such was the reverence paid him that though not a bishop, but merely a presbyter and monk, the entire province with its bishops was subject to him and his successors. The Pictish monarch was so impressed with a sense of his wisdom and worth that he held him in the highest honor, and the neighboring chiefs and princes sought his counsel and availed themselves of his judgment in settling their disputes.

When Columba landed on Iona he was attended by twelve followers whom he had formed into a religious body of which he was the head. To these, as occasion required, others were from time to time added, so that the original number was always kept up. Their institution was called a monastery and the superior an abbot, but the system had little in common with the monastic institutions of later times. The name by which those who submitted to the rule were known was that of Culdees, probably from the Latin "cultores Dei"—worshippers of God. They were a body of religious persons associated together for the purpose of aiding each other in the common work of preaching the gospel and teaching youth, as well as maintaining in themselves the fervor of devotion by united exercises of worship. On entering the order certain vows were taken by the members, but they were not those which were usually imposed by monastic orders, for of these, which are three, celibacy, poverty, and obedience, the Culdees were bound to none except the third. To poverty they did not bind themselves; on the contrary they seem to have labored diligently to procure for themselves and those dependent on them the comforts of life. Marriage also was allowed them, and most of them seem to have entered into that state. True their wives were not permitted to reside with them at the institution, but they had a residence assigned to them in an adjacent locality. Near Iona there is an island which still bears the name of "Eilen nam ban," women's island, where their husbands seem to have resided with them, except when duty required their presence in the school or the sanctuary.

Campbell, in his poem of "Reullura," alludes to the married monks of Iona:

> "—The pure Culdees
>   Were Albyn's earliest priests of God,
> Ere yet an island of her seas
>   By foot of Saxon monk was trod,
> Long ere her churchmen by bigotry
> Were barred from holy wedlock's tie.
> 'Twas then that Aodh, famed afar,
>   In Iona preached the word with power,
> And Reullura, beauty's star,
>   Was the partner of his bower."

In one of his "Irish Melodies," Moore gives the legend of St. Senanus and the lady who sought shelter on the island, but was repulsed:

> "O, haste and leave this sacred isle,
>   Unholy bark, ere morning smile;
> For on thy deck, though dark it be,
>   A female form I see;
> And I have sworn this sainted sod
> Shall ne'er by woman's foot be trod."

In these respects and in others the Culdees departed from the established rules of the Romish Church, and consequently were deemed heretical. The consequence was that as the power of the latter advanced that of the Culdees was enfeebled. It was not however till the thirteenth century that the communities of the Culdees were suppressed and the members dispersed. They still continued to labor as individuals, and resisted the inroads of Papal usurpation as they best might till the light of the Reformation dawned on the world.

Iona, from its position in the western seas, was exposed to the assaults of the Norwegian and Danish rovers by whom those seas were infested, and by them it was repeatedly pillaged, its dwellings burned, and its peaceful inhabitants put to the sword. These unfavorable circumstances led to its gradual decline, which was expedited by the subversion of the Culdees through Scotland. Under the reign of Popery the island became the seat of a nunnery, the ruins of which are still seen. At the Reformation, the nuns were allowed to remain, living in community, when the abbey was dismantled.

Iona is now chiefly resorted to by travellers on account of the numerous ecclesiastical and sepulchral remains which are found upon it. The principal of these are the Cathedral or Abbey Church, and the Chapel of the Nunnery. Besides these remains of ecclesiastical antiquity, there are some of an earlier date, and pointing to the existence on the island of forms of worship and belief different from those of Christianity. These are the circular Cairns which are found in various parts, and which seem to have been of Druidical origin. It is in reference to all these remains of ancient religion that Johnson exclaims, "That man is little to be envied whose patriotism would not gain force upon the plains of Marathon, or whose piety would not grow warmer amid the ruins of Iona."

In the "Lord of the Isles," Scott beautifully contrasts the church on Iona with the cave of Staffa, opposite:

"Nature herself, it seemed, would raise
A minister to her Maker's praise!
Not for a meaner use ascend
Her columns, or her arches bend;
Nor of a theme less solemn tells
That mighty surge that ebbs and swells,
And still between each awful pause,
From the high vault an answer draws,
In varied tone, prolonged and high,
That mocks the organ's melody;
Nor doth its entrance front in vain
To old Iona's holy fane,
That Nature's voice might seem to say,
Well hast thou done, frail child of clay!
Thy humble powers that stately shrine
Tasked high and hard—but witness mine!"

·······

Proverbial Expressions

No. 1. Page 44.

Materiem superabat opus.—*Ovid*

The workmanship surpassed the material.

No. 2. Page 44.

Facies non omnibus una,
Nec diversa tamen, qualem decet esse sororum.—*Ovid*

Their faces were not all alike, nor yet unlike, but such as those of
sisters ought to be.

No. 3. Page 46.

Medio tutissimus ibis.—*Ovid*

You will go most safely in the middle.

No. 4. Page 48.

Hic situs est Phaeton, currus auriga paterni,
Quem si non tenuit, magnis tamen excidit ausis.—*Ovid*

Here lies Phaeton, the driver of his father's chariot, which if he
failed to manage, yet he fell in a great undertaking.

No. 5. Page 102.

Imponere Pelio Ossam.—*Virgil*

To pile Ossa upon Pelion.

No. 6. Page 178.

Timeo Danaos et dona ferentes.—*Virgil*

I fear the Greeks even when they offer gifts.

No. 7. Page 179.

Non tali auxilio nec defensoribus istis
Tempus eget.—*Virgil*

Not such aid nor such defenders does the time require.

No. 8. Page 189.

Incidit in Scyllam, cupiens vitare Charybdim.

He runs on Scylla, wishing to avoid Charybdis.

No. 9. Page 199.

Monstrum horrendum, informe, ingens, cui lumen
ademptum.—*Virgil*

A horrible monster, misshapen, vast, whose only eye had been
put out.

No. 10. Page 200.

Tantæne animis cœlestibus iræ?—*Virgil*

In heavenly minds can such resentments dwell?

No. 11. Page 201.

Haud ignara mali, miseris succurrere disco.—*Virgil*

Not unacquainted with distress, I have learned to succor the
unfortunate.

No. 12. Page 201.

Tros, Tyriusve mihi nullo discrimine agetur.—*Virgil*

Whether Trojan or Tyrian shall make no difference to me.

No. 13. Page 203.

Facilis descensus Averni;
Noctes atque dies patet atri janua Ditis;
Sed revocare gradum, superasque evadere ad auras,
Hoc opus, hic labor est.—*Virgil*

The descent of Avernus is easy; the gate of Pluto stands open
night and day; but to retrace one's steps and return to the upper
air—that is the toil, that the difficulty.

No. 14. Page 203.

Uno avulso non deficit alter.—*Virgil*

When one is torn away another succeeds.

No. 15. Page 202.

Tu ne cede malis, sed contra audentior ito.—*Virgil*

Yield thou not to adversity, but press on the more bravely.

No. 16. Page 214.

Quadrupedante putrem sonitu quatit ungula campum.—*Virgil*

Then struck the hoofs of the steeds on the ground with a four-
footed trampling.

No. 17. Page 216.

Sternitur infelix alieno vulnere, cœlumque
Adspicit et moriens dulces reminiscitur Argos.—*Virgil*

He falls, unhappy, by a wound intended for another; looks up
to the skies, and dying remembers sweet Argos.

Index of Names

Absyrtus, 113
Aby'dos, 90
Ace'tes, 130
Acha'tes, 213
Achelo'us, 141
Achilles, 166
Acis, 163
Acon'teus, 101
Actæon, 40
Adme'ta, 118
Adme'tus, 142
Ado'nis, 63
Adrastus, 144
Æ'acus, 83
Æe'tes, 107
Æge'us, 122
Ægis, 98
Ægisthus, 181
Æne'as, 166-197
Æ'olus, 185-200
Æscula'pius, 106, 226
Æson, 110
Æthiopians, 18-47
Æthra, 122
Agame'des, 225
Agamemnon, 166-180
Aga've, 132
Age'nor, 81
Agla'ia, 22
Agni, 242
Ah'riman, 241
Ajax, 166-177
Alces'tis, 142
Alci'des, 120
Alcin'o-us, 191
Alcme'na, 117
Alecto, 22
Alexander. See Paris

Alfa'dur, 249
Alphe'us, 57
Althæ'a, 113
Amalthe'a, 142
Am'azons, 118, 124
Ambro'sia, 18
Ammon, 102
Amphiara'us, 144
Amphi'on, 96, 151
Amphitri'te, 138
Ampyx, 101
Amri'ta, 243
Amymo'ne, 117
Anaxar'ete, 71-72
Ance'us, 114
Anchi'ses, 198
Andræ'mon, 62
Androm'ache, 166, 199
Androm'eda, 99
Anemo'ne, 64
Antæ'us, 119
Ante'a, 104
An'teros, 21
Antig'one, 144
Anti'ope, 124, 151
Anu'bis, 222
Aphrodi'te, 21
Apis, 223, 226
Apollo, 20, 30, 64
Aq'uilo, 140
Arach'ne, 92
Arcas, 40
Areop'agus, 181
Ares, 20
Arethu'sa, 55
Argo, 108
Ar'gonauts, 108
Argus, 37, 108, 196
Ariad'ne, 123, 132

Arima'nes, 240
Arimas'pians, 107
Ari'on, 153
Aristæ'us, 147, 149
Ar'temis, 21
Asgard, 248
Aske, 248
Astræ'a, 27
Asty'ages, 101
Atalan'ta, 113
Ate, 173
Atlan'tis, 208
Ath'amas, 107
Athe'ne, 21
Atlas, 99
At'ropos, 22
Audhum'bla, 248
Au'geas, 118
Aulis, 166
Auro'ra, 162
Auster, 140
Av'atar, 242
Bacchanals, 130
Bacchus, 22, 129
Baldur, 258
Bards, 266
Basilisk, 236
Baucis, 50
Beller'ophon, 104
Bello'na, 23
Beltane, 264
Ber'oe, 129
Bifrost, 249
Bo'reas, 140
Bragi, 250
Brahma, 242
Brazen age, 26
Bria'reus, 102
Brise'is, 168
Buddha, 245

·······
ESSAYS
·······

Myths and the Modern World

by Michael Grant

The myths told by the Greeks and Romans are as important as history for our understanding of what those peoples, ancestors of our own civilization, believed and thought and felt, and expressed in writing and in visual art. For their mythologies were inextricably interwoven, to an extent far beyond anything in our own experience, with the whole fabric of their public and private lives.

And then without these myths we should be hard put to it to understand the arts and literature and ways of thinking of the west, and of many other parts of the world as well, during the centuries that have passed since the classical world came to an end. Time after time these products of ancient imagination have been used to inspire fresh creative efforts, which amount to a substantial part of our whole cultural inheritance. Such renewals and adaptations have often seemed far removed, in character and spirit, from the original tradition; yet they stem directly from it, and are unimaginable without it.

> The intelligible forms of ancient poets,
> The fair humanities of old religion,
> The Power, the Beauty, and the Majesty,
> That had their haunts in dale, or piny mountain,
> Or forest by slow stream, or pebbly spring,
> Or chasms and watery depths: all these have vanished.
> They live no longer in the faith of reason!
> But still the heart doth need a language, still
> Doth the old instinct bring back the old names . . .

And so even communities professing that quite different code of beliefs which is Christianity have, after various struggles, found it impracticable to dispense with the classical stories. Today new political systems have fabricated their own myths which Coleridge, writing those lines under the Graeco-Roman spell, had never imagined. Yet twentieth-century writers, from tragic theatre to comic strip, have continued to employ the archetypes with renewed vigour. These dramatic, concrete, individual, insistently probing ancient myths still supplement the deductions of science as clues to much in the world that does not alter.

The atmosphere to which they translate us is life-enhancing; for it gives us fresh strength by providing a route of escape. The escape is from day-to-day reality, of which, as we know, it is not possible to endure very much. Yet this is not escapism of any ordinary kind, for the road leads to another sort of reality, a more imposing sort, than the reality which dominates our ordinary lives. At times, in receptive conditions, these myths generate and throw off potent, almost violent, flashes of inextinguishable, universal truths. Those are not of course, as far as we are concerned, the religious truths which (among much else) the Greeks and Romans saw in their mythology. However they are truths that still impinge, sometimes with ungovernable force, upon the mind and feelings, and illuminate aspects of our human condition.

This particular brand of enlightenment is difficult or impossible to grasp by more logical and rational means, and would elude nonmythical presentation. Yet it would be wrong to say that myths seem modern or topical; they are as relevant to our time as to any other, no more, no less. That is to say, they are not specifically antique either. They are ostensibly lodged, it is true, within a certain framework of the remote past, but that does not impede their perpetual compulsive tenacity. Indeed, their relevance to life's basic, continuing situations is sharpened into high relief by this setting which, though ancient in origin and form, remains unaffected by temporal circumstances.

For the images of myth, once they have stirred our perceptions, precipitate them into a new, unforeseen dimension outside time. The Greeks and Romans, although in different epochs they saw mythology in different lights, were by training and inclination ready to enter this exciting, unearthly dimension of timelessness, this

> Dark, illimitable ocean, without bound,
> Without dimension, where length and breadth and height,
> And time and place, are lost.

Heavy with unplumbed meaning is this ocean—beckoning, inviting immersion and obsession. Perhaps after so long a time we can only reach its shallows; yet we shall be losing an irreplaceable experience if we do not go as deep as we can. But we need, for this enterprise, a more detailed preparation than the ancients needed.

Each myth means something different to everybody who reads and studies it. The stories are hard to forget; feelings about them come unpredictably. Their underlying qualities do not readily yield to definition or classification—still less to weird searches for mystic hidden meanings and anachronistic allegories. Above all, as I hope will become clear, they are varied. *No single theory*, however valuably suggestive, will suffice to explain the whole range of Greek and Roman mythology, or even a major proportion of its content. Indeed, such all-embracing theories (of which there are many), whether put forward by anthropologists or classicists or psychoanalysts or scholars of religion, present the most dangerous hazard which students of this strange subject will encounter. And in this field we are exceptionally vulnerable to hazards, since we almost all come to it after an education in which the myths are neglected or, to the accompaniment of gutless illustrations, reduced to whimsical travesty.

So the only safe hope would seem to be the Horatian maxim:

> Ask not, to what Doctors I apply;
> Sworn to no Master, of no Sect am I.

Or, better, go to as many of the doctors as one can, and sit at their feet, and from all of them accept something—though (since they contradict one another) obviously not everything. For each of these different kinds of scholar that I mentioned has during the present century, in spite of these all too comprehensive theories, added to our realization that mythology is something far more serious than the primitive, unreflecting, childish precursor of science or of developed religion that it was formerly believed to be. Indeed, the revitalizing of the classical myths can be claimed as the most significant of all the impacts that the Graeco-Roman world has made upon modern thought . . .

Michael Grant is a contemporary English writer and historian whose works include *History of Rome; The Estruscans;* and *Myths of the Greeks and Romans,* from which this essay is excerpted.

Greek Myth and the Poets

by Charles Grosvenor Osgood

Many readers or students of poetry in this latter day undoubtedly consider the use of Greek myth by English poets merely an annoyance. A poet's references to unfamiliar and rather absurd tales and persons as if they were known to every reader may serve to exhibit his erudition, but they are a hindrance to the full enjoyment of his poetry. Either they interrupt the music until they can get themselves explained, or they are passed over and discounted as unintelligible. Or so it may seem.

Earlier poets might have retorted—rather obviously—that when they sang, the myths were a matter of common knowledge, common to them and to their audiences. Present-day poets, however, cannot offer this retort because, for some unhappy reason, the knowledge has ceased to be common. The twilight of the gods has deepened into almost total darkness....

Certainly, whether or not we believe the gods are dead, what we unluckily have come to call "myth," or, worse, "mythology," is not dead. It can perish only with the human spirit itself, for we are all inveterate makers and partakers of myth. We may have exchanged the glorious Athene for the Powerful Katrinka, or Zeus and Hera for Joe and Vi Green, but we *must* have our mythology.

One bright morning a little boy ran out to play, shouting,

Sun a-calling, Wind a-calling;
Coming, Wind! Coming, Sun!

Happy young mythmaker, all unconscious of the primitive, perennial instinct that moved him to song! This is what the learned call animism. It is really myth in its genesis. Who is not at times beguiled or bewitched or baffled or rebuffed by that form of life other than ourselves that we call Nature—so alluring, so evasive, so inscrutable? We instinctively try to break down the barrier, or rend the curtain, by giving her forms like our own—anything to make her more familiar, more friendly, more companionable. But we are like the clumsy, oafish Cyclops on the beach, pining in love for the beautiful, milk-white Galatea (sea foam) leaping and playing beside him. "She flies when thou art wooing her, when thou woo'st not, she pursues thee."*

So would we clothe the mystery in human shape in vane hope of exploring it—sun, moon, stars, night, day, storm, sea, mountain, streams, spring, autumn.

Yet other mysteries confront us, too, more intimate and often more

*Theocritus, *Idyll* 6.

terrifying—the mysteries concerning life and death, and the compelling instincts, such as love, hate, greed, hope, despair, and the sense of justice; and the other mysteries concerning the many activities and occupations that spring from these first mysteries and take possession of us, such as wooing, homemaking, war, arts, government, and reform. These, too, assume human, even divine, shape in man's imagination. Hence in time there is an accumulation that we call a mythology; hence Aphrodite, Ares, Athene, Themis, Prometheus, Orpheus, and Zeus.

All peoples with any trace of civilization have thus tried to cope with the mysteries of Nature and life, sometimes grossly and crudely, to be sure. At first local and scattered, the stories—or the best of them—tended to grow and improve and merge with the growth of a people or nation. Our *good* old stories are a survival of the fittest, that is, of the most beautiful and most expressive myths. The poorer stories fade from memory.

As children we wanted our favorite stories repeated always without variation, and this conservative instinct survives in us all. Yet every good storyteller will try to improve his stories every time he tells them, if only with an added or altered detail, or tone of voice, or timing here and there. Between these two unceasing contrary forces, conservative and progressive, each surviving legend has been ground and polished like a bit of quartz in a glacier until it has emerged in perfectly rounded form. Thus the story fit to survive loses nought by the telling, except what is not worth keeping, and through generations of repetition grows refined and charged with accretions of truth from its conveyors until it becomes a myth that man does not willingly let die.

In this matter of polishing, the Greeks of all peoples have been the most successful. Greek myth embodies the genius and wisdom of a most enlightened nation with a vast experience in living—a balance of elements in life both grave and gay. It is charged with high literary potentialities that have been expressed in epic, dramatic, and lyric forms and that are still capable of high expression. Thus the Greeks' endeavor to clothe the mysteries of Nature and life in human form and event—their mythology—has survived not only the Greeks themselves but all tumults of civilization to our own day and has saturated the imagination and poetry of the centuries. And it has survived,not primarily because the stories are beautiful or quaint or entertaining, but because they impart some essence of vital truth. Says Milton:

> 'Tis not vain or fabulous,
> (Though so esteem'd by shallow ignorance)
> What the sage poets taught by the Heavenly Muse,
> Storied of old in high immortal verse,
> Of dire Chimeras and enchanted isles,
> And rifted rocks whose entrance leads to Hell,
> For such there be, but unbelief is blind.

No doubt in earlier stages of culture people grew up with belief in the literal truth of these stories. How much they realized of the original truth and the power of mystery that had first inspired the myths, who shall say? But as a nation or people grows more sophisticated and the old literal belief fades, intelligent men still discern the original elements of truth and beauty in the myths and cling to them as vehicles of truths far more compelling and acceptable than mere abstract statements. Indeed these myths in time become universal symbols.

To the poet, though, whether he is ancient or modern, a myth is not static and fixed. In his mind it takes new root and blooms again. He keeps up the old practice of mythmaking. The story of Circe in Spenser's or in Milton's hands, the stories of Prometheus or Arethusa in Shelley's, of Endymion in Keats', of Atalanta in Swinburne's, undergo transmutations that to the old intrinsic truth add new significance distilled in the poet's genius. The old legend receives new life from his handling. Thus by the very vitality of its inherent truth and beauty the best of the old lore has survived.

At least it survived until the last hundred years or so. Then the mystery that inspired and clothed the old tales evaporated under the literal sunlight of science, and in the pride of our new knowledge we discarded them as mere superstitions and supercargo. What part, we ask, can they take in the pursuit of science, theoretical or applied, in economics, or in the currently fashionable "social" studies?

Oddly enough, this question is not new. It has been asked in one form or another for hundreds of years. And the answer is always the same, for there is only one. The old myth, even the Nature myth, is primarily concerned with human life—with those eternal aspects of it that will elude scientific scrutiny for ever and baffle us with their mystery. Further, it is concerned with human life in a competent way. The perennial issue between youth and age, between radical and conservative, with all its confusion of folly and wisdom, of suffering and defeat, of wrong and right on both sides, is grandly intrinsic in the story of Prometheus. In Ulysses, Tennyson reads the unquenchable and tragic thirst of the human soul for knowledge, and in Prometheus, Shelley sees the agony of genius confined in a conventional world—he sees, in fact, his own agony. This habit or instinct of a man steeped in ancient myths to identify his own plight or career with a mythical instance is not uncommon.

Of course earlier poets were well aware of this community with hearers who had assimilated a knowledge of the old myths almost with their mothers' milk. Most people appropriated their knowledge of Greek myths from reading Ovid and Virgil in school, but we who have put away such reading are more or less disqualified from this community. Hence we need handbooks of mythology.

We sometimes speak of a big assignment as a Herculean task or of a brawny football guard as rearing the shoulders of Atlas. Hercules and Atlas are familiar superstandards of prowess and strength, much more telling than mere statistics and physical measurements; for they at once stir and release the imagination and carry it back along the course of an age-old human tradition to a transcendent human being at the other end. Thus Hercules and Atlas have become communal symbols with an invariable value.

These, then, are some of the uses of classic myths to the poet. They serve to establish community of mind, of imagination, and of life between him and his hearers. In similes they become standard measures of size, or grace, or beauty, or power, or heroism. They draw us into closer and more sympathetic relation with external Nature by humanizing her and thus generating community of understanding and imagination between poet, listener, and Nature herself. Moreover, they also embody the elements of great moral ideas and values invariable in human life. In the story of Dionysus as god of inspiration, ecstasy, and mysticism, his conflict with the literal myopic common sense of the human majority is highly significant to any man keenly aware of unseen impulses. In the fate of the poet Orpheus, who sang so ravishingly as to draw all Nature after him—

> Such strains as would have won the ear
> Of Pluto to have quite set free
> His half-regained Eurydice,

had he not faltered and looked back—yet who was torn asunder by an infuriated and stupid mob that had no ear for music, a great neglected poet is sure to recognize his own suffering.

> What could the Muse herself that Orpheus bore,
> The Muse herself for her enchanting son,
> Whom universal Nature did lament,
> When by the rout that made the hideous roar
> His gory visage down the stream was sent,
> Down the swift Hebrus to the Lesbian shore.

The struggle of Prometheus for the enlightenment of mankind with the static paralysis of things as they are, his sufferings, his ultimate if partial triumph—what is this but a supreme example of the course of human progress in all generations? As such it has been rehearsed by poet after poet, in dramatic, narrative, and lyric verse.

Charles Grosvenor Osgood (1871–1964), Professor Emeritus at Princeton University, was co-author of *Tradition of Virgil,* and edited many other works of criticism and poetry.